The Squaw Man (1905)	Edwin M
Brewster's Millions (1906)	Winchell Smith (1871-1933)
Forty-Five Minutes from Broadway (1906) *Seven Keys to Baldpate* (1913)	George M. Cohan (1878-1942)
The Great Divide (1906)	William Vaughn Moody (1869-1910)
The Rose of the Rancho (1906)	Richard W. Tully (1877-1945)
The Man of the Hour (1907)	George H. Broadhurst (1866-1952)
The Piper (1907)	Josephine Preston Peabody (1874-1922)
The Easiest Way (1909)	Eugene Walter (1874-1941)
The Arrow Maker (1911)	Mary Austin (1868-1934)
The Scarecrow (1911)	Percy MacKaye (1875-1956)
Peg o' My Heart (1912)	J. Hartley Manners (1870-1928)
The Broker of Bogota (1913) *The Gladiator* (1931)	Robert Montgomery Bird (1806-1854)
Romance (1913)	Edward Sheldon (1886-1946)
Why Marry? (1917)	Jesse Lynch Williams (1871-1929)
Lightnin' (1918)	Winchell Smith (1871-1933) Frank Bacon (1864-1922)
A Woman's Honor (1918) *Alison's House* (1930)	Susan Glaspell (1882-1948)
Aria da Capo (1919)	Edna St. Vincent Millay (1892-1950)
Déclassée (1919) *The Old Maid* (1935)	Zoe Akins (1886-1958)
Clarence (1919)	Booth Tarkington (1869-1946)
Miss Lulu Bett (1919)	Zona Gale (1874-1939)
The Sign on the Door (1919)	Channing Pollock (1880-1946)
Beyond the Horizon (1920) *The Hairy Ape* (1922) *Strange Interlude* (1928) *The Iceman Cometh* (1946) *Long Day's Journey into Night* (1956)	Eugene O'Neill (1888-1954)
Detour (1921) *Icebound* (1923)	Owen Davis (1874-1956)
Hellbent for Heaven (1922)	Hatcher Hughes (1886?-1945)
Seventh Heaven (1922)	Austin Strong (1881-1952)
Wild Birds (1922)	Dan Totheroh (1895-)
The Adding Machine (1923) *Street Scene* (1929)	Elmer Rice (1892-1967)
Sunup (1923)	Lula Vollmer (1898-1955)
Abie's Irish Rose (1924)	Anne Nichols (1895-1966)

See back cover for continuation of this chart.

Reader's Bookshelf of American Literature

American Drama, edited by Alan S. Downer

American Literary Essays, edited by Lewis Leary

American Poetry, edited by Karl Shapiro

American Short Novels, edited by R. P. Blackmur

American Short Stories, edited by Ray B. West, Jr.

GENERAL EDITOR: WILLIAM VAN O'CONNOR

American Drama

Edited by Alan S. Downer

Thomas Y. Crowell Company · New York · Established 1834

Designed by Laurel Wagner
Library of Congress Catalog Card Number: 60-6315
Manufactured in the United States of America
By Kingsport Press, Inc., Kingsport, Tennessee

Acknowledgments

Acknowledgment is gratefully made as follows on pages iv–v for permission to reprint copyrighted plays:

James A. Herne, *Shore Acres:* Revised and edited, 1928, by Mrs. James A. Herne. Copyright, 1928, by Katherine C. Herne. Copyright, 1956 (in renewal), by John T. Herne. CAUTION: Professionals and amateurs are hereby warned that *Shore Acres,* being fully protected under the copyright laws of the United States of America, the British Empire, including the Dominion of Canada, and all other countries of the Copyright Union, is subject to a royalty. All rights, including professional, amateur, motion pictures, recitation, public reading, radio and television broadcasting and the rights of translation into foreign languages are strictly reserved. Amateurs may produce this play upon payment of a royalty of Fifty Dollars for each performance, payable one week before the play is to be given to Samuel French, Inc., at 25 West 45th St., New York 36, N.Y., or 7623 Sunset Blvd., Hollywood 46, Calif., or if in Canada, to Samuel French (Canada) Ltd., at 27 Grenville St., Toronto, Ont.

William Vaughn Moody, *The Great Divide:* Copyright, 1906, by William Vaughn Moody, under the title *A Sabine Woman*. Copyright, 1934 (in renewal), in the name of Charlotte E. Moody, Henrietta Moody Fawcett, and Julia Moody Schmalz. CAUTION: Professionals and amateurs are hereby warned that *The Great Divide,* being fully protected under the copyright laws of the United States of America, the British Empire, including the Dominion of Canada, and all other countries of the Copyright Union, is subject to a royalty. All rights, including professional, amateur, motion pictures, recitation, public reading, radio and television broadcasting and the rights of translation into foreign lan-

To my students at the University of Copenhagen, 1953–1954, and the Salzburg Seminar in American Studies, 1959:

Nec levis, ingenuas pectus coluisse per drama
Cura sit; et linguas edidicisse duas.

A.S.D.

Contents

AMERICAN DRAMA

Introduction

On the Development of an American Dramatic Art

To constitute an American work, something more than the mere name is necessary: it seems to us that it should appeal more or less to the national feelings, and exhibit some degree of individuality. . . .

National feeling is exemplified, not by empty boasting, clamorous avidity for praise, or childish impatience of censure, but by a calm, quiet, manly independence of thought and action, by a deep feeling of inborn, long-cherished preference, which is indicated on all proper occasions, by a general tone of affectionate devotion, that no one can mistake, as arising from any other source than genuine patriotism. It is not precisely the exclusive patriotism of the English, which approaches to that bigotry which allows of no salvation out of its own creed . . . and still less is it the patriotism of our own country, which appears principally to consist in bringing down the standard of European excellence as low as possible, and then making it the object of our most abject imitation. . . . The best foundation for true patriotism is a clear, rational perception of the just claims of our country to our attachment and devotion. . . .

American literature must possess some striking features to distinguish it from the literature of any other country, or it can assert no claim to the distinction of nationality. It must be sufficiently original to claim some degree of individuality, and identify its nativity, either by certain peculiarities in opinion, certain preferences for things not especially relished by other nations, occasional traces of a departure from the old beaten track, and especially by local allusions, descriptions, references, and attachments, which cannot be mistaken in their origin.

The Knickerbocker, V (1835), 380–383.

THE STAGE AS MODEL

The essayist of *The Knickerbocker,* issuing a manifesto for a national literature in America, was far from a solitary voice. As early as 1790, Noah Webster had exhorted the citizens of the new nation to "*believe,* and act from the belief, that it is dishonorable to waste life in mimicking the follies of other nations and basking in the sunshine of foreign glory." For such writers, the Revolution had created not just a new nation but the possibility of a new national character, not just a new political establishment but the possibility of a new system of beliefs and ideals. The function of literature, they asserted, was to formulate and teach this new system; the secondary function of art as a mirror was for the remote future.

But the reiteration of Webster's doctrine during the next half century suggests that professional authors in the United States continued to practice a kind of literary colonialism, that the theatre was holding the mirror up to the nature of London audiences rather than those of New York or Philadelphia. Patriotic commentators were able to find virtue even in this defect. Acknowledging that "a taste for the belles-lettres, including under that description dramatic poetry as well as all others, is very low in America generally," the novelist John P.

Kennedy points out that "ours are a grave and saturnine people," affecting "a thoughtful and reserved demeanour in society, unlike the free and careless undress of social life in Europe." It was thus entirely proper that our stages should be occupied with the products or imitations of the products of this carefree society (European, 1812) while our native talents were "naturally directed to the cultivation of that knowledge which most effectually answers the common purposes of life." Not only the plays but the players were imported from the British theatre, and as late as 1821 an English actor reported that there were not enough American actors on the whole continent to form a company; "fortunately for the young population of that day," he adds piously, "they had something better to do."

Yet it would be strange if a new nation which was very conscious that it was the end product of all the progressive forces of a century of extensive theorizing about politics and society, of a revolution whose prologue included the radical doctrine that every man was entitled to life, liberty, and the pursuit of happiness, and whose epilogue declared that it had been fought to form a more perfect union, establish justice, promote the general welfare, and secure the blessings of liberty—it would be strange if this new and self-conscious nation would accept without criticism the moral and social values that underlay the theatrical literature of the Old World.

Therefore it is important to read with more care than their aesthetic qualities warrant the earliest plays of the American repertory. At first sight they appear merely imitative of what was currently popular in Germany and in London with a certain amount of Columbianism—speeches celebrating the new nation—thrust upon them. But on closer reading it becomes apparent that the imitation is of the *form* rather than the attitudes or subject matter of the European originals. Form, after all, is rarely an invention; it is a growth. And the basic forms of European drama, both classical and modern, had slowly evolved through centuries from religious rituals, the Greek festivals of Dionysos, the rites of the Christian church. No such rituals lay in the American past to provide a vehicle for the expression of those truths we held to be self-evident. It was necessary to take what vehicles were available—English comedy of manners, German sentimental drama, French romantic tragedy—and convert them to the uses of the republic. For this was to be drama with a purpose, the high, noble, and difficult purpose of making good citizens out of its audiences. William Dunlap, the first historian of the American theatre and an early play maker, wrote in 1821 of the relationship between form and subject matter:

> Inasmuch as we may hereafter deviate from the models left us by our ancestors, it will only be, as we hope, in a more severe and manly character, induced by our republican institutions, and approaching the high tone of the Greek drama. A character created by our free government and the absence of debasing aristocratic grades in our society already marks our travellers in every European country they visit. Surely, if any people on earth can hope to rival the works of Sophocles and Euripides, it is that country which is destined to look back to the annals of long past ages for a record that ever a slave or a master polluted her soil. A people literally self-governed, and guided by the experience and accumulated science of Asia, Africa, and Europe, must appreciate liberty and feel patriotism as no other people ever did. . . .
>
> The first efforts at dramatic literature in this country were wild. The essays of youth, not sufficiently instructed in any thing, and deficient in literary education, and though received favorably by a people beginning to feel that they were called to a new state of existence, and wishing a literature identified with themselves, and distinct from that of

Europe, both the dramatists and the people they addressed had not yet sufficiently matured their notions of the result of the great political changes which had taken place to know how far to assert independence in literature or government, or how far to imitate their European ancestors. . . .

When the whole character of our literature shall have received the impress of our republican government, when our writers, wherever they may lay the scene or plot of their works, shall warn mankind of the evils of government usurped over the people, then our drama will be national and distinct from that of countries not blessed by liberty of thought.

If this seems a heavy burden to place upon an art that professes to offer pastime with good company, it might be noted that in 1787, the very year in which the first wholly original play written by a citizen of the United States was performed in New York, the citizens of Philadelphia were beguiled into attending an English classic by the announcement that the theatre was presenting a concert of music. "Between the parts of the concert," the announcement added, "will be introduced a moral and instructive *tale,* called Filial Piety Exemplified in the History of the Prince of Denmark."

Royall Tyler, graduate of Harvard College, army officer, public-minded leading citizen of Vermont, is generally considered to be the first American playwright, that is, the first man with so completely an American background to present a play to the theatre after the completion of the Revolution. Far from being a dramatist by profession or vocation, he wrote *The Contrast* to criticize his fellow Americans and to convert them to his own view of the noble goals of the republic.

The Contrast, composed in a few days during a business trip to New York, is a comedy much after the manner of the eighteenth-century English comedy of manners; like its audience and its author it had neither the time nor the instinct to see life in the new nation as offering possibilities for tragic contemplation. The action contrasts the behavior of two young Americans, one a citizen of New York who idolizes the manner and attitudes of his British cousins, and one a citizen of Massachusetts who personifies the homespun virtues and manly sentiments learned under the command of General Washington as a soldier in the Revolutionary War. The New England officer, Colonel Manly, is openly critical of his fellow men who have failed to sever the bonds with England. Further he is romantically idealistic about the future of his country, and democratic in his enthusiasm for the capacities of the common man.

At the very outset, Tyler outlines the path that the early American drama was to follow. The dramatic form may have been English, but the comic attitude was American. Where Tyler's model, Sheridan in *The School for Scandal,* criticized those who deviated from the accepted morals and behavior of good society, Tyler directs his criticism against the conformist, against the man who follows the accepted social pattern rather than declaring his independence and virility of action and thought. Tyler's hero draws his moral principles from his own experience rather than Lord Chesterfield's *Letters to His Son,* models himself on the new but firmly established mythical ideal of George Washington, and behaves always with the narrow but ardent convictions of a Puritan-turned-Yankee. He is accompanied by a character who in the British original would be a servant ridiculed for aping his master or tolerated for being sufficiently ungenteel to get his master out of difficulties in which his own social niceness has entangled him. But Jonathan, though a comic figure, is a "waiter," not a servant; he is baffled by, but rises superior to, the un-American degeneracy of the city. *The Contrast* is hardly a play that the modern reader can take very seriously as dramatic art, but there is scarcely a subject or an attitude that was to form a part of the later American repertory that Tyler does not at least touch upon.

The reasons for this are not wholly nationalistic. The attitudes which the American drama was to reflect were in the air, were as much a part of the *Weltanschauung* as the nation itself. America was born at the beginning of the era of the common man, in social and political thinking, and during the Romantic Revival in literature and art.

Attention had occasionally been visited upon common men in the European theatre: George Lillo had tried to make a merchant's clerk into a tragic hero in *George Barnwell,* Diderot had evoked tears with sentimental family tales, and the time was not far off when Hebbel would turn from Biblical and historical subject matter to the life of the humble in *Maria Magdalene.* France discovered the *peau-rouge,* noblest of savages, and William Wordsworth was only one of the many poets to exercise his gifts on workingmen, farmers, and the poor. This new choice of subject matter was, of course, not merely influenced by the awakening interest in the common man, but by the spirit of romanticism.

Romanticism can mean so many things that it is almost useless as a term; however, as it is related to this particular period and to the drama of the period, it may be taken to involve a sense of closeness to nature, a sense of the importance of the individual's peculiar self (as opposed to some ideal entity), a taste and an enormous capacity for sensory, emotional reaction to events. Pity and sentimentality are never remote from the romantic, nor are other extremes: exaltation and a grotesque sense of comedy. But perhaps the greatest usefulness of the romantic spirit for the drama is its instinct for mythmaking.

Behind every great dramatic repertory there lies a body of myth, stories invented by the people to explain some mystery of nature or of their own racial personality. Myths explain in human terms what the social group believes to be true and they determine the basic patterns of action and the characteristic features of the heroes and villains of the more sophisticated art which develops out of them. Myths have thus both a social and a literary function, and if there are none buried in a nation's past, it is necessary to invent them. For this invention, the romantic spirit is well qualified.

It was this spirit that determined the character and the consistency of the character of the early American popular stage hero. He wore many different costumes: sometimes he was a revolutionary veteran (like Colonel Manly in *The Contrast*), sometimes an Indian chief, sometimes a Yankee peddler, or a frontiersman, or a farmer. But whatever the costume, beneath it was the same man, the same hero, the patriotic American's image of himself, a mythical figure as universally accepted as any derived from more ancient civilizations and cultures. This is the more remarkable since all Americans were immigrants and brought with them the centuries-old cultures of their European homelands; yet they almost at once began thinking of themselves as something unique, not just a nation but a race or culture apart.

Since Americans thought of themselves as "different" it is not surprising that one of the first disguises the popular hero assumed should have been the Indian chief, a character native to the drama of no European land. But the stage Indian was hardly to be found in the forests of America, either. What the playwrights depicted was not the savage nomad whom the settlers had cheated, fought, outwitted, and driven from the land which supported him to unproductive, unwanted territory. The stage Indian was rather the crystallization of an ideal:

he was the unconquerable underdog. Outnumbered, perhaps defeated by his enemies (British or Spanish but never American), he was firm in his conviction of the justice of his cause and in the determination to fight for his rights against the encroachment of non-Indian (that is to say, non-American) influences. He was proud, self-reliant, conscious of his worth as an individual, aware that his strength came to him from nature and nature's God rather than from the artificial codes of the civilization that oppressed him. He was, in fact, Colonel Manly without his regimentals.

Close to the stage Indian in popularity with early audiences stood his comic coadjutor, the Yankee peddler. As is proper in comedy, the peddler is perhaps a little closer to reality than is the heroic redskin. He appears as a traveling salesman, pack on back, dispensing wooden nutmegs and sanded sugar, but also coming to the rescue of distressed maidens, dispossessed widows, and deserted orphans. Like his prototype he was at first tolerated, then welcomed, and finally admired. He was tolerated as an individual who faced the world with nothing but his own ingenuity, he was welcomed because he brought to the pioneers the gossip, news, and stories of the communities they had left behind, and he was admired for his willingness to take on the rich, the strong, or the politically important with only his wit as an offensive weapon.

As the country moved westward, the stage Yankee shifted his costume to that of the stage frontiersman, and the ability to outtalk, outbuy, and outsell any other mortal was translated into the ability to outbrag and outshoot any man and outwit any natural phenomenon. Such a character was Davy Crockett, whose actual biography was completely ignored by the playwright in favor of a mythical figure complete with proverbial wisdom, fantastic skills as hunter and woodsman, and a dramatic action that crosses the story of Young Lochinvar with Paul Bunyan. Such a character too was Rip Van Winkle, first portrayed by Washington Irving as a shiftless, worthless vagabond, but translated by the dramatist into a victim of evil social forces who emerges triumphant through his own shrewdness.

Such heroes and their actions suggest, if they do not directly present, a critical attitude toward American life. It is, to be sure, not satire and not social drama in the later sense. But neither the tragedy of the stage Indian nor the triumph of Yankee ingenuity could exist if the forces that led to tragedy or comedy were not present. Colonel Manly inveighs against conformity, the peddler outwits a conventional vested interest. Later actions would show the corruption of rural virtue by the fashions of the Big City, or the destruction of manly independence by the Demon Rum. The point of the comic action was always the defeat of evil through exercise of ingenuity uncorrupted by the false values of an increasingly industrial civilization. Joe Morgan, village drunkard, harkens in time to the pleas of his dying child, signs a temperance pledge, and is returned to domestic felicity. Adam Trueman, the old farmer from Cattaraugus, visiting his former neighbor who has become a metropolitan merchant, finds him the victim of an ambitious wife, a pretended nobleman, and a blackmailing clerk, and contrives to set all right in the last scene. For associated with the mythical hero was an equally mythical conviction: you have only to go back, to the farm, to the domestic hearth, to be as it were recreated in virtue. If this early popular drama is critical in that it raises questions about some of the values of American life, they are all questions that can be answered. The Garden of Eden was not permanently closed.

It was, of course, a heavily moral drama. Like all institutions in a new country it must serve the nation, convince the audiences that the principles by which they were supposed to act were the true principles. So audiences wept for the noble savage and applauded the defeat of crafty landlords and evil innkeepers. If these plays appear in the mid-twentieth century as naïve and cluttered with sentimentality and easy optimism, they reflect very precisely—as the drama must always be expected to do—the inner spirit of the nation that furnished its audiences.

The theatre itself, where these plays were the staple of the repertory, was naïve in quite another way. It took the greatest delight in displaying an increasing illusion of reality for its own sake. Painted flats were replaced with rooms constructed on the stage, with real furniture, with real rugs, and real potted palms. Plays became long run successes because they set before the eyes of bedazzled spectators real boats foundering in waves of agitated canvas (soon to be replaced by real water), real locomotives and real sawmills; the time would come when the manager had only to announce that Edison's Incandescent Lamp would be used in a parlor scene for audiences to flock to his box office.

A romantic action in a setting of apparent realism created a shambling kind of spectacle that was increasingly unsatisfactory to the more critical spectators. In 1845, Edgar Allan Poe put together a long article which he entitled "The American Drama." The plays which he was able to discuss as examples of the native repertory were all failures, either with Poe or the audiences; but the principles which he laid down for a drama which would be essentially American in something more than its hero, its setting, or its subject matter are of considerable interest, particularly since they anticipate by some years the reforms actually effected by Ibsen and other continental dramatists. Poe declared,

The first thing necessary is to burn or bury the "old models," and to forget as quickly as possible, that ever a play has been penned. The second thing is to consider *de novo* what are the *capabilities* of the drama—not merely what hitherto have been its conventional purposes. The third and last point has reference to the composition of a play (showing to the fullest extent these capabilities) conceived and constructed with Feeling and Taste guided and controlled in every particular by the details of Reason—of Common Sense—in a word, of a Natural Art.

THE STAGE AS MIRROR

Poe was a maker of manifestos rather than plays and it is difficult to imagine what sort of play he had in mind: one which tests to the fullest extent the capabilities of the dramatic form and represents Natural Art. While a play by Poe would hardly have followed the techniques of domestic or sensational melodrama, it would probably not have achieved that freedom suggested by his manifesto, freedom from all conventions of the older theatre, freedom to allow the subject matter and attitude to determine the form and technique; in short, that freedom which is typical of the American drama after 1916.

Before this freedom could be achieved, playwrights had to learn to realize the full capabilities of the physical medium: the acting ensemble and the theatre itself, with its increasingly illusionistic scenery. Turning from the spectacular romantic play and the play of domestic sensibility, they had to explore the uses of that mode which is most characteristic of the nineteenth-century theatre: realism.

There are three stages in the development of realism from a technique to an art in playwrighting. The first, already alluded to, was well under way by mid-century; this was the realism of surfaces, the attempt to reproduce actuality in stage setting, and its fuller achievement waited upon scientific and mechanical progress. The second stage, realism of content, was only beginning to be experimented with. Characters tended more and more to be chosen from the lower ranks of society and to be involved in situations that the common man in the audience would recognize as the daily concerns of himself and his fellows. But always they were glamorized by the resounding presence of an "old school" actor, larger than life, or by a resort to fantasy that permitted playwright and playgoer to escape the responsibility of facing squarely the situation.

Three plays from this period will illustrate how far the American theatre had to go to reach the second stage of realism. *Rip Van Winkle* (1865) was put together by a skillful writer of melodrama, Dion Boucicault, and a popular character actor, Joseph Jefferson, from a story by Washington Irving. Jefferson invented the character and Boucicault much of what happened to it; Irving's responsibility was little more than the idea of the twenty-year sleep. The basic situation of the play is an interesting one: the village ne'er-do-well, driven from his home by his (justifiably) exasperated wife, wanders off into the woods. Before he can fall asleep, however, he finds himself in a cluster of dwarfs who prove to be the spirits of Henry Hudson and his men, still drinking schnapps and bowling in the Catskills. Rip drinks himself into his twenty-year sleep and returns to the village just in time to save his property from the machinations started by the villain two decades ago, to be reunited with his loving child, and to accept the apologies of his wife. What began as an interesting study of the effect of a lovable but worthless man on his family and community was hastily diverted into the actual fantasy of Hudson's dwarfs and the conventional fantasy of native wit and humble virtue triumphing over evil.

Similarly, Augustin Daly in *Horizon* (1871) poses questions of both immediate and enduring interest in American life, only to drop his final curtain without developing, to say nothing of answering, them. He takes a group of cultured Easterners into the rough life of the western frontier. But the clash of cultures is treated, when it is treated at all, solely for comedy, and the playwright is principally interested in revealing the noble heart under the black suit of a Bret-Hartean gambler, and in demonstrating that the true cause of the Indian uprisings was the hopeless pursuit of the heroine (The White Flower of the Plains) by Wannemucka, an Indian brave. The implications of the title are completely ignored.

In *The Old Homestead* (1886) Denman Thompson created a play whose title has become almost a symbol of a way of life. And both the opening situation (a group of city dwellers interfering with the orderly business of farming) and its main plot line (the rescue of a farm boy who has gone wrong in the big city) are related to one of the major issues in American life in the last part of the nineteenth century. But Thompson is content, on the one hand, with the photographic realism of wash basins and milk pails, and on the other, with the sentimental fantasy of a reunion at New Year's on the farm. The play exploits the realism of its setting and the sentimentality of its situations without going beyond the easiest laughter and the most willing tears.

It was an actor-playwright, James A. Herne, who took the final step to inner realism. Herne had been raised in the older theatre, he knew the conventions of character and situation to which audiences were accustomed, but he was also aware of developments in the other arts. As a friend of such literary men as William Dean Howells and Hamlin Garland, he observed that the literature of the stage was a drama of plot rather than purpose, and that the pleasures to be derived from it were the pleasures of ingenuity, craftsmanship, and execution. It was, he says, rather surprisingly, "art for art's sake." He declares himself boldly on the side of art for truth's sake which

> emphasizes humanity. It is not sufficient that the subject be attractive or beautiful, or that it does not offend. It must first of all express some *large* truth. That is to say, it must always be representative. Truth is not always beautiful, but in art for truth's sake it is indispensable.
>
> Art for truth's sake is serious. Its highest purpose has ever been to perpetuate the life of its time.

More than half a century and a revolution in dramatic art intervene between the first performance of Herne's *Shore Acres* in 1892 and the present-day reader. The survivals of the older theatre in it will perhaps be more apparent to us than will Herne's originality. We will see melodrama in the cast-out daughter and the averted shipwreck, farce in some of the incidents of the dooryard, and sentimentality in some of the character relationships. Yet the author's stage directions, his constant insistence on "playing down," indicate that these are only the familiar materials, not the purpose of his play. Love is more than a theatrical device to spin the plot, and the farm is more than a colorful background for theatrical high jinks. The final pantomimic scene, an astonishing *tour de force* in a theatre that had always insisted on a thrilling curtain line, has been several times compared with the ending of Chekhov's Russian classic, *The Cherry Orchard*, as a summary and symbol of the "large truth" with which the play is ultimately concerned.

It is through symbolism, of course, that the realistic drama achieves universality, the status of art. The European theatre discovered this in the plays of Ibsen. It remained for Herne to show the American theatre that settings and properties could be something more than inanimate actors, could be useful vehicles for expressing theme and attitude. What this can mean in the creation of dramatic art can be easily demonstrated by comparing one of the older western plays, *Horizon*, for example, or such a modern melodrama as David Belasco's *The Girl of the Golden West* (1905), with William Vaughn Moody's *The Great Divide* (1906). Both Belasco and Moody began with an actual event which would have been incredible in any locale other than the frontier west of the Rockies. Belasco had heard of a sheriff's discovery of a hidden desperado when some drops of blood fell on his handkerchief from the criminal's hiding place. Moody had heard of three men fighting for possession of a woman in a lonely cabin. Belasco makes his incident the climax of his play, a drama of causes; Moody makes his the inciting incident for a drama of effects. Belasco's incident suggested to him a thrilling action, Moody's suggested a *myth* (he originally called the play *The Sabine Woman*), that is, a story devised to explain human conduct. In *The Great Divide* the interplay of east and west, proposed in *Horizon*, is followed through as the central theme, and the play makes a statement about American life and about human relationships of both historical and general truth.

With the plays of Herne and Moody and some of their contemporaries the American theatre had reached the final stage in the progress toward realism. It was now ready to consider *de novo* the larger "*capabilities* of the drama."

THE CREATIVE THEATRE

Between 1900 and 1916 there were many tentative steps and several real advances toward freeing the dramatist from the conventions that not only past centuries but the more recent school of realism had imposed upon him. But perhaps the clearest program for the future, returning almost literally to the very beginnings of drama for fresh inspiration, was set forth by George Cram Cook as he announced the foundation of the Provincetown Players in 1916. He wrote,

> Primitive drama, the expression of the communal or religious life of the organic human group, the tribe, had spontaneously the unity of a pure art. There may be two hundred actors dramatically dancing the conflict of winter and spring, but all that all of them do in that drama springs from one shared fund of feelings, ideas, impulses. Unity is not imposed on them by the will of one of their number, but comes from that deep level in each where all their spirits are one. The aim of the founder of the Provincetown Players is to make all hands work from that level and to do it by recreating in a group of modern individuals, individuals far more highly differentiated than primitive people, a spiritual unity underlying their differences, a unity resembling the primitive unity of the tribe, a unity which may spontaneously create the unity necessary to the art of the theatre.

This is neither pedantry nor empty rhetoric.

Cook is, of course, referring to the anthropologist's explanation of the origins of dramatic art in tribal ritual, but a glance at the history of this theatre group will show that something quite concrete and American lay behind his words.

The Provincetown was one of many "off-Broadway" dramatic troupes organized in various communities by people to whom the restrictions, both economic and artistic, of the commercial theatre had become irksome. These groups were not necessarily "arty" or amateur. The Provincetown, for instance, was established in a fishing village at the tip of Cape Cod, under the aegis of Cook, by a variety of artists: they were poets and painters and writers of fiction, and an actor or two. They wrote, produced, and acted in their own plays in a theatre they had fashioned out of an old fishing shack. Among their first plays was Susan Glaspell's *Suppressed Desires,* a good-humored satire on psychiatry which has held the stage to this day; and among their first discoveries was Eugene O'Neill, generally considered the leading playwright of the modern American theatre.

O'Neill himself is perhaps the best proof that this new drama was professional and traditional and at the same time determined to discover the capabilities of the medium. His father was a popular actor who had toured the country for years in romantic melodrama. Eugene had traveled with his father as a boy and played a minor role in a vaudeville version of *The Count of Monte Cristo.* His first attempts at playwriting generally involved a series of violent actions leading up to a strong situation. Unlike his father, however, he came to know and be strongly attracted to the contemporary drama of Europe, in particular the naturalistic and symbolic plays of August Strindberg, and this new influence is apparent in his first produced work, the one-act plays of the sea, *Beyond the Horizon,* and in particular *Anna Christie* and *The Straw.* Once freed from the conventions of the past, O'Neill went on to create his own forms and techniques, as he does with originality and confidence in *The Hairy Ape.* Yet, while exploiting the capabilities of the drama to the full, he does not completely abandon the American tradition. What was useful to him, he preserved, and this included characters, situations, techniques, and attitudes.

Shortly after the first performance of *The Emperor Jones,* a symbolic drama of man's quest for the ultimate springs of action in his own subconscious and his racial past which had taxed the resources and the creative ingenuity of the Provincetown Playhouse to the utmost, O'Neill received a suggestion from his father's former manager that he rewrite *The Count of Monte Cristo,* adjusting the old melodrama to the tastes of the new theatre and its audience. Instead of ridiculing or scorning the idea, O'Neill replied:

I can only imagine one way in which the project would call forth any genuine creative interest on my part. If I could say to myself: Throw everything overboard—all precedent, all existing dogmas of what is practicable and what is not in the theatre of today, all well-regulated ideas of what a play is or isn't, etc. Create your own form just as you did in *The Emperor Jones.* Rely on, and *demand,* as you did in that play, a new ingenuity and creative collaboration on the part of the producer—a new system of staging of extreme simplicity and flexibility which, combined with art in the lighting, will permit of many scenes and instantaneous changes, a combination of the scope of the movies with all that is best in spoken drama. But keep all this within the realms of theatrical possibility as you understand it. Don't write closet drama.

In that letter O'Neill expresses the principles that have governed both himself and his successors in the American theatre. In addition he calls attention to some of the things that have made those principles practicable: the advances in stagecraft, the greater flexibility of the physical medium through the introduction of electric lighting, and the rediscovery of the possibilities of panoramic structure in the motion picture scenario.

In scene design, in acting technique, in lighting, and most particularly in elevating the director into the chief force for producing a finished and total unit in a dramatic production, the American theatre in the decade after 1916 quickly caught up with the theatres of western Europe which had led the way. The readiness of American playwrights to seize the new tools they had been offered and their willingness to experiment with dramatic technique soon produced a repertory able for the first time to take its place in the great repertory of the world theatre. And from his first production, as play followed play, success or failure, Eugene O'Neill was recognized as the leader in the renaissance of American drama.

He was a restless experimenter. Although his themes, or "large ideas," are unchanging, he was constantly seeking new vehicles for communicating with his audience. He began with various kinds of realism: now broadly reportorial as in the sea plays, now highly selective as in *Beyond the Horizon.* He tried symbolism, as in *The Hairy Ape,* and symbolism combined with realism, as in *The Emperor Jones.* He adapted the techniques of the older theatre—masks, asides, illusionistic scenery—not for the sake of novelty but for their symbolic value in revealing the ultimate meaning and increasing the texture of the dramatic experience for the audience. For he was never concerned with individual or temporal problems, with the rehabilitation of drunkards or wastrel sons, with the rights of labor or class distinctions, with conformity and independence. He was concerned only with revealing as intimately and expressively as he could the inner nature of man and his search for identity in a mysterious universe.

While Thornton Wilder is not to be thought of as a disciple of O'Neill, in following him into the theatre he inevitably benefited from the atmosphere of experimentation which O'Neill made almost the identifying characteristic of modern American drama. If O'Neill may be thought of as a writer who makes original and creative use of the older techniques of the theatre, Wilder plays philosophically with the oldest conventions of the drama itself, with the Aristotelian unities of time and place. His relativistic treatment of time in *The Long Christmas Dinner* is a good instance: he does not ignore time as did the Greek playwrights, he does not make it his fool, to run fast or slow at his bidding, as did the Elizabethans, and he is not bound by clock and calendar as were the writers of the well-made play. Instead he presents time as a symbolic force in American life, his action flows in generations, and the audience, experiencing the history of an American family, experiences also the revelation of a truth at once pathetic, profound, and universal.

There is nothing in this, or Wilder's other plays, that is experimental to the point of being unstageworthy. To paraphrase O'Neill, everything is kept within the realms of theatrical possibility as he understands it. *The Happy Journey to Trenton and Camden* takes a father, a mother, a son, and a daughter on a short automobile trip between the two cities without illusionistic scenery, without even an automobile. Place and movement through space are both indicated to the imagination of the audience by the actors, by action, speech, and gesture. *The Pullman Car Hiawatha* reveals not only the actions of the characters and their inner thoughts but the thoughts of the places through which they rush in the night express, and finally the enveloping thoughts of the great philosophers and poets who have shaped all men's lives without their awareness. Wilder's long plays, for example, his famous *Our Town,* exhibit his continuing determination to exploit the capabilities of the stage, to express basic truths about human experience in terms of the dramatist's chief and unique tool, the actor, his physical presence, his human art.

Wilder and O'Neill share the experimentalism that is characteristic of the modern American theatre; they have not infrequently turned for their subject matter to those characters and situations which have concerned the American drama since its post-Revolutionary beginnings. The isolation of peculiarly American characteristics in the farmer and the villager—Colonel Manly and Jonathan in *The Contrast,* Adam Trueman in *Fashion,* Josh Whitcomb in *The Old Homestead,* Uncle Dan'l in *Shore Acres*—is echoed in Wilder's *Our Town,* and with a different evaluation in O'Neill's *Desire under the Elms.* The combination of criticism and idealism appears in *The Skin of Our Teeth* and *Ah, Wilderness!* To Wilder the American dream is a recoverable reality; if O'Neill is among the disenchanted, he at least knows the reality of what has been lost.

Disenchantment of a different sort dominates the theme and action of *The Petrified Forest.* Robert E. Sherwood thought of himself as both a liberal and an intellectual, and on such men the impact of the last years of the twenties and the early years of the thirties was stunning. In the preface to *Reunion in Vienna* he observed that ahead of modern man was only

> black doubt, punctuated by brief flashes of ominous light, whose revelations are not comforting. Behind him is nothing but the ghastly wreckage of burnt bridges. As an alternative to cynicism is the sentimentalism which derives exquisite anguish from an acknowledgment of futility.—Democracy—liberty—equality, fraternity, and the pursuit of happiness. Peace and prosperity! Emancipation by enlightenment! All the distillations of man's maturing intelligence have gone sour.

Looking back, it is apparent that this black despair was at least in part the result of losing contact with the characteristic impulses of American life, impulses that could still be perceived by such different playwrights as Lynn Riggs in his folk-comedy *Roadside,* and George Kaufman and Moss Hart in their urban fantasy *You Can't Take It with You.* But the temporary paralysis which the depression inflicted not just on the economic but on the intellectual life of the country is well represented by *The Petrified Forest.*

To escape the paralysis a good many artists turned to Marxism or some other gospel of determinism. Sherwood, however, is not trying to propagandize for the few but to reflect the many. He dismisses communism in his opening scene, dwells at some length on the then more immediate evil of fascism, but is principally concerned with "the wreckage of burnt bridges." This had been the chief subject of the European expressionists, but Sherwood does not find it necessary to venture beyond the conventional form of the popular theatre of his time—the well-made play.

The well-made play in its origin was a tidy and economical structure for setting up a dramatic conflict, increasing it by mechanical turns of plotting, and resolving it in a thrilling but logical climax. In the hands of Ibsen it became the vehicle for a drama of social and philosophical questioning; in the hands of lesser men it degenerated into a convenient technique to support hackneyed ideas.

The Petrified Forest escapes from the empty slickness of its conventional form and from the exquisite anguish of an acknowledgment of futility in theme through symbolism. The scene is a *paysage moralisé;* the characters, who could have stepped from the picture-page of a newspaper, are chosen to represent carefully differentiated ideas; the action is a controlled allegory. The play thus becomes a revealing social and historical document, though the principal characters, Gabby, Squier, and Duke Mantee, are drawn with such sympathy that the work has achieved a life and importance of its own. The despair that envelopes Sherwood's Wasteland is never so black that the individual is incapable of positive action, and if Alan Squier alludes to The Hollow Men, he is able in the end to step out of their company and find his place with those American heroes whose principle was formulated by Davy Crockett: Make sure you're right, then go ahead.

The end of the Second World War brought new vigor to the American drama, particularly in the plays of Tennessee Williams and Arthur Miller. With a strong sense of the American past and a sharp eye on the present they spoke effectively and directly not just to Broadway and the hinterland but to vast audiences abroad. Indeed, since 1946, America has been the chief source of new plays in the repertory of the world theatre.

Not because ours has become any less a national drama. The heroes of *Death of a Salesman* or *The Glass Menagerie* could only have been produced by the particular forces of American life. If they have found an understanding audience away from Broadway it is because they have been drawn so completely and so honestly that the playgoer cannot turn his back on the human truth they project.

Human truth, directly experienced: that is the characteristic of the most vigorous American drama after nearly two centuries of development. It is not, of course, the sole "capability" of the form. The drama can sport with human follies, it can moralize; it can sigh over the futility of existence, it can puzzle the will; it can reiterate the received truths, it can propound radical doctrines. But the American playwright, jealous of his freedom to assume what attitudes he chooses, to draw his characters from the national life as he perceives it, and above all to make almost impossible demands upon the creativity of his collaborators in the theatre, has been able to provide for his audiences a dramatic experience comparable in intensity and illumination with all but the greatest masterpieces of this most complex of the narrative arts.

Royall Tyler

✻ 1757-1826

Royall Tyler, the first citizen of the United States to write a play performed by a professional American company, was born in Boston and educated at Harvard College. Upon his graduation in 1776 he was also awarded a degree by Yale College as a mark of singular intellectual promise. He took up the study of the law, but found time to associate himself with a group of young Cambridgeites who were preoccupied with writing, painting, and politics, and was admitted to the bar in 1780.

In 1786 he was appointed a major in the company of General Benjamin Lincoln and sent into western Massachusetts to aid in putting down Shays's Rebellion, which had been organized by a large group of farmers in protest against the taxes and customs duties imposed by the state government. Apparently Tyler's eloquence in addressing the rebels had much to do with their surrender, and in March, 1787, he was sent by the governor to New York on official business. Here he visited the playhouse in John Street, became acquainted with the chief low comedian of the company, Thomas Wignell, and saw such plays as THE SCHOOL FOR SCANDAL *and John O'Keeffe's* THE POOR SOLDIER.

Shays's Rebellion, the official trip to New York, the theatre in John Street, Wignell, and the plays he had seen all became a part of his own first play, THE CONTRAST, *produced at that theatre and with Wignell as Jonathan on April 16, 1787. It was repeated five times in New York and was also played in Baltimore, Philadelphia, Boston and Charleston—the only theatrical "centers" of the new nation. In May, Tyler furnished the players with a comic opera,* MAY DAY IN TOWN, OR, NEW YORK IN AN UPROAR, *and ten years later his* GEORGIA SPEC, OR LAND IN THE MOON *was performed in Boston.*

He wrote other plays (not produced) and a variety of miscellaneous verse and essays, and one novel, THE ALGERINE CAPTIVE *(1792). Meanwhile he continued his practice of the law, became chief justice of the Vermont Supreme Court and professor of jurisprudence at the University of Vermont. He died in Brattleboro.*

The text of THE CONTRAST *here reprinted is taken from the original edition published by Thomas Wignell in Philadelphia in 1790. Tyler's name does not appear on the title page, the authorship being credited only to "*A CITIZEN OF THE UNITED STATES.*"*

The Contrast

A COMEDY IN FIVE ACTS

Characters

COL. MANLY	CHARLOTTE
DIMPLE	MARIA
VAN ROUGH	LETITIA
JESSAMY	JENNY
JONATHAN	*Servants*

SCENE, *New-York*

PROLOGUE

[*Written by a Young Gentleman of New-York, and Spoken by Mr. Wignell*]

Exult each patriot heart!—this night is shewn
A piece, which we may fairly call our own;
Where the proud titles of "My Lord! Your Grace!"
To humble Mr. and plain Sir give place.
Our Author pictures not from foreign climes
The fashions or the follies of the times;
But has confin'd the subject of his work
To the gay scenes—the circles of New-York.
On native themes his Muse displays her pow'rs;
If ours the faults, the virtues too are ours.
Why should our thoughts to distant countries roam,
When each refinement may be found at home?
Who travels now to ape the rich or great,
To deck an equipage and roll in state;
To court the graces, or to dance with ease,
Or by hypocrisy to strive to please?
Our free-born ancestors such arts despis'd:
Genuine sincerity alone they priz'd;
Their minds, with honest emulation fir'd,
To solid good—not ornament—aspir'd;
Or, if ambition rous'd a bolder flame,
Stern virtue throve, where indolence was shame.
But modern youths, with imitative sense,
Deem taste in dress the proof of excellence;
And spurn the meanness of your homespun arts,
Since homespun habits would obscure their parts;
Whilst all, which aims at splendour and parade,
Must come from Europe, and be ready made.
Strange! we should thus our native worth disclaim,
And check the progress of our rising fame.
Yet one, whilst imitation bears the sway,
Aspires to nobler heights, and points the way.
Be rous'd, my friends! his bold example view;
Let your own Bards be proud to copy you!
Should rigid critics reprobate our play,
At least the patriotic heart will say,
"Glorious our fall, since in a noble cause.
"The bold attempt alone demands applause."
Still may the wisdom of the Comic Muse
Exalt your merits, or your faults accuse.
But think not, 'tis her aim to be severe;—
We all are mortals, and as mortals err.
If candour pleases, we are truly blest;
Vice trembles, when compell'd to stand confess'd.
Let not light Censure on your faults, offend,
Which aims not to expose them, but amend.
Thus does our Author to your candour trust;
Conscious, the free are generous, as just.

ACT I SCENE 1

An Apartment at CHARLOTTE'S

[CHARLOTTE *and* LETITIA *discovered.*]

LETITIA. And so, Charlotte, you really think the pocket-hoop unbecoming.

CHARLOTTE. No, I don't say so. It may be very becoming to saunter round the house of a rainy day; to visit my grand-mamma, or to go to Quakers' meeting: but to swim in a minuet, with the eyes of fifty well-dressed beaux upon me, to trip it in the Mall, or walk on the battery, give me the luxurious, jaunty, flowing, bell-hoop. It would have delighted you to have seen me the last evening, my charming girl! I was dangling o'er the battery with Billy Dimple; a knot of young fellows were upon the platform; as I passed them I faultered with one of the most bewitching false steps you ever saw, and then recovered myself with such a pretty confusion, flirting my hoop to discover a jet black shoe and brilliant buckle. Gad! how my little heart thrilled to hear the confused raptures of—*"Demme, Jack, what a delicate foot!" "Ha! General, what a well-turned——"*

LETITIA. Fie! fie! Charlotte [*stopping her mouth*], I protest you are quite a libertine.

CHARLOTTE. Why, my dear little prude, are we not all such libertines? Do you think, when I sat tortured two hours under the hands of my friseur, and an hour more at my toilet, that I had any thoughts of my aunt Susan, or my cousin Betsey? though they are both allowed to be critical judges of dress.

LETITIA. Why, who should we dress to please, but those who are judges of its merit?

CHARLOTTE. Why, a creature who does not know *Buffon* from *Souflée*—Man!—my Letitia—Man! for whom we dress, walk, dance, talk, lisp, languish, and smile. Does not the grave Spectator assure us that even our much bepraised diffidence, modesty, and blushes are all directed to make ourselves good wives and mothers as fast as we can? Why, I'll undertake with one flirt of this hoop to bring more beaux to my feet in one week than the grave Maria, and her sentimental circle, can do, by sighing sentiment till their hairs are grey.

LETITIA. Well, I won't argue with you; you always out-talk me; let us change the subject. I hear that Mr. Dimple and Maria are soon to be married.

CHARLOTTE. You hear true. I was consulted in the choice of the wedding clothes. She is to be married in a delicate white satin, and has a monstrous pretty brocaded lutestring for the second day. It would have done you good to have seen with what an affected indifference the dear sentimentalist turned over a thousand pretty things, just as if her heart did not palpitate with her approaching happiness, and at last made her choice and arranged her dress with such apathy as if she did not know that plain white satin and a simple blond lace would show her clear skin and dark hair to the greatest advantage.

LETITIA. But they say her indifference to dress, and even to the gentleman himself, is not entirely affected.

CHARLOTTE. How?

LETITIA. It is whispered that if Maria gives her hand to Mr. Dimple, it will be without her heart.

CHARLOTTE. Though the giving the heart is one of the last of all laughable considerations in the marriage of a girl of spirit, yet I should like to hear what antiquated notions the dear little piece of old-fashioned prudery has got in her head.

LETITIA. Why, you know that old Mr. John-Richard-Robert-Jacob-Isaac-Abraham-Cornelius Van Dumpling, Billy Dimple's father (for he has thought fit to soften his name, as well as manners, during his English tour), was the most intimate friend of Maria's father. The old folks, about a year before Mr. Van Dumpling's death, proposed this match: the young folks were accordingly introduced, and told they must love one another. Billy was then a good-natured, decent-dressing young fellow, with a little dash of the coxcomb, such as our young fellows of fortune usually have. At this time, I really believe she thought she loved him; and had they then been married, I doubt not they might have jogged on, to the end of the chapter, a good kind of a sing-song lack-a-daysaical life, as other honest married folks do.

CHARLOTTE. Why did they not then marry?

LETITIA. Upon the death of his father, Billy went to England to see the world and rub off a little of the patroon rust. During his absence, Maria, like a good girl, to keep herself constant to her *nown true-love,* avoided company, and betook herself, for her amusement, to her books, and her dear Billy's letters. But, alas! how many ways has the mischievous demon of inconstancy of stealing into a woman's heart! Her love was destroyed by the very means she took to support it.

CHARLOTTE. How?—Oh! I have it—some likely young beau found the way to her study.

LETITIA. Be patient, Charlotte; your head so runs upon beaux. Why, she read Sir Charles Grandison, Clarissa Harlow, Shenstone, and the Sentimental Journey; [1] and between whiles, as I said, Billy's letters. But, as her taste improved, her love declined. The contrast was so striking betwixt the good sense of her books and the flimsiness of her love-letters, that she discovered she had unthinkingly engaged her hand without her heart; and then the whole transaction, managed by the old folks, now appeared so unsentimental, and looked so like bargaining for a bale of goods, that she found she ought to have rejected, according to every rule of romance, even the man of her choice, if imposed upon her in that manner. Clary Harlow would have scorned such a match.

CHARLOTTE. Well, how was it on Mr. Dimple's return? Did he meet a more favourable reception than his letters?

LETITIA. Much the same. She spoke of him with respect abroad, and with contempt in her closet. She watched his conduct and conversation, and found that he had by travelling acquired the wickedness of Lovelace without his wit, and the politeness of Sir Charles Grandison without his generosity. The ruddy youth, who washed his face at the cistern every morning, and swore and looked eternal love and constancy, was now metamorphosed into a flippant, palid, polite beau, who devotes the morning to his toilet, reads a few pages of Chesterfield's letters, and then minces out, to put the infamous principles in practice upon every woman he meets.

CHARLOTTE. But, if she is so apt at conjuring up these sentimental bugbears, why does she not discard him at once?

LETITIA. Why, she thinks her word too sacred to be trifled with. Besides, her father, who has a great respect for the memory of his deceased friend, is ever telling her how he shall renew his years in their union, and repeating the dying injunctions of old Van Dumpling.

CHARLOTTE. A mighty pretty story! And so you would make me believe that the sensible Maria would give up Dumpling manor, and the all-accomplished Dimple as a husband, for the absurd, ridiculous reason, forsooth, because she despises and abhors him. Just as if a lady could not be privileged to spend a man's fortune, ride in his carriage, be called after his name, and call him her *nown dear lovee* when she wants money, without loving and respecting the great he-creature. Oh! my dear girl, you are a monstrous prude.

LETITIA. I don't say what I would do; I only intimate how I suppose she wishes to act.

CHARLOTTE. No, no, no! A fig for sentiment. If she breaks, or wishes to break, with Mr. Dimple, depend upon it, she has some other man in her eye. A woman rarely discards one lover until she is sure of another. Letitia little thinks what a clue I have to Dimple's conduct. The generous man submits to render himself disgusting to Maria, in order

[1] *Sir Charles Grandison, Clarissa Harlowe,* sentimental novels by Samuel Richardson; William Shenstone, poet of sentimentalized nature; *The Sentimental Journey,* novel by Laurence Sterne.

that she may leave him at liberty to address me. I must change the subject. [*Aside, and rings a bell.*]

[*Enter* SERVANT.]

Frank, order the horses to.——Talking of marriage, did you hear that Sally Bloomsbury is going to be married next week to Mr. Indigo, the rich Carolinian?

LETITIA. Sally Bloomsbury married! —why, she is not yet in her teens.

CHARLOTTE. I do not know how that is, but you may depend upon it, 'tis a done affair. I have it from the best authority. There is my aunt Wyerly's Hannah. You know Hannah; though a black, she is a wench that was never caught in a lie in her life. Now, Hannah has a brother who courts Sarah, Mrs. Catgut the milliner's girl, and she told Hannah's brother, and Hannah, who, as I said before, is a girl of undoubted veracity, told it directly to me, that Mrs. Catgut was making a new cap for Miss Bloomsbury, which, as it was very dressy, it is very probable is designed for a wedding cap. Now, as she is to be married, who can it be to but to Mr. Indigo? Why, there is no other gentleman that visits at her papa's.

LETITIA. Say not a word more, Charlotte. Your intelligence is so direct and well grounded, it is almost a pity that it is not a piece of scandal.

CHARLOTTE. Oh! I am the pink of prudence. Though I cannot charge myself with ever having discredited a tea-party by my silence, yet I take care never to report any thing of my acquaintance, especially if it is to their credit,—*discredit,* I mean,—until I have searched to the bottom of it. It is true, there is infinite pleasure in this charitable pursuit. Oh! how delicious to go and condole with the friends of some backsliding sister, or to retire with some old dowager or maiden aunt of the family, who love scandal so well that they cannot forbear gratifying their appetite at the expense of the reputation of their nearest relations! And then to return full fraught with a rich collection of circumstances, to retail to the next circle of our acquaintance under the strongest injunctions of secrecy,—ha, ha, ha!—interlarding the melancholy tale with so many doleful shakes of the head, and more doleful "Ah! who would have thought it! so amiable, so prudent a young lady, as we all thought her, what a monstrous pity! well, I have nothing to charge myself with; I acted the part of a friend, I warned her of the principles of that rake, I told her what would be the consequence; I told her so, I told her so."—Ha, ha, ha!

LETITIA. Ha, ha, ha! Well, but, Charlotte, you don't tell me what you think of Miss Bloomsbury's match.

CHARLOTTE. Think! why I think it is probable she cried for a plaything, and they have given her a husband. Well, well, well, the puling chit shall not be deprived of her plaything: 'tis only exchanging London dolls for American babies.—Apropos, of babies, have you heard what Mrs. Affable's high-flying notions of delicacy have come to?

LETITIA. Who, she that was Miss Lovely?

CHARLOTTE. The same; she married Bob Affable of Schenectady. Don't you remember?

[*Enter* SERVANT.]

SERVANT. Madam, the carriage is ready.

LETITIA. Shall we go to the stores first, or visiting?

CHARLOTTE. I should think it rather too early to visit, especially Mrs. Prim; you know she is so particular.

LETITIA. Well, but what of Mrs. Affable?

CHARLOTTE. Oh, I'll tell you as we go; come, come, let us hasten. I hear Mrs. Catgut has some of the prettiest caps arrived you ever saw. I shall die if I have not the first sight of them. [*Exeunt.*]

SCENE 2

A Room in VAN ROUGH'S *House*

[MARIA *sitting disconsolate at a Table, with Books, &c.*]

SONG

I.

The sun sets in night, and the stars shun the day;
But glory remains when their lights fade away!
Begin, ye tormentors! your threats are in vain,
For the son of Alknomook shall never complain.

II.

Remember the arrows he shot from his bow;
Remember your chiefs by his hatchet laid low:
Why so slow?—do you wait till I shrink from the pain?
No—the son of Alknomook will never complain.

III.

Remember the wood where in ambush we lay,
And the scalps which we bore from your nation away:
Now the flame rises fast, you exult in my pain;
But the son of Alknomook can never complain.

IV.

I go to the land where my father is gone;
His ghost shall rejoice in the fame of his son:
Death comes like a friend, he relieves me from pain;
And thy son, Oh Alknomook! has scorn'd to complain.

There is something in this song which ever calls forth my affections. The manly virtue of courage, that fortitude which steels the heart against the keenest misfortunes, which interweaves the laurel of glory amidst the instruments of torture and death, displays something so noble, so exalted, that in despite of the prejudices of education I cannot but admire it, even in a savage. The prepossession which our sex is supposed to entertain for the character of a soldier is, I know, a standing piece of raillery among the wits. A cockade, a lapell'd coat, and a feather, they will tell you, are irresistible by a female heart. Let it be so. Who is it that considers the helpless situation of our sex, that does not see that we each moment stand in need of a protector, and that a brave one too? Formed of the more delicate materials of nature, endowed only with the softer passions, incapable, from our ignorance of the world, to guard against the wiles of mankind, our security for happiness often depends upon their generosity and courage. Alas! how little of the former do we find! How inconsistent! that man should be leagued to destroy that honour upon which solely rests his respect and esteem. Ten thousand temptations allure us, ten thousand passions betray us; yet the smallest deviation from the path of rectitude is followed by the contempt and insult of man, and the more remorseless pity of woman; years of penitence and tears cannot wash away the stain, nor a life of virtue obliterate its remembrance. Reputation is the life of woman; yet courage to protect it is masculine and disgusting; and the only safe asylum a woman of delicacy can find is in the arms of a man of honour. How naturally, then, should we love the brave and the generous; how gratefully should we bless the arm raised for our protection, when nerv'd by virtue and directed by honour! Heaven grant that the man with whom I may be connected —may be connected! Whither has my imagination transported me—whither does it now lead me? Am I not indissolubly engaged, "by every obligation of honour which my own consent and my father's approbation can give," to a man

ALKNOMOOK

The Death Song of the CHEROKEE INDIANS.

NEWYORK Printed+ſold by G.GILFERT.Nº177 BROADWAY.
Likewise to be had at P. A.VONHAGENS. Muſicſtore. Nº3.Cornhill. BOSTON

who can never share my affections, and whom a few days hence it will be criminal for me to disapprove—to disapprove! would to heaven that were all—to despise. For, can the most frivolous manners, actuated by the most depraved heart, meet, or merit, anything but contempt from every woman of delicacy and sentiment?

[VAN ROUGH *without.* Mary!]

Ha! my father's voice—Sir!——

[*Enter* VAN ROUGH.]

VAN ROUGH. What, Mary, always singing doleful ditties, and moping over these plaguy books.

MARIA. I hope, Sir, that it is not criminal to improve my mind with books, or to divert my melancholy with singing, at my leisure hours.

VAN ROUGH. Why, I don't know that, child; I don't know that. They us'd to say, when I was a young man, that if a woman knew how to make a pudding, and to keep herself out of fire and water, she knew enough for a wife. Now, what good have these books done you? have they not made you melancholy? as you call it. Pray, what right has a girl of your age to be in the dumps? haven't you everything your heart can wish; an't you going to be married to a young man of great fortune; an't you going to have the quit-rent of twenty miles square?

MARIA. One-hundredth part of the land, and a lease for life of the heart of a man I could love, would satisfy me.

VAN ROUGH. Pho, pho, pho! child; nonsense, downright nonsense, child. This comes of your reading your story-books; your Charles Grandisons, your Sentimental Journals, and your Robinson Crusoes, and such other trumpery. No, no, no! child; it is money makes the mare go; keep your eye upon the main chance, Mary.

MARIA. Marriage, Sir, is, indeed, a very serious affair.

VAN ROUGH. You are right, child; you are right. I am sure I found it so, to my cost.

MARIA. I mean, Sir, that as marriage is a portion for life, and so intimately involves our happiness, we cannot be too considerate in the choice of our companion.

VAN ROUGH. Right, child; very right. A young woman should be very sober when she is making her choice, but when she has once made it, as you have done, I don't see why she should not be as merry as a grig; I am sure she has reason enough to be so. Solomon says that "there is a time to laugh, and a time to weep." Now, a time for a young woman to laugh is when she has made sure of a good rich husband. Now, a time to cry, according to you, Mary, is when she is making choice of him; but I should think that a young woman's time to cry was when she despaired of *getting* one. Why, there was your mother, now: to be sure, when I popp'd the question to her she did look a little silly; but when she had once looked down on her apron-strings, as all modest young women us'd to do, and drawled out ye-s, she was as brisk and as merry as a bee.

MARIA. My honoured mother, Sir, had no motive to melancholy; she married the man of her choice.

VAN ROUGH. The man of her choice! And pray, Mary, an't you going to marry the man of your choice—what trumpery notion is this? It is these vile books [*throwing them away*]. I'd have you to know, Mary, if you won't make young Van Dumpling the man of *your* choice, you shall marry him as the man of *my* choice.

MARIA. You terrify me, Sir. Indeed, Sir, I am all submission. My will is yours.

VAN ROUGH. Why, that is the way your mother us'd to talk. "My will is yours, my dear Mr. Van Rough, my will is yours"; but she took special care to have her own way, though, for all that.

MARIA. Do not reflect upon my mother's memory, Sir——

VAN ROUGH. Why not, Mary, why not? She kept me from speaking my mind all her *life,* and do you think she shall henpeck me now she is *dead* too? Come, come; don't go to sniveling; be a good girl, and mind the main chance. I'll see you well settled in the world.

MARIA. I do not doubt your love, Sir, and it is my duty to obey you. I will endeavour to make my duty and inclination go hand in hand.

VAN ROUGH. Well, well, Mary; do you be a good girl, mind the main chance, and never mind inclination. Why, do you know that I have been down in the cellar this very morning to examine a pipe of Madeira which I purchased the week you were born, and mean to tap on your wedding day?—That pipe cost me fifty pounds sterling. It was well worth sixty pounds; but I over-reach'd Ben Bulkhead, the supercargo. I'll tell you the whole story. You must know that——

[*Enter* SERVANT.]

SERVANT. Sir, Mr. Transfer, the broker, is below. [*Exit.*]

VAN ROUGH. Well, Mary, I must go. Remember, and be a good girl, and mind the main chance. [*Exit.*]

MARIA [*Alone*]. How deplorable is my situation! How distressing for a daughter to find her heart militating with her filial duty! I know my father loves me tenderly; why then do I reluctantly obey him? Heaven knows! with what reluctance I should oppose the will of a parent, or set an example of filial disobedience; at a parent's command, I could wed awkwardness and deformity. Were the heart of my husband good, I would so magnify his good qualities with the eye of conjugal affection, that the defects of his person and manners should be lost in the emanation of his virtues. At a father's command, I could embrace poverty. Were the poor man my husband, I would learn resignation to my lot; I would enliven our frugal meal with good humour, and chase away misfortune from our cottage with a smile. At a father's command, I could almost submit to what every female heart knows to be the most mortifying, to marry a weak man, and blush at my husband's folly in every company I visited. But to marry a depraved wretch, whose only virtue is a polished exterior; who is actuated by the unmanly ambition of conquering the defenceless; whose heart, insensible to the emotions of patriotism, dilates at the plaudits of every unthinking girl; whose laurels are the sighs and tears of the miserable victims of his specious behaviour,—can he, who has no regard for the peace and happiness of other families, ever have a due regard for the peace and happiness of his own? Would to heaven that my father were not so hasty in his temper? Surely, if I were to state my reasons for declining this match, he would not compel me to marry a man, whom, though my lips may solemnly promise to honour, I find my heart must ever despise. [*Exit.*]

End of the First Act

ACT II SCENE 1

[*Enter* CHARLOTTE *and* LETITIA.]

CHARLOTTE [*At entering*]. Betty, take those things out of the carriage and carry them to my chamber; see that you don't tumble them. My dear, I protest, I think it was the homeliest of the whole. I declare I was almost tempted to return and change it.

LETITIA. Why would you take it?

CHARLOTTE. Didn't Mrs. Catgut say it was the most fashionable?

LETITIA. But, my dear, it will never fit becomingly on you.

CHARLOTTE. I know that; but did not you hear Mrs. Catgut say it was fashionable?

LETITIA. Did you see that sweet airy cap with the white sprig?

CHARLOTTE. Yes, and I longed to take it; but, my dear, what could I do? Did not Mrs. Catgut say it was the most fashionable; and if I had not taken it, was not that awkward gawky, Sally Slender, ready to purchase it immediately?

LETITIA. Did you observe how she tumbled over the things at the next shop, and then went off without purchasing anything, nor even thanking the poor man for his trouble? But, of all the awkward creatures, did you see Miss Blouze endeavouring to thrust her unmerciful arm into those small kid gloves?

CHARLOTTE. Ha, ha, ha, ha!

LETITIA. Then did you take notice with what an affected warmth of friendship she and Miss Wasp met? when all their acquaintance know how much pleasure they take in abusing each other in every company.

CHARLOTTE. Lud! Letitia, is that so extraordinary? Why, my dear, I hope you are not going to turn sentimentalist. Scandal, you know, is but amusing ourselves with the faults, foibles, follies, and reputations of our friends; indeed, I don't know why we should have friends, if we are not at liberty to make use of them. But no person is so ignorant of the world as to suppose, because I amuse myself with a lady's faults, that I am obliged to quarrel with her person every time we meet: believe me, my dear, we should have very few acquaintance at that rate.

[SERVANT *enters and delivers a letter to* CHARLOTTE, *and exits.*]

CHARLOTTE. You'll excuse me, my dear. [*Opens and reads to herself.*]

LETITIA. Oh, quite excusable.

CHARLOTTE. As I hope to be married, my brother Henry is in the city.

LETITIA. What, your brother, Colonel Manly?

CHARLOTTE. Yes, my dear; the only brother I have in the world.

LETITIA. Was he never in this city?

CHARLOTTE. Never nearer than Harlem Heights,[2] where he lay with his regiment.

LETITIA. What sort of a being is this brother of yours? If he is as chatty, as pretty, as sprightly as you, half the belles in the city will be pulling caps for him.

CHARLOTTE. My brother is the very counterpart and reverse of me: I am gay, he is grave; I am airy, he is solid; I am ever selecting the most pleasing objects for my laughter, he has a tear for every pitiful one. And thus, whilst he is plucking the briars and thorns from the path of the unfortunate, I am strewing my own path with roses.

LETITIA. My sweet friend, not quite so poetical, and a little more particular.

CHARLOTTE. Hands off, Letitia. I feel the rage of simile upon me; I can't talk to you in any other way. My brother has a heart replete with the noblest sentiments, but then, it is like—it is like—Oh! you provoking girl, you have deranged all my ideas—it is like—Oh! I have it—his heart is like an old maiden lady's bandbox; it contains many costly things, arranged with the most scrupulous nicety, yet the misfortune is that they are too delicate, costly, and antiquated for common use.

LETITIA. By what I can pick out of your flowery description, your brother is no beau.

CHARLOTTE. No, indeed; he makes no pretension to the character. He'd ride, or rather fly, an hundred miles to relieve a distressed object, or to do a gallant act in the service of his country; but should you drop your fan or bouquet in his presence, it is ten to one that some beau at the farther end of the room would have the honour of presenting it to you before he had observed that it fell. I'll tell you one of his antiquated, anti-gallant notions. He said once in my presence, in a room full of company,—would you believe it?—in a large circle of ladies, that the best evidence a gentleman could give a young lady of his respect and affection was to endeavour in a friendly manner

[2] Scene of a military engagement in the Revolution.

to rectify her foibles. I protest I was crimson to the eyes, upon reflecting that I was known as his sister.

LETITIA. Insupportable creature! tell a lady of her faults! if he is so grave, I fear I have no chance of captivating him.

CHARLOTTE. His conversation is like a rich, old-fashioned brocade,—it will stand alone; every sentence is a sentiment. Now you may judge what a time I had with him, in my twelve months' visit to my father. He read me such lectures, out of pure brotherly affection, against the extremes of fashion, dress, flirting, and coquetry, and all the other dear things which he knows I dote upon, that I protest his conversation made me as melancholy as if I had been at church; and heaven knows, though I never prayed to go there but on one occasion, yet I would have exchanged his conversation for a psalm and a sermon. Church is rather melancholy, to be sure; but then I can ogle the beaux, and be regaled with "here endeth the first lesson"; but his brotherly *here,* you would think had no end. You captivate him! Why, my dear, he would as soon fall in love with a box of Italian flowers. There is Maria, now, if she were not engaged, she might do something. Oh! how I should like to see that pair of pensorosos together, looking as grave as two sailors' wives of a stormy night, with a flow of sentiment meandering through their conversation like purling streams in modern poetry.

LETITIA. Oh! my dear fanciful——

CHARLOTTE. Hush! I hear some person coming through the entry.

[*Enter* SERVANT.]

SERVANT. Madam, there's a gentleman below who calls himself Colonel Manly; do you choose to be at home?

CHARLOTTE. Show him in. [*Exit* SERVANT.] Now for a sober face.

[*Enter* COLONEL MANLY.]

MANLY. My dear Charlotte, I am happy that I once more enfold you within the arms of fraternal affection. I know you are going to ask (amiable impatience!) how our parents do,—the venerable pair transmit you their blessing by me. They totter on the verge of a well-spent life, and wish only to see their children settled in the world, to depart in peace.

CHARLOTTE. I am very happy to hear that they are well. [*Coolly.*] Brother, will you give me leave to introduce you to our uncle's ward, one of my most intimate friends?

MANLY [*Saluting* LETITIA]. I ought to regard your friends as my own.

CHARLOTTE. Come, Letitia, do give us a little dash of your vivacity; my brother is so sentimental and so grave, that I protest he'll give us the vapours.[3]

MANLY. Though sentiment and gravity, I know, are banished the polite world, yet I hoped they might find some countenance in the meeting of such near connections as brother and sister.

CHARLOTTE. Positively, brother, if you go one step further in this strain, you will get me crying, and that, you know, would spoil my eyes; and then I should never get the husband which our good papa and mamma have so kindly wished me—never be established in the world.

MANLY. Forgive me, my sister,—I am no enemy to mirth, I love your sprightliness; and I hope it will one day enliven the hours of some worthy man; but when I mention the respectable authors of my existence,—the cherishers and protectors of my helpless infancy, whose hearts glow with such fondness and attachment that they would willingly lay down their lives for my welfare,—you will excuse me if I am so unfashionable as to speak of them with some degree of respect and reverence.

CHARLOTTE. Well, well, brother; if you won't be gay, we'll not differ; I will be as grave as you wish. [*Affects gravity.*] And so, brother, you have come to the

[3] A state of depression.

city to exchange some of your commutation notes [4] for a little pleasure?

MANLY. Indeed you are mistaken; my errand is not of amusement, but business; and as I neither drink nor game, my expenses will be so trivial, I shall have no occasion to sell my notes.

CHARLOTTE. Then you won't have occasion to do a very good thing. Why, here was the Vermont General—he came down some time since, sold all his musty notes at one stroke, and then laid the cash out in trinkets for his dear Fanny. I want a dozen pretty things myself; have you got the notes with you?

MANLY. I shall be ever willing to contribute, as far as it is in my power, to adorn or in any way to please my sister; yet I hope I shall never be obliged for this to sell my notes. I may be romantic, but I preserve them as a sacred deposit. Their full amount is justly due to me, but as embarrassments, the natural consequences of a long war, disable my country from supporting its credit, I shall wait with patience until it is rich enough to discharge them. If that is not in my day, they shall be transmitted as an honourable certificate to posterity, that I have humbly imitated our illustrious WASHINGTON, in having exposed my health and life in the service of my country, without reaping any other reward than the glory of conquering in so arduous a contest.

CHARLOTTE. Well said heroics. Why, my dear Henry, you have such a lofty way of saying things, that I protest I almost tremble at the thought of introducing you to the polite circles in the city. The belles would think you were a player run mad, with your head filled with old scraps of tragedy; and as to the beaux, they might admire, because they would not understand you. But, however, I must, I believe, introduce you to two or three ladies of my acquaintance.

[4] Scrip given to American soldiers in lieu of pay at the end of the war.

LETITIA. And that will make him acquainted with thirty or forty beaux.

CHARLOTTE. Oh! brother, you don't know what a fund of happiness you have in store.

MANLY. I fear, sister, I have not refinement sufficient to enjoy it.

CHARLOTTE. Oh! you cannot fail being pleased.

LETITIA. Our ladies are so delicate and dressy.

CHARLOTTE. And our beaux so dressy and delicate.

LETITIA. Our ladies chat and flirt so agreeably.

CHARLOTTE. And our beaux simper and bow so gracefully.

LETITIA. With their hair so trim and neat.

CHARLOTTE. And their faces so soft and sleek.

LETITIA. Their buckles so tonish and bright.

CHARLOTTE. And their hands so slender and white.

LETITIA. I vow, Charlotte, we are quite poetical.

CHARLOTTE. And then, brother, the faces of the beaux are of such a lily-white hue! None of that horrid robustness of constitution, that vulgar corn-fed glow of health, which can only serve to alarm an unmarried lady with apprehension, and prove a melancholy momento to a married one, that she can never hope for the happiness of being a widow. I will say this to the credit of our city beaux, that such is the delicacy of their complexion, dress, and address, that, even had I no reliance upon the honour of the dear Adonises, I would trust myself in any possible situation with them, without the least apprehensions of rudeness.

MANLY. Sister Charlotte!

CHARLOTTE. Now, now, now, brother [*interrupting him*], now don't go to spoil my mirth with a dash of your gravity; I am so glad to see you, I am in tip-top spirits. Oh! that you could be with us at a little snug party. There is Billy Simper, Jack Chaffé, and Colonel Van Titter, Miss Promonade, and the two Miss Tambours, sometimes make a party, with some other ladies, in a side-box [5] at the play. Everything is conducted with such decorum. First we bow round to the company in general, then to each one in particular, then we have so many inquiries after each other's health, and we are so happy to meet each other, and it is so many ages since we last had that pleasure, and if a married lady is in company, we have such a sweet dissertation upon her son Bobby's chin-cough; then the curtain rises, then our sensibility is all awake, and then, by the mere force of apprehension, we torture some harmless expression into a double meaning, which the poor author never dreamt of, and then we have recourse to our fans, and then we blush, and then the gentlemen jog one another, peep under the fan, and make the prettiest remarks; and then we giggle and they simper, and they giggle and we simper, and then the curtain drops, and then for nuts and oranges, and then we bow, and it's pray, Ma'am, take it, and pray, Sir, keep it, and oh! not for the world, Sir; and then the curtain rises again, and then we blush and giggle and simper and bow all over again. Oh! the sentimental charms of a side-box conversation! [*All laugh.*]

MANLY. Well, sister, I join heartily with you in the laugh; for, in my opinion, it is as justifiable to laugh at folly as it is reprehensible to ridicule misfortune.

CHARLOTTE. Well, but, brother, positively I can't introduce you in these clothes: why, your coat looks as if it were calculated for the vulgar purpose of keeping yourself comfortable.

MANLY. This coat was my regimental coat in the late war. The public tumults of our state have induced me to buckle on the sword in support of that government which I once fought to establish. I can only say, sister, that there was a time when this coat was respectable, and some people even thought that those men who had endured so many winter campaigns in the service of their country, without bread, clothing, or pay, at least deserved that the poverty of their appearance should not be ridiculed.

CHARLOTTE. We agree in opinion entirely, brother, though it would not have done for me to have said it: it is the coat makes the man respectable. In the time of the war, when we were almost frightened to death, why, your coat was respectable, that is, fashionable; now another kind of coat is fashionable, that is, respectable. And pray direct the tailor to make yours the height of the fashion.

MANLY. Though it is of little consequence to me of what shape my coat is, yet, as to the height of the fashion, there you will please to excuse me, sister. You know my sentiments on that subject. I have often lamented the advantage which the French have over us in that particular. In Paris, the fashions have their dawnings, their routine, and declensions, and depend as much upon the caprice of the day as in other countries; but there every lady assumes a right to deviate from the general *ton* as far as will be of advantage to her own appearance. In America, the cry is, what is the fashion? and we follow it indiscriminately, because it is so.

CHARLOTTE. Therefore it is, that when large hoops are in fashion, we often see many a plump girl lost in the immensity of a hoop-petticoat, whose want of height and *en-bon-point* would never have been remarked in any other dress. When the high head-dress is the mode, how then do we see a lofty cushion, with a profusion of gauze, feathers, and ribband, supported by a face no bigger than an apple! whilst a broad full-faced lady, who really would have appeared tolerably handsome in a large

[5] The fashionable section of the theatre.

head-dress, looks with her smart chapeau as masculine as a soldier.

MANLY. But remember, my dear sister, and I wish all my fair countrywomen would recollect, that the only excuse a young lady can have for going extravagantly into a fashion is because it makes her look extravagantly handsome.—Ladies, I must wish you a good morning.

CHARLOTTE. But, brother, you are going to make home with us.

MANLY. Indeed I cannot. I have seen my uncle and explained that matter.

CHARLOTTE. Come and dine with us, then. We have a family dinner about half-past four o'clock.

MANLY. I am engaged to dine with the Spanish ambassador. I was introduced to him by an old brother officer; and instead of freezing me with a cold card of compliment to dine with him ten days hence, he, with the true old Castilian frankness, in a friendly manner, asked me to dine with him to-day—an honour I could not refuse. Sister, adieu—Madam, your most obedient——[*Exit.*]

CHARLOTTE. I will wait upon you to the door, brother; I have something particular to say to you. [*Exit.*]

LETITIA [*Alone*]. What a pair!—She the pink of flirtation, he the essence of everything that is *outré* and gloomy.—I think I have completely deceived Charlotte by my manner of speaking of Mr. Dimple; she's too much the friend of Maria to be confided in. He is certainly rendering himself disagreeable to Maria, in order to break with her and proffer his hand to me. This is what the delicate fellow hinted in our last conversation. [*Exit.*]

SCENE 2

The Mall

[*Enter* JESSAMY.]

Positively this Mall is a very pretty place. I hope the cits [6] won't ruin it by repairs. To be sure, it won't do to speak of in the same day with Ranelagh or Vauxhall; [7] however, it's a fine place for a young fellow to display his person to advantage. Indeed, nothing is lost here; the girls have taste, and I am very happy to find they have adopted the elegant London fashion of looking back, after a genteel fellow like me has passed them.—Ah! who comes here? This, by his awkwardness, must be the Yankee colonel's servant. I'll accost him.

[*Enter* JONATHAN.]

JESSAMY. Votre très-humble serviteur, Monsieur. I understand Colonel Manly, the Yankee officer, has the honour of your services.

JONATHAN. Sir!——

JESSAMY. I say, Sir, I understand that Colonel Manly has the honour of having you for a servant.

JONATHAN. Servant! Sir, do you take me for a neger,—I am Colonel Manly's waiter.

JESSAMY. A true Yankee distinction, egad, without a difference. Why, Sir, do you not perform all the offices of a servant? Do you not even blacken his boots?

JONATHAN. Yes; I do grease them a bit sometimes; but I am a true blue son of liberty, for all that. Father said I should come as Colonel Manly's waiter, to see the world, and all that; but no man shall master me. My father has as good a farm as the colonel.

JESSAMY. Well, Sir, we will not quarrel about terms upon the eve of an acquaintance from which I promise myself so much satisfaction;—therefore, sans ceremonie——

JONATHAN. What?——

JESSAMY. I say I am extremely happy to see Colonel Manly's waiter.

JONATHAN. Well, and I vow, too, I am pretty considerably glad to see you;

[6] The civic-minded members of the middle class.

[7] Fashionable London pleasure gardens.

but what the dogs need of all this outlandish lingo? Who may you be, Sir, if I may be so bold?

JESSAMY. I have the honour to be Mr. Dimple's servant, or, if you please, waiter. We lodge under the same roof, and should be glad of the honour of your acquaintance.

JONATHAN. You a waiter! by the living jingo, you look so topping, I took you for one of the agents to Congress.

JESSAMY. The brute has discernment, notwithstanding his appearance.—Give me leave to say I wonder then at your familiarity.

JONATHAN. Why, as to the matter of that, Mr. ——; pray, what's your name?

JESSAMY. Jessamy, at your service.

JONATHAN. Why, I swear we don't make any great matter of distinction in our state between quality and other folks.

JESSAMY. This is, indeed, a levelling principle.—I hope, Mr. Jonathan, you have not taken part with the insurgents.

JONATHAN. Why, since General Shays has sneaked off and given us the bag to hold, I don't care to give my opinion; but you'll promise not to tell—put your ear this way—you won't tell?—I vow I did think the sturgeons were right.

JESSAMY. I thought, Mr. Jonathan, you Massachusetts men always argued with a gun in your hand. Why didn't you join them?

JONATHAN. Why, the colonel is one of those folks called the Shin—Shin—[8] dang it all, I can't speak them lignum vitæ words—you know who I mean—there is a company of them—they wear a china goose at their button-hole—a kind of gilt thing.—Now the colonel told father and brother,—you must know there are, let me see—there is Elnathan, Silas, and Barnabas, Tabitha—no, no, she's a she—tarnation, now I have it—there's Elnathan, Silas, Barnabas, Jonathan, that's I—seven of us, six went into the wars, and I stayed at home to take care of mother. Colonel said that it was a burning shame for the true blue Bunker Hill sons of liberty, who had fought Governor Hutchinson, Lord North, and the Devil, to have any hand in kicking up a cursed dust against a government which we had, every mother's son of us, a hand in making.

JESSAMY. Bravo!—Well, have you been abroad in the city since your arrival? What have you seen that is curious and entertaining?

JONATHAN. Oh! I have seen a power of fine sights. I went to see two marblestone men and a leaden horse that stands out in doors in all weathers; and when I came where they was, one had got no head, and t'other weren't there. They said as how the leaden man was a damn'd tory, and that he took wit in his anger and rode off in the time of the troubles.

JESSAMY. But this was not the end of your excursion?

JONATHAN. Oh, no; I went to a place they call Holy Ground. Now I counted this was a place where folks go to meeting; so I put my hymn-book in my pocket, and walked softly and grave as a minister; and when I came there, the dogs a bit of a meeting-house could I see. At last I spied a young gentlewoman standing by one of the seats which they have here at the doors. I took her to be the deacon's daughter, and she looked so kind, and so obliging, that I thought I would go and ask her the way to lecture, and—would you think it?—she called me dear, and sweeting, and honey, just as if we were married: by the living jingo, I had a month's mind to buss her.

JESSAMY. Well, but how did it end?

JONATHAN. Why, as I was standing talking with her, a parcel of sailor men and boys got round me, the snarl-headed curs fell a-kicking and cursing of me at such a tarnal rate, that I vow I was glad to take to my heels and split home, right

[8] The Society of the Cincinnati, a hereditary order of Revolutionary officers.

off, tail on end, like a stream of chalk.

JESSAMY. Why, my dear friend, you are not acquainted with the city; that girl you saw was a —— [*Whispers.*]

JONATHAN. Mercy on my soul! was that young woman a harlot!—Well! if this is New-York Holy Ground, what must the Holy-day Ground be!

JESSAMY. Well, you should not judge of the city too rashly. We have a number of elegant, fine girls here that make a man's leisure hours pass very agreeably. I would esteem it an honour to announce you to some of them.—Gad! that announce is a select word; I wonder where I picked it up.

JONATHAN. I don't want to know them.

JESSAMY. Come, come, my dear friend, I see that I must assume the honour of being the director of your amusements. Nature has given us passions, and youth and opportunity stimulate to gratify them. It is no shame, my dear Blueskin, for a man to amuse himself with a little gallantry.

JONATHAN. Girl huntry! I don't altogether understand. I never played at that game. I know how to play hunt the squirrel, but I can't play anything with the girls; I am as good as married.

JESSAMY. Vulgar, horrid brute! Married, and above a hundred miles from his wife, and thinks that an objection to his making love to every woman he meets! He never can have read, no, he never can have been in a room with a volume of the divine Chesterfield.—So you are married?

JONATHAN. No, I don't say so; I said I was as good as married, a kind of promise.

JESSAMY. As good as married!——

JONATHAN. Why, yes; there's Tabitha Wymen, the deacon's daughter, at home; she and I have been courting a great while, and folks say as how we are to be married; and so I broke a piece of money with her when we parted, and she promised not to spark it with Solomon Dyer while I am gone. You wouldn't have me false to my true-love, would you?

JESSAMY. May be you have another reason for constancy; possibly the young lady has a fortune? Ha! Mr. Jonathan, the solid charms, the chains of love are never so binding as when the links are made of gold.

JONATHAN. Why, as to fortune, I must needs say her father is pretty dumb rich; he went representative for our town last year. He will give her—let me see—four times seven is—seven times four—nought and carry one,—he will give her twenty acres of land—somewhat rocky though—a Bible, and a cow.

JESSAMY. Twenty acres of rock, a Bible, and a cow! Why, my dear Mr. Jonathan, we have servant-maids, or, as you would more elegantly express it, waitresses, in this city, who collect more in one year from their mistresses' cast clothes.

JONATHAN. You don't say so!——

JESSAMY. Yes, and I'll introduce you to one of them. There is a little lump of flesh and delicacy that lives at next door, waitress to Miss Maria; we often see her on the stoop.

JONATHAN. But are you sure she would be courted by me?

JESSAMY. Never doubt it; remember a faint heart never—blisters on my tongue—I was going to be guilty of a vile proverb; flat against the authority of Chesterfield. I say there can be no doubt that the brilliancy of your merit will secure you a favourable reception.

JONATHAN. Well, but what must I say to her?

JESSAMY. Say to her! why, my dear friend, though I admire your profound knowledge on every other subject, yet, you will pardon my saying that your want of opportunity has made the female heart escape the poignancy of your penetration. Say to her! Why, when a man goes a-courting, and hopes for success, he must begin with doing, and not saying.

JONATHAN. Well, what must I do?

JESSAMY. Why, when you are introduced you must make five or six elegant bows.

JONATHAN. Six elegant bows! I understand that; six, you say? Well——

JESSAMY. Then you must press and kiss her hand; then press and kiss, and so on to her lips and cheeks; then talk as much as you can about hearts, darts, flames, nectar, and ambrosia—the more incoherent the better.

JONATHAN. Well, but suppose she should be angry with I?

JESSAMY. Why, if she should pretend—please to observe, Mr. Jonathan—if she should pretend to be offended, you must—— But I'll tell you how my master acted in such a case: He was seated by a young lady of eighteen upon a sofa, plucking with a wanton hand the blooming sweets of youth and beauty. When the lady thought it necessary to check his ardour, she called up a frown upon her lovely face, so irresistibly alluring, that it would have warmed the frozen bosom of age; remember, said she, putting her delicate arm upon his, remember your character and my honour. My master instantly dropped upon his knees, with eyes swimming with love, cheeks glowing with desire, and in the gentlest modulation of voice he said: My dear Caroline, in a few months our hands will be indissolubly united at the altar; our hearts I feel are already so; the favours you now grant as evidence of your affection are favours indeed; yet, when the ceremony is once past, what will now be received with rapture will then be attributed to duty.

JONATHAN. Well, and what was the consequence?

JESSAMY. The consequence!—Ah! forgive me, my dear friend, but you New England gentlemen have such a laudable curiosity of seeing the bottom of everything;—why, to be honest, I confess I saw the blooming cherub of a consequence smiling in its angelic mother's arms, about ten months afterwards.

JONATHAN. Well, if I follow all your plans, make them six bows, and all that, shall I have such little cherubim consequences?

JESSAMY. Undoubtedly.—What are you musing upon?

JONATHAN. You say you'll certainly make me acquainted?—Why, I was thinking then how I should contrive to pass this broken piece of silver—won't it buy a sugar-dram? [9]

JESSAMY. What is that, the love-token from the deacon's daughter?—You come on bravely. But I must hasten to my master. Adieu, my dear friend.

JONATHAN. Stay, Mr. Jessamy—must I buss her when I am introduced to her?

JESSAMY. I told you, you must kiss her.

JONATHAN. Well, but must I buss her?

JESSAMY. Why kiss and buss, and buss and kiss, is all one.

JONATHAN. Oh! my dear friend, though you have a profound knowledge of all, a pugnency of tribulation, you don't know everything. [*Exit.*]

JESSAMY [*Alone*]. Well, certainly I improve; my master could not have insinuated himself with more address into the heart of a man he despised. Now will this blundering dog sicken Jenny with his nauseous pawings, until she flies into my arms for very ease. How sweet will the contrast be between the blundering Jonathan and the courtly and accomplished Jessamy!

End of the Second Act

ACT III SCENE 1

DIMPLE'S *Room*

[DIMPLE, *discovered at a Toilet, reading.*]

DIMPLE. "Women have in general but one object, which is their beauty."

[9] Glass of punch.

Very true, my lord; positively very true. "Nature has hardly formed a woman ugly enough to be insensible to flattery upon her person." Extremely just, my lord; every day's delightful experience confirms this. "If her face is so shocking that she must, in some degree, be conscious of it, her figure and air, she thinks, make ample amends for it." The sallow Miss Wan is a proof of this. Upon my telling the distasteful wretch, the other day, that her countenance spoke the pensive language of sentiment, and that Lady Wortley Montague declared that if the ladies were arrayed in the garb of innocence, the face would be the last part which would be admired, as Monsieur Milton expresses it, she grinn'd horribly a ghastly smile. "If her figure is deformed, she thinks her face counterbalances it."

[*Enter* JESSAMY *with letters.*]

DIMPLE. Where got you these, Jessamy?

JESSAMY. Sir, the English packet [10] is arrived.

DIMPLE [*Opens and reads a letter enclosing notes*].

"Sir,

"I have drawn bills on you in favour of Messrs. Van Cash and Co. as per margin. I have taken up your note to Col. Piquet, and discharged your debts to my Lord Lurcher and Sir Harry Rook. I herewith enclose you copies of the bills, which I have no doubt will be immediately honoured. On failure, I shall empower some lawyer in your country to recover the amounts.

"I am, Sir,

"Your most humble servant,

"JOHN HAZARD."

Now, did not my lord expressly say that it was unbecoming a well-bred man to be in a passion, I confess I should be ruffled. [*Reads.*] "There is no accident so unfortunate, which a wise man may not turn to his advantage; nor any accident so fortunate, which a fool will not turn to his disadvantage." True, my lord; but how advantage can be derived from this I can't see. Chesterfield himself, who made, however, the worst practice of the most excellent precepts, was never in so embarrassing a situation. I love the person of Charlotte, and it is necessary I should command the fortune of Letitia. As to Maria!—I doubt not by my *sang-froid* behaviour I shall compel her to decline the match; but the blame must not fall upon me. A prudent man, as my lord says, should take all the credit of a good action to himself, and throw the discredit of a bad one upon others. I must break with Maria, marry Letitia, and as for Charlotte—why, Charlotte must be a companion to my wife.—Here, Jessamy!

[*Enter* JESSAMY.]

[DIMPLE *folds and seals two letters.*]

DIMPLE. Here, Jessamy, take this letter to my love. [*Gives one.*]

JESSAMY. To which of your honour's loves?—Oh! [*reading*] to Miss Letitia, your honour's rich love.

DIMPLE. And this [*delivers another*] to Miss Charlotte Manly. See that you deliver them privately.

JESSAMY. Yes, your honour. [*Going.*]

DIMPLE. Jessamy, who are these strange lodgers that came to the house last night?

JESSAMY. Why, the master is a Yankee colonel; I have not seen much of him; but the man is the most unpolished animal your honour ever disgraced your eyes by looking upon. I have had one of the most *outré* conversations with him!—He really has a most prodigious effect upon my risibility.

DIMPLE. I ought, according to every rule of Chesterfield, to wait on him and insinuate myself into his good graces.——Jessamy, wait on the colonel with my compliments, and if he is disengaged

[10] Express boat.

I will do myself the honour of paying him my respects.—Some ignorant, unpolished boor——

[JESSAMY *goes off and returns.*]

JESSAMY. Sir, the colonel is gone out, and Jonathan his servant says that he is gone to stretch his legs upon the Mall.—Stretch his legs! what an indelicacy of diction!

DIMPLE. Very well. Reach me my hat and sword. I'll accost him there, in my way to Letitia's, as by accident; pretend to be struck by his person and address, and endeavour to steal into his confidence. Jessamy, I have no business for you at present. [*Exit.*]

JESSAMY [*taking up the book*]. My master and I obtain our knowledge from the same source;—though, gad! I think myself much the prettier fellow of the two. [*Surveying himself in the glass.*] That was a brilliant thought, to insinuate that I folded my master's letters for him; the folding is so neat, that it does honour to the operator. I once intended to have insinuated that I wrote his letters too; but that was before I saw them; it won't do now; no honour there, positively.—"Nothing looks more vulgar, [*reading affectedly*] ordinary, and illiberal than ugly, uneven, and ragged nails; the ends of which should be kept even and clean, not tipped with black, and cut in small segments of circles."—Segments of circles! surely my lord did not consider that he wrote for the beaux. Segments of circles; what a crabbed term! Now I dare answer that my master, with all his learning, does not know that this means, according to the present mode, let the nails grow long, and then cut them off even at top. [*Laughing without.*] Ha! that's Jenny's titter. I protest I despair of ever teaching that girl to laugh; she has something so execrably natural in her laugh, that I declare it absolutely discomposes my nerves. How came she into our house! [*Calls.*] Jenny!

[*Enter* JENNY.]

JESSAMY. Prithee, Jenny, don't spoil your fine face with laughing.

JENNY. Why, mustn't I laugh, Mr. Jessamy?

JESSAMY. You may smile, but, as my lord says, nothing can authorise a laugh.

JENNY. Well, but I can't help laughing.—Have you seen him, Mr. Jessamy? ha, ha, ha!

JESSAMY. Seen whom?

JENNY. Why, Jonathan, the New England colonel's servant. Do you know he was at the play last night, and the stupid creature don't know where he has been. He would not go to a play for the world; he thinks it was a show, as he calls it.

JESSAMY. As ignorant and unpolished as he is, do you know, Miss Jenny, that I propose to introduce him to the honour of your acquaintance?

JENNY. Introduce him to me! for what?

JESSAMY. Why, my lovely girl, that you may take him under your protection, as Madame Rambouillet did young Stanhope; that you may, by your plastic hand, mould this uncouth cub into a gentleman. He is to make love to you.

JENNY. Make love to me!——

JESSAMY. Yes, Mistress Jenny, make love to you; and, I doubt not, when he shall become *domesticated* in your kitchen, that this boor, under your auspices, will soon become *un amiable petit Jonathan.*

JENNY. I must say, Mr. Jessamy, if he copies after me, he will be vastly, monstrously polite.

JESSAMY. Stay here one moment, and I will call him.—Jonathan!—Mr. Jonathan!—[*Calls.*]

JOHNATHAN [*within*]. Holla! there. —[*Enters.*] You promise to stand by me —six bows you say. [*Bows.*]

JESSAMY. Mrs. Jenny, I have the honour of presenting Mr. Jonathan, Colonel Manly's waiter, to you. I am extremely happy that I have it in my power to make two worthy people acquainted with each other's merits.

JENNY. So, Mr. Jonathan, I hear you were at the play last night.

JOHNATHAN. At the play! why, did you think I went to the devil's drawing-room?

JENNY. The devil's drawing-room!

JONATHAN. Yes; why an't cards and dice the devil's device, and the play-house the shop where the devil hangs out the vanities of the world upon the tenter-hooks of temptation? I believe you have not heard how they were acting the old boy one night, and the wicked one came among them sure enough, and went right off in a storm, and carried one quarter of the play-house with him. Oh! no, no, no! you won't catch me at a play-house, I warrant you.

JENNY. Well, Mr. Jonathan, though I don't scruple your veracity, I have some reasons for believing you were there: pray, where were you about six o'clock?

JONATHAN. Why, I went to see one Mr. Morrison, the *hocus pocus* man; they said as how he could eat a case knife.

JENNY. Well, and how did you find the place?

JONATHAN. As I was going about here and there, to and again, to find it, I saw a great crowd of folks going into a long entry that had lanterns over the door; so I asked a man whether that was not the place where they played *hocus pocus*? He was a very civil, kind man, though he did speak like the Hessians; he lifted up his eyes and said, "They play *hocus pocus* tricks enough there, Got knows, mine friend."

JENNY. Well——

JONATHAN. So I went right in, and they showed me away, clean up to the garret, just like meeting-house gallery. And so I saw a power of topping folks, all sitting round in little cabins, "just like father's corn-cribs"; and then there was such a squeaking with the fiddles, and such a tarnal blaze with the lights, my head was near turned. At last the people that sat near me set up such a hissing—hiss—like so many mad cats; and then they went thump, thump, thump, just like our Peleg threshing wheat, and stampt away, just like the nation; and called out for one Mr. Langolee,—I suppose he helps act the tricks.

JENNY. Well, and what did you do all this time?

JONATHAN. Gor, I—I liked the fun, and so I thumpt away, and hiss'd as lustily as the best of 'em. One sailor-looking man that sat by me, seeing me stamp, and knowing I was a cute fellow, because I could make a roaring noise, clapt me on the shoulder and said, "You are a d——d hearty cock, smite my timbers!" I told him so I was, but I thought he need not swear so, and make use of such naughty words.

JESSAMY. The savage!—Well, and did you see the man with his tricks?

JONATHAN. Why, I vow, as I was looking out for him, they lifted up a great green cloth and let us look right into the next neighbor's house. Have you a good many houses in New-York made so in that 'ere way?

JENNY. Not many; but did you see the family?

JONATHAN. Yes, swamp it; I see'd the family.

JENNY. Well, and how did you like them?

JONATHAN. Why, I vow they were pretty much like other families;—there was a poor, good-natured, curse of a husband, and a sad rantipole of a wife.

JENNY. But did you see no other folks?

JONATHAN. Yes. There was one youngster; they called him Mr. Joseph; [11] he talked as sober and as pious as a minister; but, like some ministers that I

[11] Joseph Surface, the pious hypocrite in *The School for Scandal.*

know, he was a sly tike in his heart for all that. He was going to ask a young woman to spark it with him, and—the Lord have mercy on my soul!—she was another man's wife.

JESSAMY. The Wabash!

JENNY. And did you see any more folks?

JONATHAN. Why, they came on as thick as mustard. For my part, I thought the house was haunted. There was a soldier fellow, who talked about his row de dow, dow, and courted a young woman; but, of all the cute folk I saw, I liked one little fellow——

JENNY. Aye! who was he?

JONATHAN. Why, he had red hair, and a little round plump face like mine, only not altogether so handsome. His name was—Darby;—that was his baptizing name; his other name I forgot. Oh! it was Wig—Wag—Wag-all, Darby Wag-all,—pray, do you know him?—I should like to take a sling with him, or a drap of cider with a pepper-pod in it, to make it warm and comfortable.

JENNY. I can't say I have that pleasure.

JONATHAN. I wish you did; he is a cute fellow. But there was one thing I didn't like in that Mr. Darby; and that was, he was afraid of some of them 'ere shooting irons, such as your troopers wear on training days. Now, I'm a true born Yankee American son of liberty, and I never was afraid of a gun yet in all my life.

JENNY. Well, Mr. Jonathan, you were certainly at the play-house.

JONATHAN. I at the play-house!—Why didn't I see the play then?

JENNY. Why, the people you saw were players.

JONATHAN. Mercy on my soul! did I see the wicked players?—Mayhap that 'ere Darby that I liked so was the old serpent himself, and had his cloven foot in his pocket. Why, I vow, now I come to think on't, the candles seemed to burn blue, and I am sure where I sat it smelt tarnally of brimstone.

JESSAMY. Well, Mr. Jonathan, from your account, which I confess is very accurate, you must have been at the play-house.

JONATHAN. Why, I vow, I began to smell a rat. When I came away, I went to the man for my money again; you want your money? says he; yes, says I; for what? says he; why, says I, no man shall jocky me out of my money; I paid my money to see sights, and the dogs a bit of a sight have I seen, unless you call listening to people's private business a sight. Why, says he, it is the School for Scandalization.—The School for Scandalization!—Oh! ho! no wonder you New-York folks are so cute at it, when you go to school to learn it; and so I jogged off.

JESSAMY. My dear Jenny, my master's business drags me from you; would to heaven I knew no other servitude than to your charms.

JONATHAN. Well, but don't go; you won't leave me so——

JESSAMY. Excuse me.—Remember the cash. [*Aside to him, and exits.*]

JENNY. Mr. Jonathan, won't you please to sit down? Mr. Jessamy tells me you wanted to have some conversation with me. [*Having brought forward two chairs, they sit.*]

JONATHAN. Ma'am!——

JENNY. Sir!——

JONATHAN. Ma'am!——

JENNY. Pray, how do you like the city, Sir?

JONATHAN. Ma'am!——

JENNY. I say, Sir, how do you like New-York?

JONATHAN. Ma'am!——

JENNY. The stupid creature! but I must pass some little time with him, if it is only to endeavour to learn whether it was his master that made such an abrupt entrance into our house, and my young mistress's heart, this morning.

[*Aside.*] As you don't seem to like to talk, Mr. Jonathan—do you sing?

JONATHAN. Gor, I—I am glad she asked that, for I forgot what Mr. Jessamy bid me say, and I dare as well be hanged as act what he bid me do, I'm so ashamed. [*Aside.*] Yes, Ma'am, I can sing—I can sing Mear, Old Hundred, and Bangor.

JENNY. Oh! I don't mean psalm tunes. Have you no little song to please the ladies, such as Roslin Castle, or the Maid of the Mill?

JONATHAN. Why, all my tunes go to meeting tunes, save one, and I count you won't altogether like that 'ere.

JENNY. What is it called?

JONATHAN. I am sure you have heard folks talk about it; it is called Yankee Doodle.

JENNY. Oh! it is the tune I am fond of; and if I know anything of my mistress, she would be glad to dance to it. Pray, sing!

JONATHAN [*Sings*].

Father and I went up to camp,
Along with Captain Goodwin;
And there we saw the men and boys,
As thick as hasty-pudding.
Yankee doodle do, etc.

And there we saw a swamping gun,
Big as log of maple,
On a little deuced cart,
A load for father's cattle.
Yankee doodle do, etc.

And every time they fired it off
It took a horn of powder,
It made a noise—like father's gun,
Only a nation louder.
Yankee doodle do, etc.

There was a man in our town,
His name was——

No, no, that won't do. Now, if I was with Tabitha Wymen and Jemima Cawley down at father Chase's, I shouldn't mind singing this all out before them—you would be affronted if I was to sing that, though that's a lucky thought; if you should be affronted, I have something dang'd cute, which Jessamy told me to say to you.

JENNY. Is that all! I assure you I like it of all things.

JONATHAN. No, no; I can sing more; some other time, when you and I are better acquainted, I'll sing the whole of it—no, no—that's a fib—I can't sing but a hundred and ninety verses; our Tabitha at home can sing it all. [*Sings.*]

Marblehead's a rocky place,
And Cape Cod is sandy;
Charlestown is burnt down,
Boston is the dandy.
Yankee doodle, doodle do, etc.

I vow, my own town song has put me into such topping spirits that I believe I'll begin to do a little, as Jessamy says we must when we go a-courting.—[*Runs and kisses her.*] Burning rivers! cooling flames! red-hot roses! pig-nuts! hasty-pudding and ambrosia!

JENNY. What means this freedom? you insulting wretch. [*Strikes him.*]

JONATHAN. Are you affronted?

JENNY. Affronted! with what looks shall I express my anger?

JONATHAN. Looks! why as to the matter of looks, you look as cross as a witch.

JENNY. Have you no feeling for the delicacy of my sex?

JONATHAN. Feeling! Gor, I—I feel the delicacy of your sex pretty smartly [*rubbing his cheek*], though, I vow, I thought when you city ladies courted and married, and all that, you put feeling out of the question. But I want to know whether you are really affronted, or only pretend to be so? 'Cause, if you are certainly right down affronted, I am at the end of my tether; Jessamy didn't tell me what to say to you.

JENNY. Pretend to be affronted!

JONATHAN. Aye, aye, if you only pretend, you shall hear how I'll go to work to make cherubim consequences. [*Runs up to her.*]

JENNY. Begone, you brute!

JONATHAN. That looks like mad; but I won't lose my speech. My dearest Jenny—your name is Jenny, I think?—My dearest Jenny, though I have the highest esteem for the sweet favours you have just now granted me—Gor, that's a fib though, but Jessamy says it is not wicked to tell lies to the women. [*Aside.*] I say, though I have the highest esteem for the favours you have just now granted me, yet you will consider that, as soon as the dissolvable knot is tied, they will no longer be favours, but only matters of duty and matters of course.

JENNY. Marry you! you audacious monster! get out of my sight, or, rather, let me fly from you. [*Exit hastily.*]

JONATHAN. Gor! she's gone off in a swinging passion, before I had time to think of consequences. If this is the way with your city ladies, give me the twenty acres of rock, the Bible, the cow, and Tabitha, and a little peaceable bundling.

SCENE 2

The Mall

[*Enter* MANLY.]

MANLY. It must be so, Montague! [12] and it is not all the tribe of Mandevilles [13] that shall convince me that a nation, to become great, must first become dissipated. Luxury is surely the bane of a nation: Luxury! which enervates both soul and body, by opening a thousand new sources of enjoyment, opens, also, a thousand new sources of contention and want: Luxury! which renders a people weak at home, and accessible to bribery, corruption, and force from abroad. When the Grecian states knew no other tools than the axe and the saw, the Grecians were a great, a free, and a happy people. The kings of Greece devoted their lives to the service of their country, and her senators knew no other superiority over their fellow-citizens than a glorious pre-eminence in danger and virtue. They exhibited to the world a noble spectacle,—a number of independent states united by a similarity of language, sentiment, manners, common interest, and common consent, in one grand mutual league of protection. And, thus united, long might they have continued the cherishers of arts and sciences, the protectors of the oppressed, the scourge of tyrants, and the safe asylum of liberty. But when foreign gold, and still more pernicious foreign luxury, had crept among them, they sapped the vitals of their virtue. The virtues of their ancestors were only found in their writings. Envy and suspicion, the vices of little minds, possessed them. The various states engendered jealousies of each other; and, more unfortunately, growing jealous of their great federal council, the Amphictyons, they forgot that their common safety had existed, and would exist, in giving them an honourable extensive prerogative. The common good was lost in the pursuit of private interest; and that people who, by uniting, might have stood against the world in arms, by dividing, crumbled into ruin;—their name is now only known in the page of the historian, and what they once were is all we have left to admire. Oh! that America! Oh! that my country, would, in this her day, learn the things which belong to her peace!

[*Enter* DIMPLE.]

DIMPLE. You are Colonel Manly, I presume?

MANLY. At your service, Sir.

DIMPLE. My name is Dimple, Sir. I have the honour to be a lodger in the

[12] Edward Montagu, author of *Reflections on the Rise and Fall of the Ancient Republics.*

[13] Bernard Mandeville, author of *The Fable of the Bees, or Private Vices, Public Benefits.*

same house with you, and; hearing you were in the Mall, came hither to take the liberty of joining you.

MANLY. You are very obliging, Sir.

DIMPLE. As I understand you are a stranger here, Sir, I have taken the liberty to introduce myself to your acquaintance, as possibly I may have it in my power to point out some things in this city worthy your notice.

MANLY. An attention to strangers is worthy a liberal mind, and must ever be gratefully received. But to a soldier, who has no fixed abode, such attentions are particularly pleasing.

DIMPLE. Sir, there is no character so respectable as that of a soldier. And, indeed, when we reflect how much we owe to those brave men who have suffered so much in the service of their country, and secured to us those inestimable blessings that we now enjoy, our liberty and independence, they demand every attention which gratitude can pay. For my own part, I never meet an officer, but I embrace him as my friend, nor a private in distress, but I insensibly extend my charity to him.——I have hit the Bumpkin off very tolerably. [*Aside.*]

MANLY. Give me your hand, Sir! I do not proffer this hand to everybody; but you steal into my heart. I hope I am as insensible to flattery as most men; but I declare (it may be my weak side) that I never hear the name of soldier mentioned with respect, but I experience a thrill of pleasure which I never feel on any other occasion.

DIMPLE. Will you give me leave, my dear Colonel, to confer an obligation on myself, by showing you some civilities during your stay here, and giving a similar opportunity to some of my friends?

MANLY. Sir, I thank you; but I believe my stay in this city will be very short.

DIMPLE. I can introduce you to some men of excellent sense, in whose company you will esteem yourself happy; and, by way of amusement, to some fine girls, who will listen to your soft things with pleasure.

MANLY. Sir, I should be proud of the honour of being acquainted with those gentlemen:—but, as for the ladies, I don't understand you.

DIMPLE. Why, Sir, I need not tell you, that when a young gentleman is alone with a young lady he must say some soft things to her fair cheek—indeed, the lady will expect it. To be sure, there is not much pleasure when a man of the world and a finished coquette meet, who perfectly know each other; but how delicious is it to excite the emotions of joy, hope, expectation, and delight in the bosom of a lovely girl who believes every tittle of what you say to be serious!

MANLY. Serious, Sir! In my opinion, the man who, under pretensions of marriage, can plant thorns in the bosom of an innocent, unsuspecting girl is more detestable than a common robber, in the same proportion as private violence is more despicable than open force, and money of less value than happiness.

DIMPLE. How he awes me by the superiority of his sentiments. [*Aside.*] As you say, Sir, a gentleman should be cautious how he mentions marriage.

MANLY. Cautious, Sir! No person more approves of an intercourse between the sexes than I do. Female conversation softens our manners, whilst our discourse, from the superiority of our literary advantages, improves their minds. But, in our young country, where there is no such thing as gallantry, when a gentleman speaks of love to a lady, whether he mentions marriage or not, she ought to conclude either that he meant to insult her or that his intentions are the most serious and honourable. How mean, how cruel, is it, by a thousand tender assiduities, to win the affections of an amiable girl, and, though you leave her virtue unspotted, to betray her into the appearance of so many tender partialities, that every man of delicacy would suppress his inclination towards her, by supposing her heart engaged! Can any man, for the trival gratification of his leisure hours, affect the happiness of a whole life! His not having spoken of marriage may add to his perfidy, but can be no excuse for his conduct.

DIMPLE. Sir, I admire your sentiments;—they are mine. The light observations that fell from me were only a principle of the tongue; they came not from the heart; my practice has ever disapproved these principles.

MANLY. I believe you, Sir. I should with reluctance suppose that those pernicious sentiments could find admittance into the heart of a gentleman.

DIMPLE. I am now, Sir, going to visit a family, where, if you please, I will have the honour of introducing you. Mr. Manly's ward, Miss Letitia, is a young lady of immense fortune; and his niece, Miss Charlotte Manly, is a young lady of great sprightliness and beauty.

MANLY. That gentleman, Sir, is my uncle, and Miss Manly my sister.

DIMPLE. The devil she is! [*Aside.*] Miss Manly your sister, Sir? I rejoice to hear it, and feel a double pleasure in being known to you.——Plague on him! I wish he was at Boston again, with all my soul. [*Aside.*]

MANLY. Come, Sir, will you go?

DIMPLE. I will follow you in a moment, Sir. [*Exit* MANLY.] Plague on it! this is unlucky. A fighting brother is a cursed appendage to a fine girl. Egad! I just stopped in time; had he not discovered himself, in two minutes more I should have told him how well I was with his sister. Indeed, I cannot see the satisfaction of an intrigue, if one can't have the pleasure of communicating it to our friends. [*Exit.*]

End of the Third Act

ACT IV SCENE 1

CHARLOTTE's *Apartment*

[CHARLOTTE *leading in* MARIA.]

CHARLOTTE. This is so kind, my sweet friend, to come to see me at this moment. I declare, if I were going to be married in a few days, as you are, I should scarce have found time to visit my friends.

MARIA. Do you think, then, that there is an impropriety in it?—How should you dispose of your time?

CHARLOTTE. Why, I should be shut up in my chamber; and my head would so run upon—upon—upon the solemn ceremony that I was to pass through!—I declare, it would take me above two hours merely to learn that little monosyllable—*Yes.* Ah! my dear, your sentimental imagination does not conceive what that little tiny word implies.

MARIA. Spare me your raillery, my sweet friend; I should love your agreeable vivacity at any other time.

CHARLOTTE. Why, this is the very time to amuse you. You grieve me to see you look so unhappy.

MARIA. Have I not reason to look so?

CHARLOTTE. What new grief distresses you?

MARIA. Oh! how sweet it is, when the heart is borne down with misfortune, to recline and repose on the bosom of friendship! Heaven knows that, although it is improper for a young lady to praise a gentleman, yet I have ever concealed Mr. Dimple's foibles, and spoke of him as of one whose reputation I expected would be linked with mine; but his late conduct towards me has turned my coolness into contempt. He behaves as if he meant to insult and disgust me; whilst my father, in the last conversation on the subject of our marriage, spoke of it as a matter which lay near his heart, and in which he would not bear contradiction.

CHARLOTTE. This works well; oh! the generous Dimple. I'll endeavour to excite her to discharge him. [*Aside.*] But, my dear friend, your happiness depends on yourself. Why don't you discard him? Though the match has been of long standing, I would not be forced to make myself miserable: no parent in the world should oblige me to marry the man I did not like.

MARIA. Oh! my dear, you never lived with your parents, and do not know what influence a father's frowns have upon a daughter's heart. Besides, what have I to allege against Mr. Dimple, to justify myself to the world? He carries himself so smoothly that every one would impute the blame to me, and call me capricious.

CHARLOTTE. And call her capricious! Did ever such an objection start into the heart of woman? For my part, I wish I had fifty lovers to discard, for no other reason than because I did not fancy them. My dear Maria, you will forgive me; I know your candour and confidence in me; but I have at times, I confess, been led to suppose that some other gentleman was the cause of your aversion to Mr. Dimple.

MARIA. No, my sweet friend, you may be assured, that though I have seen many gentlemen I could prefer to Mr. Dimple, yet I never saw one that I thought I could give my hand to, until this morning.

CHARLOTTE. This morning!

MARIA. Yes; one of the strangest accidents in the world. The odious Dimple, after disgusting me with his conversation, had just left me, when a gentleman, who, it seems, boards in the same house with him, saw him coming out of our door, and, the houses looking very much alike, he came into our house instead of his lodgings; nor did he discover his mistake until he got into the parlour, where I was; he then bowed so gracefully, made such a genteel apology, and looked so manly and noble!——

CHARLOTTE. I see some folks, though it is so great an impropriety, can praise a gentleman, when he happens to be the man of their fancy. [*Aside.*]

MARIA. I don't know how it was,— I hope he did not think me indelicate,— but I asked him, I believe, to sit down, or pointed to a chair. He sat down, and, instead of having recourse to observations upon the weather, or hackneyed criticisms upon the theatre, he entered readily into a conversation worthy a man of sense to speak, and a lady of delicacy and sentiment to hear. He was not strictly handsome, but he spoke the language of sentiment, and his eyes looked tenderness and honour.

CHARLOTTE. Oh! [*eagerly*] you sentimental, grave girls, when your hearts are once touched, beat us rattles a bar's length. And so you are quite in love with this he-angel?

MARIA. In love with him! How can you rattle so, Charlotte? am I not going to be miserable? [*Sighs.*] In love with a gentleman I never saw but one hour in my life, and don't know his name! No; I only wished that the man I shall marry may look, and talk, and act, just like him. Besides, my dear, he is a married man.

CHARLOTTE. Why, that was good-natured—he told you so, I suppose, in mere charity, to prevent you falling in love with him?

MARIA. He didn't tell me so; [*peevishly*] he looked as if he was married.

CHARLOTTE. How, my dear; did he look sheepish?

MARIA. I am sure he has a susceptible heart, and the ladies of his acquaintance must be very stupid not to——

CHARLOTTE. Hush! I hear some person coming.

[*Enter* LETITIA.]

LETITIA. My dear Maria, I am happy to see you. Lud! what a pity it is that you have purchased your wedding clothes.

MARIA. I think so. [*Sighing.*]

LETITIA. Why, my dear, there is the sweetest parcel of silks come over you ever saw! Nancy Brilliant has a full suit come; she sent over her measure, and it fits her to a hair; it is immensely dressy, and made for a court-hoop. I thought they said the large hoops were going out of fashion.

CHARLOTTE. Did you see the hat? Is it a fact that the deep laces round the border is still the fashion?

[DIMPLE *within.*] Upon my honour, Sir.

MARIA. Ha! Dimple's voice! My dear, I must take leave of you. There are some things necessary to be done at our house. Can't I go through the other room?

[*Enter* DIMPLE *and* MANLY.]

DIMPLE. Ladies, your most obedient.

CHARLOTTE. Miss Van Rough, shall I present my brother Henry to you? Colonel Manly, Maria,—Miss Van Rough, brother.

MARIA. Her brother! [*Turns and sees* MANLY.] Oh! my heart! the very gentleman I have been praising.

MANLY. The same amiable girl I saw this morning!

CHARLOTTE. Why, you look as if you were acquainted.

MANLY. I unintentionally intruded into this lady's presence this morning, for which she was so good as to promise me her forgiveness.

CHARLOTTE. Oh! ho! is that the case! Have these two penserosos been together? Were they Henry's eyes that looked so tenderly? [*Aside.*] And so you promised to pardon him? and could you be so good-natured? have you really forgiven him? I beg you would do it for my sake [*whispering loud to* MARIA]. But, my dear, as you are in such haste, it would be cruel to detain you; I can show you the way through the other room.

MARIA. Spare me, my sprightly friend.

MANLY. The lady does not, I hope, intend to deprive us of the pleasure of her company so soon.

CHARLOTTE. She has only a mantua [14] maker who waits for her at home. But, as I am to give my opinion of the dress, I think she cannot go yet. We were talking of the fashions when you came in, but I suppose the subject must be changed to something of more importance now. Mr. Dimple, will you favour us with an account of the public entertainments?

DIMPLE. Why, really, Miss Manly, you could not have asked me a question more *mal-apropos.* For my part, I must confess that, to a man who has travelled, there is nothing that is worthy the name of amusement to be found in this city.

CHARLOTTE. Except visiting the ladies.

DIMPLE. Pardon me, Madam; that is the avocation of a man of taste. But for amusement, I positively know of nothing that can be called so, unless you dignify with that title the hopping once a fortnight to the sound of two or three squeaking fiddles, and the clattering of the old tavern windows, or sitting to see the miserable mummers, whom you call actors, murder comedy and make a farce of tragedy.

MANLY. Do you never attend the theatre, Sir?

DIMPLE. I was tortured there once.

CHARLOTTE. Pray, Mr. Dimple, was it a tragedy or a comedy?

DIMPLE. Faith, Madam, I cannot tell, for I sat with my back to the stage all the time, admiring a much better actress than any there—a lady who played the fine woman to perfection; though, by the laugh of the horrid creatures round me, I suppose it was comedy. Yet, on second thoughts, it might be some hero in a tragedy, dying so comically as to set the whole house in an uproar. Colonel, I presume you have been in Europe?

[14] Cloak.

MANLY. Indeed, Sir, I was never ten leagues from the continent.

DIMPLE. Believe me, Colonel, you have an immense pleasure to come; and when you shall have seen the brilliant exhibitions of Europe, you will learn to despise the amusements of this country as much as I do.

MANLY. Therefore I do not wish to see them; for I can never esteem that knowledge valuable which tends to give me a distaste for my native country.

DIMPLE. Well, Colonel, though you have not travelled, you have read.

MANLY. I have, a little; and by it have discovered that there is a laudable partiality which ignorant, untravelled men entertain for everything that belongs to their native country. I call it laudable; it injures no one; adds to their own happiness; and, when extended, becomes the noble principle of patriotism. Travelled gentlemen rise superior, in their own opinion, to this; but if the contempt which they contract for their country is the most valuable acquisition of their travels, I am far from thinking that their time and money are well spent.

MARIA. What noble sentiments!

CHARLOTTE. Let my brother set out where he will in the fields of conversation, he is sure to end his tour in the temple of gravity.

MANLY. Forgive me, my sister. I love my country; it has its foibles undoubtedly;—some foreigners will with pleasure remark them—but such remarks fall very ungracefully from the lips of her citizens.

DIMPLE. You are perfectly in the right, Colonel—America has her faults.

MANLY. Yes, Sir; and we, her children, should blush for them in private, and endeavour, as individuals, to reform them. But, if our country has its errors in common with other countries, I am proud to say America—I mean the United States—has displayed virtues and achievements which modern nations may admire, but of which they have seldom set us the example.

CHARLOTTE. But, brother, we must introduce you to some of our gay folks, and let you see the city, such as it is. Mr. Dimple is known to almost every family in town; he will doubtless take a pleasure in introducing you.

DIMPLE. I shall esteem every service I can render your brother an honour.

MANLY. I fear the business I am upon will take up all my time, and my family will be anxious to hear from me.

MARIA. His family! but what is it to me that he is married! [*Aside.*] Pray, how did you leave your lady, Sir?

CHARLOTTE. My brother is not married [*observing her anxiety*]; it is only an odd way he has of expressing himself. Pray, brother, is this business, which you make your continual excuse, a secret?

MANLY. No, sister; I came hither to solicit the honourable Congress, that a number of my brave old soldiers may be put upon the pension list, who were, at first, not judged to be so materially wounded as to need the public assistance. My sister says true [*to* MARIA]: I call my late soldiers my family. Those who were not in the field in the late glorious contest, and those who were, have their respective merits; but, I confess, my old brother-soldiers are dearer to me than the former description. Friendships made in adversity are lasting; our countrymen may forget us, but that is no reason why we should forget one another. But I must leave you; my time of engagement approaches.

CHARLOTTE. Well, but, brother, if you will go, will you please to conduct my fair friend home? You live in the same street——I was to have gone with her myself—[*Aside*]. A lucky thought.

MARIA. I am obliged to your sister, Sir, and was just intending to go. [*Going.*]

MANLY. I shall attend her with

pleasure. [*Exit with* MARIA, *followed by* DIMPLE *and* CHARLOTTE.]

MARIA. Now, pray, don't betray me to your brother.

CHARLOTTE. [*Just as she sees him make a motion to take his leave*]. One word with you, brother, if you please. [*Follows them out.*]

[*Manent,* DIMPLE *and* LETITIA.]

DIMPLE. You received the billet I sent you, I presume?

LETITIA. Hush!—Yes.

DIMPLE. When shall I pay my respects to you?

LETITIA. At eight I shall be unengaged.

[*Reënter* CHARLOTTE.]

DIMPLE. Did my lovely angel receive my billet? [*To* CHARLOTTE.]

CHARLOTTE. Yes.

DIMPLE. What hour shall I expect[15] with impatience?

CHARLOTTE. At eight I shall be at home unengaged.

DIMPLE. Unfortunate! I have a horrid engagement of business at that hour. Can't you finish your visit earlier and let six be the happy hour?

CHARLOTTE. You know your influence over me.

[*Exeunt severally.*]

SCENE 2

VAN ROUGH'S *House*

VAN ROUGH [*Alone*]. It cannot possibly be true! The son of my old friend can't have acted so unadvisedly. Seventeen thousand pounds! in bills! Mr. Transfer must have been mistaken. He always appeared so prudent, and talked so well upon money matters, and even assured me that he intended to change his dress for a suit of clothes which would not cost so much, and look more substantial, as soon as he married. No, no, no! it can't be; it cannot be. But, however, I must look out sharp. I did not care what his principles or his actions were, so long as he minded the main chance. Seventeen thousand pounds! If he had lost it in trade, why the best men may have ill-luck; but to game it away, as Transfer says—why, at this rate, his whole estate may go in one night, and, what is ten times worse, mine into the bargain. No, no; Mary is right. Leave women to look out in these matters; for all they look as if they didn't know a journal from a ledger, when their interest is concerned they know what's what; they mind the main chance as well as the best of us. I wonder Mary did not tell me she knew of his spending his money so foolishly. Seventeen thousand pounds! Why, if my daughter was standing up to be married, I would forbid the banns, if I found it was to a man who did not mind the main chance.—Hush! I hear somebody coming. 'Tis Mary's voice; a man with her too! I shouldn't be surprised if this should be the other string to her bow. Aye, aye, let them alone; women understand the main chance.—Though, i'faith, I'll listen a little. [*Retires into a closet.*]

[MANLY *leading in* MARIA.]

MANLY. I hope you will excuse my speaking upon so important a subject so abruptly; but, the moment I entered your room, you struck me as the lady whom I had long loved in imagination, and never hoped to see.

MARIA. Indeed, Sir, I have been led to hear more upon this subject than I ought.

MANLY. Do you, then, disapprove my suit, Madam, or the abruptness of my introducing it? If the latter, my peculiar situation, being obliged to leave the city in a few days, will, I hope, be my excuse; if the former, I will retire, for I am sure I would not give a moment's inquietude to her whom I could devote my life to please. I am not so indelicate as to seek your immediate approbation; permit me only to be near you, and by a thousand tender assiduities

[15] Await.

to endeavour to excite a grateful return.

MARIA. I have a father, whom I would die to make happy; he will disapprove——

MANLY. Do you think me so ungenerous as to seek a place in your esteem without his consent? You must—you ever ought to consider that man as unworthy of you who seeks an interest in your heart contrary to a father's approbation. A young lady should reflect that the loss of a lover may be supplied, but nothing can compensate for the loss of a parent's affection. Yet, why do you suppose your father would disapprove? In our country, the affections are not sacrificed to riches or family aggrandizement: should you approve, my family is decent, and my rank honourable.

MARIA. You distress me, Sir.

MANLY. Then I will sincerely beg your excuse for obtruding so disagreeable a subject, and retire. [*Going.*]

MARIA. Stay, Sir! your generosity and good opinion of me deserve a return; but why must I declare what, for these few hours, I have scarce suffered myself to think?—I am——

MANLY. What?

MARIA. Engaged, Sir; and, in a few days, to be married to the gentleman you saw at your sister's.

MANLY. Engaged to be married! And have I been basely invading the rights of another? Why have you permitted this? Is this the return for the partiality I declared for you?

MARIA. You distress me, Sir. What would you have me say? You are too generous to wish the truth. Ought I to say that I dared not suffer myself to think of my engagement, and that I am going to give my hand without my heart? Would you have me confess a partiality for you? If so, your triumph is complete, and can be only more so when days of misery with the man I cannot love will make me think of him whom I could prefer.

MANLY [*After a pause*]. We are both unhappy, but it is your duty to obey your parent—mine to obey my honour. Let us, therefore, both follow the path of rectitude; and of this we may be assured, that if we are not happy, we shall, at least, deserve to be so. Adieu! I dare not trust myself longer with you. [*Exeunt severally.*]

End of the Fourth Act

ACT V SCENE 1

DIMPLE'S *Lodgings*

[JESSAMY *meeting* JONATHAN.]

JESSAMY. Well, Mr. Jonathan, what success with the fair?

JONATHAN. Why, such a tarnal cross tike you never saw! You would have counted she had lived upon crab-apples and vinegar for a fortnight. But what the rattle makes you look so tarnation glum?

JESSAMY. I was thinking, Mr. Jonathan, what could be the reason of her carrying herself so coolly to you.

JONATHAN. Coolly, do you call it? Why, I vow, she was fire-hot angry: may be it was because I buss'd her.

JESSAMY. No, no, Mr. Jonathan; there must be some other cause; I never yet knew a lady angry at being kissed.

JONATHAN. Well, if it is not the young woman's bashfulness, I vow I can't conceive why she shouldn't like me.

JESSAMY. May be it is because you have not the graces, Mr. Jonathan.

JONATHAN. Grace! Why, does the young woman expect I must be converted before I court her?

JESSAMY. I mean graces of person: for instance, my lord tells us that we must cut off our nails even at top, in small segments of circles—though you won't understand that; in the next place, you must regulate your laugh.

JONATHAN. Maple-log seize it! don't I laugh natural?

JESSAMY. That's the very fault, Mr. Jonathan. Besides, you absolutely misplace it. I was told by a friend of mine that you laughed outright at the play the other night, when you ought only to have tittered.

JONATHAN. Gor! I—what does one go to see fun for if they can't laugh?

JESSAMY. You may laugh; but you must laugh by rule.

JONATHAN. Swamp it—laugh by rule! Well, I should like that tarnally.

JESSAMY. Why, you know, Mr. Jonathan, that to dance, a lady to play with her fan, or a gentleman with his cane, and all other natural motions, are regulated by art. My master has composed an immensely pretty gamut, by which any lady or gentleman, with a few years' close application, may learn to laugh as gracefully as if they were born and bred to it.

JONATHAN. Mercy on my soul! A gamut for laughing—just like fa, la, sol?

JESSAMY. Yes. It comprises every possible display of jocularity, from an *affettuoso* smile to a *piano* titter, or full chorus *fortissimo* ha, ha, ha! My master employs his leisure hours in marking out the plays, like a cathedral chanting-book, that the ignorant may know where to laugh; and that pit, box, and gallery may keep time together, and not have a snigger in one part of the house, a broad grin in the other, and a d——d grum look in the third. How delightful to see the audience all smile together, then look on their books, then twist their mouths into an agreeable simper, then altogether shake the house with a general ha, ha, ha! loud as a full chorus of Handel's at an Abbey commemoration.

JONATHAN. Ha, ha, ha! that's dang'd cute, I swear.

JESSAMY. The gentlemen, you see, will laugh the tenor; the ladies will play the counter-tenor; the beaux will squeak the treble; and our jolly friends in the gallery a thorough base, ho, ho, ho!

JONATHAN. Well, can't you let me see that gamut?

JESSAMY. Oh! yes, Mr. Jonathan; here it is. [*Takes out a book.*] Oh! no, this is only a titter with its variations. Ah, here it is. [*Takes out another.*] Now, you must know, Mr. Jonathan, this is a piece written by Ben Jonson,[16] which I have set to my master's gamut. The places where you must smile, look grave, or laugh outright, are marked below the line. Now look over me. "There was a certain man"—now you must smile.

JONATHAN. Well, read it again; I warrant I'll mind my eye.

JESSAMY. "There was a certain man, who had a sad scolding wife,"—now you must laugh.

JONATHAN. Tarnation! That's no laughing matter though.

JESSAMY. "And she lay sick a-dying"; —now you must titter.

JONATHAN. What, snigger when the good woman's a-dying! Gor, I——

JESSAMY. Yes, the notes say you must—"and she asked her husband leave to make a will,"—now you must begin to look grave;—"and her husband said"——

JONATHAN. Ay, what did her husband say? Something dang'd cute, I reckon.

JESSAMY. "And her husband said, you have had your will all your lifetime, and would you have it after you are dead, too?"

JONATHAN. Ho, ho, ho! There the old man was even with her; he was up to the notch—ha, ha, ha!

JESSAMY. But, Mr. Jonathan, you must not laugh so. Why you ought to have tittered *piano*, and you have laughed *fortissimo*. Look here; you see these marks, A, B, C, and so on; these are the references to the other part of the book. Let us turn to it, and you will see the directions how to manage the muscles. This [*turns over*] was note D

[16] Elizabethan comic dramatist.

you blundered at.—You must purse the mouth into a smile, then titter, discovering the lower part of the three front upper teeth.

JONATHAN. How? read it again.

JESSAMY. "There was a certain man" —very well!—"who had a sad scolding wife,"—why don't you laugh?

JONATHAN. Now, that scolding wife sticks in my gizzard so pluckily that I can't laugh for the blood and nowns of me. Let me look grave here, and I'll laugh your belly full, where the old creature's a-dying.

JESSAMY. "And she asked her husband" [*Bell rings.*] My master's bell! he's returned, I fear.—Here, Mr. Jonathan, take this gamut; and I make no doubt but with a few years' close application, you may be able to smile gracefully. [*Exeunt severally.*]

SCENE 2

CHARLOTTE'S *Apartment*

[*Enter* MANLY.]

MANLY. What, no one at home? How unfortunate to meet the only lady my heart was ever moved by, to find her engaged to another, and confessing her partiality for me! Yet engaged to a man who, by her intimation, and his libertine conversation with me, I fear, does not merit her. Aye! there's the sting; for, were I assured that Maria was happy, my heart is not so selfish but that it would dilate in knowing it, even though it were with another. But to know she is unhappy!—I must drive these thoughts from me. Charlotte has some books; and this is what I believe she calls her little library. [*Enters a closet.*]

[*Enter* DIMPLE *leading* LETITIA.]

LETITIA. And will you pretend to say now, Mr. Dimple, that you propose to break with Maria? Are not the banns published? Are not the clothes purchased? Are not the friends invited? In short, is it not a done affair?

DIMPLE. Believe me, my dear Letitia, I would not marry her.

LETITIA. Why have you not broke with her before this, as you all along deluded me by saying you would?

DIMPLE. Because I was in hopes she would, ere this, have broke with me.

LETITIA. You could not expect it.

DIMPLE. Nay, but be calm a moment; 'twas from my regard to you that I did not discard her.

LETITIA. Regard to me!

DIMPLE. Yes; I have done everything in my power to break with her, but the foolish girl is so fond of me that nothing can accomplish it. Besides, how can I offer her my hand when my heart is indissolubly engaged to you?

LETITIA. There may be reason in this; but why so attentive to Miss Manly?

DIMPLE. Attentive to Miss Manly! For heaven's sake, if you have no better opinion of my constancy, pay not so ill a compliment to my taste.

LETITIA. Did I not see you whisper her to-day?

DIMPLE. Possibly I might—but something of so very trifling a nature that I have already forgot what it was.

LETITIA. I believe she has not forgot it.

DIMPLE. My dear creature, how can you for a moment suppose I should have any serious thoughts of that trifling, gay, flighty coquette, that disagreeable——

[*Enter* CHARLOTTE.]

DIMPLE. My dear Miss Manly, I rejoice to see you; there is a charm in your conversation that always marks your entrance into company as fortunate.

LETITIA. Where have you been, my dear?

CHARLOTTE. Why, I have been about to twenty shops, turning over pretty things, and so have left twenty visits unpaid. I wish you would step into the carriage and whisk round, make my apology, and leave my cards where our friends are not at home; that, you know, will serve as a visit. Come, do go.

LETITIA. So anxious to get me out! but I'll watch you. [*Aside.*] Oh! yes, I'll go, I want a little exercise. Positively [DIMPLE *offering to accompany her*], Mr. Dimple, you shall not go; why, half my visits are cake and caudle visits; it won't do, you know, for you to go. [*Exit, but returns to the door in the back scene and listens.*]

DIMPLE. This attachment of your brother to Maria is fortunate.

CHARLOTTE. How did you come to the knowledge of it?

DIMPLE. I read it in their eyes.

CHARLOTTE. And I had it from her mouth. It would have amused you to have seen her! She, that thought it so great an impropriety to praise a gentleman that she could not bring out one word in your favour, found a redundancy to praise him.

DIMPLE. I have done everything in my power to assist his passion there: your delicacy, my dearest girl, would be shocked at half the instances of neglect and misbehaviour.

CHARLOTTE. I don't know how I should bear neglect; but Mr. Dimple must misbehave himself indeed, to forfeit my good opinion.

DIMPLE. Your good opinion, my angel, is the pride and pleasure of my heart, and if the most respectful tenderness for you, and an utter indifference for all your sex besides, can make me worthy of your esteem, I shall richly merit it.

CHARLOTTE. All my sex besides, Mr. Dimple!—you forgot your tête-à-tête with Letitia.

DIMPLE. How can you, my lovely angel, cast a thought on that insipid, wry-mouthed, ugly creature!

CHARLOTTE. But her fortune may have charms?

DIMPLE. Not to a heart like mine. The man, who has been blessed with the good opinion of my Charlotte, must despise the allurements of fortune.

CHARLOTTE. I am satisfied.

DIMPLE. Let us think no more on the odious subject, but devote the present hours to happiness.

CHARLOTTE. Can I be happy when I see the man I prefer going to be married to another?

DIMPLE. Have I not already satisfied my charming angel, that I can never think of marrying the puling Maria? But, even if it were so, could that be any bar to our happiness? for, as the poet sings,

Love, free as air, at sight of human ties,
Spreads his light wings, and in a moment flies.

Come, then, my charming angel! why delay our bliss? The present moment is ours; the next is in the hand of fate. [*Kissing her.*]

CHARLOTTE. Begone, Sir! By your delusions you had almost lulled my honour asleep.

DIMPLE. Let me lull the demon to sleep again with kisses. [*He struggles with her; she screams.*]

[*Enter* MANLY.]

MANLY. Turn, villain! and defend yourself.——[*Draws.*]

[VAN ROUGH *enters and beats down their swords.*]

VAN ROUGH. Is the devil in you? are you going to murder one another? [*Holding* DIMPLE.]

DIMPLE. Hold him, hold him,—I can command my passion.

[*Enter* JONATHAN.]

JONATHAN. What the rattle ails you? Is the old one in you? Let the colonel alone, can't you? I feel chock-full of fight,—do you want to kill the colonel?——

MANLY. Be still, Jonathan; the gentleman does not want to hurt me.

JONATHAN. Gor! I—I wish he did; I'd show him Yankee boy's play, pretty quick.—Don't you see you have frightened the young woman into the *hystrikes?*

VAN ROUGH. Pray, some of you explain this; what has been the occasion of all this racket?

MANLY. That gentleman can explain it to you; it will be a very diverting story for an intended father-in-law to hear.

VAN ROUGH. How was this matter, Mr. Van Dumpling?

DIMPLE. Sir,—upon my honour,—all I know is, that I was talking to this young lady, and this gentleman broke in on us in a very extraordinary manner.

VAN ROUGH. Why, all this is nothing to the purpose; can you explain it, Miss? [*To* CHARLOTTE.]

[*Enter* LETITIA *through the back scene.*]

LETITIA. I can explain it to that gentleman's confusion. Though long betrothed to your daughter [*to* VAN ROUGH], yet, allured by my fortune, it seems (with shame do I speak it) he has privately paid his addresses to me. I was drawn in to listen to him by his assuring me that the match was made by his father without his consent, and that he proposed to break with Maria, whether he married me or not. But, whatever were his intentions respecting your daughter, Sir, even to me he was false; for he has repeated the same story, with some cruel reflections upon my person, to Miss Manly.

JONATHAN. What a tarnal curse!

LETITIA. Nor is this all, Miss Manly. When he was with me this very morning, he made the same ungenerous reflections upon the weakness of your mind as he has so recently done upon the defects of my person.

JONATHAN. What a tarnal curse and damn, too!

DIMPLE. Ha! since I have lost Letitia, I believe I had as good make it up with Maria. Mr Van Rough, at present I cannot enter into particulars; but, I believe, I can explain everything to your satisfaction in private.

VAN ROUGH. There is another matter, Mr. Van Dumpling, which I would have you explain. Pray, Sir, have Messrs. Van Cash & Co. presented you those bills for acceptance?

DIMPLE. The deuce! Has he heard of those bills! Nay, then, all's up with Maria, too; but an affair of this sort can never prejudice me among the ladies; they will rather long to know what the dear creature possesses to make him so agreeable. [*Aside.*] Sir, you'll hear from me. [*To* MANLY.]

MANLY. And you from me, Sir——

DIMPLE. Sir, you wear a sword——

MANLY. Yes, Sir. This sword was presented to me by that brave Gallic hero, the Marquis de la Fayette. I have drawn it in the service of my country, and in private life, on the only occasion where a man is justified in drawing his sword, in defence of a lady's honour. I have fought too many battles in the service of my country to dread the imputation of cowardice. Death from a man of honour would be a glory you do not merit; you shall live to bear the insult of man and the contempt of that sex whose general smiles afforded you all your happiness.

DIMPLE. You won't meet me, Sir? Then I'll post you for a coward.

MANLY. I'll venture that, Sir. The reputation of my life does not depend upon the breath of a Mr. Dimple. I would have you to know, however, Sir, that I have a cane to chastise the insolence of a scoundrel, and a sword and the good laws of my country to protect me from the attempts of an assassin——

DIMPLE. Mighty well! Very fine, indeed! Ladies and gentlemen, I take my leave; and you will please to observe in the case of my deportment the contrast between a gentleman who has read

Chesterfield and received the polish of Europe and an unpolished, untravelled American. [*Exit.*]

[*Enter* MARIA.]

MARIA. Is he indeed gone?——

LETITIA. I hope, never to return.

VAN ROUGH. I am glad I heard of those bills; though it's plaguy unlucky; I hoped to see Mary married before I died.

MANLY. Will you permit a gentleman, Sir, to offer himself as a suitor to your daughter? Though a stranger to you, he is not altogether so to her, or unknown in this city. You may find a son-in-law of more fortune, but you can never meet with one who is richer in love for her, or respect for you.

VAN ROUGH. Why, Mary, you have not let this gentleman make love to you without my leave?

MANLY. I did not say, Sir——

MARIA. Say, Sir!——I—the gentleman, to be sure, met me accidentally.

VAN ROUGH. Ha, ha, ha! Mark me, Mary; young folks think old folks to be fools; but old folks know young folks to be fools. Why, I knew all about this affair. This was only a cunning way I had to bring it about. Hark ye! I was in the closet when you and he were at our house. [*Turns to the company.*] I heard that little baggage say she loved her old father, and would die to make him happy! Oh! how I loved the little baggage! And you talked very prudently, young man. I have inquired into your character, and find you to be a man of punctuality and mind the main chance. And so, as you love Mary and Mary loves you, you shall have my consent immediately to be married. I'll settle my fortune on you, and go and live with you the remainder of my life.

MANLY. Sir, I hope——

VAN ROUGH. Come, come, no fine speeches; mind the main chance, young man, and you and I shall always agree.

LETITIA. I sincerely wish you joy [*advancing to* MARIA]; and hope your pardon for my conduct.

MARIA. I thank you for your congratulations, and hope we shall at once forget the wretch who has given us so much disquiet and the trouble that he has occasioned.

CHARLOTTE. And I, my dear Maria, —how shall I look up to you for forgiveness? I, who, in the practice of the meanest arts, have violated the most sacred rights of friendship? I can never forgive myself, or hope charity from the world; but, I confess, I have much to hope from such a brother; and I am happy that I may soon say, such a sister.

MARIA. My dear, you distress me; you have all my love.

MANLY. And mine.

CHARLOTTE. If repentance can entitle me to forgiveness, I have already much merit; for I despise the littleness of my past conduct. I now find that the heart of any worthy man cannot be gained by invidious attacks upon the rights and characters of others;—by countenancing the addresses of a thousand;—or that the finest assemblage of features, the greatest taste in dress, the genteelest address, or the most brilliant wit, cannot eventually secure a coquette from contempt and ridicule.

MANLY. And I have learned that probity, virtue, honour, though they should not have received the polish of Europe, will secure to an honest American the good graces of his fair countrywomen, and, I hope, the applause of THE PUBLIC.

The End

James A. Herne

✻ 1839-1901

James A. Herne, who changed his name from Aherne for reasons of euphony, was born in Cohoes, New York, left school at the age of thirteen to earn his living, and was almost at once bitten by the theatrical bug. Having saved his money, he bought a theatrical wardrobe and joined the stock company in Troy, playing in UNCLE TOM'S CABIN *and other "standard" dramas. He soon established himself as a useful player and was engaged by Lucille Western, a popular star of the day, as leading man for a nationwide tour. In San Francisco he accepted the job of stage director at the Baldwin Theatre, married Katherine Corcoran, who was to be both his leading lady and the dominant influence on his writing, and collaborated with David Belasco on his first plays. One of these, a melodrama, he later reshaped into* HEARTS OF OAK, *which he and his wife took on tour for seven years. It was a simple, sentimental play, without a villain, and acted with that realism or underplaying of which the Hernes were pioneers.*

After several more plays of the same type, Herne boldly undertook a serious treatment of marital infidelity in MARGARET FLEMING. *In this he was strongly supported by his wife and by the leaders of American naturalism, but violently rejected by the managers of playhouses. He finally staged the play himself in Lynn, Massachusetts, in 1890, and in a concert hall in Boston, but it was many years before the play could be accepted by the general public. Two years later the quiet realism of* SHORE ACRES *(in spite of the sensation scene in the third act) met the same rejection. However, a friendly Chicago manager staged the play in 1892, to no great acclaim, and in the next year it was brought out in Boston with some revisions and at once found its audience. Herne played it throughout the country for five years.*

In 1899 he produced GRIFFITH DAVENPORT *in Washington, possibly the first play to treat the Civil War as something more than an occasion for melodrama or romance. His last play,* SAG HARBOR, *opened in Boston in the same year. It is a reworking of an older play in the style that Herne had made his own, and it was destined for the success of* SHORE ACRES *when the actor-playwright suffered a breakdown and died in New York City.*

Many of Herne's manuscripts were lost in a fire that destroyed his home; of GRIFFITH DAVENPORT *only one act survives, while* MARGARET FLEMING *was reconstructed from memory by his wife.* SHORE ACRES *was first printed in a collection of three plays revised by Katherine C. Herne. It is particularly interesting for the stage directions, which indicate both what the actor is expected to convey in the often semi-articulate speeches and how he is expected to avoid the conventions of the older school of rhetorical or romantic interpretation.*

Shore Acres

A COMEDY IN FOUR ACTS

Characters

MARTIN BERRY, *owner of "Shore Acres" and keeper of Berry Light*
NATHAN'L BERRY, *"Uncle Nat," his elder brother*
JOEL GATES, *a grass widower*
JOSIAH BLAKE, *postmaster and store-keeper*
SAM WARREN, *a young physician*
CAPTAIN BEN HUTCHINS, *skipper of the* "Liddy Ann"
DR. LEONARD
SQUIRE ANDREWS
TIM HAYES
YOUNG NAT BERRY
IKE RICHARDS, LEM CONANT, ABE HIGGINS, STEVE BAILEY — *"Kinder work around"*
DAVE BURGESS, GABE KILPATRICK, BILL HODGEKINS — *Fishermen, crew of the* "Liddy Ann"
BOB BERRY
THE MAIL CARRIER
ANN BERRY, *Martin's wife*
HELEN BERRY, *Martin's daughter*
LIDDY ANN NYE
MRS. ANDREWS
MRS. LEONARD
PERLEY, *Mrs. Berry's hired girl*
MARY BERRY
MILLIE BERRY
MANDY GATES
BOB LEONARD, SIS LEONARD — *The twins*

ACT I. View of "Shore Acres Farm," near Bar Harbor
"Hayin' Time"

ACT II. The Berry farmhouse kitchen
"The Silver Weddin'"

ACT III. Scene 1. Interior of Berry Lighthouse
"Havin' an Understandin'"

Scene 2. Exterior of Berry Lighthouse
"The 'Liddy Ann' in a Sou'-easter"

ACT IV. Same as Act II. Fifteen months later
"Me an' the Children"

TIME—1891

PLACE—Berry, on Frenchman's Bay, near Bar Harbor, on the coast of Maine

ACT I

"Hayin' Time"

View of "Shore Acres Farm," near Bar Harbor.

Scene: Frenchman's Bay, with Mount Desert Island and its range of grandly picturesque hills in the distance. Away off to the right are the stately Schoodac Mountains, veiled in mist.

On the right of the stage, at the back, on a rocky bluff dotted with dwarf pines, and overlooking the bay, is Berry Light. It is separated from the farmhouse by a shady road, which runs across the stage from left to right. The farmhouse, on the right, is barely visible, being hidden in a profusion of shrubs and flowers. Trees overhang the roof; a white-washed fence divides the door yard from the road. Several shining milk pails are hanging on the fence, and on one of the palings hangs a small weatherbeaten mail bag; near it hangs a battered tin horn. The door yard is filled with old-fashioned flowers.

To the left of the stage is an old barn, its doors open, its littered yard enclosed by a rail fence. A dove cote is built into the peak of its gabled roof, and doves come and go leisurely.

Outside the fence, at the upper end, is a pump, beneath which is a trough filled

with water. Against the lower end of the fence lies a plough. Trees overhang the roof of the barn, and join those overhanging the house from the other side. At right centre is a gnarled old tree, and beneath it is a bench. Down left, below the fence, is a wheelbarrow.

At the rise of the curtain, and until the act is well in progress, the wind gently sways the foliage with a slightly rustling sound. Birds sing, and flit to and fro. The sound of multitudinous insects is the one distinct note of the scene. The bay is calm, quiet, and in the distance a catboat is occasionally seen sailing lazily, appearing and disappearing among the islands. A tiny steam launch appears once, about the middle of the act, and is seen no more. A mowing machine is heard at work in the distance off left. It stops, turns, goes on again, while the voice of the driver is heard guiding his horses, with "Whoa! Stiddy! Get up! Whoa Bill!" (All this must be very distant.)

At the rise of the curtain, MILLIE, *a little girl about four years old, is sitting down left near the plough, playing in the sand with clam shells and pieces of old crockery. She wears a quaint little calico dress, and has a small white flannel shawl around her shoulders, crossed in front and tied behind her back. Her shoes are very dusty, her little hands are dirty.*

On the road, off stage to the right, a horse and wagon can be heard driving up and stopping outside; and presently the MAIL CARRIER *appears, with a mail bag and a basket of groceries. He is a kindly-looking man of middle age, wearing a linen duster, driving gloves and a straw hat. He goes to the bag hanging on the fence, takes two letters from it, and puts in a newspaper wrapped for mailing. He drops the letters into his own bag, and places the basket of groceries beside the fence.*

MAIL CARRIER [*Putting his hands to his mouth, calls*]. Whoop! Whoop! Whoop!

[*At his call,* MILLIE *leaves her play and runs to him. They are evidently good friends.*]

MILLIE. Hello!

MAIL CARRIER. Hello, Millie! I swan I'm afeared I've fergot yeh this mornin'.

MILLIE. Oh! Hev yeh?

MAIL CARRIER. Well, not quite. [*Feels in his coat pocket, gets out a piece of candy as if it were the usual thing, and gives it to her.*]

MILLIE [*Pleased*]. Thank yeh.

MAIL CARRIER. Hain't yeh got a kiss fer me?

MILLIE. I guess so. [*Lifts up her face; he kisses her.*]

MAIL CARRIER. I'll bring yeh a bigger piece tomorry. Good-by. [*He goes off right, and is heard driving away.*]

[MILLIE *nibbles the candy as she watches him out of sight, then she resumes her play.*

[*After the mail wagon drives away,* HELEN *enters, left, followed by* UNCLE NAT. HELEN *is a girl of seventeen, with a frank yet thoughtful manner, indicating a girl of advanced ideas. She has golden-red hair and brown eyes; she is picturesquely dressed, and wears a sunbonnet. She carries a small pail full of berries, and a tin cup hangs from a crooked finger.*

[UNCLE NAT *is a man of sixty, and his large sturdy frame shows signs of toil. His eyes, of a faded blue-gray, have the far-seeing look common to sailors. He wears his yellow-white hair rather long, and he is clean-shaven save for the tippet of straw-white beard that seems to grow up from his chest and to form a sort of frame for his benevolent, weather-beaten old face.* UNCLE NAT *is of the soil, yet there is an inherent poise and dignity about him that are typical of the men who have mastered their environment. He has great cheerfulness and much sly, quiet humor. He wears overalls of a faded blue, a blue checked jumper, beneath which one glimpses a red flannel shirt, and on his head is a farmer's much-battered wide straw hat. His sleeves are rolled back, and he carries a pitchfork in his hand.*

[*As the scene progresses, one is impressed by the frank comradeship between the old man and the girl. On his part there is tenderness, and a deep interest in her problems; there is admiration too for her fine spirit of independence.* HELEN *shows a suppressed feeling of bitterness as she talks. She is high-spirited and proud, yet simple and direct. They pause a little above center as they talk.*]

HELEN [*Talking as she enters*]. Yes, I know, Uncle Nat, perhaps I oughtn't. But Father makes me mad when he talks as he does about Sam.

UNCLE NAT [*Soothingly*]. Well, now, things'll come out all right ef you'll only hev patience. You're young, so's Sam. I told 'im so t'other day. Sez I, "Sam Warren," sez I, "you hain't got a mite o' sense," I sez.

HELEN [*In the same manner*]. Father says—if he catches me speaking to him again, he'll——

UNCLE NAT. You mustn't let 'm ketch yeh! [*Chuckles.*] Law sakes, ef I couldn't spark a fellah athout my father ketchin' me at it, I'd bag my head.

HELEN [*With gentle reproach*]. I can't bear deceit——

UNCLE NAT. Neither kin I, but what yeh goin' to do about it—give Sam up?

HELEN [*Determinedly*]. No! [*She crosses to the right, and sits on the bench under the tree, and says with an undercurrent of defiance*] I'll never give him up—I'll leave home first.

UNCLE NAT [*teasingly*]. Oh, Nell! You wouldn't hev spunk enough fer that.

HELEN [*Half smiling, then thoughtfully*]. Wouldn't I——

UNCLE NAT. No sirree! [*Crosses to the left and places the pitchfork against the fence.*]

HELEN. You'll see—it'll be his own fault if I do. [*Rising and going toward him.*] Uncle Nat, if you were my father, would you——

UNCLE NAT [*Wistfully, with a tender cadence in his voice*]. Ef I was yer father, Nell? Ef I was yer father, I'm afeared I'd let you do jes' about's you'd a mind to. Allus *did* seem es ef you was my baby anyway, an' I'd give the two eyes out'n my head to see you an' Sam happy. But I ain't yer father, Nell—I ain't yer father. [*The last with a regretful sigh.*]

HELEN [*Softly*]. I sometimes wish you were.

UNCLE NAT [*Goes to her and places his hands affectionately on her shoulders*]. Now, hol' on! Thet ain't right. No sirree! Thet ain't right, an' you know it.

HELEN. Father's changed. [*Leaves him and goes slowly back to the bench.*] He never takes me on his knee any more. [*With a slight shade of resentment.*]

UNCLE NAT [*Smiling, and looking at her admiringly*]. You're gittin' too heavy I guess.

HELEN. No, it isn't that. Mother's noticed it, and she feels pretty bad about it too, although she pretends not to see it.

UNCLE NAT. Of course she dooze. She ain't a-goin' to see no changes in a man she's been married to nigh on to twenty-five year, not ef she kin help it.

HELEN [*Rises, and as she does so she sees* MR. BLAKE's *buggy, which is supposedly standing offstage, right. Immediately her whole manner changes, and she says with an impatient tone in her voice*]. There's Mr. Blake's buggy again! [*Shrugging her shoulders.*] He's here about all the time lately.

UNCLE NAT [*Rather seriously*]. He *is*

here pooty consid'ble, ain't he? What's he after I wonder?

HELEN [*Resentfully*]. Principally—me.

UNCLE NAT [*Surprised, but rather amused*]. He ain't!

HELEN [*With finality*]. Yes he is. Father wants me to marry him.

UNCLE NAT [*Frightened*]. He don't!

HELEN [*In the same manner*]. Yes, he does. Mr. Blake told me as much the other day.

UNCLE NAT. My! My! Thet's too bad. I swan thet's too bad. I'm afeared yer father don't understand yeh, Helen. Has he said anythin' to yeh about 't himself?

HELEN [*Still standing by the bench*]. No, not yet—but he will, and then—well—[*Half savagely.*] He'll find out I'm not Mother——

UNCLE NAT. Tut—tut—tut—there yeh go—Thet's yer father all over again—thet's yer father all over again.

[JOEL GATES *drifts into the farmyard from the road, left. Little* MANDY *drifts in after him.* GATES *is dressed in dark overalls, with suspenders, a soiled white shirt, no vest, and an old drab soft hat. He carries a scythe, the snath under his left arm, the blade to the ground with the point off to the left, and he has a whetstone in his right hand. He looks as if life had battered him mercilessly. He is small and slight, his face weather-washed, kindly; his keen little eyes seem to be as a child's with a question in them, always asking "What is it all about any-how!—I d'know!" He is never seen with-out* MANDY. *Her whole little personality is part of his; the nondescript, faded clothing, the rhythm of movement. The far-away look in the old face is repeated in the apple-blossom beauty of the child. He rarely addresses her or seems aware of her presence.*]

GATES [*In a drawl*]. Good day, Nathan'l.

UNCLE NAT. Hello, Joel!

GATES [*Talking as he walks across the stage toward the right*]. Why ain't yeh in th' hay field?

UNCLE NAT. Ben there good part th' mornin'. Who be you a-cuttin' fer t'day, Joel?

GATES. Simm'ns. Jes' got done. Goin' t' cut m'own now. Can't afford to lose this weather.

UNCLE NAT. No; too good weather to lose, an' no mistake.

[GATES *is about to exit, with* MANDY *behind him, when he stops abruptly near the bench.* MANDY *pauses also.*]

GATES. Oh, Nathan'l! Will yeh lend me yer gun fer a day 'r two?

UNCLE NAT [*Reluctantly*]. Yes—I guess'o. What fer? [*Coming down center.*]

GATES. There's a fox 'r suthin' a-playin' ol' Nick with my chickings.

UNCLE NAT. Thet so? Helen, git me ol' Uncle Sam'l, will yeh? She's a-standin' in her corner in the kitchen. [HELEN *goes into the house.*] Hello, Mandy! [*Chuckles.*] How d'yeh do?—You ben in the hay field too? [*The child nods.*] By George—you're a great haymaker. I'll tell you what—when you git a scythe inter yer hands th' grasshoppers is got to jump over the fence an' no mistake, ain't they, Joel? [*Chuckles.*] Will yeh shake hands with me? [*Urging the child kindly.*]

GATES. Go on—shake hands.

[MANDY *shyly creeps behind her father.*]

UNCLE NAT. Bashful, ain't she?

GATES [*Reaching around to where the child stands behind him, and pressing her closer to him*]. Yes—she's a shy sort o' critter. Don't never seem t' want t' play with nobody nor nothin' but me.

UNCLE NAT. She's a-growin' ain't she—growin' jes' like a weed. My—my! How like her mother she dooze look, don't she?

GATES [*With a break in his voice and a catch in his breath, placing his hand on *her head and looking at her*]. Yeh. Gits to look more an' more like her every day in the week.

UNCLE NAT [*Hesitatingly, as if loth to arouse unhappy memories*]. I suppose —yeh hain't never heard nothin' of her —sence—hev yeh, Joel?

GATES [*Out of the depths of pitiful memories*]. No—nothin. [*With a great sigh.*]

[HELEN *returns with the gun and crosses to* UNCLE NAT. GATES *also crosses to* UNCLE NAT, *leaving* MANDY *in front of the bench. After* HELEN *gives* UNCLE NAT *the gun, she goes over to* MILLIE, *who has been playing in the sand, all unconscious of things that have been going on about her, and sits down beside her and plays with her.* MANDY *timidly sits on the edge of the bench; she watches her father intently, with a look of trust and affectionate content which one sees in a dearly loved dog when near his master.*

[*The attitude of* GATES *and* UNCLE NAT *in the episode of the gun is that of two boys gloating over a treasure.*]

UNCLE NAT. Well—here's ol' Uncle Sam'l. Take good keer of 'r. I set a good deal o' store by Sam'l. [*He hands* GATES *the gun.*]

GATES [*Putting the stone in his pocket, laying down his scythe and taking the gun*]. Is she—eh—ludded?

UNCLE NAT. Yes, I allus keep 'r ludded.

GATES. Doos she—eh—kick?

UNCLE NAT. She never kicked me, d'know what she might do to a feller she didn't like.

GATES [*Handling the gun with pride, as though it were a great privilege, his eyes traveling the length of it admiringly, and then looking at* UNCLE NAT *with his face aglow*]. Fit all through the war with 'r, didn't yeh?

UNCLE NAT. Yeh.

GATES. Sixth Maine?

UNCLE NAT [*His hands clasped behind him, shoulders thrown back, his head high in the air, teeters to and fro on his heels and toes*]. Yeh—Sixth Maine, Company A. Her 'n me's tramped a good many miles together, one way 'nother. [*His voice is quiet and his face tense with memories.*]

GATES [*In an awed hushed voice*]. Did yeh ever—kill a rebel 'th her?

UNCLE NAT [*In a matter-of-fact tone*]. Don't know. I used t' jes' p'int 'er, shet both my eyes 'n let 'r do her own work.

GATES [*Reflectively*]. I guess thet's 'bout as good a way as any fer me t'kill thet 'ere fox. [*He is fussing with the gun and unconsciously aims it at* UNCLE NAT.]

UNCLE NAT [*Taking hold of the gun and pushing it aside*]. Hol' on, yeh danged ol' fool— Didn't I jes' tell yeh she was ludded?

GATES. What yer skeered of? I wa'n't a-goin' to pull the trigger—I was only jes' aimin' 'r.

UNCLE NAT. Well, aim 'r at somebody else.

GATES. There ain't nobody else handy.

UNCLE NAT. I swan thet's too bad.

GATES. Well, good day. [*Takes up the scythe, and puts the gun over his shoulder.*] I'll bring 'r back safe an' sound.

[GATES *goes off right.* MANDY *quietly slips from the bench and slowly drifts after him.* UNCLE NAT *attracts her attention by playfully snapping his fingers at her, and she turns and shows quite a little interest in his kindly friendliness. She passes on, her eyes fixed wonderingly upon him.* UNCLE NAT *is amused and chuckles. After they go off, he seats himself on the bench under the tree.*]

HELEN. Oh, Uncle Nat! Have you and Sam done anything more about your back pension?

UNCLE NAT. Well, Sam got me t' sign some papers over at the Squire's t'other day—but—I d'want him to do nothin' about my back pension. [*With mock indignation.*] What do you an' him take me fur? One o' them 'ere pension grabbers?

HELEN [*Going up left*]. Well, Sam says you're entitled to it, and he's going to try and get it for you too.

UNCLE NAT. Sam says lots o' things asides his prayers, don't he, Nell?

HELEN [*Pausing and leaning over the fence*]. I guess he does. [*They laugh together softly with amused understanding.*]

UNCLE NAT. Where yeh goin'?

HELEN. Oh, I don't know. Just for a stroll. [*And much occupied with her problems, she disappears down the road to the left.*]

UNCLE NAT [*Rises from the bench a little stiffly, as if checked by a slight rheumatic twinge, goes down left and gets the wheelbarrow. He starts off as if he might be going to get fodder for the noon meal of the animals, when he notices* MILLIE *and says jovially*]. Well, Millie, d'yeh want a ride?

MILLIE [*Dropping her play and brushing off her frock, eagerly*]. Yes.

UNCLE NAT. Well, climb into the kerridge an' don't keep the ol' hoss waitin'. Yeh know how to git into a kerridge?

MILLIE. Yes. [*She sits on the edge of the wheelbarrow.*]

UNCLE NAT. Well, I don't know whether yeh do or not. Take a back seat. [*He tips the wheelbarrow gently so that she slides into the back of it. She is a bit startled for a moment.*] You see, I knew yeh didn't know how to git into a kerridge. The fust thing yeh know this ol' hoss'll kick up and knock the dashboard out, an' spill yeh all over the place, an' yeh won't like thet a bit. [*He wheels her off, right.*]

[BLAKE *enters from the barn. He is a man of forty years; he has black hair, and his side-whiskers are close cut. The rest of his face is cleanly shaven. He is dressed in a gray business suit, "store made"; the coat is a single-breasted frock, very slightly cutaway, buttoned with one button at the breast. He wears a white laundered shirt, and a rather high standing collar with a black ready-made tie. His hat is a silk one, old, but not battered, brown at the edges of the crown and brim. His shoes have been home-polished, but are dusty. He has drab castor gloves, not new; he carries a buggy whip, an old white one. He has a black silk ribbon watch guard around his neck, and a gold watch. He is portly and well-to-do, but jovial. He is rather good-looking, and has the air of a contented, cheerful businessman, shrewd, but not cunning or mean; he is always smiling. He passes through the gate of the barnyard, and goes right center.*

[*He is followed by* MARTIN, *a heavy robust man of fifty. He is slow and deliberate in manner and speech. His face and hands are weather-beaten, his hair is sandy-gray and cropped, and he has a short stubby beard. He wears pepper-and-salt trousers tucked into his boots, a black vest, and an open white, home-made and home-laundered shirt with collar attached. His shirt sleeves are rolled up a trifle, showing red flannel beneath. He has a black silk sailor handkerchief, and a black soft hat, well worn. He carries a jackknife in his right hand, and is opening and shutting the blade with his thumb as he walks along, "clicking" it. His left hand is behind his back, and his head is down, as if in deep thought. He stops inside the rail fence.*

[*At the same time enters from the house,* PERLEY, *the "hired girl," a strong muscular girl of about twenty, in a calico dress, with her sleeves rolled up to her shoulders, showing her red powerful arms. She pays no attention to* BLAKE *or* MARTIN *and goes to the mail bag, takes it down, takes out the paper, crosses over and gives it to* MARTIN, *who mechan-*

ically looks at the address as if he knew what it was, as it is a regularly "subscribed for" paper. She crosses back to the basket of provisions, puts the bag into the basket, stands with her back to the men, with her hands on her hips, and looks up and down the road for a moment. She then takes up the basket and goes into the house.

[*The dialogue between* MARTIN *and* BLAKE *has gone on right through the action, from the moment they entered.*]

BLAKE. No, sirree. I tell yeh, Martin, the day o' sentiment's gone. We're livin' in a practical age. Any man's liable to go to bed poor 'n wake up a milli'naire. Ef I'd had a friend to give me such a boost and such advice's I've given you I'd hev owned half the State o' Maine, I believe.

MARTIN [*At the lower end of the fence, and facing the audience; putting the paper in the watch pocket of his vest*]. Why, yeh see's I told yeh, Mother left the place to me 'n Nathan'l, an' we sort o' promised 'er we'd never sell it an——

BLAKE. Sentiment! All sentiment! Any man thet'll hang on to an old farm jes' 'cause—[*goes to the pump, takes the cup and pumps water into it*] he sort o' promised his dead mother he'd never sell it, ain't got no business to live in this bustlin', go-ahead, money-makin', devil-take-the-hinder-most day of ours—[*drinks*] thet's all I've got to say. [*Laughs. Pours the balance of the water into the trough, replaces the cup, and wipes his mouth.*]

MARTIN [*Casually*]. P'r'aps you never sot much store b'your mother, Mr. Blake.

BLAKE. I never hed no mother—thet is not to speak of. You know all about thet as well as I do. [*He returns to* MARTIN.]

MARTIN. Thet mus' be the reason yeh can't understand——

BLAKE [*Patronizingly*]. I kin understand this. [*Leaning with his back to the fence, both elbows on the top rail.*] "Shore Acres" is a good enough farm as Maine farms go—yeh manage by hard work to make a livin' fer yerself an' family——

MARTIN [*Defensively, nodding his head at* BLAKE]. A good—comfortable —livin'! [*He puts his foot upon the middle rail.*]

BLAKE [*Admitting the correction good-naturedly*]. A good comfortable livin'! [*Switching the whip up and down.*]

MARTIN [*With quiet dignity*]. An' pay my debts.

BLAKE. An' pay—your debts.

MARTIN [*Complacently*]. Don't owe no man nothin', an' kin sleep nights.

BLAKE [*Patronizingly, agreeing with him*]. From sundown to cockcrow—I ain't a-goin' to dispute thet, thet's a-l-l right. Well, now, you happen to hev a hundred an' sixty rod, more or less, of about the sightliest shore front to be found on the coast. Yeh didn't know thet till I told yeh, did yeh?

MARTIN. No, I didn't. [*Climbs up, sits on the rail fence, facing the house, and sticks the knife into the rail between his legs.*]

BLAKE. Well! This shore front makes your land val'able. [*Turning and putting his foot on the bottom rail.*] Not to plant potatoes in—but to build summer cottages on. I tell yeh, the boom's a-comin' here jes' as sure as you're born. [*Carried away by his own enthusiasm.*] Bar Harbor's got s' high, yeh can't touch a foot of it—not by coverin' it with gold dollars. This has got to be the next p'int. [*Goes to the bench, right, and sits down.*]

MARTIN [*He is impressed by* BLAKE'S *enthusiasm, but there is caution in his immediate response*]. Seems so—the way you put matters.

BLAKE. Seems so? 'Tis so. You pool your land in with mine— [*He talks with a confident, good-natured, yet shrewd business air. He lays out a plan on the grass with the end of his whip.*] We'll lay out quarter-acre lots, cut avenoos, plant trees, build a driveway to the shore, hang on to all the shore front an' corner lots—sell every one o' the others, see!!! They'll build on 'em an' that'll double the value of ours—see!—they'll have to pay the heft o' the taxes 'cause they've built; we'll be taxed light 'cause we didn't—see?

MARTIN [*In the same manner*]. I d'know as I jes' see.

BLAKE [*Confidentially*]. If we can get holt of half a dozen just the right sort o' fellahs—city fellahs—yeh know—fellahs that hev got inflooance to bring folks down here—we can afford to give 'em each an inside lot, here an' there, provided they'll guarantee to build, lay out their grounds, an' help to make the place attractive. That'll give us a kind of starter—see? [*Chuckles.*]

MARTIN [*Warming a bit at* BLAKE's *confident statements*]. Seems es ef thet wouldn't be a bad idee.

BLAKE. *Bad* idee? It's *the* idee! [*Rising and going to* MARTIN, *confidentially.*] Let me show you——

[*He takes a notebook from his pocket, and begins to show* MARTIN *some calculations he has jotted down. They become so absorbed in this that they do not notice* GATES, *who enters right, followed by* MANDY.]

GATES [*Smiling ingratiatingly*]. How d' do? [*If encouraged he would stop, but they merely nod.*] I hear you fellahs is a-goin' to boom things here 'n the spring. [*He goes quite close to* BLAKE *and* MARTIN, *who are deep in discussion. He tries to peer over their shoulders, and raises his voice as if they were deaf.*] Is thet so thet Jordan Ma'sh's [1] comin' down here to go inter business? [*He pauses, inviting a response; again braces up a bit and makes another effort, now in a manner implying that he is doing them a great favor.*] I wouldn't mind sellin' thet seven acre o' mine—ef I thought I could git rich out 'n it.

[BLAKE *looks over his shoulder as if a puff of wind or something had disturbed him, then pointedly resumes his talk with* MARTIN. GATES *is crestfallen, and turns away.*]

GATES. Gosh! How some folks kin get stuck up 's soon as they git a little mite rich—I never see—— [*He shuffles off left, with mingled dignity and resentment, followed by* MANDY.]

BLAKE. I tell yeh, Martin, I've got the scheme! You go in with me an' in less than a year I'll make you so rich you can live in Bangor. Move your mother's remains up there, an' have 'em buried in one o' them fine cemet'ries, an' put a handsome stun over her as you'd ought to do.

MARTIN. Nathan'l an' me 's ben savin' up fer a stun. I guess we've got most enough now to git one—money's scurse with us—we don't see much *real* cash.

BLAKE. I'll tell you what I'll do. I'll take a mortgage on the farm for the money to start you—an' you kin sell the lots.

MARTIN [*Hesitatingly*]. I'll talk to Nathan'l an' Ann.

BLAKE. Talk to 'em—of course—but don't let 'em talk you out of the scheme. There's a good deal of sentiment in Nathan'l.

MARTIN. It'd make me pooty rich, wouldn't it?

BLAKE. Rich? Well, I guess. Yeh wouldn't hev to be borrowin' nobody else's chaise to go to meetin' in.

MARTIN. Seems es though it hed ought to be done, don't it? Yet it seems a kind o' pity to——

BLAKE. To get rich, eh? [*Laughs.*] Say, look a-here! Honest now—wouldn't you like to live better 'n you do? Now Honest Injun, wouldn't yeh?

[1] Jordan Marsh—a Boston department store.

MARTIN [*A bit warmed by* BLAKE's *suggestions*]. I suppose I would.

BLAKE. Of course yeh would, an' yeh'd like to have your family live better. Helen'd ought to hev a real good syminerry eddication—she's worth it, she's a bright han'some girl—she'd ought to be a bookkeeper or suthin'. [*Complacently.*] I was a-tellin' her t'other day 'bout your a-wantin' her 'n me to git married, an'——

MARTIN [*Showing interest*]. What'd she say?

[BLAKE *purses his lips and shakes his head dubiously.*]

MARTIN. Did yeh offer her the piannah, as I told yeh to?

BLAKE. Y-e-s——

MARTIN [*Nonplussed*]. I thought she'd 'a'jumped at the piannah. She's so fond o' music.

BLAKE. I offered her everything I could think of. I offered to build her a house, an' let her paint an' paper it any way she'd a mind to.

MARTIN [*Pondering*]. I guess I'd better talk to her myself. She giner'ly does what I tell her to.

BLAKE. Yes, but you see girls are beginning to think they've a right to marry who they please.

MARTIN [*With pride in* HELEN, *and pride in his own power to control her*]. Not *my* girl.

BLAKE [*Going right, with a shade of resentment*]. I'm afraid I'll never git very close to her so long 's young Doc Warren's around.

MARTIN [*Angrily*]. Doc Warren!—She don't keep company along o' him no more? [*As if in doubt.*]

BLAKE. Don't she?

MARTIN. I guess not. I told her I didn't want she should—thet's allus ben enough.

BLAKE. Them free thinkers is hard to git shut of. They're dangerous to young folks' religion.

MARTIN. Helen's ben riz a stric' Babtis'—I guess she'll stay so; she's a pious girl.

BLAKE. Them's the wust when they do change. Sam Warren was *raised* respectable enough. His father and mother were Presbyterians.

MARTIN [*His memory carries him into the past, and a smile creeps into his face as he answers patronizingly*]. Ol' man Warren was a good-natured honest ol' soul an' all that—but I never thought he had any too much sense.

BLAKE. No! If he had he wouldn't have worked himself to a skeleton tryin' to make a doctor out of his boy. [*Laughs.*]

MARTIN [*Nodding his head wisely*]. The mother had a good deal to do with thet, I guess.

BLAKE. Six o' one an' half a dozen o' the other. What she said was law with the ol' man and what he said was gospel with her. They thought the sun jes rose an' sot in their Sam, an' now look at 'im. First he read Emanuel Swedenborg, an' he was a red-hot Swedenborgian—then he got hold of Spencer an' Darwin an' a lot o' them kind o' lunatics an' began to study frogs an' bugs an' things. [*He laughs.* MARTIN *laughs too, but not so heartily as* BLAKE *does.*] Why, sir! One mornin', a spell ago, as I was goin' to Ellsworth, I seed him a-settin' on his hunkers in the middle of the rud, watchin' a lot of ants runnin' in an' out of a hole. [*Both roar with laughter at this.*] D'yeh remember thet free lecture he gave with the magic lantern in the schoolhouse, on evolution 's he called it?

MARTIN. Yes, some of 'em wanted to tar an' feather 'im thet time.

BLAKE. Oh! Pshaw! That wouldn't 'a'done! [*A slight pause.*] Now he's come out as a home-a-pathic physician—[*Laughs.*] He ain't a doctor—he's a pheesycian—goes around wantin' to cure sick folks with sugar shot—by George! [*Both laugh heartily.*]

MARTIN. L'see—ain't he a-tendin' ol' Mis' Swazy now?

BLAKE [*Carelessly*]. Yep! Doc Leonard give her up, an' they had to have him. [*Starts to go off right, then stops.*] Oh, I'm goin' to git rid o' all my hawgs. I'd like you to have them two shoats, they're beauties!

MARTIN [*Preoccupied*]. I guess I've got all I want.

BLAKE. Well, think over thet there land business. If you want to get rich, now's your chance—if you don't, I can't help it. Good day! [MARTIN *nods.*] Good hay weather. [*Scans the sky.*]

MARTIN. Fust-rate.

BLAKE [*As he goes off right*]. Most through?

MARTIN. Finish this week ef the weather holds.

BLAKE [*Outside*]. Good day!

MARTIN. Good day! [*He looks after* BLAKE, *then slowly and thoughtfully enters the barn, head down, hands behind his back.*]

[HELEN'S *voice is heard off left. She talks as she enters; she has an arm around* YOUNG NAT, *a handsome boy of fourteen. He is an errand boy in* BLAKE'S *store. He wears knickerbockers, and a cap with no visor. He has the air of being spoiled and thoroughly selfish.* HELEN'S *manner toward him is one of amused and affectionate tolerance.*]

HELEN [*Laughing indulgently*]. La, Nat! What good would my marrying Mr. Blake do you?

YOUNG NAT. Lots o' good. You could coax money out o' him, an' give it to me.

HELEN [*Shocked*]. Oh! Nat Berry! [*Shakes her finger at him.*] Would you take that kind of money?

YOUNG NAT. I'd take any kind o' money. 'Tan't no worse than weighin' yer hand with the sugar, is it?

HELEN [*As if talking to a child, placing her hands to his face*]. Well, Natty dear——

YOUNG NAT [*Pushing her hands away*]. Don't call me Natty. Gosh, don't I hate thet! Mother makes me so 'shamed every time she comes up to Blake's. This is the last suit o' knickerbockers she gits on me. Gosh, wouldn't I have lots o' things ef you'd marry ol' Blake! [*Putting his arms around her, coaxingly.*] Say, Nell, will yeh? Marry ol' Blake—do. Jes' this once an' I'll never ask you again. Will you? I'll do as much fer you some day! Will you?

HELEN. No, I won't! I don't want to marry Mr. Blake.

YOUNG NAT [*Reproachfully; going right*]. Ain't you selfish!

HELEN. Aren't you selfish!

YOUNG NAT. You'd marry Doc Warren mighty quick ef Father'd let you.

HELEN [*Smiling proudly*]. I guess I would.

[SAM WARREN *enters by the road, right, at the back. He is tall, handsome, and manly, with an open honest face, and a frank manner. He stands for a moment, leaning over the fence, listening to* YOUNG NAT *with an amused smile.*]

YOUNG NAT [*Coming toward* HELEN]. Hands like a blacksmith, poor's Job, proud as a peacock an'—[*with awe*] don't believe there's any hell.

HELEN [*Quietly smiling*]. Well, neither do I.

YOUNG NAT. O-O-O-h!—Nell Berry! I'll tell yer father, an' then you'll find out!

[SAM *comes down and takes* YOUNG NAT *by the ear and twists it playfully.* YOUNG NAT *howls.*]

SAM. What do *you* think about it, Nat?

YOUNG NAT [*Crying*]. Ouch! L' go my ear!

HELEN [*Going to* YOUNG NAT *and folding him in her arms*]. Ah!

YOUNG NAT. An' you let go of me, too. [*Pushing her away and going up center.*]

HELEN. Sam! You've hurt him. You're too rough. Don't cry, Nat.

SAM. I didn't mean to hurt him, Nell.

He's more mad than hurt I guess, aren't you, Nat?

YOUNG NAT [*Crying*]. None of yer business! I'll get even with you fer this some day, you see if I don't! I wish I was big enough. I'd show you whether there's any hell or not, you great big blacksmith, pickin' on a little fellah like me! [*He goes off left, crying.*]

[SAM *laughs and crosses to right center, watching him.*]

HELEN [*With gentle reproach*]. You shouldn't tease Nat so, Sam. You know he doesn't like you. [*She sits beneath the tree on the bench, right. She is vibrating with content and happiness in the presence of the man she loves.*]

SAM [*Sits down on the plough lying against the barnyard fence*]. That seems to be a general complaint around these parts. A fellow that knows some things his great-great-grandfather didn't know is an object of suspicion here. [*As he talks, he picks up a handful of sand and lets it slip through his fingers.*]

HELEN [*Smiling*]. Well, what are you going to do about it?

SAM [*Cheerily*]. Keep right on knowing. Just as long as they build printing offices, we've got to know, that's all there is about that.

HELEN. I'm afraid—[*laughs softly*] *my* reading is going to get me into trouble.

SAM. How so?

HELEN [*Still amused*]. Why, the other day I was trying to tell Father something about evolution and "The Descent of Man," but he got mad and wouldn't listen.

SAM [*Laughing*]. Family pride! You know, Nell, there are lots of people who wouldn't be happy in this world if they couldn't look forward to a burning lake in the next. [*Takes a book out of his pocket and carelessly flips over the pages, looking at her as he talks.*]

HELEN. Kind of sad, isn't it?

SAM. Oh! I don't know! They take a heap of comfort preparing to keep out of it, I suppose.

HELEN [*Seeing the book in* SAM's *hand, rises and goes toward him*]. What book's that? [*Trying to read the title on the cover.*]

SAM [*Rising*]. "A Hazard of New Fortunes." [2]

HELEN. Have you read it?

SAM. Yes.

HELEN [*Eagerly, reaching for it*]. May I read it?

SAM. Yes, I brought it for you. [*He gives her the book.*]

[HELEN *delightedly takes the book and begins eagerly scanning the pages as she turns and goes back to the bench under the tree, speaking as she goes.*]

HELEN. I've been longing for this book. I read a fine article about it in the Boston paper. [*Sits down and looks at Sam with a joyous smile.*] Thank you ever so much, Sam.

SAM [*Pointing to the book*]. That's a book you won't have to hide. Your father'll listen to that. If he was a speculating man, now, it would do him good.

HELEN [*Turning the leaves of the book, and pausing here and there at a page as something interesting catches her eye*]. How's poor old Mrs. Swazy getting along?

SAM [*In a matter-of-fact way*]. Firstrate. She'll pull through this time.

[*As the scene progresses,* SAM *moves about restlessly, as though preoccupied with something. He is never far away from* HELEN *and always has his eyes and attention focused upon her.*]

HELEN [*Looking up at him with awe and wonder*]. Oh! Sam! After they'd all given her up—— [*Proudly but ingenuously.*] Well, they'll have to acknowledge that you're a great physician now.

SAM [*Laughs*]. Great fiddlesticks! Why, the folks around here wouldn't let

[2] By William Dean Howells.

me doctor a sick kitten if they could help it.

HELEN. Why, you'll get the credit of this!

SAM. Yes! Me and the Lord! [*Laughs.*] I'm satisfied so long as the old lady gets well.

[HELEN *is still sitting on the bench, glancing over the book, a look of contentment and happiness upon her face.* SAM, *who has been leaning against the barnyard fence, goes to her thoughtfully, his whole manner changed. He stands slightly above her to the left, puts one foot on the bench, leans on his knee and bends over her, and says in a rather quiet tense voice*] Nell—I want to tell you something.

HELEN [*Without looking up, says gaily as* SAM *pauses*] Something good, I hope.

SAM [*In the same manner*]. Don't I always tell you good things?

HELEN [*With a teasing little laugh, looking up at him over her shoulder*]. Most—always, Sam!

SAM [*Quietly, looking down into her eyes*]. I'm going away.

HELEN [*Seems stunned. The joy passes out of her face; her eyes are still upon him, but all the happiness is gone from them. The book drops from her hands and falls to the ground. She slowly slides along the bench away from him as though to study him better. She is pale and frightened, and in a dry voice with a low cry of pain, she says*] Oh!—Sam! [*Then, feeling it cannot be true, she leans toward him and adds in a very appealing voice*] Honest?

SAM [*Quietly*]. Honest. What's the use of my staying here? [*Sits down left of* HELEN.] Nobody'll speak to me except Nathan'l—and your mother—and you. [*Putting his arm around her.*]

HELEN [*Drawing away from him, endeavoring to overcome her emotion*]. Don't Sam—Please don't.

SAM [*With a dry laugh*]. And *you're* half afraid to.

HELEN [*Brokenly*]. No! I'm not afraid—only you know—Father says ——

SAM [*In the same manner*]. I know —they all say it. Blake says I've got dynamite in my boots. Just because I can't believe as they do—they won't any of 'em look at me if they can help it. So I'm going out West, where a fellow can *believe* as he likes and *talk* as he likes——

HELEN [*With awe, her eyes upon him*]. To—*Chicago?*

SAM [*Amused*]. Oh no—o! A fellow may *believe* what he likes in Chicago, but he mustn't *say* too much about it. I'm going a-w-a-y out West. Montana—or somewhere out that way.

HELEN [*Innocently, in a pathetic voice*]. Oh my! I'll never get so far as that, will I?

SAM [*Not heeding her, rising and walking up center*]. I want to get where I can sprout a new idea without being *sat* on.

HELEN [*In a crushed voice*]. Yes, of course—you're right.

SAM. Where I won't be hampered by dead men's laws and dead men's creeds.

HELEN [*Turning to him in a chiding manner*]. Why, you don't blame Father for believing as *his* father believed, do you?

SAM. No. But I *do* blame him for sitting down on me just because I can't believe the same way. I tell you, Nell [*he picks up a pebble*] one world at a time is good enough for me; and I've made up my mind that I'm going to *live* while I'm in this one [*he throws the pebble as far as he can reach, watching its flight*] and I'm going to do something more than practice medicine in Berry. Sitting around, waiting for patients [*rather contemptuously*] such as old Mrs. Swazy. [*He puts his hands in his pockets and turns down center.*]

HELEN [*Getting up from the bench and going to him, center*]. Yes. But—what's going to become of *me?*

[SAM *goes to her with arms outstretched, and enfolds her lovingly.*]

SAM [*Tenderly*]. You! You're going to stay right here with your mother, till I get started. Then I'm coming back to get you and take you out there and show those western fellows a *real* Yankee girl. [*Amused.*] You know, Nell, the newspapers used to print pictures of them with pants on and a stovepipe hat!

HELEN [*Making a pitiful effort to be cheerful*]. Yes! But they don't do that now, Sam.

SAM. No, they do *not* do that now. You girls have come to stay, there's no getting around that fact, and we cranks are going to help you stay here. [*He notices the book lying on the ground.*] Let me show you something in that book.

[*They walk over to the bench,* SAM'S *arm remains about* HELEN. *She sits down, he picks up the book and sits at her left, and they both become deeply absorbed in reading.*]

MARTIN [*Enters from the barn, leading a horse by the halter to water him at the trough.*[3] *His head is bent and he is in deep thought, pondering upon the idea of getting rich which* BLAKE *has suggested to him. He does not see* HELEN *and* SAM *until he turns to re-enter the barn. When his eyes rest upon them, so content and absorbed in each other, he pauses amazed, and his face flames with bitter resentment. He is unable to speak for a moment, then he blurts out harshly*] Sam Warren, hain't yeh got no more pride than to come where yeh ain't wanted?

[SAM *and* HELEN *start in surprise.* HELEN *shyly draws away from* SAM. SAM *looks up with a very affable air and says pleasantly and respectfully*] Hello, Mr. Berry! Yes sir, I have.

MARTIN [*In the same manner*]. Well, what yeh doin' here, then?

[3] NOTE: If it is not convenient to have a horse, Martin can come in with two heavy stable buckets, one in each hand, which he fills with water from the trough. J.A.H.

SAM [*Looking at* HELEN *slyly as if it were a good joke*]. I thought—I *was* wanted.

MARTIN [*Taking a menacing step toward him*]. Didn't I tell yeh yeh wa'n't?

SAM [*Smiling, but rather reluctantly*]. Yes sir,—*you* did!

[SAM *plays this scene very quietly, never losing his temper; plays it as if something else of more immediate importance were on his mind.*

[*The scene throughout is pitched in a quick staccato, which reaches its height in* HELEN'S *cry of terror as the two men clinch. Then there is a pause, and the rest of the scene, until* MARTIN *leaves the stage, is completed in tense low tones that are portentous of trouble. There is active hate on* MARTIN'S *part.* SAM'S *attitude is one of simple manly poise.*]

MARTIN. Well, ain't thet enough?

SAM [*Pleasantly*]. Yes, I suppose it is—but I thought that—maybe you'd like to know—— [*Rises and goes toward him.*]

MARTIN [*Goaded by* SAM'S *manner, fiercely*]. I don't want to know nothin'! An' I don't want *her* to know nothin' thet I don't want her to know! [*Indicating* HELEN *with a nod of his head.*]

SAM [*Making another effort to conciliate him*]. Why you see, Mr. Berry—you can't help——

MARTIN [*Breaking in and shouting at him*]. *I'm* a-bringin' up my family! An' I don't want no interference from you—nor Darwin—nor any o' the rest o' the breed! [*With a passionate sweep of his arm. He half turns as if to go.*]

SAM [*Smiling*]. Darwin's dead, Mr. Berry——

MARTIN [*Turning and interrupting, resentfully*]. Them *books* ain't dead.

SAM [*Very positive and very much satisfied with his statement*]. No! "Them books" are going to be pretty hard to kill.

MARTIN [*Sharply, turning to* HELEN, *who is still seated on the bench*]. What book's thet yeh got there now? [*Indicat-*

ing the book with a wrathful toss of his arm.]

HELEN [*Very gently*]. One of Sam's books, Father.

MARTIN [*Glaring at* SAM]. Well, give it right straight back to Sam. I don't want nothin' to do with *him* nor his books.

SAM [*Kindly, correcting him*]. It *is* my book, Mr. Berry, but it was written by a man——

MARTIN [*His temper rising steadily, flashes at him*]. I won't hev yeh a-bringin' them books here! A-learnin' my daughter a pack o' lies, about me an' my parents a-comin' from monkeys——

SAM [*His eyes twinkling with suppressed amusement, answers soothingly*]. La bless you, Mr. Berry! That was ages ago!

MARTIN [*Is goaded to the extreme by* SAM'S *manner*]. I don't care how long ago it was, I won't hev it flung in my children's faces.

HELEN [*Is much distressed by her father's bitter temper, and she suddenly attempts to calm him, and approaches* MARTIN, *who has been standing near the barnyard gate. She timidly holds out the book to him, and says pleadingly*] Father, I wish you'd let me read you this little bit——

MARTIN [*With ugly stubbornness, checks her with a sweep of his arm, as though pushing away some harmful or noxious thing*]. I don't want to hear it. I read *The Bangor Whig,* an' *The Agriculturist,* an' the Bible, an' thet's enough. There ain't no lies in *them.*

SAM [*Ironically*]. No, especially in *The Bangor Whig!*

[*Here the staccato changes to a deep ominous murmur.*]

MARTIN [*Peering at* SAM *through half-closed lids, mutters*]. I'm skeered of a man thet ain't got no religion.

SAM [*With quiet assurance*]. But, Mr. Berry, I *have* got a religion.

MARTIN [*Doubtfully, in the same manner*]. What is it?

SAM [*His manner becoming serious, in a voice warm with feeling, pointing off with a sweep of his arm*]. Do you hear those insects singing?

MARTIN [*Rather puzzled, mumbles*]. Yes—I hear 'em!

SAM [*Seriously and calmly*]. Well, that's their religion, and I reckon mine's just about the same thing.

MARTIN [*With supreme disgust and contempt in his voice and manner*]. Oh! Good Lord! [*He starts for the barn with the horse.*]

HELEN [*With tender appeal, swiftly following him*]. Father, why won't you ever let Sam tell you——

[MARTIN, *goaded to the breaking point, turns upon* HELEN, *dropping the halter and allowing the horse to go into the barn.*]

MARTIN [*Hardly able to control his rage*]. Look a-here, Nell! I've had all the words I'm goin' to hev with *you*—— [*Shaking his closed fist threateningly.*] But by the Eternal, I ain't a-goin' to hev thet fellah a-comin' here preachin' his infidelity to my family. [*Frantic with rage, he now says more than he intends to, deliberately and fiercely.*] If you *want* him you *take* him, an' clear out!

[SAM *approaches quickly, intensely moved by what* MARTIN *has said.*]

SAM. Do you mean that, Mr. Berry?

HELEN [*Her head high in the air, her whole attitude one of noble defiance*]. I will! [*As though accepting the challenge.*]

MARTIN [*Looks at* HELEN, *quite broken, all the fire of his passion in ashes, and murmurs thickly*] Yeh won't?

HELEN [*Proudly, her eyes full of burning tears, her voice vibrating with emotion*]. Won't I? You'll see whether I will or not! [*There is a challenge in her voice too.*]

SAM [*Moving toward* MARTIN, *intensely excited by his words*]. Mr. Berry—if you'll say that again——

MARTIN [*Springs at* SAM *and clutches him by the throat*]. Damn you!

SAM [*Swiftly seizes* MARTIN'S *wrist with his left hand, drawing back his right hand to strike*]. Damn you!

HELEN [*With a cry of terror, covering her face with her hands, calls out appealingly*]. Oh! Sam—don't!

[*The sound of* HELEN'S *voice brings both men to their senses, and they relax their hold upon each other. They stand silent for a moment, both a little ashamed. Then* MARTIN *says in a heartbroken manner*] D'yeh mean to steal my child from me?

SAM [*Quietly, adjusting his collar*]. I'm not going to *steal* her, Mr. Berry—I'm going out West to *earn* her!

MARTIN [*Speaking through his teeth, vehemently*]. Sam Warren, I hated you afore—but *now* you've shamed me afore my own child. Git off'n my farm an' don't yeh never set foot on't agin—— [*Quite low and passionately.*] It's dangerous fer both on us.

[MARTIN *wearily drags himself into the barn.*

[HELEN *stands dazed and heartbroken.* SAM *leans against the fence, his hands in his pockets, his head bent, deep in thought. There is a moment's pause.*

[ANN[4] *bustles cheerily out of the house. She is a woman of forty-five, handsome in a wholesome, motherly way. She is dressed in a freshly laundered, becoming calico dress, and her sleeves are rolled up beyond the elbows, showing a pair of shapely arms. She is quick and energetic in all her movements. To her, home is the most desirable place in the world, and she rules it with all the skill and love of a typical American housewife. Her manner is pleasant and happy. She is always smiling and always sees the best side of everything. Nothing disturbs her; she meets all the problems of her daily life with a quiet and unobtrusive efficiency.*]

ANN. Well Helen, I was jes' a-wonderin' what'd become o' you. Sam Warren! I hup Martin hain't seen yeh; I say, hain't seen yeh.

SAM. Yes, he has——

ANN. Didn't he hev a tantrum; I say, a tantrum?

HELEN [*Concealing her true feelings, listlessly*]. No, Mother, he didn't say much—not as much as——

ANN. I want to know! Well, there must ha' ben sumpthin' powerful on his mind; I say, on his mind.

SAM. I guess there is now, if there wasn't before. [*Sadly.*]

ANN. Well, Nell, blow the horn. Dinner's all sot an' I don't want it to git cold. Sorry I can't ask yeh to stop, Sam; I say, I'm sorry I can't ask yeh to stop. [*She goes into the house.*]

SAM. Thank you, I don't think I'd enjoy the meal. [HELEN *and he look at each other, her eyes fill with tears.*]

[HELEN *goes up to the fence, picks up the horn hanging there and blows it twice. Then she turns back to* SAM, *letting the horn slip from her hand to the ground.*]

SAM [*Slowly*]. Well, Nell, I suppose you and I might just as well say good-by now as any time——

HELEN [*Again quite overcome at the thought of parting with him, holds out her hand, which he takes*]. Good-by, Sam. [*Cries.*]

SAM [*Very tenderly*]. Good-by, Nell. [*Draws her to him.*] Don't cry! I don't know how soon I'll get away, but just as soon as I can I will. I'll try to see you before I go—if not—I'll——

HELEN [*Pleadingly*]. You can't take me with you, can you, Sam?

SAM [*Wistfully*]. No, Nell, I can't. I haven't got money enough. I ought to

[4] NOTE: Ann begins all her speeches slowly, increasing in rapidity as she progresses. She is in the habit of repeating the final words of all her speeches emphatically, as though the person she were addressing had not heard her. J.A.H.

have a hundred dollars more than I've got to get away myself. [*Meditatively.*] I wonder if Blake'd lend me a hundred dollars.

HELEN [*Still struggling with her tears*]. I wouldn't ask him—he'd only refuse you. [*She breaks down and clings to* SAM *like a child.*] It's going to be awful lonesome——

SAM [*Deeply moved*]. I know—it's going to be pretty lonesome for me too. There, now— [*Taking both her hands in his.*] I thought this was going to be one of those partings without tears—[*trying to cheer her up*] nor promises—nothing but just confidence.

HELEN [*Making an effort to overcome her grief*]. All right—Sam. [*Lifting her head and taking a deep breath to get hold of herself, bravely but still with a slight break in her voice.*] If I don't see you before you go, good-by. [*Goes to the house, as if to go inside, stops at the door, and turns as though struck by a sudden thought.*] I don't think you'd better come here again, Sam. I don't want to quarrel with Father if I can help it—— [*With a note of fatality.*] I'll have to some day I know—but I want to avoid it just as long as I can. [*She smiles and tries to brave it out, but it is plain that she is silently crying.*]

SAM [*Stands a moment, looking at her tenderly and longingly, as though loth to leave her. He cannot control his own feelings. He turns away abruptly as he says*] Good-by, Nell, keep up your courage, my girl. And remember, it isn't as though it was forever, you know. [*He goes off right above the house.*]

HELEN [*Her eyes follow him off*]. Good-by, Sam. [*Waves her hand as if in response to him and calls after him*] Take good care of yourself, won't yeh?

SAM [*Speaking off stage, as though from a little distance*]. I'll take care of myself, you take care of yourself.

[*Helen turns slowly away and drags herself, broken and weary, into the house.*

[*There is a brief pause, then* MARY BERRY, *a lively girl of about 10, comes running from the road, left, into the yard. She has a little bunch of wild flowers in her hand. She is skipping gaily, and just as she is about to enter the house,* BOB BERRY, *a sturdy little fellow of about 8 years with rosy cheeks and dancing eyes, runs on excitedly from the left, with his schoolbooks tied in a strap, and says*] Mary, Mary, take my books in the house, I'm goin' in swimmin'. [*He throws the books into her hands and runs off right, above the house.*]

MARY [*Calling after him*]. Bob Berry, if you go in swimmin' I'll tell yer Ma.

BOB [*In the distance, off right*]. Tell if yeh want to—ol' tattle tale.

MARY [*Running into the house*]. Ma, Ma, Bob's goin' in swimmin'——

[IKE RICHARDS, LEM CONANT, ABE HIGGINS, *and* STEVE BAILEY, *farmhands, enter from the left. With them is* TIM HAYES, *the hired man, a good-natured, red-headed Irishman. They are playing with an old football, laughing and scuffling in a friendly way.*

[GATES, *with* MANDY *in his wake, follows the men on, and watches them, keenly interested.*]

GATES. Give me a kick.

TIM [*Good-naturedly*]. Let the ould man have a kick.

[*The others jeer at this.*]

ABE. He can't kick it, he's too old.

GATES [*Enraged*]. Too old, am I? You jes' see. [GATES *seizes the ball and gives it a tremendous kick which sends it flying down the road. The men cheer him derisively.* GATES *picks up a chip and puts it on his shoulder.*]

GATES [*To* ABE, *assuming a defiant attitude*]. If I'm too old, you jes' knock this chip off'n my shoulder.

[ABE *hesitates, but the other men urge him on, at last forcing him into the fight. He and* GATES *have a brief rough-and-*

tumble wrestling match, which ends when GATES *ducks* ABE *in the water trough.*

[*The men greet* ABE's *defeat with shouts of laughter, and he hurries somewhat sheepishly into the house, followed by the others.* GATES *looks after them, wagging his head triumphantly.*]

GATES [*Calling after them*]. Too old, am I? They don't build houses like they used to. An' they don't make boys like they used to, nuther! [*With an air of high satisfaction he goes off, down the road, lower right, followed by* MANDY.]

[*Enter* UNCLE NAT *along the road, upper right, wheeling* MILLIE *in the barrow.* MILLIE *has a line through the rod of the barrow and is pretending to drive.*]

UNCLE NAT [*Talking as he enters*]. An' after that they lived in peace and died in Greece, an' was buried in a pot of honey.

MILLIE. What's the else of it, Uncle Nat?

UNCLE NAT. There ain't no else to it. Besides, this hoss don't do 'nother stroke of work till he gets his oats. [*He wheels the barrow down stage below the bench, right.*]

MILLIE [*Climbing out*]. Wait till I unhitch yeh——

UNCLE NAT. This is a new-fangled hoss. He can hitch himself up and unhitch himself, and currycomb himself and get his own oats, an'—— [UNCLE NAT *goes to the trough and starts to wash his hands.*]

MILLIE [*Following him up to the trough*]. Hossy want a drink?

UNCLE NAT. No—hossy don't want a drink. Hossy want to wash his hands so thet he can set down to the table like a clean respect'ble hoss. [MILLY *splashes water in his face. He staggers back, pretending to be drenched and shaking the wet off.*] Is thet what yeh call givin' hossy a drink?

MILLIE [*Chuckling*]. Yep.

UNCLE NAT. Well, the fust thing yeh know, this hoss'll duck yeh in the hoss trough.

MILLIE. No he won't.

UNCLE NAT. Won't he? You jes' see if he won't. [*He talks to* MILLIE *in the manner of one child talking to another.*] You can't throw water in a hossy's face without makin' him mad no more than yeh can give a elephant a chaw o' terbacker without makin' *him* mad. Did yeh ever give a elephant a chaw o' terbacker?

MILLIE. No!

UNCLE NAT. Well, don't yeh try it, cause I knowed a boy in a circus once that give a elephant a chaw o' terbacker, an' he didn't see thet boy agin fer more n' a hundred years. But he jes' remembered it an' he blew water all over him. I tell yeh, elephants has got good memories—— [UNCLE NAT *takes a clean bandanna handkerchief out of his pocket and wipes his hands. He is about to enter the house, when he is stopped by the voice of* MARTIN, *who comes from the barn and pauses outside the barnyard gate.*]

[MILLIE *resumes her play in the sand.*]

MARTIN [*Casually*]. Nathan'l.

UNCLE NAT [*Kindly*]. Hello, Martin.

MARTIN. Be yeh hungry?

UNCLE NAT [*Still mechanically wiping his hands*]. Not powerful, but able to git away with my rayshuns 'thout no coaxin' I guess. Why? [*Taking a step toward* MARTIN.]

MARTIN [*Still casually*]. 'Cause I'd like to talk to yeh [*studying his face closely*] an' I d'know's I'll hev a better chance.

UNCLE NAT [*Cheerily; putting his handkerchief back in his pocket*]. I d'know's yeh will, Martin. [*He moves a few steps down right;* MARTIN *is up left center near the barnyard.*]

MARTIN [*Hesitates, picks up a stick, takes out a jackknife and whittles it, looking intently at the stick and walking down a few steps toward* UNCLE NAT. *He seems rather to dread saying what is on his mind.* UNCLE NAT *looks at him furtively; this unusual request puzzles him; he is apprehensive that it is of* HELEN *and* BLAKE *that his brother wishes to talk, and a look of disapproval sweeps into his eyes. His face grows a bit stern, but his manner is kindly and attentive. After a pause* MARTIN *blurts out abruptly*] Mr. Blake's been here.

UNCLE NAT [*Gazes at him curiously, looks off right as if he could still see* BLAKE'S *buggy there, picks up a straw and chews it, and says carelessly*] Hez' 'e? [*Seats himself on the wheelbarrow.*]

MARTIN [*Seating himself on the stable bucket, which he has turned bottom upward*]. Yes. He argues that we'd ought to cut the farm up into buildin' lots.

UNCLE NAT [*Is dazed by this. It is so sudden and unexpected that he scarcely gets its full meaning, as he murmurs in a low tense voice*] Dooze 'e?

MARTIN. Y-e-s. He says there's a boom a-comin' an' the land's too val'able to work.

UNCLE NAT [*Murmurs mechanically*] Dooze—'e——?

MARTIN. Yes. He wants I should pool in with him, an' build cottages an' sell 'em at a hundred per cent more'n they cost, an' git's rich's Jay Gould.

[*Slowly it comes to* UNCLE NAT *that his brother is saying "Sell the farm." He grows cold—there is a heavy painful lump where his heart was beating a moment ago. His eyes grow dim and tired—there is no sunshine—no more music in the day. Sell the farm—the dear fields with all their slopes and undulations, the great old silver birches guarding the orchard from the pastures, the gnarled oaks along the rocky shore. He knows in a thousand aspects this old farm, summer and winter, always affable and friendly to him, and it is here he has learned to know God and love him. He answers casually enough in a tone of wonderment*] I want t' know 'f he dooze. [*A moment's pause.*] Where d's he talk o' beginnin'?

MARTIN [*Blurting out half defiantly, half shamefacedly*]. Out there at th' north end o' the short front—an' work back t' his line.

UNCLE NAT [*The numbness passes and there is a tingling in his veins. Tense set lines come into his face and his voice grows vital. He talks with his usual clear cadence and gentle rhythm*]. Yeh don't mean up yonder? [*Pointing with his thumb over his shoulder, right.* MARTIN *looks up and nods.*] Not up at the ol' pastur'?

MARTIN [*Slowly*]. Y—e—s——

UNCLE NAT [*In a tense voice*]. Dooze 'e calk'late to take in the knoll thet looks out t'Al'gator Reef?

MARTIN [*As before*]. Y-e-s—I s'pose he—dooze.

UNCLE NAT [*Rising, speaking quietly, but with a quiver of smothered feeling in his voice*]. Did yeh tell him—'bout —Mother's bein' buried there——?

MARTIN [*Sulkily*]. He knows all 'bout thet jes' as well as you do.

UNCLE NAT [*With significance, but very simply*]. Dooze. Well—what's he calk'late to do with Mother?

MARTIN. He advises puttin' on her in a cimitery up to Bangor.

UNCLE NAT [*A deprecating shadowy smile flits across his face; he shakes his head slowly and replies*]. She'd never sleep comfort'ble in no cimitery, Martin —Mother wouldn't.

MARTIN. Blake says thet's the choice bit o' the hull pa'sell.

UNCLE NAT [*Gently persuasive*]. Then who's got so good a right to it as Mother has? Yeh don't begrutch it to her, do yeh, Martin?

MARTIN. I don't begrutch nothin'. Only, Blake says folks ain't a-goin' to pay fancy prices fer lots 'thout they hev their pick.

UNCLE NAT [*Gently reproachful*].

D'ye think any fancy price had ought to buy Mother's grave, Martin?

MARTIN. Thet's sent'ment!

UNCLE NAT [*As though rebuked*]. Is it?

MARTIN. Yes, it is—Blake says——

UNCLE NAT [*Nodding his head, with a little sad half-smile*]. Dooze—well —— [*He sighs.*] P'r'aps 'tis—— [*There is a pause; then, as though a flood of memories had suddenly rushed over him.*] You don't rec'llect much about Father—de yeh, Martin?

MARTIN. No.

UNCLE NAT. You was so young—[*His eyes look far off down the years, and he tells the story simply and directly and the clear cadence and soft rhythm are like the colors in a picture*] a baby a'most, the evenin' him an' Si Leech was lost tryin' to save the crew o' thet 'ere brig—thet went to pieces on the reef yonder. [*Indicates over his shoulder with a nod of his head.*]

MARTIN [*Under the spell of* UNCLE NAT'S *mood, is touched, and replies very gently*]. No. Mother'n you never seemed to care to talk much about thet.

UNCLE NAT. Mother an' me seen the hull thing from the p'int o' thet 'ere knoll— [*With a slight indication of his head over his shoulder.*] After it was all over she sent me hum—told me to take care o' you—said thet I needn't come back—thet she'd stay there an' wait fer him. 'Twa'n't no use t'argy with Mother, y'know, an' so I went. I put you in yer cradle an' sot down alongside o' yeh. I d' know as I ever passed jes' sich a night—seemed s'kinder l-o-n-g. [*Pause.*] Jes' as soon as it was light enough to see—I went back to find out what'd come o' her—I didn't know but what she might hev—but she hadn't—she was there—jes' where I left her—I don't believe she'd moved an inch the hull night. It had been a-rainin'—— [*Pause.*] Her eyes was sot in her head and starin' right out to sea—ef I'd 'a' met her any other place but there, I swear I wouldn't 'a' know'd 'r. I took her by the hand to sort o' coax 'r away. "Nathan'l," she says, "when I die—I want yeh should bury me right here on this spot—so's ef Father ever *dooze* come back—he'll find me waitin' fer him." I hed to turn 'round an' look at 'er—her voice sounded so kinder strange—seemed as ef it come from way off somewheres. [*Pause.*] She lived a good many years after thet—but I don't believe she ever missed a day 'thout goin' over t' thet knoll. I allus sort o' imagined she wa'n't never jes' right in her head after thet night. [UNCLE NAT *is lost in memories for a moment. Then catching his breath and pulling himself together, he continues*] Well, Martin, there she is. We buried her there at last—you an' me did. I d'know, but seems to me—ef I was you—I'd kinder hate to sell thet fer a buildin' lot. Thet is, I'd want to be pooty partic'lar who I sold it to.

MARTIN [*In the manner of a spoiled child, closing his knife with a sharp click*]. I'm tired o' lightkeepin'.

UNCLE NAT [*Warmly, with quick understanding*]. I don't blame yeh. Why didn't yeh say thet afore? Yeh needn't do it no longer. Tim an' me kin take keer o' the light jes' as well's not. I only sort o' hang onto it 'cause Father had it put there, an' the Gover'ment named it after him—he used to think so much o' that.

MARTIN [*Defending himself*]. You *give* me your interest in the farm anyhow—made it all over to me the day I was married.

UNCLE NAT [*Warmly, with a fine spirit of conciliation*]. I know it an' I hain't never regretted it. I ain't a-regrettin' of it now.

MARTIN [*Peevishly*]. You seem to kind o' shameface me for wantin' to sell it.

UNCLE NAT. Didn't mean to, Martin—it's only nat'ral thet I should feel kind o' bad to see the ol' place cut up—but law sakes! Who'm I thet I should set my face agin improvements I'd like to know? [*Laughs.*] You've got a wife, an' children, an' a family, an' all thet. Mr. Blake mus' be right. So go 'head an' build, an' git rich, an' move up to Boston ef yeh want to. Only, Martin—don't sell that. [*Indicating over his shoulder, right, with his head.*] Leave me thet, an' I'll build on't an' stay an' take keer o' th' light, as long's I kin—an' after thet—why—well, after thet—yeh kin put both on us in a cimitery ef yeh hev a mind to.

[*His voice trails off into silence.* MARTIN *stands downcast.* UNCLE NAT *remains immovable, self-hypnotized by the recital of his story—somehow all the sting of it has passed and he is at peace. He is still contemplating the remote days of his boyhood, and he stands there picking a bit of string into fine shreds too deeply absorbed to be aware of the life about him.*

[MILLIE *is lying asleep on the sand.*

[ANN *enters briskly from the house.*]

ANN. Sakes alive! Martin Berry, ain't you a-comin' to yer dinner today? I say today? [*Goes up center and looks off right.*]

MARTIN [*Slowly, starting toward house*]. Yes, I was jest a-comin'. [*As he crosses to the house, he says very gently*] Nathan'l, dinner's waitin'. [*He goes slowly and thoughtfully into the house.*]

ANN [*Looking up the road and calling*]. Bob—B-o-b! Bob B-e-r-r-y—Come out o' thet water—Come to yer dinner!—Yer back'll be all blistered! [*She sees* MILLIE *lying asleep and goes down to her.*] Bless thet child, she's clean fagged out! Come to Ma, precious. [*She takes* MILLIE *tenderly in her arms.*] Come Nathan'l, your dinner'll be stun cold. I say stun cold. [*She goes into the house with the child.*]

[UNCLE NAT *stands deep in meditation.*]

The Curtain Descends Slowly

ACT II

"The Silver Weddin'"

The Berry farmhouse kitchen.

Scene: A quaint old New England farmhouse kitchen of the better class, used partly as a living room. There is a large window center, full of pots of growing flowers. Beneath the window is a table upon which HELEN *places cups and saucers and from which she serves tea during the dinner. To the right of the window is a wooden sink with an old-fashioned hand pump, and there is a large stove to the left of the window, upon which a kettle is boiling and pots are stewing. Behind it is a woodbox. On the shelf back of the stove stands an old-fashioned cuckoo clock.*

A sturdy old open stairway is against the left wall, and at the back of it is a row of pegs, where hang UNCLE NAT'S *old army coat and cap, and* HELEN'S *jacket and tam-o'-shanter. There is a door leading to the woodhouse to the left of the stove. Standing parallel to the stairs is a long dining table, covered with a white linen cloth. Against the side of the stairs is a heavy old-fashioned mahogany sideboard, from which* HELEN *later takes small articles, such as tumblers and salt and pepper holders. At the foot of the stairs a door opens into the sitting room. There is a worktable, right, below the sink, covered with material for making bread, and on it are several loaves of bread fresh from the oven. Below the worktable is a door leading outside. To the right, between the door and the sink, is an alcove where stands a large old-fashioned dresser, holding dishes, pans, and various kitchen furnishings, also several large pies.*

At the rise of the curtain, ANN, HELEN, *and* PERLEY *are in the midst of extensive preparations for dinner.* MILLIE *is down right, by a chair, making doll's bread, very intent on her work.* ANN *is hot and flustered. She is dressed in an old-*

fashioned black silk dress, open at the neck, with a white lace collar. The skirt is pinned up, showing a white petticoat underneath trimmed with home-made lace, and there is a big white apron over all. PERLEY *is cool and unconcerned.* MARY *and* BOB, *with aprons over their best clothes, are sitting on the stairs, polishing spoons and forks.* HELEN *is setting the table. She is dressed daintily in a simple muslin frock, and also wears a large apron to protect her dress. She is grave and thoughtful; the memory of the encounter with her father is still sharp upon her. She moves about, doing her work with swift deft touches.*

ANN [*At the stove, stirring the cranberry sauce*]. Sakes alive! I hup another silver weddin' won't come in this house in a hurry; I say, in a hurry. [*She goes to the table and starts sharpening a carving knife, preparatory to cutting a large loaf of bread which is on the table.*]

HELEN [*At the foot of the table, as she finishes placing the knives and forks*]. Ma, I've arranged all the presents on the center table. [*Smiling. She is very tender and sympathetic in her attitude toward her mother.*] The sitting room looks like a jewelry store. [*She goes to the sideboard, left, and takes from it a glass jar holding teaspoons, and places it on the center of the table.*]

MARY. Oh, let's go'n see! [*Runs off into the sitting room.*]

BOB. Yes, let's do. [*Follows* MARY.]

HELEN. Aren't you proud of them, Mother?

ANN [*Seriously*]. Helen, you know what the Bible says about pride's one day havin' a fall. No, I ain't proud. [*Turning and coming down slowly toward the center of the stage, absent-mindedly drawing the carving knife across the steel as she talks.*] Of course, it's nice to be so remembered by everybody, an' there's a good many nice presents there—some I ben a-wishin' fer. But I think I value yourn an' the young uns' an' Nathan'l's an' Martin's the best o' the lot. Not thet I ain't grateful, but, somehow, the nearer—— [*Fills up, hastily brushes away a tear with the back of her hand, and turns to the stove to hide her emotion. Lifts the griddle and pokes the fire.*] How like the ol' Harry this fire dooze burn! Seems es ef everythin' went agin me today; I say, today. [*Calls.*] Tim! [*To* PERLEY, *sharply.*] Tell Tim I want him. [*Puts the griddle back on the stove, and closes the damper.*]

[PERLEY *goes down to the door, right, opens it, and calls* TIM, *each time in a different and higher key.*]

PERLEY. Ti-m—T-i-m—T-i-i-m-m——

TIM [*Outside, in the distance*]. More power to ye, but it's the foine loongs ye have in ye! Fwat is it?

PERLEY. Mis' Berry wants y-o-u. [*Goes back to her work.*]

ANN. [*To* PERLEY, *handing her a saucepan of potatoes*]. Mash them 'taters; I say, mash them 'taters.

[PERLEY *gets the potato masher, takes the pan of potatoes to the sink, peels and mashes them, adding butter, salt, and a little milk.*

[TIM *appears at the door in his shirt sleeves.*]

TIM. Fwat is it, ye Andhrewscoggin' mermaid, ye? [*He starts to come into the room.*]

ANN [*Stopping him, peremptorily*]. Scrape yer feet, Tim Hayes, an' don't track the hull cow shed over my clean floor; I say, clean floor. [*She is standing near the window, center.*]

TIM [*Wipes his feet on the door mat, and speaks imgratiatingly*]. Yis ma'am. I will ma'am. Fwat can I do for ye?

ANN. I want you should split me a handful of fine wood; this 'ere fire's actin' like the very Ol' Nick today; I say, today.

[TIM *goes into the woodhouse, and reappears almost immediately with a handful of small wood which he gives to* ANN, *who puts a few pieces on the fire. He returns to the woodhouse and during the next scene he is heard splitting wood.*]

PERLEY [*Who has now finished mashing the potatoes; speaking through* TIM's *business*]. What yeh want I should do 'th these 'ere 'taters?

ANN. Put 'em in a veg'table dish an' set 'em in the ov'n to brown; I say, to brown.

[PERLEY *puts the potatoes into a vegetable dish, smooths them over, shakes two or three spots of pepper on them, and puts them in the oven. She takes plenty of time over this.*

[ANN *stirs the cranberries, tastes them, lifts up the kettle and sets it back, and puts the griddle on the hole.*

[UNCLE NAT *appears at the top of the stairs, dressed in a new "store" suit. He looks very important and proud, and glances down expecting all eyes to be upon him, but nobody notices him. He comes down a few steps. His new boots hurt him, and he pauses and bends his feet on the toes, as if to ease the boots, murmuring to himself "Gosh, but these shoes do hurt!" He straightens up, comes down a few more steps, and again eases his right boot and, making a wry face, he slips his foot partly out of the boot, and finishes the descent limping, but with a comfortable sense of relief. When he is well toward the left center of the stage, he stands, anxious to be noticed.*]

UNCLE NAT [*In a jubliant tone*]. Well, Helen, I got 'em on!

HELEN [*Coming down to his left, and speaking delightedly*]. Oh Uncle Nat! Ma, look! Isn't he sweet?

ANN [*Stops in her work at the table in front of the window, and comes down right of him*]. Well Nathan'l, how nice you do look; I say, look.

[PERLEY *comes forward a few steps and gazes at him admiringly.*]

UNCLE NAT. How do they fit me?

ANN. Jes' es ef they was made——

HELEN [*More critically*]. Turn round, Uncle Nat. [*He does so with an air of great importance, and is very happy over the impression he is creating, for it is many a long day since he had a new suit of clothes.* HELEN *smooths the back of his coat down with her hand.*] The waist might be a trifle longer. Don't you think so, Ma?

ANN [*Inspecting him carefully with her arms on her hips*]. Oh! Do you think so? Seems to me's ef 'twas meant to be jes' thet way. [*Goes back to the stove.*] I say, jes' thet way.

HELEN. Well, maybe it was. [*A pause. She returns to her work at the table.*]

UNCLE NAT [*Fingering his vest*]. Helen, there's a button come off this vest a'ready. I guess they're jes' stuck on. I wish you'd sew 'em on with thread, by 'n' by.

HELEN. All right, Uncle Nat, good strong thread.

UNCLE NAT [*With a complete change of manner, full of businesslike importance*]. Well, how be yeh gettin' along —I hope yeh hain't sp'ilt nothin' sence I ben away. Helen, will you get me my apron. [*He takes off his coat and places it carefully over the back of a chair, and comes down center.* HELEN *gets him a woman's checked apron.*] I want you should tie it in a bowknot so that when the company comes, I can get it off handy. [*He stands with arms outstretched;* HELEN *ties the apron around him just beneath his shoulders. He pushes it down.*] Not too high-waisted, not too high-waisted. [*He pushes his foot back into the boot and limps to the stove.*] How's the ol' cranberries gettin' on? [*Slight pause.*] Who sot these cranberries on the back of the stove? [*Looks around at them all accusingly.*] Don't yeh know nothin' in this house, or don't yeh? [*Lifts up the saucepan and puts it on the front of the stove. Tastes the cranberries, and says reproachfully*] Oh Ma, I'm sorry yeh put more sugar in the cranberries, yeh got 'em too sweet. I had 'em jes' right when I left 'em. [*Nobody answers.*] Ma, did you put any more sugar in them cranberries?

ANN [*Busy at the table, right, speaking over her shoulder*]. I didn't put no more sugar in 'em.

UNCLE NAT. Well somebody has. Helen, did you put any more sugar in them cranberries?

HELEN. No, Uncle Nat.

UNCLE NAT. Well, somebody did. [*Turning to* PERLEY *in an accusing manner.*] Perley, did you put any more sugar in them cranberries?

PERLEY [*A little resentfully, drawling*]. I hain't teched 'em.

UNCLE NAT [*Testily, imitating her drawl*]. Well, *some*body's teched 'em. Cranberries couldn't walk off the stove and get into the sugar bucket by themselves.

PERLEY. They wuz a-scorchin', an' I sot 'em back, thet's all I done.

UNCLE NAT [*In disgust*]. Well I wish you'd let 'em alone. I'd ruther have I don't know what around me than a lot of women when I'm a-cookin' of a dinner. [*Taking the saucepan off the stove, and setting it in the sink.*] Nell, dish out them cranberries and set 'em t' cool some place 'r other, will yeh?

HELEN. Yes, in a minute. [*Gets a preserve dish from the alcove, dishes out the berries, and sets them on the table at the window.*]

[BOB *runs on from the sitting room.*]

BOB. Ma, can we play store with the presents?

ANN. Yes, play with 'em all you like, but don't break any of 'em; I say, don't break any of 'em.

BOB. Oh, we won't break 'em. [*Runs off.*] Mary! Mary! Ma says we can play with 'em.

UNCLE NAT [*With happy expectancy*]. Now, les' see how the ol' turkey's a-gettin' on. [*Goes over to the stove, sees the damper is shut, and says indignantly*] Now, in the name of common sense, who shut up thet damper! [*Opens the damper with a jerk.*]

ANN. Yeh must 'a' done it yerself.

UNCLE NAT. Upon my word, a man can't leave a stove out of his hands five minutes without somebody a-foolin' with it. [*He opens the oven door and looks at the turkey, his face aglow with admiration. They all stand around him, very much interested.*] By George, ain't he a beauty? [*In a grieved tone.*] Who turned him on his back? I had him on his side.

HELEN. You want him to brown all over, don't you?

UNCLE NAT. See here, who's cookin' this turkey, you or me? [*Smacking his lips.*] Get the platter, he's done. Ef he stays in there any longer, he'll be burned to a crisp. [HELEN *gets a platter from the dresser.*] Ma, you get me a dishtowel.

[ANN *gives him a dishtowel. All is bustle and excitement as he lifts out the dripping pan, and sets it on top of the stove.* UNCLE NAT *is left and the women are right of the stove.*

[TIM *comes in from the woodhouse with an armful of wood, both large and small pieces, which he dumps into the woodbox, afterward brushing the chips which cling to his sleeve into the box. He stands and looks admiringly at the turkey.*]

UNCLE NAT [*Glowing with pride*]. What do you think of thet for a turkey, eh Tim?

TIM. As they say in ould Ireland, that's a burrd!

[*He goes over to* PERLEY, *who stands near the sink, right, throws his arm around her, and hugs her roughly and quickly. She hits him with a dishcloth, and he runs out down right, laughing, followed by* PERLEY *hitting the air with the dishcloth, trying to reach him. After he goes, she returns coolly to her work at the sink. This byplay is unnoticed by the others, who are intent on the turkey.*]

UNCLE NAT [*To* ANN *and* HELEN, *chuckling; speaking through* TIM'S *business*]. I wonder what they call a turkey in Ireland, a critter? Give me a large fork. [HELEN *gives him one.*] Now a big spoon. [ANN *gives him one.*]

ANN [*As* UNCLE NAT *starts to lift the turkey out with the fork and spoon*]. Be careful. Don't stick the fork into the turkey; ef you break the skin, the juice'll all run out; I say, run out.

HELEN. Be careful, Uncle Nat, don't drop him.

UNCLE NAT [*Puts the turkey back in the pan, turns from one woman to the other, and says with gentle exasperation*]. Say, if you can find anythin' to do about the house, I wish you'd go an' do it an' leave me alone. Yeh've got me s'nervous, I don't know whether I'm standin' on my head or my heels. [*Gets the turkey into the platter, and says joyously*] There he is! Now put him in the oven to keep warm, while I make the gravy. [*Proceeds to stir the gravy in the dripping pan.*] Nell, pour a little water in there, careful now. [*She pours some into the pan from the tea kettle.*] Thet's enough. Thet'll do—Thet'll do! [*He pushes the kettle spout up.*]

HELEN [*Protesting*]. Why, Uncle Nat, you won't have half gravy enough! [*Attempts to pour more in.*] Ma, I wish you'd look at this.

UNCLE NAT [*Turning to* ANN]. Ma, you attend to your own business.

[*While* UNCLE NAT *is talking to* ANN, HELEN *pours more water into the pan.* UNCLE NAT *turns and sees her doing it, and he pushes the spout up and burns his fingers.* HELEN *drops the kettle on the stove.*]

UNCLE NAT. Now you've done it, Nell! You've got enough gravy to sail a boat in. [*Blowing his scalded fingers.*]

HELEN. Well, you want to thicken it with some flour, don't you? Here! [*She takes the dredging box and sifts in the flour.*]

UNCLE NAT [*Making the best of it, stirs in the flour as she sifts*]. Thet'll do —Thet'll do—Thet'll do! Do you want to make a paste of it? Oh, Nell, don't put so much in, you've got it all full o' lumps now. [*Unconsciously blowing his scalded fingers, holding them up in the air, and then again blowing them.*]

HELEN. All right, Uncle Nat. Make the gravy yourself. [*She returns to her work.*]

UNCLE NAT [*After a slight pause. He is now stirring the gravy*]. Now gimme the giblets, an' I'll stir 'em in an' make the giblet sass. [*There is no answer. He speaks a little louder.*] I say, some one o' yeh gimme the giblets, an' I'll make the giblet sass. [*The three women stop in their work and look at one another, as if to say "What are we going to do now?"*] Come, hurry up! [*A pause,* UNCLE NAT *blows his fingers.*] Gimme the giblets I tell you! [*Silence.* HELEN *crosses over to* PERLEY. UNCLE NAT *gets impatient.*] Will yeh gimme the giblets, Ma?

ANN. I don't know where they be.

UNCLE NAT. They're in the choppin' tray, wherever you stuck it.

ANN [*Holding up the empty chopping tray, and showing it to him*]. No they ain't nuther; I say, nuther.

UNCLE NAT [*As he continues to stir the gravy*]. Well, they was there. What yeh done with 'em?

ANN. I hain't done nothin' with 'em.

UNCLE NAT [*Getting testy again*]. Well, *some*body's done suthin' with 'em. [*Turning to* HELEN.] Hev you seen 'em, Nell?

HELEN. No, Uncle Nat.

UNCLE NAT. Well, *somebody's* seen 'em. [*Turning to* PERLEY, *accusingly.*] Perley, hev you been a-monkeyin' with them giblets?

PERLEY [*Who has been trying to escape observation by violently scouring a pan at the sink, blurts out*]. I fed 'em to the chickings.

UNCLE NAT [*Dropping the spoon with utter exasperation*]. Well, of all the durn gawks I ever see you beat all! Thet ends the dinner! No giblet sass. Me a-settin' down fer half an hour a-choppin' giblets fer you to feed to the chickings. Perley, yeh're a nateral born gawk.

ANN [*Crossing to the table*]. Oh, Nathan'l, give me a hand with this table, will yeh?

UNCLE NAT [*Going to the lower end of the table*]. What yeh want to do with it, Ma?

ANN. Oh, jes' set it out a piece from the stair.

UNCLE NAT [*As they move the table slightly toward center*]. Be keerful, Ma, it fell down last Washin'ton's birthday. [*Crossing to the window and looking out.*] Looks a leetle like a shower. I hope it won't keep any of the company away.

ANN. Oh, I guess not. They ain't nuther sugar nor salt; I say, nuther sugar nor salt.

[MILLIE *by this time has made all the dough into little loaves on a tin plate, and she now takes the plate to* ANN. *She has managed to get herself pretty well messed up with flour.*]

MILLIE. Mama, please bake this for dolly'n me.

ANN. Powers above! Look at thet child! What'n the name of all possessed hev yeh been a-doin' with yerself? I say, a-doin' with yerself?

MILLIE. Makin' bwead for dolly 'n me.

ANN [*Smiling indulgently*]. Well, I should say you hed. Nathan'l, tend to thet baby; I say, thet baby. [*She takes the plate of dough from* MILLIE.]

[*During the following scene,* ANN, HELEN, *and* PERLEY *busy themselves with the dinner things.*]

UNCLE NAT. Yes, ef I didn't tend to her, I'd like to know who would. [*Crosses to the sink, takes a clean towel, and pumps water on one end of it. He then goes center to* MILLIE.] Upon my word, Millie, this is too bad. Here's company a-comin' and you think we've got nothin' to do but run after you young uns every five minutes of the day. We put yeh all three this mornin'—why didn't yeh stay put? Mussy, mussy, mussy, what a dirty child!

MILLIE. That ain't dirt, it's bwead.

UNCLE NAT [*Getting down on his knees, and beginning to clean her hands with the wet end of the towel*]. Well, it's mighty dirty bread. Who'd yeh 'spose'd eat bread from such dirty hands as those? Who you makin' bread fer?

MILLIE. Dolly.

UNCLE NAT [*Drying her hands*]. Well, it's a good thing that dolly's only got one eye. She'd never eat bread from such dirty hands, not unless you kept it on the blind side of her. [*Washing her face.*] My sakes alive, why, you'd scare all Mama's visitors out o' th' house with such a dirty face.

MILLIE [*Talking through the towel*]. Bob's got a false face.

UNCLE NAT. What's that?

MILLIE. Bob's got a false face.

UNCLE NAT [*Drying her face*]. Hez he?

MILLIE. Yes. [*Talking through the towel.*] I wish you'd buy me a false face, will yeh, Uncle Nat?

UNCLE NAT. You don't want no false face, you want yer own sweet pooty little clean face. [*Kisses her.*] Now shake yer frock. [*She shakes it in his face.*] Don't shake it in my face. Stand over there and shake it.

MILLIE. Ain't I a nice clean child now, Uncle Nat?

UNCLE NAT. You're the nicest cleanest child in the hull State of Maine.

[*As* UNCLE NAT *finishes making* MILLIE *tidy, the noise of approaching wagons is heard in the distance, and now all the guests except* BLAKE *arrive outside, amid great bustle and laughter, as if they had finished the journey in a race. Instantly all is excitement indoors.*]

UNCLE NAT. Hello, Ann, here they be! [*Crosses up left.*] Helen, take my apron off. [*She does so.* UNCLE NAT *puts on his coat quickly, and hurries off, right, leaving the door open. He is heard greeting the guests outside.*]

ANN. Mussy on me, an' I ain't fit to be seen to a nigger clambake; I say clambake! [*She takes her apron off.* HELEN *unpins her dress and smooths it down.*]

[HELEN *and* PERLEY *go to the window.* BOB *and* MARY *run in from the sitting room.* MILLIE *goes to the door, right.*]

CAPTAIN BEN [*Outside*]. Hello, Nathan'l—Many happy returns o' the day!

UNCLE NAT [*Outside*]. Don't git things mixed, Cap'n. This ain't *my* fun'ral. [*All laugh.*] Step right in. Tim an' me'll take care o' the hosses.

[*All the guests enter together, laughing and talking.* CAPTAIN BEN HUTCHINS *comes first. He is a jolly man of about fifty, half farmer, half skipper, with iron-gray hair and a full beard; he wears a blue suit with brass buttons and a peaked cap. He is accompanied by* LIDDY ANN NYE, *a motherly widow in half-mourning. They are followed by* SQUIRE ANDREWS, *a very tall, wiry, distinguished-looking man about seventy-five. He is well-preserved, and has very gray hair and a pink face. He is very deaf, and carries a tin ear-trumpet which has seen much service. With him is* MRS. ANDREWS, *a tall woman with white hair; she is dressed in good taste. The* DOCTOR, MRS. LEONARD, *and the* TWINS *enter last. The* DOCTOR *is a genial country physician. His wife is a trifle overdressed; as her husband is a professional man, she feels a bit above the farmers' wives. The* TWINS *are nicely dressed; the boy is in knickerbockers, and the little girl wears a white dress, trimmed with lace. The* DOCTOR *and the boy take off their hats as they enter. All the guests scrape their feet on the mat. They all speak at once.*]

DOCTOR. Many happy returns of the day, Mrs. Berry!

MRS. LEONARD. Returns of the day, Mrs. Berry, I'm sure.

SQUIRE ANDREWS. Many happy returns of the day, Mis' Berry!

MRS. ANDREWS. I wish you many happy returns of the day.

CAPTAIN BEN. May ye live another twenty-five years, an' invite us all agin.

MRS. NYE. Well, Ann, I swan yeh look younger'n yeh did twenty-five years ago, an' no wonder!

[*As they speak, they are all endeavoring to shake* ANN *by the hand.*]

ANN [*Shaking hands with them all, excited and happy*]. Don't come near me, if you don't want to get yer clothes spattered. This ol' stove sputters like I'd know what today. I'm greasier'n a pig. I'm 'bleeged t'yeh all fer comin'; I say, fer comin'.

CAPTAIN BEN. Oh! Ketch any of us missin' one o' *your* dinners! [*All laugh.*] I was tellin' Mis' Nye thet ef I had a cook like you aboard the "Liddy Ann," I'd stay t' sea the year 'round. [*Laughs.*]

MRS. ANDREWS. The boot's on the other leg. We're obleeged to *you* fer askin' of us.

SQUIRE ANDREWS [*With the horn at his ear*]. What do you say?

MRS. ANDREWS [*Through the trumpet*]. I said Mis' Berry's lookin' well.

SQUIRE ANDREWS. Oh yes—she allus looks well.

ANN. Well, ef you'll all step into the settin' room an' lay off yer things, I'll run upstairs an' try to make the *bride* presentable.

ALL [*Laughing*]. Certainly, certainly, by all means! [*They all go off through the door leading to the sitting room.*]

ANN. Children, take the twins in an' show 'em the presents, an' let 'em look at yer noo red albyum. [*She goes upstairs, followed by* PERLEY.]

[BOB *and* MARY, *one on each side of the* TWINS, *lead them by the hand in the direction of the sitting room. The* DOCTOR, *who is going out last, is stopped by* MILLIE, *who has a dilapidated doll, with no clothes, no hair, one eye, one arm and half a leg gone, in her arms.*]

MILLIE. Tan 'oo ture my dolly, Doctor?

DOCTOR. Cure your dolly? I guess so. What appears to be the matter with her? [*Taking the doll, and entering into the mood of the child.*]

MILLIE. She's sick.

DOCTOR. Sick! [*Looking the doll over.*] I should say she was. What's come of her other eye?

MILLIE. She swallowed it, an' it's down in her little tummick.

DOCTOR. Is *that* so? My, my! She *is* in a bad way. Well, come along, and let's see what we can do for her. [*He goes out after the others, leading* MILLIE.]

[*During this scene,* HELEN *has been busying herself with the table, putting on the bread, butter, cranberry sauce, etc.*

[MARTIN *and* BLAKE *enter through the door, right.* BLAKE *is in his best black suit, and* MARTIN *is dressed in his Sunday clothes.*]

MARTIN [*Speaking as he comes in*]. Where's Ma, Helen? [*Crosses over to the row of pegs at the back of the stairs and hangs up his hat.*]

HELEN [*Coldly*]. She'll be here in a minute. [*Shows that she and her father have not been on the best of terms since the quarrel with* SAM. *She is not rude, however.*]

[*As* BLAKE *notices* HELEN'S *manner, he draws back and pretends to be wiping his feet on the doormat, so as not to hear what passes. He does not enter the room until* MARTIN *crosses the stage for his exit.*]

MARTIN [*Pauses, and looks at* HELEN]. Hain't you got over the sulks yet?

HELEN. I'm not in any *sulks,* but I can't laugh when you stick pins in me. [*She crosses over to the stove, kneels down, opens the oven door, and looks at the turkey.*]

MARTIN. I don't want to stick pins into yeh, Nell. You give up Sam Warren, an' you an' me'll never have a word.

HELEN [*Speaking over her shoulder and temporarily stopping her work, trying to hide her feelings*]. He'll not trouble any of us much longer, I guess.

MARTIN [*Pleased.*] Hev yeh forbid him a-seein' of yeh?

HELEN. *You* have, haven't you?

MARTIN. Yes.

HELEN. Well?

MARTIN. An' ef he knows when he's well off, he'll do as I say. Company's come, I see.

HELEN [*Rising*]. Yes, they're in the sitting room.

MARTIN [*As he goes out, left*]. Come along, Mr. Blake.

BLAKE. I'll be there in a minute.

[*As* MARTIN *reaches the sitting room, he is heard saying genially*] Be yeh all here?

THE GUESTS [*Outside*]. Many happy returns of the day!

BLAKE [*Whose eyes have been fixed on* HELEN *from the moment he entered*]. Well, Helen!

HELEN [*Pleasantly, but distantly*]. How do you do, Mr. Blake.

[*During this scene,* HELEN *goes to the sideboard, gets the tumblers and salt cellars, and begins arranging them on the table. She is at the left of the table;* BLAKE *stands right center.*]

BLAKE. I suppose you'll be hevin' a silver weddin' of your own one o' these days, eh?

HELEN [*Carelessly*]. I don't know, I'm sure.

BLAKE. Did Sam tell yeh about wantin' to borry a hundred dollars o' me?

HELEN [*Interested for the first time*]. No. When?

BLAKE. Yesterday afternoon.

HELEN [*Eagerly*]. Did you lend it to him?

BLAKE. No, but I told him I'd give him a thousand if he'd pick a fuss with you, clear out, an' promise never to come back.

HELEN [*Smiling scornfully*]. What'd he say?

BLAKE [*Pauses deprecatingly*]. Said he'd—see me in hell fust.

HELEN. H'm! [*As if to say "I knew he'd say just that." She turns and busies herself near the head of the table.*]

CAPTAIN BEN [*Outside*]. I said fifty fathom.

THE GUESTS [*Outside*]. Oh! We didn't understand yeh, Cap'n Ben.

BLAKE [*Insinuatingly*]. Has yer father said anything to yeh about me *lately?*

HELEN [*With a bitter little laugh*]. No, he doesn't say much to me *lately* about anything, or anybody.

BLAKE. Well! I've got the biggest scheme fer gettin' him an' me rich! I'll tell you what I'll do with you.

HELEN [*Proudly*]. I don't want you should do anything with me, Mr. Blake. [*Crosses to the dresser, right.*]

BLAKE. Your father's set his mind on you an' me gettin' married, y'know.

HELEN. My father had better mind his own business. [*She picks up a pie and wipes the under part of the plate with a dishtowel.*]

BLAKE. His *own* business! Great Scott! D'yeh mean to say it ain't his business who his daughter marries?

HELEN. That's just exactly what I mean to say. [*Crosses to the table, left, with the pie, and sets it on the table.*]

BLAKE [*Gives a long low whistle*]. Well, Sam Warren *has* filled your head with his new-fangled ideas, an' *no* mistake.

HELEN [*Filling up with tears*]. Never mind Sam Warren, Mr. Blake. I can talk for myself.

BLAKE. That's just why I think s'much of you. Helen, I'm goin' to be awful rich. I'll give you half of every dollar I make for the next twenty years, if you'll marry me.

HELEN [*Kindly, but with finality*]. No, Mr. Blake, I can't marry you. [*She is left of the table;* BLAKE *is right, close to the table.*]

BLAKE [*Wistfully*]. Too old, I suppose?

HELEN [*Sighing heavily*]. No, it's not that. That wouldn't make any difference to *me*.

BLAKE. Too orthodox? [*With large generosity.*] You needn't go to meetin' if you don't want to. You can read all the novels you've a mind to. [*Beaming and enthusiastic, with a warm spirit of sacrifice.*] I'll read *them books* with you.

HELEN [*With a hopeless little laugh*]. Oh, Mr. Blake, you don't understand me. [*Crosses to the sink, taking off her apron.*]

BLAKE [*Intensely*]. No, nor you me. I never set my mind on a thing yet I didn't get.

HELEN [*Scornfully*]. I'm afraid you've done it this time, Mr. Blake. [*Gives her apron a vigorous and emphatic shake as she hangs it up on a peg by the sink.*]

BLAKE. No, I haven't. I'm goin' to have you, Helen, or die a-tryin'. [*She turns and looks at him; he continues quickly*] Nothin' *underhand* though—nothin' underhand.

HELEN [*With a scornful toss of her head*]. I should hope not. [*There is a note of defiance in her voice.*]

[UNCLE NAT *enters through the door, right.*]

UNCLE NAT. Helen—— [*She runs to him and he says in a tense whisper.*] Sam's out there by the wood pile. He's got the money an'——

HELEN [*Joyously*]. Got the hundred dollars? Where did he get it?

UNCLE NAT. [*Evading the question.*] He wants to see you—— [HELEN *starts to go past him out the door. He stops her.*] Not thet way. Slip out through the woodhouse. [HELEN *runs out through the woodhouse door, left.*]

BLAKE [*Suspecting something, starts to go to the window as* HELEN *crosses outside*]. What's the matter? Anything wrong?

[UNCLE NAT *stands between* BLAKE *and the window, picks up an apron, and shakes it in his face.*]

UNCLE NAT. Helen's speckled pullet's fell inter the rain barrel.

BLAKE. Oh! I hope she ain't drowned. [*Trying to see through the window.*]

UNCLE NAT. No, she ain't drownded, but she's awful wet.

[ANN *comes down the stairs, all freshened up, followed by* PERLEY.]

ANN [*Speaking as she comes down*]. Well, be we all ready, Perley?

PERLEY. Yes'm. [*Puts the potatoes on the table.*]

ANN. Well, let's have 'em in, Nathan'l.

UNCLE NAT. All right. You put the turkey on the table, an' I'll hev 'em in in three shakes of a lamb's tail.

[UNCLE NAT *goes into the sitting room. As he is supposed to open the sitting room door, a loud laugh is heard.*

[ANN *puts the turkey on the table.*]

UNCLE NAT [*Outside*]. Come, dinner's all sot, an' fetch three or four chairs with you.

ANN [*For the first time seeing* BLAKE, *who has been standing at the window, his hands behind his back*]. Good afternoon, Mr. Blake. I was 'feared you couldn't git here, yeh're such a busy man.

BLAKE [*Coming down to the table*]. I'd drop business any time to eat one o' *your* dinners, Mrs. Berry.

ANN. Well, I d'know whether the turkey sp'iled or not. Nathan'l's so fussy; I say, so fussy.

[*All the guests enter, laughing and chatting.* CAPTAIN BEN, *the* DOCTOR, *and* MARTIN *carrying chairs.* UNCLE NAT *is also carrying a chair, and is laughing heartily at some remark that has just been made. The guests stand around expectantly, waiting for* ANN *to seat them.* MARTIN *goes to the head of the table and begins to carve the turkey. The* CHILDREN *come on leading the* TWINS, *in the same manner as they went off.*]

CAPTAIN BEN [*As he enters*]. It's the pootiest kind of a trip this time o' year.

MARTIN. How long'll you be gone this time?

CAPTAIN BEN. 'Bout six weeks to two months.

UNCLE NAT. When d'ye sail, Cap'n Ben?

CAPTAIN BEN. T'night—fust o' the tide.

UNCLE NAT. I've a durn good notion t' go with yeh. D'yeh want any more hands?

CAPTAIN BEN. Yep, come on, Nathan'l. I'll give you a berth, ten dollars, an' found.

ANN. Oh, fer pity's sake, don't take him till I get these dishes washed.

MARTIN. Where'll yeh set us, Ma?

ANN [*Who has been standing at the upper end of the table on* MARTIN's *right, recollecting herself*]. Oh! Mr. Blake—— [*He does not answer. She calls again.*] Mr. Blake!

BLAKE [*Who has been at the window lost in thought, his arms folded behind him, his head bent*]. Eh? Oh, I beg pardon.

[*As* ANN *indicates each place, the guest acknowledges it with a little bow preparatory to taking his or her seat.*]

ANN [*Indicating* BLAKE's *place at her right*]. Set there please. I suppose I'd ought to make a speech—Mis' Nye—[*indicates her place at* MARTIN's *left, at the upper end of the table*] to thank yeh all —Doctor—[*indicates his place left of* MRS. NYE] for yer pooty presents—Mis' Leonard—[*indicates her place left of the* DOCTOR] but I never made a speech except once—Cap'n Ben—[*indicates his place left of* MRS. LEONARD] 'n thet was twenty-five years ago—Mis' Andrews—[*indicates her place right of* BLAKE] an' then all I said was "yes" —— [*All laugh. She shouts.*] Squire—Squire—[*he takes his place next to his wife.*] I tell Martin thet ef I do live with him twenty-five years longer—the children 'll hev t'wait——

BOB [*Stamping his foot*] Oh gosh! I wish you'd never hev any company—we allus hev t' wait! [*Goes off left, leading* SIS LEONARD *by the hand, followed by* MARY *leading* BOB LEONARD. UNCLE NAT *half follows them off, motioning them to be quiet.*]

ANN. —it'll only be 'count of the presents. [*All laugh.*] Well, set by.

[*All busy themselves at the table, and do not see* HELEN, *who enters, right, crying. She comes to* UNCLE NAT, *who draws her to the center of the stage.*]

HELEN [SOFTLY]. He *is* going tonight, Uncle Nat.

UNCLE NAT [*Tensely and quietly, soothing her*]. There, don't let 'em see you cryin'. It'll all come right some day. You wait on the table. [*Turning to* ANN *and covering up his concern for* HELEN *with a cheery manner.*] Where be yeh a-going to put me, Ma?

[*By this time everybody is seated.*]

ANN [*Pointing*]. Oh, you're down at the foot o' the class. [*All laugh.*]

UNCLE NAT. Allus was at the foot of the class—— [*Laughs, and sits down.*]

[MILLIE *enters through the door, right, with her apron full of clam shells.*]

MILLIE [*Dropping the shells on the floor*]. Where's my place, Mama?

MRS. NYE. Bless the darlin'!

CAPTAIN BEN [*Gets up and offers his chair with mock ceremony*]. Set right down here, I'll wait.

MRS. ANDREWS [*Nudging the* SQUIRE]. Look at thet child.

SQUIRE ANDREWS. Yes—I will——

[*The above exclamations are simultaneous, and all are laughing.*]

ANN. My blossom! Come to Ma, precious.

[MILLIE *goes to her;* ANN *takes her on her lap, wipes her face and hands with a napkin, and puts her in her high chair, which* PERLEY *has brought to the table.*

[MARTIN *has gone on carving.* BLAKE *has tucked his napkin in his neck, diamond-wise, and spread the ends all over his chest. The* DOCTOR *and* MRS. LEONARD *have placed their napkins in their laps.* MRS. NYE *has laid hers beside her place.* MRS. ANDREWS *fastens the* SQUIRE'S *napkin around his neck.* UNCLE NAT *sticks his in the breast of his vest like a handkerchief. All are laughing and chatting, then suddenly* MARTIN *taps on the table with the handle of his knife. They all pause instantly, and there is silence as they bow their heads in prayer. This must be done in a perfunctory manner, but in all seriousness.*]

MARTIN [*Quickly*]. Now sing out what kind uv a j'int yeh'll hev.

[*The* SQUIRE *remains with his head on the table,* UNCLE NAT *shakes him.*]

UNCLE NAT. Squire, Squire! [*The* SQUIRE *looks up and places his hand to his ear.*] Meetin's out.

MRS. ANDREWS. I'll hev secon' j'int, an' the Squire 'll hev a bit o' the breast. [MRS. ANDREWS *has the* SQUIRE'S *plate.*]

SQUIRE ANDREWS [*Puts his hand to his ear*]. Hey?—What?

MRS. ANDREWS. I said you'd hev a bit o' the breast.

MRS. NYE. I'll hev a wing.

CAPTAIN BEN [*Heartily.*] Gimme anything so's it's turkey.

BLAKE. I've no particular choice.

UNCLE NAT [*After all the others have spoken*]. Neither hev I. I'll hev the part that went over the fence last, ef nob'dy else *wants* it.

[MARTIN *helps rapidly.* ANN *serves the cranberry sauce.* PERLEY *and* HELEN *pass the vegetables, bread, and butter. They all eat heartily.*]

CAPTAIN BEN [*With his mouth full*]. Now thet's what I call turkey.

UNCLE NAT. Thet's what we cooked her fer, Cap'n Ben. Ann, don't be so stingy with yer ol' cranberry sass. [*Passes his plate.*]

ANN [*As she helps* UNCLE NAT *to cranberry sauce*]. Well, yeh can pass up again. There's plenty more in the sass dish.

UNCLE NAT. I only said that to be polite.

MARTIN. Now, folks, don't be bashful. It costs jes' the same whether yeh eat 'r not.

[*All laugh, except the* SQUIRE, *who is busy eating.*

[JOEL GATES *appears in the doorway, carrying* UNCLE NAT'S *gun, with* MANDY *beside him. He stands there and cranes his neck to look over at the table, his eyes gloating over the food. No one notices him. They are all intent upon their food.*]

UNCLE NAT. I don't believe the Squire heard a word of it. Squire, did you hear what Martin said?

SQUIRE ANDREWS [*With his hand back of his ear*]. Eh?

UNCLE NAT. He said it costs jes' the same whether yeh eat or not.

SQUIRE ANDREWS. Oh, we'll eat a lot.

UNCLE NAT. No, no— Not lot.

GATES [*Still standing at the doorway, ingratiatingly*]. How d' do?

UNCLE NAT [*Looking up and seeing him for the first time*]. Hello, Joel!

MARTIN [*With hearty hospitality*]. Hello, Joel—jes' in time. Set by an' hev some dinner with us.

[*All the guests greet* GATES.]

GATES [*Steps over the threshold, glowing at the invitation, followed by* MANDY]. I didn't know yeh hed comp'ny.

ANN. Perley, set 'm a chair; I say, a chair. [PERLEY *starts to get a chair for him.*]

GATES [*Protestingly, to* PERLEY]. No! No! [*Apologetically, to all the guests.*] I ain't fit to set down with comp'ny, I ben workin' round the barn. I jes' fetched back yer gun, Nathan'l.

HELEN. I'll take her, Mr. Gates.

GATES [*As he hands her the gun*]. Be careful, Hel'n, she's ludded.

[HELEN *sets the gun in the corner by the sink.*]

UNCLE NAT [*Casually*]. Did yeh manage to kill thet there fox, Joel?

GATES. I found out 't wa'n't a fox. [*Very much interested in the turkey and the guests' enjoyment of it.*]

UNCLE NAT. Thet so. What was it?

GATES. 'Twas a skunk.

[*A murmur of amusement goes around the table.* GATES *starts to go.*]

MARTIN. Set down an' hev some turkey.

GATES [*Deprecatingly, looking at the table longingly*]. No, I'm too s'iled. Ef I'd 'a' knowed you was hevin' turkey—I mean comp'ny, I'd 'a' cleaned myself up a bit.

UNCLE NAT [*While eating*]. Now thet yeh be here, let Ma fix some on a plate to take hum with yeh.

ANN. Yes. Here, Martin, give him this, you can fix yerself some more. [*Holds* MARTIN'S *plate;* MARTIN *fills it.*]

UNCLE NAT [*To the child*]. Mandy, you come here an' git a piece of Ma Berry's pie.

GATES [*To the child, who hesitates and looks up at him inquiringly*]. Go 'n git it, ef yeh want to.

[MANDY *goes to* UNCLE NAT, *who gives her a huge piece of pie. She returns to her father, holding the pie with both hands, her face in a glow of wonder.*]

ANN [*Giving* HELEN *a plate piled high with food*]. Helen, pass this to Mr. Gates.

GATES [*As* HELEN *gives him the plate*].

Thank yeh, thank yeh. I'll jes' step inter the woodhouse an' eat it, then I kin hand the plate back.

MARTIN. No, set down there, ef yeh won't come to the table. Hel'n, give 'im a chair.

[HELEN *places a chair, center. Her manner is very gentle and kind.*]

GATES. *Thank* yeh.

[HELEN *gets* MILLIE's *small rocking-chair for* MANDY. *She sits down in it, and slowly rocks to and fro, and for the first time a look of childish joy appears on her face.*

[GATES *settles himself in the chair carefully, with his knees drawn together and his toes resting on a rung, so as to make a table of his lap. With his shoulders hunched, he attacks the overflowing plate and becomes absorbed in the food. He eats as if he had been saving himself for this meal, and feeds the child generously with dainty morsels.*

[*Meantime, the talk at the table continues.*]

DOCTOR. Oh! By the way, Mr. Blake, did you buy the Swazy place?

BLAKE. Yes.

CAPTAIN BEN. L'see, how many acres is there in thet place?

BLAKE. Eighty-odd.

MARTIN. What'd yeh hev to pay fer it, if it's a fair question?

BLAKE. Paid enough fer it—they knew I had to hev it.

UNCLE NAT. They ain't givin' land away nowadays, be they, Mr. Blake?

DOCTOR [*To* PERLEY]. Will you give me another cup of tea, please? [*She takes his cup and fills it from the teapot on the stove.*] I'd like to sell you that ma'sh of mine, Mr. Blake.

BLAKE. How much shore front hev yeh got there?

DOCTOR. Sixty-seven rod.

BLAKE. What'll yeh take fer it?

DOCTOR. Well, I'm asking twenty-five hundred dollars for it.

BLAKE. Good Heavens! You hev sot it up. I'll give yeh a thousand fer it, half cash.

DOCTOR. The Squire's offered me more than *that* for it.

BLAKE [*Astonished*]. The Squire! What's he want with it?

SQUIRE ANDREWS [*Hearing this*]. Thet's my business. You don't s'pose you're goin' to be the only one to git rich out'n the boom, do yeh?

BLAKE. I *started* it.

SQUIRE ANDREWS. Columbus discovered Americky, but he don't *own* it. [*All laugh. The* SQUIRE *looks round the table, well satisfied.*]

UNCLE NAT [*Laughing uproariously, to the* SQUIRE *on his left*]. Squire, thet's the best thing yeh ever said in yer life—I say thet's the best—— [*Pauses, as he realizes the* SQUIRE *is paying no attention, but is busily eating.*] Yeh didn't know yeh said it, did yeh? [*The* SQUIRE *still pays no attention.* UNCLE NAT *turns to the rest of the company.*] He didn't hear himself say it. [*All laugh.*]

CAPTAIN BEN. So the Squire's got the fever too, eh?

SQUIRE ANDREWS. Yes, an' got it bad —see—— [*Pulls out an oil paper map of his farm, laid off in lots, unfolds it, and shows it to the company.*]

BLAKE. By George, he's got the start of all of us.

GATES [*Picking gingerly on a drumstick*]. Mr. Blake, I'd like t' sell yeh thet seven acre o' mine. I got a great view there. Yeh kin see fer fifty mile round, ef yer eyesight's good enough.

BLAKE. What d'yeh want fer it?

GATES [*Very importantly*]. Well, it's sort o' got round thet I sot a price. I told Gabe Kilpatrick, and he says I'd ought to git ten 'r fifteen thousand dollars fer it. [*All laugh.*] Gabe says it'd make a great buildin' site fer Vanderbilt 'r Rockenfeeder 'r any 'o them far-seein' fellers. [*All laugh.*]

ANN. Oh, Martin, thet man thet was here to see yeh yesterday was here agin today—who is he?

MARTIN [*Speaking slowly and unwillingly*]. His name's Beardsley.

UNCLE NAT [*Cheerfully and unsuspiciously*]. What is he, Martin?

MARTIN [*Ponderously*]. Surveyor!

UNCLE NAT. *Surveyor?*

MARTIN. Surveyor for this 'ere new geruntee land an' improv'ment company.

CAPTAIN BEN. Martin, will yeh gimme jes' a leetle taste more o' thet stuffin'? [*Passes his plate,* MARTIN *helps him.*]

ANN [*For the first time a little uneasy*]. What's he want here, Martin?

MARTIN [*As if forced to a stand, defiantly*]. He's goin' to survey the farm.

ANN [*Gulping down her food*]. Survey it! What fer? I say, what fer?

MARTIN [*In desperation*]. I'm goin' to cut it up into buildin' lots, ef yeh must know. [*The guests stop eating.*]

[ANN *is quite overcome at this news. She swiftly moves her chair out from the table, and stares at* MARTIN *in consternation.*]

MARTIN [*With forced change of tone*]. Hev another wing, Mis' Nye.

MRS. NYE [*Soothingly*]. Hain't et what I got on my plate yit, Martin.

[*A damper now falls on the party.*]

ANN [*Passionately*]. Martin Berry, you ain't a-goin' to sell the farm, be yeh? I say, be yeh?

MARTIN [*Stubbornly*]. You heerd what I said, didn't yeh?

ANN. Yes—I heerd yeh, but I can't *believe* yeh.

MARTIN. It's *mine,* ain't it?

ANN [*Brokenly*]. Yes, I s'pose 'tis.

MARTIN. Well, hain't I got a right to do what I like with my own?

ANN. I d'know's you got any right to turn me an' the children out o' house 'n hum.

[GATES *gently rises and gives his empty plate to* HELEN, *a look of apprehension on his face. He tiptoes from the room through the door, right, followed by* MANDY.

[UNCLE NAT *gets up and places his chair in a corner, left, and crosses to right center.*]

MARTIN. Thet's sentiment—I ain't a-goin' to turn yeh out o' nothin.' I'm a-goin' to move yeh all up to Bangor—I'm a-goin' to git rich.

ANN [*Rising and folding her arms, her head in the air, proudly and defiantly*]. You won't move *me* up to Bangor, not ef you git as rich as Methuselum.

MARTIN. I'll leave it to Mr. Blake ef I——

BLAKE. I must say I think Martin's scheme's a——

ANN [*Still with spirit, but with a break in her voice*]. I don't allow's Mr. Blake's got any right to jedge atween you an' me in this: I say, in this.

MARTIN [*Rising, and striking his fist on the table, angrily*]. Look a-here! I'm goin' to git rich in spite o' yeh. Doctor, will yeh hev another piece o' the breast? I ain't a-goin' to be browbeat.

DOCTOR. No, thank you.

MARTIN [*In a great temper by this time*]. Fust Nathan'l tries it an' then you must set up a——

UNCLE NAT [*Very tensely, but quietly*]. I hain't never browbeat yeh, Martin—I only ast yeh to leave me thet little piece up yonder.

MARTIN. I won't leave yeh nothin'! I'm durned ef I don't sell the hull thing, humstead, graveyard an' every dum——

[YOUNG NAT *enters through the door, right, out of breath and greatly agitated.*]

YOUNG NAT. Mr. Blake—Mr. Blake —Mr. Blake—— [*Breathes fast.*] You're wanted up at the store. [*All are listening.*] There's been a package o' money took out o' the safe.

BLAKE [*Swinging around in his chair so as to face* YOUNG NAT, *and resting his arms on the back as he talks*]. A package o' money! What sort of a package?

YOUNG NAT. A hundred-dollar package.

[HELEN, *who is standing a little above right center, listens intently.*]

BLAKE. Who's been in the store today, thet yeh know of?

YOUNG NAT [*Breathlessly*]. Well, there was Mis' Peasley's hired girl, but she didn't take it. Joe Bennett—Dan Nourse—Sam Warren—— [*Draws out* SAM WARREN'S *name significantly.*]

BLAKE [*Quickly*]. Sam Warren! By George! [*Hitting the back of his chair with his hand.*] *He* stole it.

HELEN [*With suppressed anger and shame*]. Oh, Mr. Blake!

BLAKE [*To* UNCLE NAT, *with a significant look*]. Thet's the speckled pullet thet fell into the rain barrel! [*To the others.*] He hed to hev a hundred dollars to go out West with. [*All the guests except* CAPTAIN BEN *nod their heads as if to say "That's so, that's bad."*] He tried to borry it o' *me.* I wouldn't lend it to him, an' so *he* stole it. [*The guests all nod "That's it."*]

HELEN [*Coming down swiftly to right center, quietly but determinedly*]. You lie!

MARTIN [*Who is still at the head of the table*]. Helen! [*A slight pause.*] How dast you call Mr. Blake a liar?

HELEN [*Her voice quivering with indignation*]. How *dare he* call Dr. Warren a thief?

BLAKE [*A little angrily*]. He *is* a——

HELEN [*Fiercely*]. You're a——

MARTIN [*In a low tense tone, approaching her angrily with his hand clenched and partly lifted*]. Helen, if you say that agin, I swear I'll——

[ANN *turns around with her back to the table, and starts crying into her apron.*]

UNCLE NAT [*Who has been standing with his fingers to his lips, trembling, fearful of* MARTIN'S *anger, goes between them and lays his hand on* MARTIN'S *shoulder*]. Martin! Don't do nothin' thet yeh'll be sorry fer all the days o' yer life.

[*All the guests have risen, rather embarrassed, but fascinated by this scene, and are standing at their places around the table.* MRS. ANDREWS *explains to the* SQUIRE *through the ear trumpet.*]

MARTIN [*Shaking* UNCLE NAT'S *hand off*]. Take yer hand off'n me. I tell yeh I won't be browbeat by you, an' I won't hev *her* [*with an angry gesture toward* HELEN] insult my friends.

HELEN [*Her voice trembling with unshed tears of rage, her face flushed with angry excitement*]. He insulted *me,* and if Sam Warren doesn't *thrash* him before night, it'll be because I can't make him do it, that's all.

[HELEN, *during this scene, shows she is the modern girl, and has the temper inherited from her father.* MRS. BERRY *is the old-fashioned, submissive wife, awed and frightened at* HELEN'S *daring to oppose her father.*]

BLAKE [*Losing his temper*]. He'll be in the lockup before night, if I can put him there. [*Picks up his hat and cane from the table by the window.*]

MARTIN [*Turning and picking up the gun from the corner by the sink, and rushing over to* BLAKE *with it*]. That's the thing to do. Git a warrant fer him an' ef he raises his hand to yeh—you—*shoot*—him.

[UNCLE NAT *has been standing at one side, his kind old face white and drawn with anguish. He now comes forward and interposes.*]

UNCLE NAT. Hol' on, Martin! Uncle Sam'l 's mine—an' she wa'n't never made fer *murderin'* folks. [*Quietly, but with authority, he takes the gun and puts it back in the corner by the sink.*]

BLAKE [*Shaking his cane, a very heavy one, threateningly*]. This'll do me!

HELEN [*Dominating the whole situation, in a low voice quivering with contempt, to* BLAKE]. Oh! You *coward!*

[*Turning to her father.*] Father, Sam's going away today. [*With tremendous authority.*] You'd better let him go if you know when you're well off.

MARTIN [*Taking her tone, tauntingly*]. You'd better not interfere if you know when *you*'re well off. I s'pose you'd like to go with him?

HELEN [*Throwing her head proudly in the air*]. Yes—I would.

MARTIN [*Beside himself*]. By God! If I lay my hands on him, I'll kill him.

HELEN. If you dare to lay a finger on him, I'll—— [*Springs toward* MARTIN *as she speaks, with hands clenched.* UNCLE NAT *catches her and puts his hand over her mouth. The tension is broken, and* HELEN *bursts into tears, her head resting on* UNCLE NAT*'s breast.*]

[*The guests now quietly leave the room, one by one, by the door left.* MRS. NYE *takes* MILLIE*'s hand and follows the others.*

[PERLEY, *during all this, has gone on clearing away the table as if nothing had happened, only occasionally glancing in the direction of* HELEN *and* MARTIN. *She now goes into the woodhouse, taking the platter with the turkey on it, as if to have her dinner there.*]

MARTIN [*Crossing to the door, right, as he speaks*]. You'll find out that I've got something to say about what you'll do and what you won't do! Who you'll marry and who you won't marry! [*He starts to go out.* YOUNG NAT *blocks his way, and he pushes him roughly outside.*] Come along, Mr. Blake! [BLAKE *passes out ahead of* MARTIN, *who turns and gives a last fierce fling at* HELEN.] You're not of age yet, my lady. I'll show Sam Warren thet ef my grandfathers *was* monkeys, they wa'n't thieves. [*He goes out.*]

[*As* HELEN *hears their receding footsteps, she runs to the window, and watches them out of sight. She is in a bitter, angry mood, and tears fill her eyes.*

[UNCLE NAT *sinks wearily and despondently into a chair, left center.*

[ANN *is still standing with her back to the audience, crying into her apron. She is dazed and broken.*]

UNCLE NAT. Well, Ann, it seems es ef our turkey'd come to a sort of an ontimely *end,* hain't she?

[HELEN *leaves the window, takes a cup and saucer from the table, goes to the stove, pours out a cup of tea and comes down stage, slowly and listlessly, and seats herself left of the table. She mechanically reaches well across the table for the milk and sugar, stirs the tea, sips it, and nibbles a crust of bread.*]

ANN [*Turning, her voice tremulous with tears*]. Oh, Nathan'l, I'm so *'shamed.* I'll never look a neighbor in the face agin. Twenty-five years married, an' nothin' like this ever happened afore. [*Begins to cry.*] To think o' the dinner all sp'iled after me cookin' myself hoarse over it. [*Starts toward the sitting room door.*] It's enough to provoke a saint out of Heaven; I say, a saint out of Heaven. [*She goes off into the sitting room.*]

UNCLE NAT [*In a quick decisive voice*]. Well, Helen, I guess Sam'd better git right away from here jes' 's quick 's he kin.

HELEN [*Frightened, quickly, in an awed whisper*]. Do you think he took the money, Uncle Nat?

UNCLE NAT [*Rising and going center*]. 'Tain't thet, but there'll be trouble ef him an' Martin comes together. [*He takes off his coat, doubles it up, and throws it in a chair, and begins to clear the table, first gathering the napkins, then the knives and forks, as he talks.*]

HELEN. He *has* got a hundred dollars, y'know.

UNCLE NAT [*Continuing with his work at the table*]. I know thet. [*Reluctantly.*] I let him hev the biggest part of it myself.

HELEN [*Amazed*]. You?

UNCLE NAT. It's the money me 'n Martin's ben a-savin' up to buy a tombstun fer Mother.

HELEN [*Rising, and striking the table with her fist*]. Then he shan't stir—one—single—step. [*Determined, her eyes flashing.*]

UNCLE NAT [*Dropping the knives and forks he has in his hand, and leaning over the table, appealingly*]. I beg of yeh, Nell—git him away from here. There'll be murder ef yeh don't! [*Crosses to the right with two chairs.*]

HELEN. I don't *care*. They *shan't* call him a thief.

UNCLE NAT [*Stops and turns*]. Now—now—Haven't they called 'im everything they could lay their tongues to a'ready? Don't yeh see thet I dasn't tell Martin I let Sam hev thet money? [*Puts the chairs down and goes back to the table.*] Don't yeh see thet it won't do fer Martin an' *me* to come together? [*Taps the table with his forefinger.*] Things hes gone too fur now.

HELEN. That's so—he's got to go. He's got to pay that money back.

UNCLE NAT [*Under the stress of deep conflict and emotion, half turns away from the table with the napkins in his hands; then he turns around again and drops the napkins back on the table*]. Yes, but he's jes' as pig-headed as any of the rest of us, an' if he knowed the money was Martin's he wouldn't tech a cent of it, not with a forty-foot pole. He'd want to stay right here an' fight it out—I'm 'feared. [*Picks up a chair and goes toward right center with it.*]

HELEN [*With quick decision*]. He mustn't do that. I'd go with him if it weren't for Mother.

UNCLE NAT [*Putting down the chair and, turning around amazed and awed, whispers quickly*]. Would yeh, Nell? [*He comes back to the table.*]

HELEN [*Bitterly*]. This'll never be a home to me any more.

UNCLE NAT [*Taking another chair and going to the window*]. It'll never be a hum to anybody any more, Nell. It's goin' to be all cut up into buildin' lots anyway.

[*By this time* HELEN *has worked her way round to the foot of the table. She now goes to* UNCLE NAT *and says*] If it weren't for Mother, I wouldn't stay here another minute. [*Appealingly.*] Would you blame me, Uncle Nat?

UNCLE NAT [*Down left, goes to her and they meet center. He says tenderly*] How could I blame yeh, Helen? Things'll never be the same here agin, an' Sam'd be all upsot out there athout you—an' you'd never be satisfied here athout him. [*With gentle insinuation.*] Now would yeh? He might get goin' to the dogs out there, an' then yeh'd worry—an' blame herself—an'—— [*Persuasively.*] I d'know—seems to me—'s ef——

HELEN [*Taking fire from his suggestion, is all eagerness and determination*]. How can we get away? They'd see us on the train.

UNCLE NAT [*Consideringly*]. Oh, you mustn't go by no train. I'll drive yeh over as far as Ellsworth, an'——

[*At this moment,* CAPTAIN BEN *passes the window.* UNCLE NAT *glances up and sees him, over his shoulder. He is struck by a sudden idea, and goes toward the window and calls.*]

UNCLE NAT. Oh, Cap'n Ben!—Cap'n Ben! [*As* UNCLE NAT *calls,* CAPTAIN BEN *turns and stands leaning on the window-sill, looking into the room.*] When did yeh say yeh was a-goin' t' sail?

CAPTAIN BEN. 'Bout an hour'r so—ef it don't come on to blow—looks kinder as ef we *might* git a sou'easter afore mornin'. [*Turns and starts to go, scanning the sky.*]

UNCLE NAT [*Stopping him again in a voice of hushed anxiety*]. Cap'n Ben! [CAPTAIN BEN *again pauses, and looks at* UNCLE NAT.] Helen an' Sam 's ben a-thinkin' o' takin' a trip down the coast fer quite a spell—— [*Looks and nods at him significantly.*] Would you mind droppin' 'em at St. Andrews's 'r somewheres along there?

CAPTAIN BEN [*Taken aback for a moment, then, comprehending the situation, answers with bluff heartiness*]. No, plenty o' room an' plenty o' grub aboard.

UNCLE NAT. Kin they go aboard now an' be stowed away somewheres?

CAPTAIN BEN. Yes, I guess so. Nell, yeh kin come right along with me now in my buggy. [*He leaves the window and continues off, right.*]

[*During this scene,* HELEN *has been standing tense as she begins to realize the significance of* UNCLE NAT'S *talk with* CAPTAIN BEN. *Now she turns and darts toward the pegs beside the woodhouse door, where hang her jacket and tam-o'-shanter. She pulls the cap quickly on her head, thrusts her arms into the sleeves of her jacket, and dashes swiftly to the door, right.* UNCLE NAT *checks her flight.*]

UNCLE NAT. Helen!—Helen!

HELEN [*Stopping*]. What is it, Uncle Nat?

[*There is a moment's pause as they both stand looking at each other. Then* HELEN *comes slowly back.*]

UNCLE NAT [*Significantly, taking a plain little silver ring off his finger*]. Thet's my mother's weddin' ring. You give it to Sam, an' tell 'im to use it the fust chance he gits. [*He takes her hand, puts the ring into it, and folds her fingers around it.*] Now run along. Cap'n Ben's a-waitin'. [*He pushes her gently toward the door, and goes quickly to the table as though to hide his emotion.*]

[HELEN *walks slowly to the door, looking at the ring. She stops, and a sudden sense of loss seizes her. She turns, and, with a cry, goes back to* UNCLE NAT.]

HELEN. Oh, Uncle Nat, I don't believe I *can* leave you and Mother—not even for him. [*Flings herself into his arms and bursts into tears.*]

UNCLE NAT [*Folding her in his arms, his voice shaking with tears*]. There now, don't talk l'k thet—Don't yeh start me a-cryin', 'cause ef yeh do, I'm afeared I won't let yeh go. [*As he talks, he turns and moves with her very slowly toward the door. His tone is the soothing one he would use to a child.*] Now, see here. To-night's my watch at the light, an' when you an' Sam an' Cap'n Ben an' all on yeh is a-sailin' down the harbor, a-singin' an' a-laughin' an' enj'yin' yerselves—jes' as yeh git to the light, you look over there an' sez you to Sam, sez you—There's ol' Uncle Nat' eye, sez you—He's a-winkin' an' a-blinkin' an' a-thinkin' of us, sez you.

HELEN. Good-by, Uncle Nat.

UNCLE NAT. No! We ain't a-goin' t' say good-by; we're jes' a-goin' to say good afternoon, thet's all! [*Tries to laugh.*] P'r'aps I'll come out there and see yeh one o' these days.

HELEN [*Who has been comforted by* UNCLE NAT'S *words, laughs at him almost joyously through her tears*]. Oh!—Will you, Uncle Nat?

UNCLE NAT [*His face taking on a look of longing, with something of renunciation*]. I said—p'r'aps—— [*A pause.*] In thet there palace o' yourn yeh used to talk s'much about when yeh was little. Remember when yeh was little how yeh used to say thet when yeh growed up, yeh'd marry a prince an' live in a gol' palace, an' I was to come an' see yeh, an' yeh was to dress me all up in silks, an' satins, an' di'monds, an' velvets——

[*He half laughs, half cries, kisses her, almost pushes her out of the door, closes the door and bursts into tears, leaning his two arms on the door and burying his face in them.*]

Curtain

ACT III SCENE 1

"Havin' an Understandin'"
Interior of Berry Lighthouse.

Scene: The room is octagonal in shape, with walls of white-washed stone, and its chief feature is an iron stairway leading to the tower above. This stairway starts well down left, then makes a turn, and extends up and across the back wall. There are small windows at intervals along the stairway. Beneath the stairs, about center, is a small, high, barred window, through which a terrific storm is seen raging. At intervals waves dash against the window.

The entrance to the lighthouse is through a door on the right; it is made of heavy planks, and has a large latch and a heavy, old-fashioned lock (NOTE: *This door must be framed and set so as to slam with force.*)

The whole room has an oily look and smell. On a shelf to the right of the window, about eighteen inches from the floor, is an oil barrel with a brass cock; beside it are some oil cans and a brass gallon measure for filling the lighthouse lamps. There is a brass pan on the floor beneath the barrel to catch the drip. Beside it is a wooden bucket. There is a shears for trimming the lamps on the floor at the foot of the stairway, and near it lies a coil of life-saving rope. A ship's glass, a sou'wester, an oilskin coat, and a pair of oilskin overalls hang on pegs on the wall, left. Leaning against the wall are oars and a boat hook. Several unlighted lanterns are standing about the floor.

The light from above shines down on the room.

At the rise of the curtain rain is heard falling in torrents outside. The wind howls, lightning flashes, and thunder crashes at intervals.

UNCLE NAT *is discovered down left sweeping the floor. He has the dirt in a little heap and is getting it into a shovel with a broom. His actions are mechanical and his manner is preoccupied. He has on his working clothes and his trousers are tucked into high boots.*

MARTIN *enters hurriedly from the right. He wears oilskins and carries a lighted lantern. He is pale and excited. As he opens the door, the rain, wind, and thunder can be heard outside. He slams the door behind him, puts the lantern on the floor, right, and stands a picture of excited anger.*

MARTIN [*Standing down right*]. Helen's gone!

UNCLE NAT [*Who has looked up over his shoulder as* MARTIN *entered, and then immediately resumed his work, quietly says*] Y—e—s.

MARTIN. Along with Sam Warren. [UNCLE NAT *looks up, concludes not to speak and continues his work.*] Did you know she was a-goin'?

UNCLE NAT [*Without looking up*]. Yeh.

MARTIN. Why didn't yeh tell me?

UNCLE NAT [*Has got all the dirt on the shovel by this time; now he empties it into the bucket, right, sweeping off the shovel so that no dust will remain on it. He speaks as he does this*]. 'Cause yeh didn't desarve to be told!

MARTIN [*Striking a clenched fist against his open palm*]. I'm her father, ain't I?

UNCLE NAT [*Drily as he hangs the shovel against the wall*]. Yeh didn't act's ef yeh was, today.

MARTIN [*Who is still standing down right*]. Then yeh blame me?

UNCLE NAT [*Quietly*]. Well, I ain't a-goin' to lie about it, Martin. [*He hangs up the broom.*]

MARTIN. An' yeh uphold her?

UNCLE NAT. Yeh didn't know your own child, Martin, thet's all. Ef yeh hed yeh'd 'a' knowed thet yeh might jest's well 'a' stuck thet there gaft [*points to the boat hook*] inter her heart as to hev said what yeh did 'bout Sam Warren. [*He knocks on the oil barrel to see how much it contains.*]

MARTIN [*With concentrated bitterness*]. He's a thief.

UNCLE NAT. Tut! Tut! Tut! He ain't. An' you know it jes' as well 's I do. [*He takes up the pan from beneath the barrel, pours the drippings into an oil can, wipes the pan with a bunch of waste, then wipes the cock of the barrel.*] Yeh unly said it 'cos yeh was crazy, crazier'n a loon. I knowed she wouldn't stay here long after thet. Yeh see, she ain't me, Martin—she's young, an'—— [*Slight pause.*]

MARTIN. Where's Tim?

UNCLE NAT. Tim went to Ells'orth this evenin', hain't got back yit.

MARTIN. How'd they go?

UNCLE NAT. 'Long o' the mail. [*Crosses to the window, wipes the pane and peers out at the storm.*]

MARTIN. I said how'd *they* go?

UNCLE NAT. Oh! Cap'n Ben took 'em in the "Liddy Ann."

MARTIN [*Still standing right*]. What time'd they start?

UNCLE NAT [*Up center near the window*]. Fust o' the ebb.

MARTIN [*Slowly and with hate*]. I hope they sink afore ever they pass the light.

UNCLE NAT [*Quietly, turning and looking at* MARTIN]. I wouldn't say thet if I was you, Martin—— [*There is a brilliant flash of lightning followed by a loud crash of thunder.* UNCLE NAT *nods toward the window, indicating the storm, and adds*] You mought git yer wish.

MARTIN [*As before*]. I mean ev'ry word I say. She's *disgraced* me.

UNCLE NAT [*Never losing his tone of patient gentleness*]. You've disgraced yourself, Martin, I guess. [*He is wiping the things on the bench with the waste.*]

MARTIN [*Slowly, through his teeth*]. Be they married?

UNCLE NAT. No!

MARTIN [*With a sneer*]. Humph!

UNCLE NAT. Not—yit.

MARTIN [*Bitterly*]. An' never will be.

UNCLE NAT [*With quiet confidence; he is down left*]. Oh yes, they will. [*Thunder and lightning.*] Ef they ever live to git to any place. Helen ain't a-goin' to forgit thet she's got a mother an' sisters —an'——

MARTIN [*Going to him left, and laughing derisively*]. You're tryin' to make me believe 'twas me that made her go —d'ye think I'm blind? She went 'cause she hed to go to hide suthin' wuss from her mother 'n me; she went 'cause she couldn't 'a' held up 'r head much longer here—she's——

UNCLE NAT [*Dropping his work and turning on him and for the first time showing deep feeling*]. Martin, don't yeh dare say it! Fer ef yeh do, I swear I'll strangle yeh right where yeh stand. [*The light from the tower grows dim.*]

[NOTE: *This must be worked very gradually.*]

MARTIN [*Stubbornly standing his ground*]. It's true an' you know it. Thet's why yeh hurried 'em away.

UNCLE NAT [*Making a movement as though to spring at* MARTIN'S *throat, shrieks hoarsely*] Martin, you've got to take thet back! [*The light in the tower flickers and goes almost out. There is the distant sound of a ship's gun.*]

UNCLE NAT [*With a sudden change of manner, in a quick, startled voice, as he glances up at the light*]. Good land, what's the matter with the light? [*He crosses down right, and picks up the lighted lantern which* MARTIN *placed there on his entrance, speaking as he does so.*] Tim's fergot to trim thet lamp, sure's you're born. [*Lantern in hand, he turns to go up the stairs. At the same moment* MARTIN *seizes the boat hook and stands in front of the stairs, barring* UNCLE NAT'S *way.*]

MARTIN [*Hoarsely, but determined*]. Yeh shan't go up them stairs.

UNCLE NAT [*Paralyzed with horror*]. Martin!

[*The ship's gun is heard again; it is nearer this time.*]

MARTIN [*In cold and measured tones*]. I say yeh shan't go up them stairs.

[*Again the gun sounds outside.*]

UNCLE NAT [*Almost beside himself*]. Why, Martin!—Thet's the "Liddy Ann"! [*The gun is heard once more.*] Thet's her gun!

MARTIN [*Stolid, quiet, intense*]. I know it.

UNCLE NAT [*With a cry of protest and unbelief*]. She'll go to pieces on the reef!

MARTIN [*Grimly*]. Let her go.

UNCLE NAT [*Half crazed*]. Yes—but —Helen'll go with 'er! [*He starts for the stairs.*]

MARTIN [*Stopping him*]. Keep away, Nathan'l. I tell yeh thet light ain't a-goin' to be lit.

UNCLE NAT [*Frantically pleading, his voice broken with emotion*]. Martin, f'r God's sake, list'n to *me!*

MARTIN [*Doggedly*]. I won't listen to nothin'.

UNCLE NAT [*Walking firmly over to him, speaking as he does so*]. You've *got* to listen. [MARTIN *makes an angry movement.*] I say—you've got to listen! We've got to hev an understandin' right here and now. [MARTIN *submits sullenly, and* UNCLE NAT *continues to talk in hurried, nervous tones, pacing up and down the space between* MARTIN *and the door, like a caged lion, rolling and unrolling the sleeves of his red flannel shirt.*] I've ben playin' secon' fiddle to you long enough, Martin Berry, ever sence yeh was born. When yeh was a baby I walked the floor with yeh, an' sung yeh t' sleep night after night. At school I fit yer battles fer yeh, an' once I saved yer life.

[*The gun is heard outside.*]

MARTIN. Yeh needn't throw thet in my face.

UNCLE NAT. I hain't a-throwin' it in yer face. I only want yeh not to forgit to remember it, thet's all. [*He goes to the window and peers out.*]

MARTIN [*Doggedly*]. I know all about thet, I tell yeh.

UNCLE NAT. Do yeh? Well, then I'll tell yeh somethin, yeh didn't know. [*Walks over and deliberately faces him, and says emphatically*] Did yeh ever know thet I might 'a' married your wife Ann?

MARTIN [*Raising the boat hook, making a step toward him, white with rage, almost shrieks*] W—h—a—t?

UNCLE NAT [*Hurried, tense, and almost hysterical*]. Hol' on—I ain't through yit. I thought more o' her than ever a miser did o' money. But when I see thet you liked her too—I jes' went off t' the war—an' I let yeh hev her! [*Taps* MARTIN'S *chest with his forefinger.*] An' thet's sumpthin' yeh didn't know all about—wa'n't it, Martin Berry? [*The gun is heard outside.*] But thet's neither here nor there—her child is out there—my child by rights! [*With sudden sublime conviction, almost heaven-inspired.*] Martin, thet light hez got to be lit! [*With an angry snarl.*] I give yeh the mother, but I'm damned ef I'm a-goin' to let yeh murder the child! Come away from them stairs, Martin—come away from them stairs, I say!

[UNCLE NAT *seizes* MARTIN, *and the two men have a quick struggle. Then* UNCLE NAT *with almost superhuman strength throws* MARTIN *the whole length of the room.* MARTIN *is dazed; he reels and staggers like a drunken man toward the door by which he entered, and blindly gropes his way out into the storm.*

[UNCLE NAT *seizes the lantern and starts to crawl up the stairs. It is hard work to climb them, the excitement has been too much for him. He gets up a few steps, then slips down again; he crawls up again on hands and knees, and once more slips down. He makes still another effort, falters, staggers, and, with a heartbreaking cry, falls and rolls down the stairs.*]

UNCLE NAT. God help me! I hain't got the strength!

[*The thunder crashes, the sea roars, the lightning flashes.*

[*The stage darkens as the light above goes completely out.*]

End of Scene 1

ACT III SCENE 2

"The 'Liddy Ann' in a Sou'easter"

Exterior of Berry Lighthouse.

(NOTE: *The storm noises are well worked up before the scene opens. The stage is completely dark, as is the front of the theatre.*)

Scene: An expanse of wild, storm-tossed waves, with the lighthouse, a dark, shadowy bulk, rising from the rocky coast on the left. The rain is pouring in torrents, the thunder roars, the lightning flashes. The boom of a ship's gun is heard above the din of the storm, and in the darkness, the "Liddy Ann," sloop-rigged and under reefed jib, makes her way slowly through the heavy seas, from right to left. She is off her course and perilously near the rocks. At intervals her gun booms and she sends up distress signals. The figures of CAPTAIN BEN, DAVE BURGESS, GABE KILPATRICK, *and* BILL HODGEKINS, *as well as* SAM *and* HELEN, *can be dimly discerned on board. The shouts of* CAPTAIN BEN *giving orders, and the replies of the crew are drowned by the noise of the storm.*

For a few moments the "Liddy Ann" tosses helplessly in the darkness. Then a tiny light appears in the lowest window of the lighthouse. For a second it wavers, then slowly it rises from window to window, as UNCLE NAT *climbs the stairs to the tower. In another moment the light in the tower blazes forth, showing the "Liddy Ann" her course. A shout of relief goes up from those on the boat, and as the "Liddy Ann" makes her way safely past the rocks*

The Curtain Descends

ACT IV

"Me an' the Children"

The scene is the same as in Act II. It is fifteen months later.

Scene: Snow is falling heavily outside. The wind is howling; a little drift of snow can be seen on the window sash. A fire burns briskly in the stove and everything has the appearance of the day's work being over. The leaves of the table are folded, and a red checked cloth covers the table on which is a lighted lamp. The tea kettle is singing on the fire. UNCLE NAT'S *gun is in its place in the corner by the sink, and his old army coat and cap are hanging on the pegs under the stairs, as in Act II. There is a large rocking chair up right, and a small one stands above the table, left. At the rise of the curtain,* YOUNG NAT *is seated reading a book at the upper end of the table; he now wears long trousers instead of knickerbockers. From time to time he turns a page but instantly resumes his position to preserve the idea that he is very intent on the story before him. His elbows are resting on the table at either side of the book and his head is supported by both hands.*

MARTIN *is seated on a chair, which is tilted back against the wall below the door, right. On his knees lies a blueprint map of his farm, which has been surveyed and laid off in lots. He is very dejected and in deep thought. Without realizing it he is grieving over the absence of his daughter, filled with bitter remorse for having driven her out of her home.*

ANN *is sitting at the right of the table, mending stockings. She wears a warm-*

colored woolen dress, with a white embroidered collar, and a crisp white apron.

UNCLE NAT *and* PERLEY *are preparing the* CHILDREN *for bed.* UNCLE NAT *is seated, center, and* PERLEY *stands beside him.* UNCLE NAT *is just finishing buttoning up* MILLIE'S *nightdress, while* PERLEY *is helping* MARY.

The CHILDREN *all have nightdresses and worsted slippers on, and their clothes are lying in little heaps, one in front of each child, as though they had just stepped out of them.* MILLIE'S *hair is in curl papers.* MARY'S *hair is braided and tied. The children's nightdresses are made of Canton flannel, with legs and arms, covering them from the neck to the ankles, and they button at the back,* MARY'S *and* BOB'S *straight up and down, and* MILLIE'S *with a little fall behind to let down.*

UNCLE NAT, PERLEY, *and the* CHILDREN *are having a great deal of fun as the curtain goes up.*

YOUNG NAT [*Looking up from his book, as though continuing a conversation*]. I tell yeh there ain't no Santy Claus! It's y'r father and mother!

MILLIE. They is too a Santy Claus, ain't they, Uncle Nat?

UNCLE NAT. Of course there is. See here, Nat, you jest read your book. When a boy gits too big to know there ain't no Santy Claus, he ought to know enough to keep his thumb out'n the Christmas puddin'.

[YOUNG NAT *laughs and resumes his reading.*]

MILLIE. Did yeh ever see him, Uncle Nat?

UNCLE NAT. See'm? Yes, sir, I seen him—lots o' times.

BOB [*Smiling*]. When was it, Uncle Nat? [*The* CHILDREN *surround* UNCLE NAT, *scenting a story.*]

UNCLE NAT. It was a g-r-e-a-t many years ago, when I was a little boy, not near so big's as you be, Bob.

MILLIE. Was you ever as big as Bob?

UNCLE NAT. Yes, sir, an' bigger. I was as big as you be once, an' once I was as little as Mis' Pearce's new baby. [*The* CHILDREN *all laugh.*]

MILLIE. An' didn't have no more hair on yer head?

UNCLE NAT [*Chuckling*]. I hain't got much more now. [*The* CHILDREN *all laugh.*]

ANN [*Looking up from her mending*]. Now young uns, hang up yer stockin's an' go to bed, I say go to bed. [*The* CHILDREN, *all excitement, prepare to hang up their stockings.*]

BOB. I'm goin' to hang up my pants.

UNCLE NAT. You give me a piece of string an' I'll tie up one leg an' you tie up t'other, an' thet way we'll get done quicker. [BOB *ties up one leg,* UNCLE NAT *the other.*]

MILLIE [*Watching enviously*]. I wish I wore pants.

UNCLE NAT. Do yeh, Millie? Well yeh may yit afore yeh die. Don't you git discouraged. Things is comin' your way mighty fast. I tell you what you do. You give me yer petticoat and I'll tie up the skirt and make as good a bag as Bob's pants. That'll beat yer stockin's.

[*The* CHILDREN *all agree to this enthusiastically.*]

ANN [*While* UNCLE NAT *is busy tying* MILLIE'S *petticoat*]. Mary, ain't you goin' to hang up yourn?

MARY. Yes, Mother. [*With a smile.*] But I'm afeared I won't get anything.

[*The* CHILDREN *remove some towels which have been hanging on a line at the back of the stove, to make room for their stockings.*]

UNCLE NAT. Now come on, git some pins. Bob, you get some clothespins. [*They rush to* ANN, *who gives them pins.*] We'll hang Millie in the middle—jes' like a fiddle. Gimme a couple o' them pins, Mary. Bob, you go over there—[*Hanging* BOB'S *knickerbockers on the line right.*] You got the clothespins, Bob? [BOB *rushes into the woodhouse, and comes back with two clothespins.* UNCLE NAT *fastens his knickerbockers to the line with them.*] Mary, where'll you go?—oh, over here—— [*He hangs* MARY'S *stocking, left.*]

[*During this scene* PERLEY *has lighted a candle and stands waiting to show the children to bed.* ANN *watches* UNCLE NAT *and the children with amused interest.*]

UNCLE NAT. Nat, ain't you goin' to hang up?

YOUNG NAT. Naw! 'Cause I know there ain't no Santy Claus.

MILLIE [*Crossing to him and almost crying*]. They is too, Nat Berry—you won't go to heaven ef you say thet.

UNCLE NAT. He won't go to heaven at all ef he don't say his prayers. Come now, gether up yer duds an' be off to bed.

[*The* CHILDREN *all pick up their clothes and shoes.* MARY *and* BOB *say "Good night" and kiss their* UNCLE NAT, *then their father, who is moody, and their mother last. She kisses them tenderly. They go upstairs.* PERLEY *stands at the foot of the stairs, lighting them up.*]

MILLIE [*To* UNCLE NAT, *who picks her up in his arms, clothes and all*]. I wish you'd sleep with me tonight, Uncle Nat.

UNCLE NAT. Oh! My suz! I couldn't git inter *your* bed—be yeh skeered?

MILLIE. Jes' a 'ittle teeny might. [*Hides her head in his neck.*]

UNCLE NAT. No, yeh ain't nuther. Yeh jes' want t' git me to try to git my long legs inter thet trundle bed o' yourn [*puts her down*] and then kick me out on the floor like yeh did las' Sunday mornin'. But yeh ain't a-goin' to do it tomorry mornin'. [*Spanks her playfully.*] Go 'long with yeh, yeh little hypocrite.

MILLIE [*Goes over and stands by her father demurely, with her clothes under her arm*]. Good night, Papa. [MARTIN *picks her up by her elbows, takes her in his arms, and kisses her, quite tenderly, and unconsciously lets the map fall to the floor, where it lies unobserved. Then he sets* MILLIE *down and becomes once more lost in his thoughts.*]

[MILLIE *moves a few steps away from* MARTIN, *then turns and looks at him and says softly and shyly*]. I wish you a Merry Kiss'mus.

[MARTIN *makes no response, and* MILLIE *turns to* UNCLE NAT *lingeringly, as though loth to go to bed.*] I wish it was mornin' so's I could see what's in my petticoat.

UNCLE NAT [*Dogmatically*]. Oh! Yeh do—do yeh? Tell yeh what yeh do, Millie. Yeh go to bed an' sleep till mornin' and then t'will be mornin' in the mornin'.

MILLIE [*Going over to her mother*]. Good night, Mama. [*Kisses her.*]

ANN. Good night, I say good night. [*Bends over and kisses her tenderly.*]

MILLIE [*Full of Old Nick*]. Good night, Uncle Nat. [*Going to him.*]

UNCLE NAT. Good night.

MILLIE. Sleep tight.

UNCLE NAT. Go t' bed, yeh little baggage yeh! Be yeh going to bed 'r not? [*Shoos her away.*]

MILLIE [*Goes to the foot of stairs, and stops suddenly*]. Oh! Uncle Nat?

UNCLE NAT. What is it?

MILLIE [*In a mysterious whisper*]. Look what's behind yeh!

UNCLE NAT [*Entering into her play*]. Oh, I'm skeered to look—what is it?

MILLIE [*In the same manner*]. Santy Claus!

UNCLE NAT [*Pretending to be frightened, jumps*]. Where? [MILLIE *laughs.*] Ain't yeh 'shamed to skeer me like thet—I've a good mind to—— [*He runs after her, she runs and laughs.*]

MILLIE. Yeh can't ketch me! [*Laughs and runs around the table.* BOB *and* MARY *appear at the top of the stairs laughing and say "Run, Millie, quick, Millie!"* UNCLE NAT *pretends he can't catch* MILLIE.]

UNCLE NAT [*At last catching* MILLIE *by the waist of her nightdress at the back, and carrying her as he would a carpet bag. She laughs very heartily all through the scene*]. Now, my young lady, I've got yeh and I'll see whether yeh'll go to bed or not! [*Carries her upstairs triumphantly, followed by* PERLEY *with the candle. He is heard talking all the way up the stairs;* MILLIE *is laughing.*] I bet I'll put yeh to bed—or I'll know the reason why. [UNCLE NAT, PERLEY, *and the* CHILDREN *go off through the door at the top of the stairs, and their voices die away in the distance.*]

ANN [*Calling after them*]. I swan, Nathan'l, you're wuss 'n the young uns—I say wuss 'n the young uns! [*Gets up and goes to the window and looks out at the storm.*] Mussy on me, what a night! I pity anybody thet's got to be out on sech a night as this. [*She turns from the window and notices* MARTIN, *who sits brooding.*] Martin, ain't you well—I say ain't you well?

MARTIN [*Gloomily, not crossly*]. Oh yes, I s'pose I'm well enough.

ANN [*Crosses to him and smooths his hair*]. Yeh worry too much—'tain't a mite o' use to worry. I wish you'd take some o' thet pikrey—I know it'd do you good—I say I know it'd do you good.

MARTIN. I d'want n-o—pik-rey. Pikrey won't do me no good.

ANN [*Goes back to the table and resumes her work*]. Thet's jes' what Cap'n Ben Hutchins said last spring. But Liddy Ann managed to git some on't inter his vittels right along athout his knowin' of it an' it cured him. He was mad's a hornet when he found it out. I've half a mind to try it—I say, to try it.

MARTIN [*In the same manner*]. Don't you put no pikrey inter my vittels if you know when you're well off.

ANN. [*Gently, with placid confidence and assurance*]. Well, Martin, jes' as soon as you sell a few o' them lots yeh got laid off—yeh said yeh was goin' to sell a couple a hundred of 'em in the spring, didn't yeh? I say didn't yeh? [*Absorbed in her mending.*]

MARTIN [*As if evading the question*]. I said I *hoped* I'd sell some on 'em in the spring.

ANN [*Gently*]. Well I sh'd hope so, now thet you've cut the farm all up inter griddle cakes. Well soon's yeh do—I'm goin' to hev yeh go up t' Boston an' see a *reel* doctor. Not but what Dr. Leonard's good enough, but now thet we're goin' to git rich, we kin afford a little better one. You ain't right an' I know it—I say, an' I know it. [*There is a tremendous burst of laughter from upstairs. Then* UNCLE NAT *comes flying down, followed by all the clothes, shoes, etc. the children had carried up. He half falls, and lands sitting on the bottom step. The children all appear at the top of the stairs with* PERLEY, *laughing.* MARTIN *jumps.* ANN *gives a scream and rises.*] Mussy on me—I tho't 'twas an earthquake! I say an earthquake! What in time's the matter with yeh?

UNCLE NAT [*Looking up with an apologetic air*]. Me'n the children hevin' a little fun, thet's all.

ANN. I should think yeh was. [*She crosses over to the stairs and calls up to the* CHILDREN.] Ef I come up there 'th my slipper I'll give you southin' to cut up about. Go to bed this minute, every man jack o' yeh, an' don't let me hear another word out o' yeh this night. [*As* ANN *speaks there is a dead silence and the children all sneak away on tiptoe.*] Perley, come and git these duds. I say git these duds. [PERLEY *comes down and gathers up the clothes and goes off with them upstairs.* ANN *sits down to her darning again, and for the first time observes* YOUNG NAT.] Nat Berry, ben't you goin' to bed tonight?

YOUNG NAT [*Absorbed in his book; without looking up*]. Jes's soon's I finish this chapter. The Black Ranger's got the girl in his power an' Walter Danforth's on his trail.

ANN. Le'see. [*She seizes the book and becomes absorbed in it.* YOUNG NAT *thrums on the table; he is impatient, but polite; finally he falls into a reverie over what he has been reading.]*

[*During the talk between* YOUNG NAT *and his mother,* UNCLE NAT *slowly rises from the stairs. Now he goes up stage and peers out of the window, speaking as he does so.*]

UNCLE NAT. By George—we'll hev sleighin' tomorry an' *no* mistake, ef this keeps on! [*He comes down stage and addresses the rest of the speech directly to* MARTIN, *who pays no attention to him.* UNCLE NAT *takes a chair and sits a little to the right of center. He lifts his left leg with his hands to cross it over his right, but a rheumatic twinge stops him. He tries a second time, and succeeds in crossing his legs; his hands are clasped over his knee. His half-furtive glances at* MARTIN, *now and then, are full of affection and sympathy. The desire to engage his brother's attention is the persistent note of his mood, and* MARTIN'S *rebuffs only act as a stimulus to his efforts. Now he looks expectantly at* MARTIN, *who continues to ignore him. Then he becomes interested in his shoe as he detects a broken place in it. He examines it carefully, and runs his finger over it. There is a slight pause and again he resumes his efforts to break down his brother's sullen resentment. There is an intimate tone in his voice as he remarks*] I hain't seen sech a storm—not sence I d'know when. Not sence thet *big* snowstorm we had 'way back in '59. [*He looks at* MARTIN'S *blank face as if for confirmation, but there is no response.*] Thet *was* a snowstorm! Couldn't see no fences n'r nothin'. Mail didn't git along here fer more'n a week. [*He looks at* MARTIN *as before. The same forbidding mask meets his inviting smile. He shakes his foot meditatively as if to gain sympathy from it; then he gives a long sigh.*] Ol' Sam Hutchins was a-haulin' wood, an' got snowed in, an' when they dug him out he was friz stiffer'n a poker, a-settin' right on his lud. [*A pause. He steals a quick, inquiring glance at his brother's immobile face, then with the manner of one who finds himself in pleasant company, he remarks with fine unction*] I kinder like to see snow on Christmas. It kinder—I d'know—seems kinder sorter more Christmassier—somehow. [*He gives another glance at the unresponsive* MARTIN, *then he rises. He leans heavily on his right foot, then he moves the foot up and down, his shoe creaking loudly as he does so. He goes up to the window and looks out once more at the storm.*] Phew! Ain't she a-comin' down! The ol' woman up in the sky's pluckin' her geese tonight fur all she's worth an' no mistake. [*He comes down, sees the map* MARTIN *has dropped, and picks it up. He handles it as though it were something precious. He looks at it a moment, and then bends his eyes upon his brother in a fine pride, as having in this map achieved a rare and wonderful thing. Then he sets himself in the same chair as before and looks over the map.*] Treemont Str—eet. [*Tracing the map with his forefinger.*] Corn—hill Str—eet. [*With a glance of pride at* MARTIN.] Wash—in'—ton Str—eet. [*There is a long pause, then* UNCLE NAT *glances about the room.*] 'Y George, Washin'ton Street's a-goin' to run right straight through the kitchen here, ain't she? [*He looks at* MARTIN, *who, for the first time meets* UNCLE NAT'S *eye, and shifts uneasily in his chair.*] Haw—thorne Av—en—oo. [*He traces the map with his forefinger.* MARTIN *casts impatient furtive glances at him from under his eyebrows; then he gets up and goes toward* UNCLE NAT.] Hawthorne Avenoo begins at the northeast end o' the ol' barn an' runs due east to——

MARTIN [*Quietly taking the map from him, folding it up and putting it in the breast pocket of his coat*]. Ef you hain't got nuthin' better t' do than to set there a-devilin' me, I'd advise you to go to bed. [*He returns to his chair and lapses into his former mood.*]

[UNCLE NAT *and* ANN *exchange glances of wonderment and pleasure at the thought of* MARTIN'S *having spoken to* UNCLE NAT. *It is a big moment for them.* ANN *catches her breath and a look of surprise and delight crosses her face. She starts to speak, but* UNCLE NAT *motions her to be quiet by putting his right hand over his lips and waving his left hand at her for additional emphasis. Then he rises and takes a few steps toward* MARTIN. *His face is illumined and quivers with joy, he speaks feelingly.*]

UNCLE NAT. Martin—thet's the fust word you've spoke to me in over fifteen months. [MARTIN *remains stolid and silent.* UNCLE NAT *continues half sadly, half jokingly*] Don't you think I've wore black fer you long enough? [*Wistfully.*] Say, Martin, let's you and me shake hands and wish each other Merry Christmas tomorry, jes' like we used to—when we was boys together—will yeh?

MARTIN. I don't care nuthin' 'bout Christmas—one day's good another t' me.

UNCLE NAT [*Gently*]. 'Twa'n't allus so.

MARTIN. Well it's so now. Merry Christmas—Humph! I'd like t'know what I've got to be merry about.

UNCLE NAT. Yeh've got *me*—ef yeh'll hev me——

MARTIN [*Significantly*]. Humph!

UNCLE NAT. You've got Ann. [MARTIN *looks up.* UNCLE NAT *continues quickly as if he should not have said that.*] You've got the children.

MARTIN [*Half bitterly*]. Yes, till they git big enough to be some help, then they'll clear out an' leave me as their sister did.

UNCLE NAT [*Very gently*]. Now—now—now—Helen didn't clear out an' leave *you.* She never'd 'a' gone ef you hadn't 'a'—said what yeh said about——

MARTIN [*Murmurs almost inaudibly.*] There now.

UNCLE NAT [*Finishing the sentence under his breath*]. Sam Warren.

MARTIN. I don't want to git inter no argument 'th you tonight! I know what I done an' I know what *she* done.

UNCLE NAT. Yeh never will let me tell yeh nothin'.

MARTIN. I don't want to *know* nothin'——

UNCLE NAT [*With a quizzical smile*]. Well—yeh come pooty nigh a-knowin' of it. I never see a man s' fond o' huggin' a sore thumb 's you be. [*With a complete change of tone.*] Will yeh help me to fill the children's stockin's?

MARTIN [*Half softening*]. I hain't got nothin' to put in 'em.

UNCLE NAT. Well, I hain't got much, but what I hev got 's a-goin' in. Come, Ma, let's you and me play Santa Claus, then I'll go to bed. [ANN *makes no reply.* UNCLE NAT *sees that she is absorbed in her book, chuckles, and decides to leave her alone. He passes* YOUNG NAT, *flicking him on the shoulder with his handkerchief as he does so, and says*] Nat, come out in the woodhouse and lend 's a hand here, will yeh?

[UNCLE NAT *goes off into the woodhouse.* YOUNG NAT *gives his mother an impatient look, then shrugs his shoulders resignedly and follows* UNCLE NAT *off. They return almost immediately, carrying between them a large woodbasket containing a lot of bundles, which they place down center.* UNCLE NAT *sits in the same chair as before,* YOUNG NAT *kneels at his left, and they begin to undo the presents. There are dolls, slates, picture books, big candy canes, a sleigh, a pair of skates, mittens, comforters, and any quantity of cheap toys, also a new dress pattern. As the things begin to reveal themselves,* MARTIN *is interested in spite of himself.*]

YOUNG NAT [*With a note of triumph in his voice*]. I *told* yeh 't was yer father an' mother all the time.

UNCLE NAT [*Continuing with his work*]. Did yeh? Well, yeh didn't know's much as yeh thought yeh did, old smarty. It ain't yer father an' mother *this* time—it's yer Uncle Nat, by George! [*They both laugh.*]

MARTIN. I hope yeh hain't been a-runnin' yerself in debt agin fer them children.

UNCLE NAT. No, I hain't run in debt this time. I paid spot cash *this time.* Thet's how I got such good bargains. [*Shows a harlequin with a string to make it jump.*] Jes' look at thet now fer five cents. [*Pulls the string and laughs.*] It's wuth more'n thet to see Millie pull the string jes' once. [*Chuckling.*]

MARTIN. I didn't know yeh had any money by yeh.

UNCLE NAT. I hadn't. I got Blake t' cash my pension warrant. [*He says this without making any boast of it.*]

MARTIN. An' spent the hull on't on the young uns as usual, I s'pose.

UNCLE NAT [*Still busy with the things; in a matter-of-fact tone*]. Yep!

MARTIN. *Eight dollars* on sech foolishness—it's wicked.

UNCLE NAT [*For the first time stopping his work and looking up*]. Say, what d'yeh s'pose I stood up to be shot at fer thirteen dollars a month fer, ef it wa'n't t' hev a little fun on my income? Think I'm a-carryin' around this bullet in my shoulder all these years f'r nuthin'? Not much, Johnny Roach! [*Goes back to his work.*]

MARTIN [*Gently*]. Yeh might 'a' bought yerself an overcut——

UNCLE NAT. Overcut—such weather as this? [*Holding up a candy cane.*] Not while candy canes is a-sellin' b'low cost. What's the matter with the one I've got?

MARTIN. Thet ol' army cut? It's patched from one end to t'other.

UNCLE NAT. Thet makes it all the warmer. [*With humor.*] 'Sides, yeh mustn't never despise a man jes' 'cause he wears a ragged cut.

ANN [*Slamming the book shut with a sense of supreme satisfaction*]. There! Ef ever a mean, contemptible houn' got his jest deserts thet Black Ranger got his'n—I say thet Black Ranger got his'n. Walter Danforth jes'——

YOUNG NAT [*With loud protest*]. Oh, *Mother,* don't tell! I want to read it myself. [*Goes back to the table, sits down, and resumes reading.*]

ANN. I swan ef I didn't forgit it was Christmas Eve—an' all about the stockin's. Nat Berry—don't you ever bring another one o' them books inside these doors when I've got work to do. [*Jumps up and begins helping* UNCLE NAT.] Ain't thet a pooty dolly—I say a pooty dolly!

[*They now proceed to fill the* CHILDREN'S *clothes, and hang things on the outside of them. There must be enough stuff to pack them. At the same time footsteps are heard on the porch outside, there is a stamping of feet as if to knock off the snow, and* BLAKE *enters. The snow drifts in as he opens the door and the wind howls. He is covered with snow and well muffled up.* MARTIN, *who has been half interested in the business of the Christmas presents, rises.* ANN *and* UNCLE NAT *stop in their work.* YOUNG NAT *looks up from his reading.* UNCLE NAT *takes the empty basket and puts it back in the woodhouse.*]

BLAKE. Too blizzardy to stop to knock. By George, what a night! I hain't seen such a storm since I dunno when. [*He is about to shake the snow from his clothing when* ANN *stops him.*]

ANN. Don't shake it off on my clean floor, Mr. Blake. Nathan'l, git a broom.

[UNCLE NAT *gets the broom, takes* BLAKE *upstage and sweeps the snow from his clothes, as the dialogue continues.*

[PERLEY *comes downstairs with the lighted candle and puts it on the table. Then she crosses over to help with the presents.*]

BLAKE. Didn't think I'd ever git here—by George. The snow's waist deep—[*To* UNCLE NAT.] Thank yeh, thet'll do I guess.

UNCLE NAT [*Hanging up the broom*].

Set down by the fire an' warm yerself. [*He places a chair for* BLAKE.] Ef yer feet are cold stick 'em in the oven an' toast 'em a bit.

BLAKE. I'll thaw out my back first. [*Stands in front of the stove with his coat tails drawn apart and warms his back.* UNCLE NAT *and* ANN *resume their work,* PERLEY *helping them.* BLAKE *observes them a moment in silence.*] Well, y're at it I see. [*He watches them with a tinge of sadness in his face.*]

UNCLE NAT. Yep! Christmas only comes oncet a year, y'know, in this family.

ANN [*Displaying the dress pattern*]. Thet's a-goin' to make Millie an awful pooty dress. Nathan'l, what was thet a yard?

UNCLE NAT. I d'know—I never ask no prices.

ANN [*Contemplating the dress pattern*]. Won't Millie be proud o' thet! I'll have it made up jes' 's stylish 's kin be. [*Puts it in* MILLIE'S *skirt, or beneath it.*] I say jes' 's stylish 's kin be.

UNCLE NAT. I heerd yeh—I *heard* yeh——

BLAKE. By George, Martin, I'd give all I'm wuth in the world to hev jes' *one* stockin' a-hangin' in my chimney corner tonight.

ANN. You'd ought t' got married long ago, Mr. Blake.

BLAKE. I never saw but one girl wuth *hevin'* and she wouldn't hev *me*. [*Sighing.*] I'll never git married now.

ANN. It must be kinder lunsome athout no children nor nothin', specially at Christmas. I say at Christmas.

BLAKE. I never noticed how lunsome it was till I see you a-fillin' them stockin's. I've ben s' busy all my life makin' *money* I hain't hed time to git lunsome. Now I'm gittin' old, I begin to see thet p'r'aps I might—— [*He shakes off his retrospective mood.*] Oh, Martin! [*He sets a chair down stage in front of* MARTIN, *sits astride it, and leans his hands on the back. They talk in low tones while* ANN, PERLEY, *and* UNCLE NAT *continue their work.* BLAKE'S *tone now is tense and low.*] Did you hear about the Land Company's bustin'?

MARTIN [*Alarmed*]. Bustin'? What? When? How? [*He starts to rise.* BLAKE *motions him back in his chair and hushes him.*]

BLAKE [*As if discharging a disagreeable duty*]. Sh! Yes sir, busted cleaner'n a whistle. Opposition fellers done it. They've bought up Lemoine, an' thrown it on the Boston market way down. Got a lot of Boston big bugs goin' to build there soon's the weather breaks.

MARTIN. Then *your* boom's over?

BLAKE. Yes, for five years anyway. [*Apologetically.*] Folks ain't a-goin' to come here when they can go to Lemoine for the same money'r less.

MARTIN [*With finality*]. An' I'm ruined.

BLAKE [*Really sorry*]. Looks thet way—now—I'm sorry to say.

MARTIN [*Slowly*]. With my farm mortgaged to you for fifteen hundred dollars, an' the money spent in cuttin' it up inter buildin' lots. [BLAKE *drums on the back of the chair with his fingers.* MARTIN *rises as if to spring at him and says between his teeth but in a low tone.*] Damn you—I——

BLAKE [*Quieting him in the same way as before*]. Hol' on. [*Points to* ANN *and* UNCLE NAT.] Yeh don't want them t' know, do yeh?

MARTIN [*Sinking back in his chair and covering his face with his hands*]. No, not tonight, don't tell 'em tonight.

[HELEN *and* SAM *appear at the window.* HELEN *has a baby in her arms.* UNCLE NAT *looks up, sees them, gives a start.*]

UNCLE NAT. Oh! My! [*They cross the window and disappear.*]

ANN. What in time is the matter with you?

[BLAKE *looks up,* MARTIN *does not stir.*]

UNCLE NAT. A tech of rheumatiz I guess. [*Rubs his shoulder.*]

ANN. La! You sot my heart right in my mouth.

[BLAKE *resumes his former attitude,* UNCLE NAT *whispers in* ANN's *ear. She starts to scream, and he claps his hand over her mouth then he motions her toward the woodhouse door.* ANN *runs out.* PERLEY *comes over to* UNCLE NAT *to find out what is the matter. He whispers to her also, she gives a little scream and he claps his hand over her mouth and cautions her to be quiet.* UNCLE NAT *goes out through the woodhouse door, followed by* PERLEY. *All this is unobserved by* BLAKE *and* MARTIN.]

BLAKE [*In an undertone to* MARTIN; *this can just be heard by the audience*]. Don't worry, Martin, mebbe things'll come out all right.

[MARTIN *shakes his head without looking up.*]

BLAKE. All yeh've got to do is to keep up the interest—y'know.

MARTIN [*Without looking up*]. Interest—how'm I goin' t' pay interest an' the farm all cut up?

BLAKE. I know, it's goin' to be a tough job. You'll hev to begin all over agin—seed down the avenoos—cut down the shade trees—an' plow up the hotel site.

[*Enter* UNCLE NAT *from the woodhouse, carrying a baby, and followed by* ANN. MARTIN *and* BLAKE *are so absorbed in their talk that they do not see them.*]

MARTIN. I wish you'd ben struck dumb afore ever you come here to set us all by the ears with y'r blame land scheme—I hain't had a minute's peace sence you fust put it inter my head.

BLAKE [*Good-naturedly*]. Thet's right, blame me. *Blame me.*

MARTIN [*Flaming up in bitterness*]. Who else *should* I blame? Ef it hadn't 'a' ben fer you, I'd 'a' ben satisfied as I was. [UNCLE NAT *comes to center and* ANN *takes the baby, takes the shawl from around it and hands it back to* UNCLE NAT, *who comes slowly down center.*] Helen'd never left hum ef it hadn't 'a' ben fer you—— [*Raising his head aloft.*] I wish I was dead. I'm ashamed to look my wife an' children in the face. [*Just at this moment he sees* UNCLE NAT, *who has been drawing near, the baby in his arms.* MARTIN *rises, and pauses, startled.*] What's thet——?

UNCLE NAT [*Beaming, his voice almost choking with joy*]. Kinder sorter looks like a baby—don't it——?

MARTIN [*Puzzled*]. Whose is it?

UNCLE NAT [*Looking down at the baby and rocking it back and forth in his arms*]. I d'know's I jes know!

MARTIN [*Looks all round the room*]. Where'd it come from?

UNCLE NAT. I got it—out on the doorstep jes' now.

MARTIN. Well, put it right straight back on the doorstep—I ain't the poormaster.

UNCLE NAT. This baby ain't lookin' fer no poorhouse—this baby's goin' to stay right here.

MARTIN. There's too many babies here now.

UNCLE NAT. No there ain't nuther. Yeh can't hev too many babies in a home. [*He crosses and sits in chair center, and rocks the baby in his arms.*]

BLAKE [*Hungrily, coming forward*]. Give it to me. By George, I'll take it!

ANN [*Coming down to* MARTIN, *and speaking gently, her voice full of tears*]. Martin, won't yeh guess whose baby this is?

MARTIN. I ain't a-guessin' babies.

ANN [*Twining her arms around his neck*]. Guess this one, jes' fer me, Martin. Jes' as a sort of a Christmas present.

MARTIN [*Looks at her earnestly, then says softly*]. Tain't—Nell's——?

ANN [*Drops her eyes to the floor,*

afraid of how he will take her answer]. Yes—It's poor Nell's.

MARTIN [*In a fierce loud whisper*]. Poor Nell's? Yeh don't mean to say thet he didn't marry her?

[UNCLE NAT *draws the baby close to his breast as if to shield it from even that thought.*]

ANN. Oh yes, Martin, he married her.

MARTIN [*Misinterpreting her words and her action, aghast, slowly, in a loud whisper*]. You don't mean to say she's *dead?*

ANN. No, Martin, she ain't dead.

MARTIN [*After a pause*]. Where is she?

ANN [*Points to the woodhouse*]. Out there.

[MARTIN *looks from* ANN *to* UNCLE NAT, *and back to* ANN. *Then he walks slowly up stage toward the woodhouse. At the door he pauses, hesitates, and finally says*]. Nathan'l—be keerful—don't drop that baby. [*He goes slowly out through the woodhouse door.*]

[UNCLE NAT, *still seated, continues to rock the baby back and forth,* ANN *looks down into the baby's face.* BLAKE *goes to the stove and stands with his back to it, and his coattails parted behind him, absorbed in thought.*]

UNCLE NAT [*As* MARTIN *goes out, with quiet, sly humor*]. I've held you many a time an' I never dropped you. [*Pause.*] Well, Ma, I s'pose you're awful proud 'cause you're a gran'mother. [*Reflectively.*] Seems only the day 'fore yist'day sence Nell was a baby herself.

[*The woodhouse door opens and* MARTIN *enters slowly, leading* HELEN *by the hand. She looks dazed, but very happy to be back in her home. They are followed by* SAM, *now a bearded handsome man who appears to be perfectly happy and gratified that* HELEN'S *wish to bring her baby home has been fulfilled.* SAM *has returned from the West a prosperous, successful man; they are both well dressed and have an air of achievement.* PERLEY *follows* SAM *into the room, her face beaming with joy. There is a long pause; everybody's eyes are on* MARTIN *and* HELEN. *He leads her proudly and slowly down the stage before he speaks.*]

MARTIN. Nell—my girl—I'm glad to see yeh back, thet's all I got to say.

[*It is with difficulty that* MARTIN *can get these words out. Tears are in his eyes and voice. He kisses her.* BLAKE *has been standing spellbound, and now he blows his nose to hide his emotion.* HELEN *creeps into her father's embrace, puts her arms around his neck, and looks pleadingly first at him and then at* SAM, *as though to say "Father, haven't you got a word for Sam?"* MARTIN'S *gaze follows hers and he sees* SAM. HELEN *draws away a little and* MARTIN *moves toward* SAM. ANN *goes to* HELEN *and puts her arms about her; both women are tense, expectantly waiting to see what* MARTIN *will do.*]

MARTIN [*Making a big effort to conquer his pride*]. Sam, I don't b'lieve I acted jes's a father ought to hev acted towards Nell, an' I didn't treat you quite right I know—I—— [*Hesitantly stretches out his hand which* SAM *takes in a hearty grasp, and the two men shake hands.*]

[ANN *and* HELEN, *in great relief, embrace each other joyously.*]

SAM [*In a big warmhearted manner*]. Oh! That's all right, Mr. Berry! You didn't quite understand me, that's all.

MARTIN [*Introspectively*]. Thet must 'a' ben it, I didn't understand yeh. [*Then with a complete change of manner* MARTIN *turns briskly to* UNCLE NAT, *who is still seated in the chair nursing the baby, and in an almost boyish manner, says to him with an air of ownership*] Give me thet baby!

[*During the scene* HELEN *and* SAM *go up left center to* YOUNG NAT *and greet him affectionately. He proudly displays his long trousers. Then they turn to* PERLEY, *who stands above the table and greet her warmly. She helps* HELEN *off with her things, also takes* SAM'*s hat and coat and hangs them up on the pegs beside the woodhouse door.*]

UNCLE NAT [*Imperturbably*]. No sir, this baby goes right straight back on the doorstep where it come from——

MARTIN. Give me thet baby I tell yeh——

UNCLE NAT [*Rocking the baby in his arms*]. No sir! there's too many babies here now. This ain't no poorhouse.

MARTIN. You give me thet baby.

UNCLE NAT [*Getting up and handing him the baby*]. All right—take y'r ol' baby—I'm durned ef I don't hev a baby o' my own one o' these days—yeh see ef I don't—an' then I'm durned ef I'll lend her to any of yeh—— [*He goes up stage.*]

[*During the next scene,* ANN *goes up stage, pokes the fire, and puts the kettle, which is on the back of the stove, in one of the front holes, where it at once begins to sing; she bustles about, gets the tea-pot and makes some tea.* MARTIN *is standing center, holding the baby in his arms, with* SAM *on one side and* HELEN *on the other.*]

MARTIN [*Looking down at the baby*]. How old is it?

HELEN. Three months last Sunday.

MARTIN. Thet so? [*Looking down at it and smiling proudly.*] It's a pooty baby. [*A pause.*] What is it?

SAM [*Proudly*]. Boy!

MARTIN. Thet so? [*Glancing up.*] H-h-hev—yeh—named him yit?

HELEN. Sam calls him Martin.

MARTIN. Thet so! [*Calls to* UNCLE NAT, *full of pride.*] Nathan'l, he's a boy an' his name's Martin.

UNCLE NAT. Oh! Good Lord! I knowed all 'bout thet long ago. [*Sits in the rocking-chair.*]

MARTIN. Thet so—I thought I was tellin' yeh news.

UNCLE NAT. Yeh wa'n't tellin' me no news, was he, Nell?

HELEN. No, indeed.

MARTIN. Gimme that rockin' chair.

UNCLE NAT [*Getting up from the rocking chair and placing it in the middle of the stage*]. Give him the rockin' chair —he's a grandfather. He owns the *house* now——

[MARTIN *seats himself in the rocking chair with the baby on his knee.* UNCLE NAT *sits in the chair down right formerly occupied by* MARTIN.]

ANN [*Bringing the pot of tea and cups and saucers over to the table*]. Here, Hel'n, you an' Sam drink this cup o' tea.

[HELEN *and* SAM *sit down at the table,* SAM *at the upper end and* HELEN *on his right.* YOUNG NAT *is seated on the left of the table. During the preceding scene,* BLAKE *has been hovering on the outskirts of the group, forgotten for the moment by all, profoundly moved at what is taking place. He now musters up his courage to speak to* SAM.]

BLAKE. Dr. Warren! Oh, Dr. Warren!

SAM [*Rises and goes to him*]. Hello, Mr. Blake. Helen, here's Mr. Blake.

HELEN [*Bows pleasantly*]. Why, how do you do, Mr. Blake?

BLAKE. Oh, I'm feeling pretty good for an old man. [*Turning to* SAM.] Dr. Warren, I'm awfully ashamed of the part I had in drivin' you away. It was small potatoes an' few in a hill.

SAM [*With the same hearty manner in which he spoke to* MARTIN]. Oh, that's all right, Mr. Blake. You folks around here didn't understand fellows like me, that's all.

BLAKE. Well, I'm ashamed of it all the same. [*He crosses to* HELEN.] Helen —I mean Mrs. Warren—will you shake hands with me?

HELEN. Why certainly, Mr. Blake. [*They shake hands.*] Oh, by the way, Mr. Blake, did you ever find out who stole your hundred dollars that time?

[*All listen.*]

BLAKE [*Ashamed*]. Well to tell the truth it never *was* stole.

ALL. What!

HELEN [*Amazed*]. Never was stolen?

BLAKE. No! We found it stuck away in the back part o' the safe—among a lot of papers.

YOUNG NAT [*Rising and standing left below the table, half grinning and half ashamed, with a sort of bravado*]. That was some o' *my* work. I hid it there.

HELEN. You——?

ANN. You—what fer—I say what fer?

YOUNG NAT [*Half crying*]. I wanted to git even with Sam Warren fer pullin' my ear—I heerd him ask Mr. Blake fer a hundred dollars an' I hid the package. I was sorry the minute I done it and I'd 'a' told long ago only I was afraid of a lickin'.

ANN. Well, I swan to goodness ef you ain't wuss'n the Black Ranger—I say wuss'n the Black Ranger! G' long up to bed this minute an' not a dough-nut nor a mouthful o' pie do you git fer a week—I say fer a week!

YOUNG NAT [*Picking up his book, and taking the candle which* PERLEY *hands him, crying*]. I won't stay here after tomorry—you see if I do—I'll go out West an' be a cowboy 'r somethin'—you see if I don't! [*He stamps upstairs in a rage.*]

ANN [*Calling after him*]. Gimme thet book—I say gimme thet book!

YOUNG NAT [*At the top of the stairs, throws the book, which almost strikes* PERLEY]. Take yer ol' book! I don't want it! [*He tramps off, banging the door.*]

ANN. Perley—put thet book in the fire. [PERLEY *picks up the book, starts to the stove with it, opens it, becomes absorbed in it, backs to the small rocking chair above the table, sits down, and reads it.*] Martin Berry, be you a-goin' to let thet boy go out West an' be a cowboy or somethin'—I say or somethin'? [*Her voice rises in an angry shriek.*]

UNCLE NAT [*Who is still seated down right*]. You set him to milkin' ol' Brindle tomorry—she'll knock all the cowboy out'n him.

[*They all laugh.*]

BLAKE. Meanness is like a kickin' gun, ain't it? A feller never knows when it's goin' to knock him over.

MARTIN [*Curiously*]. Ef it's a fair question, Sam, where did yeh git the hundred dollars yeh went away with?

SAM [*Pointing to* UNCLE NAT]. Didn't he ever tell you?

UNCLE NAT. I let him hev ninety-two dollars an' eight cents of it.

MARTIN [*Surprised*]. Where'd *you* get it?

UNCLE NAT. I borrowed the ninety-two dollars. Borrowed it off'n you an' me an' Mother. I knowed Mother wouldn't mind waitin' a month or two longer an'—it's all paid back long ago, Martin. It's in the ol' bean pot in the pantry there. [*To* BLAKE.] Mr. Blake, thet was the speckled pullet thet fell into the rain barrel thet time.

BLAKE. Well, I don't know as it's goin' to do any good to stand here callin' ourselves hard names. Martin, I wish you'd let me hold thet baby jes' a minute.

[SAM *leans over to* HELEN *as if to say "Don't let him, he might drop it."*]

MARTIN. No, *sir*——

ANN. Be keerful, you ain't used to handlin' babies, Mr. Blake, I say babies.

BLAKE. I suppose I could learn, same's the rest of yeh, if I had a chance, couldn't I? [*He takes the baby carefully in his arms, and looks lovingly at it.*] Mrs. Warren, I hope you won't bias me with the Junior here—I feel's if me an' the Junior was goin' to be great cronies. [*Leans over the baby.*] Look here, if they're mean to you here, you jes' come up to Blake's an' yeh can hev all the candy an' apples an' crackers yeh can lug off.

UNCLE NAT [*With concern*]. See here, Blake, you mustn't go to feedin' thet baby on green apples up to thet store——

BLAKE [*To* HELEN, *a little wistfully*]. I suppose I can come over an' see him once in a while?

HELEN. Certainly!

BLAKE. Thank yeh. [*He looks at her.* ANN *comes and takes the baby. A knock is heard at the door, right.*]

ANN. Come in—I say, come in.

[*Enter* GATES *and* MANDY, *both muffled up to their chins in worn, ragged garments, and covered with snow.* MANDY'S *eyes instantly fall on the presents hanging by the stove, and throughout the scene she continues to stare wistfully at them.*]

GATES [*Speaking as he enters*]. How d'do? [*He sees* HELEN *and* SAM, *and his tone changes to one of surprise.*] Why, *how*' d'do? I'd no idee *you'd* got back. Ef I'd 'a' knowed thet, I'd ben over afore —— [*He sees* ANN *with the baby in her arms.*] What's thet?

ANN. A baby—what'd yeh suppose 'twas? [*She crosses down left and seats herself in a low chair by the sitting room door, rocking the baby on her knees.* UNCLE NAT *goes back to his work with the presents.*]

GATES [*Confusedly*]. I wa'n't supposin' nothin'. I hadn't heerd any rumors afloat 'bout your havin'—— [*The mistake dawns upon the characters, who look from one to the other and burst into a laugh, not sudden, but gradual.* GATES *is nonplussed.*] Uh—whose is it?

HELEN. Mine.

GATES. *Yourn?* Well, who'd ever 'a' thought o' *your* havin' a baby? I tell yeh what, Nathan'l, thet West *is* a growin' country an' *no* mistake! [*To* ANN.] I jes' come over to see ef I could leave Mandy here a spell tomorry—I got a job over t' Pearce's thet's *got* to be done tomorry, an' they got measles over there an' I'm skeered to take'r with me——

ANN. What'n the name o' common sense'd yer want to fetch'r out such a night's this fur? D'yeh want to kill'r—I say kill'r?

GATES. Kill'r? Gosh, I guess not. [*He pats* MANDY *lovingly.*] She wouldn't stay t'hum.

ANN. Lunsome I guess, I say lunsome.

GATES. I guess'o—she's allus lunsome. Seems lunsomer Christmasses than any other time.

ANN. Let'r stay here now. She can sleep with the children, I say with the children.

GATES. Want to, Mandy? [*She looks up at him, he leans down to her and she whispers in his ear. With an apologetic smile*] Says she'd ruther sleep with me.

ANN. Well, she mustn't be lunsome tomorry—she must come over an' spend this Christmas with us——

UNCLE NAT [*Coming down from the stove, where he has been working with the presents, with a doll which he gives to* MANDY]. Here's a dolly fer yeh, Mandy. This's goin' t'be the jolliest Christmas we've had fer many a year.

MARTIN [*Suddenly remembering*]. An' the last one we'll ever hev in this ol' house.

SAM. The last—I hope not.

HELEN [*At the same time*]. Why, Father, what do you mean?

[UNCLE NAT *looks at* MARTIN *in amazement.*]

MARTIN. My durn land boom's busted.

ANN [*Looking over at him full of sympathy*]. An' thet's what's been a-worryin' of yeh! Poor Martin, I say poor Martin!

[*All the faces change; all are silent for a moment.*]

GATES [*Tc* BLAKE]. Is thet *so?*

BLAKE [*Earnestly and sympathetically*]. That's 'bout so.

GATES. Then yeh ain't a-goin' t'build thet there Opperry House?

BLAKE. Well—no—not right off—I guess.

GATES. Sorry. I'd like t'seen thet Opperry House. Them plans was beautiful. Knocks me out'n a job too—[*Chuckles.*] I guess I got 'bout th' unly farm in the county thet hain't ben surveyed 'r cut up fer sumpthin' 'r other.

[UNCLE NAT *places a chair for him, right center.* GATES *sits with* MANDY *standing between his knees.* UNCLE NAT *goes back to his work.*]

MARTIN. Hel'n, I'm poorer'n I was the day I come into the world. Blake owns "Shore Acres" now—or will by spring when his mortgage comes due.

SAM. How much is it mortgaged for, Mr. Berry?

BLAKE. All it's wuth.

ANN. Fifteen hundred dollars!

MARTIN. It'd take me ten years to lift it.

GATES [*Shakes his head*]. Yeh, couldn't do it in ten year. [*Reflectively.*] No *sir*—fifteen hundred dollars!

[*During the above scene* SAM *has been talking to* HELEN *in a whisper, unheard by the audience.*]

SAM. Nell, what d'you say if we mortgage our home and lend the money to your father?

HELEN [*Delighted*]. Of course—that's the thing to do——

SAM. We may lose it——

HELEN. No we won't—and if we do we're young—we'll get another.

SAM. Shall I tell him——?

HELEN. Yes.

SAM. All right, here goes. [*Aloud.*] Father—I mean Mr. Berry—we can help you *some.* We can reduce the principal a little and keep up the interest for you. Nell and I have scraped a little home together out there. We'd hate to lose it, but we'll borrow what we can on it and——

MARTIN [*Deeply moved*]. No—you shan't do thet—let the ol' place go——

SAM. Come out West with us and make a fresh start.

HELEN [*Eagerly*]. Oh yes, Father—do!

MARTIN. No, I'm 'feared I hain't got spunk enough. I'll stay here. Mother'n the children an' Nathan'l can go ef they've a mind to——

ANN [*Her voice breaking*]. Martin Berry, I didn't marry yeh to leave yeh. I'll stay right here with yeh. We'll live in the lighthouse ef we hev to, I say, ef we hev to.

UNCLE NAT [*In a gentle drawl*]. Well, ef you think yeh're a-goin' to get red o' me—yeh're mighty much mistaken. Mother allus told me to watch out fer yeh, an' now by George thet yeh're gettin' into yer secon' childhood, I'm a-goin' to do it——

SAM. Mr. Blake won't foreclose—will you, Mr. Blake?

BLAKE [*Regretfully*]. I'm sorry, but it's out o' my hands. I'm as bad off as Martin is. I've bought, and mortgaged, and borrowed on everything I had—I can't realize fifty cents on the dollar. I'm simply land poor. Interest a-eatin' me up, principal a-comin' due—I don't know which way to turn. My lawyers advise me to make an assignment the first o' the year. Well, I guess I'll be a-joggin' along hum——

UNCLE NAT. What's yer hurry, Mr. Blake?

BLAKE [*With a big sigh*]. Well—it's a-gettin' late—an' I don't feel jes' right somehow—— [*He gets into his coat and hat,* UNCLE NAT *helping him.*]

HELEN. Better let Sam prescribe for you, Mr. Blake.

BLAKE [*Glancing at her and then at the baby, says gently*] He *has*—that's what ails me I guess.

John Henry (Manly), Mrs. Morris (Charlotte), Thomas Wignell (Jonathan), Owen Morris (Van Rough), Lewis Hallam (Dimple) in *The Contrast,* Act V. Jonathan: "I feel chock-full of fight,—do you want to kill the colonel?——" (See p. 45) Drawn from the original production by William Dunlap.

Top panel: Robert Fischer (Martin) and James A. Herne (Uncle Nat) in *Shore Acres,* Act III, Scene 1. Uncle Nat: "I give yeh the mother, but I'm damned ef I'm a-goin' to let yeh murder the child!" (See p. 88); Act II. Uncle Nat: "Who sot these cranberries on the back of the stove?" (See p. 70); Act I. Uncle Nat: "Ef I was yer father, Nell?" (See p. 51). Bottom panel: Act IV. Martin: "She'd ought to 'a' had you. 'Twan't jes' right somehow——" (See p. 105)

Henry Miller (Ghent) and Margaret Anglin (Ruth) in *The Great Divide,* Act II. Ruth: "I held myself so dear!" (See p. 128) Photograph from the William Seymour Theatre Collection, Princeton University Library.

Louis Wolheim (Yank) in *The Hairy Ape,* Scene 1. An action photograph of the original performance by the Provincetown Players. (See p. 141) Photograph by Francis Brugière.

Humphrey Bogart (Duke), Blanche Sweet (Mrs. Chisholm), Leslie Howard (Squier), and Peggy Conklin (Gabby) in *The Petrified Forest,* Act II. Mrs. Chisholm: "You haven't the remotest conception of what's inside me . . ." (See p. 201) Photograph by Vandamm.

Anthony Ross (Jim), Laurette Taylor (Amanda), Eddie Dowling (Tom), and Julie Hayden (Laura) in *The Glass Menagerie,* Act II, Scene 8. Jim: "Here's to the old South." (See p. 249) Performance photograph, courtesy of the Theater Collection, the New York Public Library.

SAM. I can fetch you around all right, Mr. Blake.

BLAKE [*Hunting in his coat pockets for his gloves, and laughing in an effort to assume his old, cheery manner*]. What with, sugar shot? No, by George, I hain't got t' thet yet—— [*He pulls out his gloves, and with them a letter post-marked and stamped, and addressed to* NATHANIEL BERRY.] Oh, Nathan'l, here's a letter come for you this evenin'. It's postmarked Washington, D.C. Weather bein' so bad I thought I'd bring it over.

UNCLE NAT [*Taking letter, mildly surprised and interested*]. Much obleeged, but I dunno who'd write me from Washington.

ANN. The Pres'dent mebbe, wishin' yeh a Merry Christmas.

GATES. Yes! The Pres'dent ginerally wishes everybody a Merry Christmas—specially ef it's a-comin' on election time.

UNCLE NAT [*Turning the letter over and over*]. Nell, would you mind a-readin' this? Your eyes is younger'n mine. [*Gives her the letter.*]

HELEN [*Opens the letter and reads it aloud. The letter is written on a letter sheet with a small printed heading, such as is used by attorneys at law, not a commercial letterhead*]. "Washington, D.C., December 18, 1892. Nathaniel Berry Esquire, Berry, Maine. Sir: Dr. Samuel Warren of Trinidad, Colorado, some months ago commissioned us to present your claim to back pension. We are pleased to inform you that our efforts on your behalf have been successful and that your claim amounting to $1,768.92 has been finally allowed. We have this day written Dr. Warren. Awaiting your further pleasure, we are. Very truly yours, Higgins and Wells, Attorneys at law."

Oh! Uncle Nat!

[*There is a general murmur of amazement.*]

UNCLE NAT [*Who is standing beside* HELEN]. Well, I won't tech it. I d'want no back pension, an' I don't want nothin' to do with no durn lawyers. A pension grabber's next thing to a bounty jumper, an' I'll be jiggered ef I tech it.

ANN [*Still sitting down left with the baby*]. Why not? I say why not?

UNCLE NAT. 'Cause I never fit fer no back pension. I fit—'Cause—— [*He catches* ANN's *eye and stops.* ANN *looks at him significantly, and then at* MARTIN, *who sits, the picture of dejection.* UNCLE NAT *glances around at the others, and reads the same implication in all their eyes. He wavers and finishes lamely.*] 'Cause I fit.

ANN. Yeh airned it—didn't yeh? I say yeh airned it?

SAM. You know there's a good deal of difference between earning a pension and grabbing a pension.

GATES. Oh! My—yes—heaps. Seems to me—ef I was you—— [*No one pays any attention to* GATES *and his voice trails off into silence.*]

UNCLE NAT. Thet's so—I didn't think o' thet. Le's see— [*His face is illumined with a rarely beautiful smile.*] Tomorry's Christmas, ain't it? Ma, I hain't made you a *reel* Christmas present—not sence the day you was merried, hev I?

ANN [*Smiling at him*]. Thet wa'n't Christmas.

UNCLE NAT [*Chuckling*]. Jes' as good —wa'n't it? I'll tell yeh what I'll do—ef Martin'll make the place over to you—I'll take the back pension.

MARTIN [*Broken and greatly touched by* UNCLE NAT's *generosity*]. I'd know as I've got a right to say either yes or no. I'll do whatever you and Mother wants I should. I hain't got a word to say.

UNCLE NAT [*Going to* MARTIN *and clapping him on the back*]. Yeh don't need to say another word, Martin, not another blessed word. [*Turning to* HELEN.] Helen, git me ol' Uncle Sam'l. Say, Martin, Uncle Sam'l's the gal thet won the pension, an' she's the feller thet ought to hev it. [HELEN *brings the gun down to* UNCLE NAT, *who is standing center. He takes it, and speaks to it affectionately, half crying, half laughing.*] Well, ol' gal, yeh've got yer deserts at last. Yeh not only saved the Union, but, by gosh, yeh've saved this hull family! [*Still holding the gun,* UNCLE NAT *starts to go through the Manual of Arms, while* GATES *watches him and imitates him.*] Attention! [*He comes stiffly to attention.* GATES *does the same.*] Shoulder-r-r Arms! [*He brings the gun to his shoulder.* GATES *pretends to do the same thing.*] Carr-r-r-y Arms! Pre-e-sent Arms!

[*As* UNCLE NAT *starts to present arms, the gun goes off suddenly. It must be loaded so as to make a great smoke and not too much noise. There is a movement of general excitement and panic.* HELEN'S *first thought is for her baby, and she rushes over to* ANN *and takes it in her arms.* GATES *picks up* MANDY, *heels in the air, and head down, and rushes to the door, right, as if to save her anyway. He stands frantically pawing the door in the attempt to find the latch and escape with* MANDY *out of harm's way, giving frightened little gasps as he does so. As the smoke clears away, the others all gather around* UNCLE NAT, *who explains that the explosion was an accident. They are all excitedly talking and laughing, and completely oblivious of* GATES, *who, as the panic dies down, comes to his senses and turns his attention to* MANDY. *She is completely enveloped in her wraps and he has some difficulty in getting her right side up. When he finally discovers her feet, he sets her on the ground, frees her head from its wrappings, smooths her hair, feels her body to assure himself that no bones are broken, kisses her, and croons over her.* UNCLE NAT, *still holding the gun, comes down to him, and starts to explain, but, at his approach* GATES *has another attack of fright, and seizing* MANDY, *he starts to back toward the door, waving* UNCLE NAT *away.*]

UNCLE NAT [*Laughing*]. That's the fust time Uncle Sam'l ever kicked me!

GATES [*Putting his fingers in his ears*]. Gosh, that deefened me! [*Then, as if to test his hearing, he cries*] Oh! Oh! Oh!

[*Everyone laughs. They have all recovered their spirits as readily as they became depressed.*]

BLAKE [*Who has got to the door by this time*]. Well, good night. [*He goes out.*]

GATES [*Who is still nervous*]. I go your way a piece, Mr. Blake. [*He hurries after* BLAKE, *dragging* MANDY *with him.* UNCLE NAT *shows them out, closes the door and locks it after them.*]

ALL [*Calling after them*]. Good night, good night.

ANN. Come now, it's bedtime, I say bedtime.

[*There is a general movement.* UNCLE NAT *puts the gun away, then he turns and begins the task of locking up for the night, plodding slowly and methodically about the room.* PERLEY *lights a candle, and goes upstairs and off.* ANN *lights a candle which she leaves on the table for* UNCLE NAT, *and picks up the lamp. She and* HELEN *move toward the door down left.*]

HELEN. Yes—I'm pretty tired. Shall we sleep in my old room?

ANN. O'course.

HELEN [*As she goes off left*]. Are all the children well?

ANN [*Following* HELEN *off*]. You'd 'a' thought so if you'd seen'm trainin' around here this evenin' [*outside*] with Nathan'l.

[SAM *and* MARTIN *come down left, following* ANN *and* HELEN. MARTIN *has his arm around* SAM'S *shoulders.*]

MARTIN. So you're a-doin' well out there, eh Sam?

SAM. First rate. That's country for a young man.

MARTIN. I s'pose 'tis. Chicago must be a great city.

SAM. A wonderful city. Why don't you come out for the World's Fair? [*He goes off through the door lower left.* MARTIN *pauses at the door, turns, and looks at* UNCLE NAT.]

MARTIN [*In a low voice*]. Nathan'l. [UNCLE NAT *looks up.*] Yeh never told Ann about that night in the lighthouse —did yeh?

UNCLE NAT [*Coming down a few steps toward him; in a deep whisper*]. I never told her nothin'.

MARTIN [*After a pause*]. She'd ought to 'a' had you. 'Twan't jes' right somehow—— [*He goes slowly off, lower left, closing the door.*]

[UNCLE NAT *stands looking after* MARTIN, *his face lighted up by an inner glow of peace and happiness. His thoughts are reflected in his face, but not a word is spoken. The scene is played in absolute silence.*]

[*He sinks into the rocking chair close by with a sigh of content and satisfaction. He settles himself comfortably, with his chin resting in his right hand as he thinks.*]

UNCLE NAT [*He thinks this*]. Well, everythin's all right again. [*He nods his head approvingly.*] I wonder how long Nel 'n' Sam's a-goin' to stay? A month 'r two anyway. [*Then a soft, tender smile creeps slowly into his face at the thought of the baby.*] Bless thet baby! I wonder what the young uns'll say in the mornin'? It'll be better'n a circus here when Millie sees thet baby. [*He chuckles softly at the thought. Then suddenly he scans the door, wondering if he locked it. He rises slowly, easing himself on the arms of the chair, and plods to the door; he tries the lock, then tucks the doormat snugly against the sill to keep the snow from drifting in. Then he goes to the window, rubs the pane to clear the frost from it, and peers out.*] Gracious! What a night! [*He stoops down, and looks up to find the lighthouse beacon. He nods his head.*] Ol' Berry's all right—Tim's there. [*As he turns from the window, shrugging his shoulders and shivering a little*] Snow'll be ten foot deep in the mornin'. [*He goes to the stove and sets the kettle back, lifts one of the lids and looks at the fire. A thought strikes him.*] By George, it's a-goin' to be pooty hard work to git the ol' farm inter shape agin! [*He shuts the damper.*] Well, hard work never skeered me—— [*He goes to the woodhouse door and fastens the bolt. Coming down to the table he picks up the candle which* ANN *left there for him and starts to go up the stairs. At the foot he pauses, then he moves down to the door, softly pushes it open, and stands there for a moment looking off. He smiles to himself as he thinks*] I wonder what the young uns'll say in the mornin'? [*For a moment he is lost in thought; his right arm slowly relaxes. Then he turns and starts to climb slowly up the stairs, his heavy footfalls echoing through the empty room. The wind howls outside; the sharp snow tinkles rhythmically upon the windowpane. The stage darkens slightly. He reaches the top of the stairs and goes off, closing the door after him. The stage is left in darkness except for the firelight flickering through the chinks of the stove. The cuckoo clock strikes twelve and the curtain slowly descends.*]

The End of the Play

William Vaughn Moody

✻ 1869-1910

William Vaughn Moody, educator and poet as well as playwright, was born in Spencer, Indiana, where he taught in the public school to raise money to go to Harvard. In college he worked furiously, completing his course in three years, but still finding time to write verse and prose for the undergraduate magazine. He took a master's degree in 1894 and began teaching at Harvard and Radcliffe. In the next year he transferred to the University of Chicago, where he remained on the faculty until 1907, when he resigned to devote himself to writing.

He thought of himself first as a poet, and his earliest publications, THE MASQUE OF JUDGEMENT *(1900),* POEMS *(1901),* and THE FIRE-BRINGER *(1904) are in verse. But of these, the first and the last are plays, and it was to the drama that his talents were ultimately directed. "I am heart and soul dedicated," he once wrote, "to the conviction that modern life can be presented on the stage in poetic mediums and adequately presented only in that way."*

However, in 1906, after a western trip, he presented Margaret Anglin with the manuscript of a play called THE SABINE WOMAN *which, though it had the intense organic unity of poetry and made eloquent use of symbols, was nonetheless written in a prose that (though stylized) had the flavor of realistic speech to which the audiences of the commercial theatre were accustomed. Miss Anglin staged the play in Chicago with Henry Miller as her leading man, and later brought it to New York as* THE GREAT DIVIDE. *The change of title is significant: an American myth has been substituted for a classical legend and much of the play's initial success can be credited to the skill with which it crystallized a basic truth about the national experience.*

Moody's last play, THE FAITH HEALER, *produced first at Harvard in 1910 and later in St. Louis and New York, failed to duplicate the success of* THE GREAT DIVIDE. *While it too deals with the conflict of ways of life, it brings together realistically portrayed characters and a miracle, the hardest of dramatic conflicts to bring off, and thus fails to achieve the mythical universality of the situation in* THE GREAT DIVIDE. *It is, however, a play of power and promise, and Moody's early death in Colorado Springs cut short a career that must certainly have had a great influence on the renaissance of drama in the United States.*

The text is taken from the edition of 1906.

The Great Divide

A PLAY IN THREE ACTS

Characters

PHILIP JORDAN
POLLY JORDAN, *Philip's wife*
MRS. JORDAN, *his mother*
RUTH JORDAN, *his sister*
WINTHROP NEWBURY
DR. NEWBURY, *Winthrop's father*
STEPHEN GHENT
LON ANDERSON
BURT WILLIAMS

DUTCH A CONTRACTOR
A MEXICAN AN ARCHITECT
A BOY

ACT I

Interior of PHILIP JORDAN'S *cabin in southern Arizona, on a late afternoon in spring. A large room rudely built, adorned with blankets, pottery, weapons, and sacred images of the local Indian tribes, and hung with trophies of the chase, together with hunting knives, saddles, bridles, nosebags for horses, lariats, and other paraphernalia of frontier life. Through a long low window at the back the desert is seen, intensely colored, and covered with the uncouth shapes of giant cacti, dotted with bunches of gorgeous bloom. The entrance door is on the left (from the spectator's standpoint), in a projecting elbow of the room; farther to the left is a door leading to the sleeping quarters. On the right is a cookstove, a cupboard for dishes and household utensils, and a chimneypiece, over which hangs a bleached cow's skull supporting a rifle.*

At a rude table in the center sits PHILIP JORDAN, *a man of thirty-four, mending a bridle.* POLLY, *his wife, kneels before an open trunk, assisted in her packing by* WINTHROP NEWBURY, *a recent graduate of an Eastern medical college.* RUTH JORDAN, PHILIP'S *sister, a girl of nineteen, stands at the window looking out.*

WINTHROP [*As he hands the last articles to Polly*]. What on earth possessed you to bring such a load of duds to Arizona?

POLLY. They promised me a good time, meaning one small shindig—one—in the three months I've spent in this unholy place.

PHILIP [*Makes an impatient movement with the bridle; speaks gruffly*]. You'd better hurry. It's getting late.

RUTH [*From the window*]. It's getting cooler, which is more to the point. We can make the railroad easily by sunrise, with this delicious breeze blowing.

POLLY [*Gives the finishing touches to the trunk and locks the lid*]. There, at last! Heaven help the contents.

PHILIP [*Gruffly, as he rises*]. Give me a lift with the trunk, Win.

[*They carry the trunk outside.* POLLY, *with the aid of a cracked mirror, puts on her traveling hat and cloak.*]

RUTH. My, Pollikins! You'll be the talk of all the jack-rabbits and sage hens between here and the railroad.

POLLY. Phil is furious at me for going, and it *is* rather mean to sneak off for a visit in a grand house in San Francisco, when you poor dears have to slave on here. But really, I can't endure this life a day longer.

RUTH. It isn't in nature that you should. Fancy *that* [*she indicates Polly with a grandiose gesture*] nourishing itself on salt pork, chickory beans, and air-tight!

POLLY. Do you really mean to say that apart from your pride in helping your brother, making the project go, and saving the family fortunes, you really *enjoy* yourself here?

RUTH. Since Phil and I came out, one day has been more radiantly exciting than the other. I don't know what's the matter with me. I think I shall be punished for being so happy.

POLLY. Punished for being happy! There's your simon-pure New Englander.

RUTH. True! I was discovered at the age of seven in the garret, perusing "The Twelve Pillars and Four Cornerstones of a Godly Life."

POLLY [*Pointing at* RUTH'S *heart, speaks with mock solemnity*]. If Massachusetts and Arizona ever get in a mixup in there, woe be!—Are you ever going to have that coffee done?

RUTH. I hope soon, before you get me analyzed out of existence.

POLLY [*As* RUTH *busies herself at the*

stove]. The main point is this, my dear, and you'd better listen to what the old lady is a-tellin' of ye. Happiness is its own justification, and it's the sacreder the more unreasonable it is. It comes or it doesn't, that's all you can say about it. And when it comes, one has the sense to grasp it or one hasn't. There you have the Law and the Prophets.

[WINTHROP *and* PHILIP *enter from outside.* RUTH, *who has set out the coffee and sandwiches on the table, bows elaborately, with napkin over arm.*]

RUTH. *Messieurs et Mesdames!*

WINTHROP. Coffee! Well, rather, with an all-night ride in the desert ahead of us. [*They drink their coffee,* PHILIP *standing sullenly apart.*] Where do we get our next feed?

RUTH. With luck, at Cottonwood Wash.

WINTHROP. And how far may Cottonwood Wash be?

RUTH. Thirty miles.

WINTHROP [*Sarcastically*]. Local measurement?

POLLY [*Poking* PHILIP]. Phil, for Heaven's sake say something. You diffuse the gloom of the Pit.

PHILIP. I've had my say out, and it makes absolutely no impression on you.

POLLY. It's the impression on the public I'm anxious about.

PHILIP. The public will have to excuse me.

POLLY. I *am* horribly sorry for you two poor dears, left alone in this dreadful place. When Dr. Newbury goes, I don't see how you'll support life. I should like to know how long this sojourn in the wilderness is going to last, anyhow.

[*During the following,* RUTH *takes a candle from the shelf, lights it, and brings it to the table. The sunset glow has begun to fade.*]

RUTH. Till Cactus Fiber makes our eternal fortune.

WINTHROP. And how long will that be?

RUTH [*Counts on her fingers*]. Two years to pay back the money we raised on Mother's estate, two years of invested profits, two years of hard luck and marking time, two years of booming prosperity. Say eight years!

POLLY. Shades of the tomb! How long do you expect to live?

RUTH. Forever!

[*The sound of a galloping horse is heard, muffled by the sand.*]

WINTHROP. Listen. What's that?

[*A boy of fifteen, panting from his rapid ride, appears at the open door.*]

PHILIP [*Rising and going toward the door*]. What's the matter?

BOY. I've come for the doctor.

PHILIP. Who wants a doctor?

BOY. Your man Sawyer, over to Lone Tree.—He's broke his leg.

RUTH. Broken his leg! Sawyer? Our foreman?

PHILIP. There's a nice piece of luck! How did it happen?

BOY. They was doin' some Navajo stunts on horseback, pullin' chickens out of the sand at a gallop and takin' a hurdle on the upswing. Sawyer's horse renigged, and lunged off agin a 'dobe wall. Smashed his leg all to thunder.

[WINTHROP *looks vaguely about for his kit and traveling necessaries, while* POLLY *gives the boy food, which he accepts shyly as he goes outside with* PHILIP. RUTH *has snatched saddle and bridle from their peg.*]

RUTH. I'll have Buckskin saddled for you in a jiffy. How long will it take you to set the leg?

WINTHROP. Perhaps an hour, perhaps three.

RUTH. It's a big detour, but you can catch us at Cottonwood Wash by sunrise, allowing three hours for Sawyer. Buckskin has done it before. [*She goes out.*]

POLLY [*Pouting*]. This will spoil all our fun! Why can't the creature wait till you get back?

WINTHROP. Did you ever have a broken leg?

POLLY. Well, no, not exactly a leg. But I've had a broken heart! In fact, I've got one now, if you're not going with us.

WINTHROP. To tell you the truth, mine is broken too. [*Pause.*] Did you ever dream of climbing a long hill, and having to turn back before you saw what was on the other side? [POLLY *nods enthusiastically.*] I feel as if I'd had my chance tonight to see what was over there, and lost it.

POLLY. You'll excuse me if it sounds personal, Dr. Newbury, but did you expect to discern a—sort of central figure in the outrolled landscape?

WINTHROP [*Embarrassed, repenting of his sentimental outburst*]. No. That is——

POLLY [*With a sweep of her arm*]. Oh, I see. Just scenery!

[*She laughs and goes into the inner room, left.* RUTH *re-enters. The sky has partly faded and a great full moon begins to rise.*]

RUTH. Buckskin is ready, and so is the moon. The boy knows the trails like an Indian. He will bring you through to Cottonwood by daylight.

WINTHROP [*Taking heart*]. We shall have the ride back together, at any rate.

RUTH. Yes.—I would go with you, and try to do something to make poor Sawyer comfortable, but we haven't another horse that can do the distance. [*She holds out her hand.*] Good-by.

WINTHROP [*Detaining her hand*]. Won't you make it up to me? [*He draws her toward him.*]

RUTH [*Gently but firmly*]. No, Win. Please not.

WINTHROP. Never?

RUTH. Life is so good just as it is! Let us not change it.

[*He drops her hand, and goes out, without looking back.* POLLY *re-enters. The women wave* WINTHROP *good-by.*]

POLLY [*Takes* RUTH *by the shoulders and looks at her severely*]. Conscience clear?

RUTH [*Humoring her*]. Crystal!

POLLY [*Counts on her fingers*]. Promising young physician, charming girl, lonely ranch, horseback excursions, spring of the year!

RUTH. Not guilty.

POLLY. Gracious! Then it's not play, it's earnest.

RUTH. Neither the one nor the other. It's just your little blonde romantic noddle. [*She takes* POLLY's *head between her hands and shakes it as if to show its emptiness.*] Do you think if I wanted to flirt, I would select a youth I've played hookey with, and seen his mother spank? [*Suddenly sobered.*] Poor dear Win! He's so good, so gentle and chivalrous. But—[*with a movement of lifted arms, as if for air*] ah me, he's—finished! I want one that isn't finished!

POLLY. Are you out of your head, you poor thing?

RUTH. You know what I mean well enough. Winthrop is all rounded off, a completed product. But the man I sometimes see in my dreams is—[*pausing for a simile*] well, like this country out here, don't you know——? [*She breaks off, searching for words, and makes a vague outline in the air, to indicate bigness and incompletion.*]

POLLY [*Drily*]. Yes, thank you. I do know! Heaven send you joy of him!

RUTH. Heaven won't, because, alas, he doesn't exist! I am talking of a sublime abstraction—of the glorious unfulfilled—of the West—the Desert.

POLLY [*Lifts* RUTH's *chin, severely*]. We haven't by chance, some spring morning, riding over to the trading-station or elsewhere—just by the merest chance *beheld* a sublime abstraction—say in blue overalls and jumper? [RUTH *shakes her head.*] Honest? [*More emphatic head shaking.* POLLY *drops* RUTH's *chin with a shrug of the shoulders.* PHILIP *enters.*]

RUTH [*Putting on her riding hat*]. Is Pinto saddled?

PHILIP. Pinto is gone.

RUTH [*Astonished*]. Gone where?

PHILIP. To that Mexican blow-out over at Lone Tree. Every manjack on the ranch has disappeared, without leave asked or notice given, except this paper which I just found nailed to the factory door. [RUTH *takes the note and reads it anxiously. Then she slowly removes her hat and lays it away.*] What are you up to now? We've no time to lose!

RUTH [*With quiet determination*]. I am not going.

POLLY [*As* PHILIP *turns in surprise*]. Not going?

RUTH. I must stay and look after the ranch.

PHILIP. Oh, come, that's out of the question!

RUTH. We have put all Mother's money into this venture. We can't take any risks.

PHILIP. The men will be back tomorrow. It's not to be thought of—your staying here all alone.

POLLY [*Seats herself with decision*]. One thing is certain: either Ruth goes or I stay.

PHILIP [*Takes off his hat and sets down the provision basket*]. That suits me perfectly!

POLLY [*Hysterical*]. But I can't stay! I shall go mad if I spend another night in this place.

RUTH. No, you mustn't stay. You would never get us worked up to the point of letting you go, another time. [*She lifts Polly, and with arm around her waist leads her to the door.*]

PHILIP. I refuse to leave you here alone, just to satisfy a whim of Polly's. That's flat!

RUTH. But, Phil, you forget the stores you're to fetch back. They will be dumped out there on the naked sand, and by tomorrow night—— [*She blows across her palm, as if scattering thistle-down.*]

PHILIP. Well, what of it? A few hundred dollars' worth of stuff!

RUTH. A few hundred dollars means sink or swim with us just now.—Besides, there's poor Sawyer. He'll be brought back here tomorrow, and nobody to nurse him. Then inflammation, fever, and good-by Sawyer.

[PHILIP, *with a gesture of accepting the inevitable, picks up the grain sacks and basket.*]

POLLY [*At the door, embracing* RUTH]. Good-by, dear. Aren't you really afraid to stay?

RUTH. I'm awfully sorry to miss the fun, but as for danger, the great Arizona Desert is safer than Beacon Hill.

POLLY. You're sure?

RUTH. If marauders prowl, I'll just fire the blunderbuss out the window, and they won't stop running this side of the Great Divide.

POLLY [*Kissing her*]. Good-by, dear.

RUTH. Good-by.

[POLLY *goes out.*]

PHILIP [*Pausing beside* RUTH, *at the door*]. Mind you put out the light early. It can be seen from the Goodwater trail. There's no telling what riff-raff will be straggling back that way after the dance.

RUTH. Riff-raff! They're my sworn knights and brothers.

PHILIP. In that case, what makes you uneasy about the property?

RUTH. Oh, property! That's different.

PHILIP. Well, you mind what I say and put out the light.

RUTH. Yours for prudence! [*She puts her arm around his waist and draws him to her, kissing him tenderly.*] Good-by, Phil. [*He kisses her and starts to go. She still detains him. When she speaks again, her voice is softened and awed.*] What a lovely night! Who would ever think to call this a desert, this moonlit ocean of flowers? What millions of cactus blooms have opened since yesterday!

PHILIP [*Looking at her dubiously*]. What's the matter with you tonight?

RUTH. Nothing. Everything. Life!—I don't know what's got into me of late. I'm just drunk with happiness the whole time.

PHILIP. Well, you're a queer one.—Good-by. I shall get back as soon as horseflesh will do it. [*He goes out.*]

RUTH [*As the rumble of the wagon is heard*]. Good-by! Good-by, Pollikins! Good-by! [*She takes the candle from the table and stands in the door for a time, then raises the light in one hand and waves her handkerchief with the other. She sets the candle again on the table, goes to the mantel shelf, and takes down a photograph.*] Dear Win! I forgot how disappointed *you* were going to be. [*Pause, during which she still gazes at the picture.*] Clear, kind heart! [*After a moment she replaces it brusquely on the mantel shelf, and raises her arms above her head with a deep breath. She stands thus, with arms crossed behind her head, looking at the photograph. Her gaze becomes amused and mischievous; she points her finger at the picture and whispers mockingly*] Finished! Finished! [*She begins to prepare for bed, taking down her hair, and re-coiling it loosely during the following. She hums a tune vaguely and in snatches, then with a stronger rhythm; at last she sings.*]

> Heart, wild heart,
> Brooding apart,
> Why dost thou doubt, and why art thou sullen?
> Flower and bird
> Wait but thy word——

[*She breaks off, picks up a photograph from the table, and looks at it for a moment in silence.*] Poor little Mother! You look out at me with such patient, anxious eyes. There are better days coming for you, and it's a troublesome me that's bringing them. Only you trust me!

[*A man's face appears at the edge of the window, gazing stealthily in. As Ruth turns, he disappears. She lays down the picture and sings again.*]

> This is the hour,
> And thine is the power.
> Heart, high heart, be brave to begin it.
> Dare you refuse?
> Think what we lose!
> Think what we gain——

[*The words grow indistinct as she takes up the candle and passes into the other room, from which her voice sounds from time to time in interrupted song. The man again appears, shading his face with a peaked Mexican hat so as to see into the darkened room. He turns and waves his hand as if signaling distant persons to approach, then enters through the open door. He looks cautiously about the room, tiptoes to the inner door and listens, then steals softly out, and is seen again at the window, beckoning. Ruth re-enters, carrying the candle. She is shod in moccasins, and clad in a loose, dark sleeping-dress, belted at the waist, with wide, hanging sleeves and open throat. As she crosses to the table she sings.*]

> Heart which the cold
> Long did enfold—
> Hark, from the dark eaves the night thaw drummeth!
> Now as a god,
> Speak to the sod,
> Cry to the sky that the miracle cometh!

[*She passes her hand over a great bunch of wild flowers on the table.*] Be still, you beauties! You'll drive me to distraction with your color and your odor. I'll take a hostage for your good behavior. [*She selects a red flower, puts it in the dark mass of her hair, and looks out at the open door.*] What a scandal the moon is making, out there in that great crazy world! Who but me could think of sleeping on such a night?

[*She sits down, folds the flowers in her arms, and buries her face in them. After a moment she starts up, listens, goes hur-

riedly to the door, and peers out. She then shuts and bolts the door, draws the curtains before the window, comes swiftly to the table, and blows out the light. The room is left in total darkness. There are muttering voices outside, the latch is tried, then a heavy lunge breaks the bolt. A man pushes in, but is hurled back by a taller man, with a snarling oath. A third figure advances to the table and strikes a match. As soon as the match is lighted RUTH *levels the gun, which she has taken from its rack above the mantel. There is heard the click of the hammer, as the gun misses fire. It is instantly struck from her hand by the first man* (DUTCH), *who attempts to seize her. She evades him, and tries to wrest a pistol from a holster on the wall. She is met by the second man* (SHORTY), *who frustrates the attempt, pocketing the weapon. While this has been going on the third man* (GHENT) *has been fumbling with the lamp, which he has at last succeeded in lighting. All three are dressed in rude frontier fashion; the one called* SHORTY *is a Mexican half-breed, the others are Americans.* GHENT *is younger than* DUTCH, *and taller, but less powerfully built. All are intoxicated, but not sufficiently so to incapacitate them from rapid action. The* MEXICAN *has seized* RUTH *and attempts to drag her toward the inner room. She breaks loose, and flies back again to the chimney-place, where she stands at bay.* GHENT *remains motionless and silent by the table, gazing at her.*]

DUTCH [*Uncorking a whiskey flask*]. Plucky little catamount. I drink its health. [*Drinks.*]

RUTH. What do you want here?

DUTCH [*Laughs, with sinister relish*]. Did you hear that, Steve? [*He drinks again, and reaches out the flask to* RUTH.] Take one, and pull in its purty little claws, eh? Jolly time. No more fuss and fury. [RUTH *reaches for a knife, hidden behind the elbow of the chimney.* DUTCH *wrests the knife from her and seizes her in his arms.*] Peppery little devil!

[*With desperate strength she breaks from his clutch and reels from him in sickness of horror.* GHENT *remains gazing at her in a fascinated semi-stupor. Meanwhile, after closing the door, the* MEXICAN *has taken dice from his pocket, and, throwing them into a small vase on the table, shakes them and holds out the vase to* DUTCH. *He takes it and turns to* GHENT; *the latter has moved a step or two toward* RUTH, *who in her retreat has reached the chimney-piece and stands at bay.*]

DUTCH. Come, get into the game, curse you, Steve! This is going to be a free-for-all, by God!

[*As he rattles the dice,* RUTH *makes a supplicating gesture to* GHENT.]

RUTH. Save me! save me! [*Her gesture is frozen by his advancing toward her. She looks wildly about, shrinking from him, then with sudden desperate resolution speaks.*] Save me, and I will make it up to you! [GHENT *again advances; she goes on pantingly, as she stands at bay.*] Don't touch me! Listen! Save me from these others, and from yourself, and I will pay you—with my life.

GHENT [*With dull wonder*]. With—your life?

RUTH. With all that I am or can be.

GHENT. What do you mean——? [*Pause.*] You mean you'll go along with me out of this? Stick to me—on the square?

RUTH [*In a tragic whisper*]. Yes.

GHENT. On the dead square?

RUTH. Yes.

GHENT. You won't peach, and spoil it?

RUTH. No.

[*Pause, during which he looks at her fixedly.*]

GHENT. Give me your hand on it!

[*She gives him her hand. The other men, at the table, have drawn their weapons, and hold them carelessly, but alert to the slightest suspicious movement on the part of* GHENT.]

DUTCH [*As* GHENT *turns to them*]. Shorty and me's sittin' in this game, and interested, eh, Shorty?

[*The* MEXICAN *nods.* GHENT *comes slowly to the table, eying the two.*]

[DUTCH *holds out the vase containing the dice.*]

Shake for her!

GHENT. Shake how?

DUTCH. Any damn way! Sole and exclusive rights. License to love and cherish on the premises!

GHENT [*Takes the vase, shakes the dice meditatively, is about to throw, then sets the vase down. He searches through his pockets and produces a few bills and a handful of silver, which he lays on the table*]. There's all I've got in my clothes. Take it, and give me a free field, will you?

DUTCH [*Leaning over the table to* GHENT, *in plaintive remonstrance*]. You don't mean me, Steve!

GHENT [*To the* MEXICAN]. Well, you, then!

[*The* MEXICAN *spreads the money carelessly with his left hand to ascertain its amount, then thrusts it away with a disgusted grunt of refusal.*]

DUTCH. Don't blame you, Shorty! A ornery buck of a dirt-eatin' Mojave'd pay more'n that for his squaw.

[RUTH *covers her face shudderingly.* GHENT *stands pondering, watching the two men under his brows, and slowly gathering up the money. As if on a sudden thought, he opens his shirt, and unwinds from his neck a string of gold nuggets in the rough, strung on a leather thread.*]

GHENT. Well, it ain't much, that's sure. But there's a string of gold nuggets I guess is worth some money. [*He throws it on the table, speaking to both men.*] Take that, and clear out.

DUTCH [*Draws up angrily*]. I've give you fair warning!

GHENT. We'll keep everything friendly between me and you. A square stand-up shoot, and the best man takes her.

DUTCH [*Mollified*]. Now you're comin' to!

GHENT [*To the* MEXICAN]. Then it's up to you, and you'd better answer quick!

THE MEXICAN [*Eying* GHENT *and* RUTH, *points to the gun lying on the floor*]. I take him, too.

GHENT. No, you don't. You leave everything here the way you found it.

THE MEXICAN. Alla right. [*He pockets the chain and starts for the door.*]

GHENT. Hold on a minute. You've got to promise to tie the man who falls, on his horse, and take him to Mesa Grande. Bargain? [*The* MEXICAN *nods.*] And mouth shut, mind you, or—— [*He makes a sign across his throat.*]

THE MEXICAN [*Nods*]. Alla right. [*He goes out.*]

GHENT [*Motioning toward the door*]. Outside.

DUTCH [*Surprised*]. What for?

GHENT [*Sternly*]. Outside!

[*They move toward the door.* DUTCH *stops and waves his hand to* RUTH.]

DUTCH. Don't worry, my girl. Back soon.

GHENT [*Threateningly*]. Cut that out!

DUTCH. What's eatin' you? She ain't yours yet, and I guess she won't be, not till hell freezes over.

[*He taps his pistol and goes out.* GHENT *picks up the rifle which has previously missed fire; he unloads it, throws it on the windowseat, and follows* DUTCH. RUTH *stands beside the table, listening. Four shots are heard. After a short time* GHENT *appears and watches from the door the vanishing horses. He comes to the table opposite* RUTH.]

RUTH [*In a low voice*]. Is he dead?

GHENT. No; but he'll stay in the coop for a while.

[*She sinks down in a chair.* GHENT *seats himself at the other side of the table, draws a whiskey flask from his pocket, and uncorks it awkwardly, using only his right hand.*]

RUTH [*As he is about to drink*]. Don't!

GHENT [*Lowers the bottle and looks at her in a dazed way*]. Is this on the square?

RUTH. I gave you my promise.

[*Gazing at her, he lets the bottle sink slowly by his side; the liquor runs out, while he sits as if in a stupor.* RUTH *glances toward the door, and half starts from her seat, sinking back as he looks up.*]

GHENT. Give me a drink of water.

[*She brings the water from a bucket in the corner. He sets the empty bottle on the table, drinks deeply of the water, takes a handkerchief from his neck, wets it, and mops his face.*]

GHENT. Where are your folks?

RUTH. My brother has gone out to the railroad.

GHENT. Him and you ranching it here by yourselves?

RUTH. Yes.

GHENT. Write him a note. [*He shoves paper, pen, and ink before her.*] Fix it up any way you like.

RUTH. Tell me first what you mean to do with me.

GHENT [*Ponders awhile in silence*]. Have you got a horse to ride?

RUTH. Yes.

GHENT. We can reach San Jacinto before sunup. Then we're off for the Cordilleras. I've got a claim tucked away in them hills that'll buy you the city of Frisco some day, if you have a mind to it! [*She shrinks and shudders.*] What you shivering at? [RUTH *does not answer, but begins to write.* GHENT, *still using only one hand, takes a pistol from his pocket, examines it, and lays it carelessly on the table, within* RUTH'S *reach. He rises and goes to the fireplace, takes a cigarette from his pocket and lights it, and examines the objects on the mantel shelf.* RUTH *stops writing, takes up the pistol, then lays it down, as he speaks without turning around.*] Read what you've written. [RUTH *about to read, snatches up the pistol again, rises, and stands trembling and irresolute.*] Why don't you shoot? [*He turns around deliberately.*] You promised on the square, but there's nothing square about this deal. You ought to shoot me like a rattlesnake!

RUTH. I know that.

GHENT. Then why don't you?

RUTH [*Slowly*]. I don't know.

GHENT. I guess you've got nerve enough, for that or anything.—Answer me; why not?

RUTH. I don't—know.—You laid it there for me.—And—you have no right to die.

GHENT. How's that?

RUTH. You must live—to pay for having spoiled your life.

GHENT. Do you think it is spoiled?

RUTH. Yes.

GHENT. And how about your life?

RUTH. I tried to do it.

GHENT. To do what?

RUTH. To take my life. I ought to die. I have a right to die. But I cannot, I cannot! I love my life, I must live. In torment, in darkness—it doesn't matter. I want my life. I will have it! [*She drops the weapon on the table, pushes it toward him, and covers her eyes.*] Take it away! Don't let me see it. If you want me on these terms, take me, and may God forgive you for it; but if there is a soul in you to be judged, don't let me do myself violence. [*She sinks down by the table, hiding her face in her hands.*] Oh, God have pity on me!

[GHENT *puts the pistol back into his belt, goes slowly to the outer door, opens it, and stands for some moments gazing out. He then closes the door, and takes a step or two toward the table. As he speaks,* RUTH'S *sobs cease, she raises her head and looks strangely at him.*]

GHENT. I've lived hard and careless, and lately I've been going down hill pretty fast. But I haven't got so low yet but what I can tell one woman from another. If that was all of it, I'd be miles away from here by now, riding like hell for liquor to wash the taste of shame out of my mouth. But that ain't all. I've seen what I've been looking the world over for, and never knew it.—Say your promise holds, and I'll go away now.

RUTH. Oh, yes, go, go! You will be merciful. You will not hold me to my cruel oath.

GHENT. And when I come back? [RUTH *does not answer. He takes a step nearer.*] And when I come back?

RUTH. You never—could—come back.

GHENT. No, I guess I never could.

RUTH [*Eager, pleading*]. You *will* go?

GHENT. For good?

RUTH. Yes.

GHENT. Do you mean that?

RUTH. [*Wildly*]. Yes, yes, ten thousand times!

GHENT. Is that your last word?

RUTH. Yes. [*Pause. She watches him with strained anxiety.*] Oh, why did you come here tonight?

GHENT. I came because I was blind drunk and sun-crazy, and looking for damnation the nearest way. That's why I come. But that's not why I'm staying. I'm talking to you in my right mind now. I want you to try and see this thing the way it is.

RUTH. Oh, that is what I want you to do! You did yourself and me a hideous wrong by coming here. Don't do us both a more hideous wrong still! I was in panic fear. I snatched at the first thing I could. Think what our life would be, beginning as we have begun! Oh, for God's pity go away now, and never come back! Don't you see there can never be anything between us but hatred, and misery, and horror?

GHENT [*Hardening*]. We'll see about that!—Are you ready to start? [RUTH, *conscious for the first time of her undress condition, shrinks, and folds her gown closer about her neck.*] Go, and be quick about it. [*She starts toward her room; he detains her.*] Where's your saddle?

[*She points at it and goes out.* GHENT *picks up the note she has written, reads it, and stands for a moment in reflection before laying it down. He gets more water from the bucket, drinks deeply, mops his face, and rolls up the sleeve of his left arm, which is soaked with blood. He tries awkwardly to stanch a wound in his forearm, gives it up in disgust, and rolls down his sleeve again. He reads the note once more, then takes* RUTH'*s saddle and bridle from the wall and goes out.* RUTH *comes in; her face is white and haggard, but her manner determined and collected. She comes to the table, and sees the bloody handkerchief and basin of water. As* GHENT *enters, she turns to him anxiously.*]

RUTH. You are hurt.

GHENT. It's no matter.

RUTH. Where? [*He indicates his left arm. She throws off her hooded riding cloak, and impulsively gathers together water, towels, liniment, and bandages; she approaches him, quite lost in her task, flushed and eager.*] Sit down.—Roll up your sleeve. [*He obeys mechanically. She rapidly and deftly washes and binds the wound, speaking half to herself, between long pauses.*] Can you lift your arm?—The bone is not touched.—It will be all right in a few days. This balsam is a wonderful thing to heal.

GHENT [*Watching her dreamily, as she works*]. What's your name?

RUTH. Ruth—Ruth—Jordan. [*Long pause.*] There, gently.—It must be very painful. [*He shakes his head slowly, with half-humorous protest.*]

GHENT. It's not fair!

RUTH. What's isn't fair?

GHENT. To treat me like this. It's not in the rules of the game.

RUTH [*As the sense of the situation again sweeps over her*]. Binding your wound? I would do the same service for a dog.

GHENT. Yes, I dare say. But the point is, I ain't a dog; I'm a human—the worst way! [*She rises and puts away the liniment and bandages. He starts up, with an impulsive gesture.*] Make this bad business over into something good for both of us! You'll never regret it! I'm a strong man! [*He holds out his right arm, rigid.*] I used to feel sometimes, before I went to the bad, that I could take the world like that and tilt her over. And I can do it, too, if you say the word! I'll put you where you can look down on the proudest. I'll give you the kingdoms of the world and all the glory of 'em. [*She covers her face with her hands. He comes nearer.*] Give me a chance, and I'll make good. By God, girl, I'll make good!—I'll make a queen of you. I'll put the world under your feet! [RUTH *makes a passionate gesture, as if to stop her ears.*] What makes you put your hands over your ears like that? Don't you like what I'm saying to you?

RUTH [*Taking the words with difficulty*]. Do you remember what that man said just now?

GHENT. What about?

RUTH. About the Indian—and—his squaw.

GHENT. Yes. There was something in it, too. I was a fool to offer him that mean little wad.

RUTH. For—me!

GHENT. Well, yes, for you, if you want to put it that way.

RUTH. But—a chain of nuggets—that comes nearer being a fair price?

GHENT. Oh, to buy off a greaser!

RUTH. But to buy the soul of a woman—one must go higher. A mining claim! The kingdoms of the world and all the glory of them! [*Breaking down in sudden sobs.*] Oh, be careful how you treat me! Be careful! I say it as much for your sake as mine. Be careful!

GHENT [*Turns from her, his bewilderment and discomfiture translating itself into gruffness*]. Well, I guess we'll blunder through.—Come along! We've no time to lose.—Where are your things? [*At her gesture, he picks up the saddle pack which she has brought out of the bedroom with her, and starts toward the door.*]

RUTH [*Taking a hammer from the window ledge and handing it to* GHENT]. Fix the bolt. My brother must not know.

[*He drives in the staple of the bolt, while she throws the blood-stained water and handkerchief into the fire. He aids her in replacing the weapons on the walls, then takes the saddle pack and stands at the door, waiting. She picks up her mother's picture, and thrusts it in her bosom. After standing a moment in hesitation, she takes the picture out, kisses it, lays it on the mantel, face down. She extinguishes the lamp, and goes out hastily. He follows, closing the door.*]

The Curtain Falls in Darkness

ACT II

STEPHEN GHENT'S *home, in the Cordilleras. At the right, crowning a rude terrace, is an adobe cabin, stained a pale buff, mellowed to ivory by sun and dust. Over it clamber vines loaded with purple bloom. The front of the cabin is turned at an angle toward the spectator, the farther side running parallel with the brink of a canyon, of which the distant wall and upper reaches are crimsoned by the afternoon light. In the level space before the rocky terrace is a stone table and seats, made of natural rocks roughly worked with the chisel. The rude materials have manifestly been touched by a refined and artistic hand, bent on making the most of the glorious natural background. Against the rocks on the left stands a large hand loom of the Navajo type, with weaving stool, and a blanket half woven. On the table lies a half-finished Indian basket, and strips of colored weaving materials lie in a heap on the ground. Cactus plants in blossom fill the niches of the rocks and lift their fantastic forms above the stones which wall the canyon brink. At one point this wall is broken, where a path descends into the canyon.*

LON ANDERSON, *a venerable-looking miner, with gray hair and beard, sits smoking before the cabin.* BURT WILLIAMS, *a younger man, peeps up over the edge of the canyon, from the path.*

BURT. Hello, Lon. Is the Missus inside? [LON *smokes on, without looking at the questioner.*] Look here, I put a nickel in you, you blame rusty old slot-machine. Push out something!

LON [*Removes his pipe deliberately*]. What you wantin' off 'n her now? A music lesson or a headache powder?

BURT. Boss's waitin' down at the mine, with a couple o' human wonders he's brought back with him from wherever he's been this time. Something doin' on the quiet.

LON. You can tell him his wife ain't nowheres about.

[BURT *produces an enormous bandana from his pocket, mounts the wall, and waves it. He sits on the wall and smokes for a moment in silence, looking down into the canyon, as if watching the approaching party. He points with his pipe at the cabin.*]

BURT. Funny hitch-up—this here one—I think.

LON [*After a pause*]. How much you gittin' a day now?

BURT. Same little smilin' helpless three and six-bits.

LON. Anything extry for thinkin'?

BURT. Nope! Throwed in. [*They smoke again.* BURT *glances down to reassure himself, then points at the loom and basket.*] Queer business—this rug-weavin' and basket-makin', ain't it?—What d' ye s'pose she wants to sit, day in and day out, like a half-starved Navajo, slavin' over them fool things fur?—Boss ain't near, is he? Don't keep her short of ice-cream sodas and trolley-rides, does 'e? [LON *rises and approaches* BURT, *regarding him grimly.*] Saw 'er totin' a lot o' that stuff burro-back over to the hotel week 'fore last.—An' Dod Ranger—you know what a disgustin' liar Dod is—he tells how he was makin' tests over in the cross-canyon, an' all of a sudden plump he comes on her talkin' to a sawed-off Mexican hobo, and when she sees Dod, she turns white 's a sheet.

LON [*With suppressed ferocity*]. You tell Dod Ranger to keep his mouth shet, and you keep yourn shet too—or by Jee—hosophat, I'll make the two of ye eat yer Adam's-apples and swaller the core!

BURT. Oh, git down off 'n yer hind legs, Lon! Nobody's intendin' any disrespect.

LON. You boys keep yer blatherin' tongues off 'n her! Or you'll get mixed up with Alonzo P. Anderson [*he taps his breast*] so's it'll take a coroner to untangle ye!

BURT [*Deprecatingly*]. I guess I'd stick up fur 'er 's quick as you would, come to that.

LON. Well, we don't need no stickin' up fur 'er. What we need is less tongue. [*He leans down and speaks lower.*] Especially when the boss is round. You tell the boys so.

[BURT *looks at him in surprise and is about to speak;* LON *makes a warning signal, indicating the approach of the party below.* BURT *descends, saluting* GHENT *respectfully.*]

GHENT [*Peeping up over the edge of the canyon*] Coast clear, eh, Lon?

LON. Yes, sir.

GHENT. Where is she?

LON [*Points along the brink of the canyon*]. Kind o' think she went out to Look-off Ledge.—Guess she didn't expect you back today.

GHENT [*Speaking below*]. Come up, gentlemen. [GHENT *emerges from the canyon, followed by an architect, a dapper young Easterner, and a contractor, a bluff Western type.* GHENT *is neatly dressed in khaki, with riding boots and broad felt hat. He has a prosperous and busy air, and is manifestly absorbed in the national game of making money.*] Take a seat.

CONTRACTOR [*Seats himself by the table*]. Don't care if I do. That new stage of yours just jumped stiff-legged from the go-off. And the trail up here from the mine is a good deal of a proposition for the see-dentary.

ARCHITECT [*As he takes in the stupendous view*]. What a wonderful place! Even better than you described it.

GHENT. Yes. My wife picked it out. —Let's see your plans. [*He removes basket from the table, where the* ARCHITECT *unrolls several sheets of blue paper.*]

ARCHITECT. I have followed your instructions to the letter. I understand that nothing is to be touched except the house.

GHENT. Not a stone, sir; not a head of cactus. Even the vines you've got to keep, exactly as they are.

ARCHITECT [*Smiling*]. That will be a little difficult.

GHENT. You can put 'em on a temporary trellis.—A little pains will do it.

CONTRACTOR. Maybe, with a man to shoo the masons off with a shotgun.

GHENT [*Over the plans*]. Provide a dozen men, if necessary, with machine guns.

CONTRACTOR. As you please, Mr. Ghent. The owner of the Verde mine has a right to his whims, I reckon.

ARCHITECT. I have designed the whole house in the Spanish style, very broad and simple. This open space where we stand [*points to the plans*] I have treated as a semi-enclosed *patio*, with arcaded porches.

GHENT [*Dubiously*]. Good.

ARCHITECT. This large room fronting the main arcade is the living room.

GHENT. I guess we'll have 'em all living-rooms. This place is to be lived in, from the word go.

ARCHITECT [*Humoring him*]. To be sure, everything cheerful and open.—Here on the left of the inner court is the library and music room.

GHENT. I'm afraid we won't have much use for that. My wife don't go in much for frills. I used to play the concertina once, but it was a long while ago.

ARCHITECT. It can be used for other purposes. For instance, as a nursery, though I had put that on the other side.

GHENT [*Embarrassed and delighted*]. Um, yes, nursery.—Stamping-ground for the——? [*The* ARCHITECT *nods; the* CONTRACTOR *follows suit, with emphasis.* LON *nods solemnly over his pipe.*] Good. [*The* ARCHITECT *bends over to make a note with his pencil.* GHENT *restrains him and says somewhat sheepishly in his ear*] You can leave it music room on the map.

ARCHITECT [*Continuing his explanation*]. This wing——

GHENT [*Interrupting him, holds the plan at arm's length, with head on one side and eyes squinted, as he looks from the drawings to the cabin and surroundings*]. Looks a little—*sprawly* on paper. I had sort of imagined something more —more up in the air, like them swell tepees on the Hill in Frisco. [*He makes a grandiose outline of high roofs and turrets in the air.*]

ARCHITECT. I think this is more harmonious with the surroundings.

CONTRACTOR [*In answer to* GHENT'S *inquiring look*]. Won't look so showy from the new hotel across yonder. [*He points to the left, down the curve of the canyon wall.*]

GHENT. What's your estimate on this plan, now you've seen the location?

CONTRACTOR. It's a long way to haul the stuff.—Say somewheres between twenty and twenty-five thousand. Twenty-five will be safe.

GHENT [*Slightly staggered*]. That's a big lot of money, my friend!

CONTRACTOR [*With cold scorn*]. I thought we was talkin' about a *house!* I can build you a good sheep corral for a right smart less.

GHENT. Well, I guess we don't want any sheep corrals.

CONTRACTOR. I should think not, with the Verde pumping money at you the way they tell she does.

GHENT [*Holds up the plans again and looks at them in perplexed silence*]. I'll tell you, gentlemen, I'll have to consult my wife about this before I decide. The fact is, I've been working the thing out on the sly, up to now.

CONTRACTOR. Expect to build it of an afternoon, while the lady was takin' her see-ester?

GHENT. I thought I'd smuggle her off somewhere for a while. [*He is silent a moment, pondering.*] No! It's her house, and she must O.K. the plans before ground is broke. [*He looks along the canyon rim.*] Would you mind waiting a few minutes till I see if I can find her? [*He starts irresolutely, then turns back.*] Or better still, leave the plans, and I'll see you at the hotel tomorrow morning. I haven't been over there since it was opened. I'd like to know what they're making of it.

CONTRACTOR [*Astonished*]. Hain't been over to the Buny Visty yet?

GHENT. Too busy.

CONTRACTOR. Well, you'll find it an up-to-date joint, and chock full of tourist swells and lungers.

GHENT. Good afternoon, gentlemen. You'll excuse me. You can find your way back all right? Take the left hand path. It's better going.

[*The* ARCHITECT *bows ceremoniously, the* CONTRACTOR *nods.* GHENT *disappears along the canyon brink behind the cabin.*]

ARCHITECT [*Has been examining the work on the loom, and has then picked up the unfinished basket, admiringly*]. What a beautiful pattern! I say, this is like those we saw at the hotel. [*To* LON.] May I ask who IS making this? [LON *smokes in silence; the* ARCHITECT *raises his voice, slightly sharp.*] May I ask who is making this?

LON [*Benignly*]. You kin, my friend, you kin!

ARCHITECT. Well, then, the question is put.

LON. And very clear-put, too. You'd ought to be in the law business, young man. [*He gets up deliberately.*] Or some other business that'd take up all yer time.

ARCHITECT [*Between wrath and amusement*]. Well, I'll be hanged! [*He follows his companion down the canyon path, stopping a moment at the brink to look around with a professional air at the house and surroundings, then at* LON.] Tart old party! [*He descends.* LON *crosses to the table, looks over the plans, makes outlines in the air in imitation of* GHENT, *then shakes his head dubiously, as he rolls up the plans.*]

[RUTH *appears, emerging from the canyon path. She wears the same dress as at the close of Act I, with a dark scarf-like handkerchief thrown over her head. She is pale and exhausted. She sinks on the rocks at the edge of the canyon.*]

LON [*Approaching her, anxiously*]. It's too much fer you, ma'am. You'd oughter let me go. [*He brings her a glass of water from an Indian water jar before the cabin.*]

RUTH [*Tasting the water*]. Oh, I thought I should never get back! [*She leans against a rock, with closed eyes, then rouses herself again.*] Lon, take the glass, and see if you can make out any one down yonder, on the nearer trail. I—I thought some one was following me.

LON [*Speaks low*]. Excuse me askin', Mis' Ghent, but is that dod-blamed Mexican a-botherin' you again?

RUTH. No. He has gone away, for good. It's some one I saw at the hotel—someone I used to know.—Look if you can make out a man's figure, coming up.

LON [*Takes the glass from the niche in the rocks, and scans the canyon path*]. Can't see nothin' but a stray burro, an' he ain't got no figger to speak of.—Might be t'other side o' Table Rock, down in the pinyon scrub. [RUTH *gets up with an effort, takes the glass and looks through it, then lays it on the ledge.*] Excuse me, ma'am, but—Mister Ghent come home this afternoon.

RUTH [*Startled*]. Where is he?

LON. Huntin' for you down Look-off Ledge way. I 'lowed you was there, not knowin' what else to say.

RUTH. Thank you, Lon.—You can go now. [*He goes down the canyon path.* RUTH *looks once more through the glass, then crosses to the table, where she sits down and begins to finger the roll of plans.* GHENT *re-enters. He approaches with soft tread and bends over* RUTH. *She starts up with a little cry, avoiding his embrace.*] You frightened me.—When did you come back?

GHENT. An hour ago.

RUTH. Was your journey successful?

GHENT. Yes. But my homecoming—that looks rather like a failure. [*Pause.*] I expected to find you out on the bluff.

RUTH. Lon was mistaken. I had gone the other way. [*As she stands at the table, she begins to unroll the plans.*] What are these papers?

GHENT. Haven't you one word of welcome for me, after five days? [RUTH *remains silent, with averted head, absently unrolling the packet.*] Not a look even? [*He waits a moment, then sighs and seats himself moodily by the table.*] I never can remember! After I've been away from you for twelve hours, I forget completely.

RUTH. Forget what?

GHENT. How it stands between us. It's childish, but for the life of me I can't help it.—After I've been away a few hours, this place gets all lit up with bright colors in my mind, like—[*searching for a simile*] well, like a Christmas tree! I daresay a Christmas tree don't amount to much in real life, but I saw one once, in a play—I was a little mining camp roustabout, so high—and ever since it has sort of stood to me for the gates o' glory.

RUTH [*With a hysterical laugh*]. A Christmas tree! [*She bows her head in her hands, and repeats the words, as if to herself, in a tone in which bitterness has given place to tragic melancholy.*] A Christmas tree! [GHENT, *watching her moodily, crumples up the plans and throws them upon the ground. He goes toward the cabin, hesitates, turns, and comes back to the table, where* RUTH *still sits with buried head. He draws from his pocket a jewel case, which he opens and lays before her.*]

GHENT. There is a little present I brought home for you. And here are some more trinkets. [*He takes out several pieces of jewelry and tumbles them together on the table.*] I know you don't care much for these things, but I had to buy something, the way I was feeling. And these papers—[*picks them up and spreads them out on the table*] these mean that you're not to live much longer in a mud shanty, with pine boxes for furniture. These are the drawings for a new house that I want to talk over with you. [*He points at the map and speaks glibly, trying to master his discomfiture at her lack of interest.*] Spanish style, everything broad and simple! Large living room opening on inner court. Library and music room, bless your heart. Bedrooms; kitchen and thereunto pertaining. Wing where the proprietor retires to express his inmost feelings. General effect sprawly, but harmonious with the surroundings. Twenty thousand estimated, twenty-five limit. Is she ours?

RUTH [*In a dead, flat tone*]. How much did you say the house is to cost?

GHENT. Twenty-five thousand dollars at the outside.

RUTH. And these—trinkets?

GHENT. Oh, I don't know.—A few hundred.

RUTH [*Draws the plans toward her and pours the jewels in a heap upon them from her lifted hands*]. Twenty-five thousand dollars and the odd hundreds! [*She laughs suddenly and jarringly.*] My price has risen! My price has risen! [*She laughs again, as she rises from the table and looks down the canyon path.*] Keep those displayed to show to our visitors! My honor is at stake. [*She points down the path.*] There is one coming now!

GHENT. Visitors? What visitors?

RUTH. Only an old school-friend of mine; a Mr. Winthrop Newbury.

GHENT. What are you talking about? Are you crazy? [*He joins her, where she stands looking down into the canyon.*] This fellow, is he really what you say? [RUTH *nods, with unnaturally bright eyes and mocking smile.*] What does this mean?

RUTH. It means that he caught sight of me, an hour ago, in the hotel.

GHENT. In the hotel? What were you doing there?

RUTH [*With biting calm*]. Nothing wicked—as yet. They don't pay twenty-five thousand dollars over there—at least not yet! [GHENT *turns sharply, as if stung by a physical blow. She raises her hands to him, in a swift revulsion of feeling.*] Oh, don't judge me! Don't listen to me! I am not in my right mind.

GHENT [*Sweeps the jewels together, and throws them over the cliff*]. Do you want me to be here, while you see him? [*She does not answer.*] Won't you answer me?

RUTH [*Again cold*]. Act as you think best.

GHENT. It's a question of what will be easiest for you.

RUTH. Oh, it's all easy for me!

[GHENT *stands irresolute, then raises his hand in a gesture of perplexity and despair, and goes into the house, closing the door.* WINTHROP NEWBURY *appears at the top of the canyon path, looks curiously about, catches sight of* RUTH'S *averted figure, and rushes toward her.*]

WINTHROP. Ruth! Is it really you?

[RUTH *starts involuntarily toward him, stretching out her arms. As he advances, she masters herself, and speaks in a natural voice, with an attempt at gaiety as she takes his hand.*]

RUTH. Well, of all things! Winthrop Newbury! How did you find your way to this eagle's nest?

WINTHROP. I—we saw you—we caught a glimpse of you at the hotel, but we weren't sure. We followed you, but lost you in the canyon.

RUTH. We? Who is we?

WINTHROP. Your brother and his wife.

RUTH [*Turning the shock, which she has been unable to conceal into conventional surprise*]. Philip and Polly here!

WINTHROP. They took the other turn, down there where the path forks. We didn't know which way you had gone.

RUTH. Yes, but why on earth are they here at all?

WINTHROP. They are on their way East. They stopped over to see me.

RUTH. To see you? Are you—living here?

WINTHROP. I have been here only a week. [*He starts impulsively, trying to break through the conventional wall which she has raised between them.*] Ruth—for God's sake—!

RUTH [*Interrupting him, with exag-*

gerated animation]. But tell me! I am all curiosity. How do you happen to be here—of all places?

WINTHROP. What does it matter? I am here. We have found you, after all these miserable months of anxiety and searching. O Ruth—why——

RUTH. I have acted badly, I know. But I wish not to talk of that. Not now. I will explain everything later. Tell me about yourself—about Philip and Polly —and Mother. I am thirsty for news. What have you been doing all these months, since—our queer parting?

WINTHROP [*Solemnly*]. Looking for you. [*Pause.*] O Ruth—how could you do it? How could you do it?

RUTH [*Touches him on the arm and looks at him with dumb entreaty, speaking low*]. Winthrop!

WINTHROP [*In answer to her unspoken words*]. As you will.

RUTH [*Resumes her hard, bright tone*]. You haven't told me about Mother. How is she?

WINTHROP. Well. Or she will be, now. Ruth, you ought at least to have written to her. She has suffered cruelly.

RUTH [*Quickly, with a nervous uplift of her arms*]. Yes, yes, I know that!— And you are—settled here? You mean to remain?

WINTHROP. I am physician at the End-of-the-Rainbow mines, three miles below. At least I—I am making a trial of it. [*Pause.*] How pale and worn you are.—Don't turn away. Look at me. [*She flinches, then summons her courage and looks him steadily in the face.*] You are— you are ill—I fear you are desperately ill!

RUTH [*Moving away nervously*]. Nonsense. I was never better in my life. [*She goes toward the canyon brink.*] You haven't praised our view. We are very proud of it.

WINTHROP [*Following her*]. Yes, very fine. Magnificent.

RUTH. But you're not looking at it at all! Do you see that bit of smoke far down yonder? That is the stamp mill of the Rio Verde mine.

WINTHROP [*Compelling himself to follow her lead*]. Yes—the Rio Verde. One of the big strikes of the region. Dispute about the ownership, I believe.

RUTH. None that I ever heard of, and I ought to know. For [*she makes a sweeping bow*] *we* are the Rio Verde, at your service.

WINTHROP. You—your—husband is the owner of the Verde mine?

RUTH. No less!

WINTHROP [*Embarrassed*]. We found the record of your marriage at San Jacinto. The name was Ghent—Stephen Ghent.

RUTH. Yes. He will be so glad to see some of my people. [WINTHROP'S *eyes have fallen on the basket at the foot of the table. He picks it up, examines it curiously, and looks meaningly at* RUTH, *who snatches it from his hand and throws it over the cliff.*] A toy I play with! You know I always have to keep my hands busy pottering at some rubbishy craft or other.

WINTHROP [*Is about to speak, but checks himself. He points at the loom*]. And the blanket, too?

RUTH. Yes, another fad of mine. It is really fascinating work. The Indian women who taught me think I am a wonder of cleverness.

WINTHROP. So do—the women— over there. [*He points across the canyon.*]

RUTH [*Flushing*]. Ah, yes, you saw some of my stuff at the hotel. You know how vain I am. I had to show it.

WINTHROP. Perhaps. But why should the wife of the man who owns the Verde mine *sell* her handiwork, and under such —such vulgar conditions?

RUTH [*Brilliantly explanatory*]. To see if it *will* sell, of course! That is the test of its merit.

[*He looks at her in mute protest, then*

with a shake of the head, rises and puts on his hat.]

WINTHROP. Do you want to see the others?

RUTH. Why, yes, to be sure I do. How should I not?

WINTHROP. You haven't seemed very anxious—these last eight months.

RUTH. True. I have been at fault. I so dread explanations. And Phil's tempests of rage! Poor boy, he must feel sadly ill used.

WINTHROP. He does. [*Hesitates.*] If there is any reason why you would rather he didn't see you, just now——

RUTH. There is no reason. At least, none valid.

WINTHROP. Then I will bring them up.

RUTH. By all means. [*She holds out her hand, smiling.*] *Auf Wiedersehen!*

WINTHROP [*Releases her hand and goes toward the canyon path. He waves, and turns to* RUTH]. They are just below. [*As* RUTH *advances he takes her hand and looks searchingly into her eyes.*] For old friendship's sake, won't you give me one human word before they come? At least answer me honestly one human question?

RUTH [*Keeping up her hard, bright gaiety*]. In the great lottery of a woman's answers there is always one such prize!

WINTHROP [*Dejectedly, as he drops her hand*]. It's no use, if that is your mood.

RUTH. My mood! Your old bugbear! I am as sober-serious as my stars ever let me be.

WINTHROP. Did you, that night you bade me good-by, know that—this was going to happen?

RUTH [*Cordially explanatory*]. No. It was half accident, half wild impulse. Phil left me at the ranch alone. My lover came, impatient, importunate, and I—went with him.

WINTHROP. And your—this man—to whom you are married—pardon me, you don't need to answer unless you wish—for how long had you known him?

RUTH [*Solemnly, as she looks him straight in the eyes*]. All my life! And for æons before. [*He looks at her for a moment, then goes toward the canyon path.* POLLY'*s voice is heard calling.*]

POLLY [*Not yet visible*]. Win! Win!

WINTHROP [*Calls down the canyon*]. Come up! Come up!

[RUTH *goes past him down the canyon path. In a moment she reappears, with* POLLY. *They are laughing and talking as they come.*]

POLLY. Ruth!

RUTH. Dear old Polly!

POLLY. You *naughty* girl!

RUTH. If our sins must find us out, you are the kind of Nemesis I choose.

POLLY. My! But you're a shady character. And sly!

[PHILIP *appears.* RUTH *hurries to embrace him, while* POLLY, *fanning herself with her handkerchief, examines the house and surroundings with curiosity.*]

RUTH. O Phil!—Dear old man! [*She covers his face lightly with her hands.*] No scolding, no frowns. This is the finding of the prodigal, and she expects a robe and a ring.

POLLY [*Seating herself on a rock*]. Heavens, what a climb!—I'm a rag.

RUTH [*Motions to the men to be seated*]. The cabin wouldn't hold us all, but there's one good thing about this place; there's plenty of outdoors.

WINTHROP [*Looking about*]. I should say there was!

POLLY. To think of our practical Ruth doing the one really theatrical thing known in the annals of Milford Corners, Mass.!—And what a setting! My dear, your stage arrangements are perfect.

RUTH. In this case Providence deserves the credit. We may have come here to have our pictures taken, but we stayed to make a living.

[PHILIP *has drawn apart, gloomy and threatening.* POLLY *keeps up her heroic efforts to give the situation a casual and humorous air.*]

POLLY [*With jaunty challenge*]. Well, where is he?

RUTH. Who?

POLLY. He! [RUTH *points at the cabin, smiling.*] Well, produce him!

RUTH [*Following, with gratitude in her eyes, the key of lightness and raillery which* POLLY *has struck*]. You insist?

POLLY. Absolutely.

RUTH. Oh, very well! [*She goes up the rocky incline, and enters the cabin, calling: "Steve! Steve!"* POLLY *goes to* PHILIP, *and shakes him.*]

POLLY. Now you behave! [*Indicates* WINTHROP.] He's behaving.

[RUTH *reappears in the doorway, followed by* GHENT.]

RUTH [*With elaborate gaiety, as they descend the rocks*]. Well, Stephen, since they've run us to earth, I suppose we must put a good face on it, and acknowledge them.—This is Polly, of whom I've talked so much. Polly the irresistible. Beware of her! [POLLY *shakes his hand cordially.*] And this is—my brother Philip. [GHENT *extends his hand, which* PHILIP *pointedly ignores.* RUTH *goes on hastily, to cover the insult.*] And this is my old school friend, Winthrop Newbury. [*They shake hands.*]

WINTHROP [*To* PHILIP, *formally explanatory*]. Mr. Ghent is the owner of the famous Verde mine.

GHENT. Part owner, sir. I hadn't the capital to develop with, so I had to dispose of a half interest.

WINTHROP. Isn't there some litigation under way?

RUTH [*Looking at* GHENT, *surprised*]. Litigation?

GHENT. Yes—a whole rigmarole.

POLLY [*Catching at a straw to make talk*]. Heaven help you if you have got entangled in the law! I can conceive of nothing more horrible or ghostly than a court of law; unless [*she glances at* PHILIP] it is that other court of high justice, which people hold in private to judge their fellows, from hearsay and half-knowledge!

RUTH [*Keeping up the play desperately, as she blesses* POLLY *with a look*] But there must be law, just the same, and penalties and rewards and all that. Else what's the use of being good?

POLLY. Like you—for instance!

RUTH. Well, yes, like me!

POLLY. You are not good, you are merely magnificent. I want to be magnificent! I want to live on the roof of the world and own a gold mine! [*To* GHENT.] Show me where the sweet thing is.

GHENT. We can get a better view of the plant from the ledge below. Will you go down? [GHENT, POLLY, *and* WINTHROP *go down the canyon path.* RUTH *takes* PHILIP *by the arm, to lead him after.*]

PHILIP. No. We must have a word together, before the gabble begins again. Winthrop has given me your explanation, which explains nothing.

RUTH [*Trying to keep up the light tone*]. Hasn't that usually been the verdict on explanations of my conduct?

PHILIP. Don't try to put me off! Tell me in two words how you came to run away with this fellow.

RUTH [*Hardening*]. Remember to whom you are speaking, and about whom.

PHILIP. I got your note, with its curt announcement of your resolve. Later, by mere accident, we found the record of your marriage at San Jacinto—if you call it a marriage, made hugger-mugger at midnight by a tipsy justice of the peace. I don't want to question its validity. I only pray that no one will. But I want to know how it came to be made, in such hurry and secrecy—how it came to be made at all, for that matter. How did you ever come to disgrace yourself and your family by clandestine meetings and a hedge-row marriage with a person of this class? And why, after the crazy leap was taken, did you see fit to hide yourself away without a word to me or your distracted mother? Though that perhaps is easier to understand!

RUTH. The manner of your questions absolves me from the obligation to answer them.

PHILIP. I refuse to be put off with any such patent subterfuge.

RUTH. Subterfuge or not, it will have to suffice, until you remember that my right to choose my course in life is unimpeachable, and that the man whose destiny I elect to share cannot be insulted in my presence.

PHILIP. Very well, I can wait. The truth will come out some day. Meanwhile, you can take comfort from the fact that your desertion at the critical moment of our enterprise has spelled ruin for me.

RUTH [*Overwhelmed*]. Philip, you don't mean—!

PHILIP. Absolute and irretrievable ruin.

RUTH. Then you are going back East —for good?

PHILIP. Yes.

RUTH. But—Mother's money! What will she do? [PHILIP *shrugs his shoulders.*] Is everything gone—everything?

PHILIP. I shall get something from the sale. Perhaps enough to make a fresh start, somewhere, in some small way.

RUTH [*Comes to him, and lays her arms on his shoulders*]. Phil, I am sorry, sorry! [*He caresses her; she bursts into suppressed convulsive weeping and clings to him, hiding her face in his breast.*]

PHILIP. Ruth, you are not happy. You have made a hideous mistake. Come home with me. [RUTH *shakes her head.*] At least for a time. You are not well. You look really ill. Come home with us, if only for a month.

RUTH. No, no, dear Phil, dear brother! [*She draws down his face and kisses him; then lifts her head, with an attempt at lightness.*] There! I have had my cry, and feel better. The excitement of seeing you all again is a little too much for me.

PHILIP. If there is anything that you want to tell me about all this, tell me now.

RUTH. Oh, there will be plenty of time for explanations and all that! Let us just be happy now in our reunion.

PHILIP. There will not be plenty of time. We leave tomorrow morning.

RUTH. Then you will take me on trust—like a dear good brother. Perhaps I shall never explain! I like my air of mystery.

PHILIP. Remember that if you ever have anything to complain of—in your life—it is my right to know it. The offender shall answer to me, and dearly, too.

RUTH [*Takes his head between her hands, and shakes it, as with recovered gaiety*]. Of course they will, you old fire-eater!

PHILIP [*Pointing to the blanket on the loom*]. Ruth, at least tell me why——

[RUTH *does not see his gesture, as she is looking at the others, who come up from below. The men linger in the background,* GHENT *pointing out objects in the landscape.*]

RUTH [*To* POLLY, *who advances*]. Well, what do you think of us, in a bird's-eye view?

POLLY. In a bird's-eye view you are superb! [*She draws* RUTH *to her, and speaks in a lower tone.*] And looked at near, you are an enthralling puzzle.

RUTH [*Half to herself*]. If you only knew how much!

POLLY [*Taking* RUTH *by the chin as in Act I*]. So you *had*—just by chance—riding over to the trading-station or so—met the glorious unfulfilled—in blue overalls and a jumper! I thought so! [RUTH *bows her head in a spasm of pain.* POLLY, *who does not see her face, goes on teasingly.*] I see now what you meant about wanting one that wasn't finished. This one certainly isn't finished. But when he is, he'll be grand! [RUTH *moves away with averted head.* POLLY *follows her, peeping round to view her face.*] Don't sulk! I meant nothing disrespectful. On the contrary, I'm crazy about him. [*In a louder tone.*] And now that I've seen the outside of you, I *must* peep into that fascinating little house!

RUTH [*To* GHENT, *who has drawn nearer*]. Polly wants to go inside the cabin. I can't let her until we have shown her what it's going to be. [*With* GHENT'S *aid she spreads out the plans, which* POLLY *examines with curiosity.*] These are the plans for our new house. You call us magnificent. We will show you that we are not. We are overwhelming!

WINTHROP [*Looking at his watch*]. I am afraid we must be getting back. It grows dark very suddenly in the canyon.

RUTH [*To* POLLY]. Well, then you may come in, if you will promise to view the simple present in the light of the ornate future. [POLLY *goes in.* RUTH, *lingering at the door for an instant, looks back anxiously at the men.*]

PHILIP [*Curtly, to* GHENT]. If you will permit me, I should like a word with you.

GHENT. Certainly. [WINTHROP *effaces himself, making and lighting a cigarette, as he looks out over the canyon.*]

PHILIP. In deference to my sister's wishes, I refrain from asking you for the explanation which is due me. [GHENT *bows in silence.*] But there is one thing which I think I am at liberty to question.

GHENT. Do so.

PHILIP. I hear of your interest in a valuable mine. I hear of plans for an elaborate house. Why, then, is my sister compelled to peddle her own handiwork in a public caravansery?

GHENT. What do you mean? I don't understand you.

PHILIP [*Points at the loom*]. Her rugs and baskets are on sale in the corridor of the hotel, fingered and discussed by the tourist mob.

GHENT [*Astonished*]. This can't be true!

PHILIP. It is, however.

GHENT. I know nothing of it. I've had to be away a great deal. I knew she worked too hard over these things, but I took it for a mere pastime. Perhaps—No, I can't understand it at all!

PHILIP. I advise you to make inquiries. She has taken pains to conceal her identity, but it is known nevertheless, and the subject of public curiosity. [POLLY *and* RUTH *come out from the cabin.*]

POLLY [*To* PHILIP]. Take me away quickly, or I shall never enjoy upholstery again! [*To* RUTH.] Please change your mind, dear, and come with us for the night.

RUTH. No. I will see you in the morning.

WINTHROP. We leave by the early stage.

RUTH [*Looking at him quickly*]. You too?

WINTHROP. Yes, I have decided so.

RUTH. I will be there in good time, trust me. [*She kisses* POLLY *and* PHILIP.] Good-by, till morning. [*Gives her hand to* WINTHROP.] Good-by.

[PHILIP *ignores* GHENT *pointedly in the leave-taking.* POLLY *bids him farewell with corresponding cordiality.*]

POLLY. Good-by, Mr. Ghent. [*As they descend the canyon path, she is heard chatting enthusiastically.*] O Phil, you ought to have seen the inside of that delightful little house! [*Her voice is heard for some time, indistinctly.* RUTH, *at the top of the path, waves to them as they descend.*]

GHENT [*Looks long at her, with deep gratitude*]. God bless you! [*She sits down on the rocks of the cabin terrace. He walks up and down in anxious thought. Once or twice he makes as if to speak. At length he stops before her.*]

You must go in and lie down. You are worn out.

RUTH [*Rousing herself*]. No, there is something I must tell you first.

GHENT [*Points at the rug*]. It's about this—work you have been doing?

RUTH [*Slightly startled*]. You know of that?

GHENT. Your brother told me. I should have found it out tomorrow anyhow. [*Pause.*] Have you wanted money?

RUTH. Yes.

GHENT. I thought I—I thought you had enough. I have often begged you to take more.

RUTH. I haven't spent what you gave me. It is in there. [*She points toward the house.*]

GHENT [*Astonished*]. You haven't spent—any of it?

RUTH. A little. Nothing for myself.

GHENT. But there has been no need to save, not after the first month or two. You surely knew that!

RUTH. Yes, I knew it. It was not economy.

GHENT [*Slowly*]. You haven't been willing to take money from me?

RUTH. No. I know it was small of me, but I couldn't help it. I have paid for everything.—I have kept account of it—oh, to the last dreadful penny! These clothes are the ones I wore from my brother's house that night. This shelter—you know I helped to raise that with my own hands. And—and some things I paid for secretly, from the little hoard I brought away with me. You were careless; you did not notice.

GHENT [*Sits down, dizzy from the shock of her words*]. I must try to grasp this! [*There is a silence, during which he sits perfectly motionless. At last he turns to her.*] Why—why did you stand up so plucky, so splendid, just now? Put a good face on everything about our life? Call me by my first name and all that—before your own people?

RUTH. We are man and wife. Beside that, my own people are as strangers.

GHENT [*Eagerly*]. You say that? You can still say that?

RUTH [*Looks up, startled*]. Can't you? [*She awaits his answer tensely.*]

GHENT [*Desperately*]. Oh, I don't know. I can't say or think anything, after what you have just told me!

RUTH [*Wails*]. You can't say it! And it isn't true! It is we who are strangers.—Worse, a thousand times worse!

GHENT [*Rises and stands over her*]. Don't let us dash ourselves to hell in one crazy minute! [*He pauses and hesitates. When he speaks again it is with wistful tenderness.*] Ruth, do you remember our journey here? [*She lifts her head, looking at him with white, thirsty face.*] I thought—it seemed to me you had—begun to care for me.

RUTH. That night, when we rode away from the justice's office at San Jacinto, and the sky began to brighten over the desert—the ice that had gathered here [*she touches her heart*] began to melt in spite of me. And when the next night and the next day passed, and the next, and still you spared me and treated me with beautiful rough chivalry, I said to myself, "He has heard my prayer to him. He knows what a girl's heart is." As you rode before me down the arroyos, and up over the mesas, through the dazzling sunlight and the majestic silence, it seemed as if you were leading me out of a world of little codes and customs into a great new world.—So it was for those first days.—And then—and then—I woke, and saw you standing in my tent door in the starlight! I knew before you spoke that we were lost. You hadn't had the strength to save us!

GHENT [*Huskily*]. Surely it hasn't all been—hateful to you? There have been times, since that.—The afternoon we climbed up here. The day we made the table; the day we planted the vines.

RUTH [*In a half whisper*]. Yes!—

Beautiful days! [*She puts her hands suddenly before her face and sobs.*] Oh, it was not my fault! I have struggled against it. You don't know how I have struggled!

GHENT. Against what? Struggled against what?

RUTH. Against the hateful image you had raised up beside your own image.

GHENT. What do you mean?

RUTH. I mean that sometimes—often—when you stand there before my eyes, you fade away, and in your place I see—the Other One!

GHENT. Speak plainly, for God's sake! I don't understand this talk.

RUTH [*Looking steadfastly, as at an invisible shape, speaks in a horrified whisper*]. There he stands behind you now!—The human beast, that goes to its horrible pleasure as not even a wild animal will go—*in pack, in pack!* [GHENT, *stung beyond endurance, rises and paces up and down.* RUTH *continues in a broken tone, spent by the violence of her own words.*] I have tried—Oh, you don't know how I have tried to save myself from these thoughts.—While we were poor and struggling I thought I could do it.—Then—[*she points toward the canyon*] then that hole down there began belching its stream of gold. You began to load me with gifts—to force easy ways upon me——

GHENT. Well, what else did I care to make money for?

RUTH [*Does not answer for a moment, then speaks slowly, taking the words with loathing upon her tongue*]. Every time you give me anything, or talk about the mine and what it is going to do, there rings in my ears that dreadful sneer: "A dirt-eating Mojave would pay more than that for his squaw!" [*She rises, lifting her arms.*] I held myself so dear! And you bought me for a handful of gold, like a woman of the street! You drove me before you like an animal from the market! [GHENT *has seated himself again, elbows on knees and face in his hands.* RUTH *takes slowly from her bosom the nugget chain and holds it crumpled up in her palm. Her tone is quiet, almost matter-of-fact.*] I have got back the chain again.

GHENT [*Looks up*]. Chain?—What chain?

RUTH [*In the same tone, as she holds it up, letting it unwind*]. The one you bought me with.

GHENT [*Dumfounded*]. Where the devil—? Has that fellow been around here?

RUTH. It would have had no meaning for me except from his hand.

GHENT. So that's what you've been doing with this rug-weaving and basket-making tomfoolery? [RUTH *does not answer, but continues looking at the chain, running it through her fingers and weighing it in her hand.*] How long has this been going on?

RUTH. How long?—How long can one live without breathing? Two minutes? A few lifetimes? How long!

GHENT. It was about a month after we came here that you began to potter with this work.

RUTH [*Draws her hand about her neck as if loosening something there; convulsively*]. Since then this has been round my neck, around my limbs, a chain of eating fire. Link by link I have unwound it. You will never know what it has cost me, but I have paid it all. Take it and let me go free. [*She tries to force it upon him, with wailing entreaty.*] Take it, take it, I beseech you!

GHENT [*Holding himself under stern control*]. You are killing yourself. You mustn't go on this way. Go and rest. We will talk of this tomorrow.

RUTH. Rest! Tomorrow! Oh, how little you have understood of all I have said! I know it is only a symbol—a make-believe. I know I am childish to ask it. Still, take it and tell me I am free.

GHENT [*Takes the chain reluctantly, stands for a moment looking at it, then speaks with iron firmness*]. As you say, your price has risen. This is not enough. [*He throws the chain about her neck and draws her to him by it.*] You are mine, mine, do you hear? Now and forever! [*He starts toward the house. She holds out her hand blindly to detain him.*]

RUTH [*In a stifled voice*]. Wait! There is—something else. [*He returns to her, anxiously, and stands waiting. She goes on, touching the chain.*] It isn't only for my sake I ask you to take this off me, nor only for your sake. There is —another life—to think of.

GHENT [*Leaning to look into her averted face*]. Ruth!—Is it true?—Thank God!

RUTH. Now will you take this off me?

GHENT [*Starts to do so, then draws back*]. No. Now less than ever. For now, more than ever, you are mine.

RUTH. But—*how* yours? Oh, remember, have pity! *How* yours?

[PHILIP *appears at the head of the canyon path. Hearing their voices, he waits, half concealed.*]

GHENT. No matter how! Bought if you like, but mine! Mine by blind chance and the hell in a man's veins, if you like! Mine by almighty Nature whether you like it or not!

RUTH. Nature! Almighty Nature! [*She takes the chain slowly from her neck.*] Not yours! By everything my people have held sacred! [*She drops the chain.*] Not yours! Not yours! [*She turns slowly.* PHILIP *has come forward, and supports her as she sinks half fainting upon his neck.*]

PHILIP [*To* GHENT]. I came back to get my sister for the night.—I don't know by what ugly spell you have held her, but I know, from her own lips, that it is broken. [*To* RUTH.] Come! I have horses below.

GHENT. No!

PHILIP [*Measuring him.*]. Yes.

[*Pause.*]

GHENT. Let her say!

RUTH [*Looks long at* GHENT, *then at the house and surroundings. At last she turns to her brother*]. Take me—with you. Take me—home!

[PHILIP, *supporting her, leads her down the canyon path.* GHENT *stands gazing after them as they disappear below the rim. He picks up the chain and goes back, looking down after the descending figures. The sunset light has faded, and darkness has begun to settle over the mountain world.*]

Curtain

ACT III

Sitting room of MRS. JORDAN'S *house at Milford Corners, Massachusetts. An old-fashioned New England interior, faded but showing signs of former distinction. The walls are hung with family portraits, several in clerical attire of the eighteenth century, one in the uniform of the Revolutionary War. Doors open right and left. At the back is a fireplace, flanked by windows, the curtains of which are drawn. On the left is a small table, with a lamp, books, and magazines; on the right, near the fireplace, a sewing table, with lamp and sewing basket. A bookcase and a writing desk occupy opposite corners of the room, forward.*

WINTHROP *and* PHILIP *stand near the desk, chatting.* POLLY *is reading a newspaper at the table, left.* RUTH *sits before the grate, sewing; her face is turned away toward the fire.*

PHILIP [*Offers* WINTHROP *his cigar case*]. Have another cigar.

WINTHROP. Well, as a celebration. [*Takes one and lights it.*]

PHILIP. Rather small business for the Jordan family, to be celebrating a bare escape from the poorhouse.

WINTHROP. Where did you scare up the benevolent uncle? I never heard of him before.

PHILIP. Nor I, scarcely. He's always

lived abroad. [WINTHROP, *strolling about, peeps over* POLLY'S *shoulder.*]

WINTHROP [*To* PHILIP, *with a scandalized gesture*]. Stock reports!

PHILIP. Her latest craze.

WINTHROP. Last week it was Japanese Samurai.

POLLY [*Crushingly*]. And next week it will be—Smart Alecks.

[*The door on the left opens, and* MRS. JORDAN *enters, with* DR. NEWBURY. *During the preceding conversation* RUTH *has sat sewing, paying no heed to the chatter.* MRS. JORDAN *and the* DOCTOR *look at her as they come in, but she does not look up.*]

MRS. JORDAN. Sit down, Doctor, at least for a moment.

DR. NEWBURY [*Seats himself,* MRS. JORDAN *near him*]. I can never resist such an invitation, in this house.

MRS. JORDAN. Dear Doctor, you've been a wonderful friend to me and mine all these years, since poor Josiah was taken.

DR. NEWBURY. But just when you needed help most——

MRS. JORDAN. I know how gladly you would have offered it, if you could.

DR. NEWBURY. Your brother-in-law in England was able to redeem the property?

MRS. JORDAN [*Hastily*]. Yes, yes.—But what we are to do for the future, with my little capital gone—— [*She speaks lower.*] Oh, that dreadful West! If my children had only stayed where they were born and bred. [*She glances at* RUTH, *who has let her sewing fall in her lap and sits staring into the fire.*]

DR. NEWBURY [*Sotto voce*]. Poor child!

POLLY [*Looks up from the newspaper excitedly, holding her finger at a place on the sheet*]. I say, Phil! Win! Look here. [PHILIP *and* WINTHROP, *who have been chatting and smoking apart, come to the table.*]

PHILIP. What is it now?

POLLY [*Tapping on the paper*]. Something about your Arizona scheme.

PHILIP [*Bending over her, reads*] "Alleghany pig-iron, 93¾, National Brick——

POLLY [*Pointing*]. No, there!

PHILIP. Arizona Cactus Fiber, 84. [*He picks up the paper, astounded.*] Cactus Fiber listed! Selling at 84! [*He tosses the paper to Winthrop.*] This is the last straw!

MRS. JORDAN [*Who has been listening anxiously*]. What does it mean, Phil?

PHILIP. Only that the people who bought our plant and patents for a song, have made a fortune out of them. [RUTH *has resumed her needlework.* WINTHROP *offers her the paper, with his finger at the line. She takes it, looks at it vaguely, and lays it on the table.*]

POLLY [*Leaning across*]. Doesn't that interest you?

RUTH [*Tonelessly*]. Oh, yes. [*She rises, lays her work aside, and goes toward the door, left.*]

DR. NEWBURY [*As she passes him*]. Won't you bid me good night, my child?

RUTH [*Giving him her hand*]. Good night, Doctor.

DR. NEWBURY [*Shaking his finger*]. Remember, no more moping! And from tomorrow, outdoors with you. [RUTH *looks at him vacantly, attempting to smile. She moves toward the door, which* WINTHROP *opens for her.*]

WINTHROP [*Holding out his hand*]. You must bid me good night, too, and good-by.

RUTH [*With a faint kindling of interest*]. Are you going away?

WINTHROP. Only back to Boston. Some time, when you are stronger, you will come down and see our new sailors' hospital.

RUTH. Yes.—Good-by. [*She goes out,* WINTHROP *closing the door.*]

WINTHROP [*To* DR. NEWBURY]. I must be going along, Father. Good night, everybody! [*Patting* PHILIP'S *shoulder.*]

Hard luck, old man! [*He goes out by the hall door on the right,* PHILIP *accompanying him.*]

DR. NEWBURY [*Looking after his son*]. Brave boy! Brave boy! He keeps up a good show.

MRS. JORDAN. You think he still grieves over her?

DR. NEWBURY. Ah, poor chap! He's made of the right stuff, if he is mine.

MRS. JORDAN. Let us not talk of it. It is too sad, too dreadful. [PHILIP *re-enters.*]

DR. NEWBURY. About part of it we must talk. [*He speaks so as to include* PHILIP *and* POLLY *in the conversation.*] Mrs. Jordan, I don't want to alarm you, but your daughter—I may as well put it bluntly—is in a dangerous state.

MRS. JORDAN [*Frightened*]. Doctor! I thought she seemed so much stronger.

DR. NEWBURY. She is, so far as her body is concerned. [MRS. JORDAN *sits in an attitude of nervous attention, gazing at the* DOCTOR *as if trying to formulate one of many questions pressing upon her.* PHILIP *comes forward and sits by the table, near them.*]

PHILIP. Don't you think that the routine of life which she has taken up will soon restore her to a normal state of mind?

DR. NEWBURY. Perhaps.—I hope so. —I would have good hope of it, if it were not for her attitude toward her child.

MRS. JORDAN [*Overwhelmed*]. You have noticed that, too! I haven't spoken to you of it, because—I haven't been willing to see it myself.

PHILIP. I can't see that there is anything particularly strange in her attitude. She takes care of the brat scrupulously enough.

POLLY. Brat!

MRS. JORDAN. Brat! [*To* DR. NEWBURY, *after a reproachful gaze at* PHILIP.] With the most watchful, the minutest care, but [*she speaks in a constrained voice, with a nervous glance at the door*] exactly as if it were a piece of machinery!—Phil, do please lay down that paper-knife before you break it! Your father brought that to me from India. [*He obeys, but picks it up again absent-mindedly, after a few seconds.*] Pardon me, Doctor. She goes about her daily business, and answers when she is spoken to, but as for her really being here—— [*She breaks out.*] Doctor, what *shall* we do?

DR. NEWBURY. She must be roused from this state, but how to do it, I don't know.

POLLY [*Rising, with heightened color and nervous emphasis*]. Well, I do!

MRS. JORDAN [*Looking at her with frightened interrogation*]. Polly——?

POLLY. What she needs is her husband, and I have sent for him!

PHILIP [*Inarticulate with surprise and anger*]. You——!

POLLY. Yes, I. He's been here a week. And he's an angel, isn't he, Mother?

[PHILIP *snaps the paper-knife in two, flings the pieces to the floor, and rises, pale with rage.*]

MRS. JORDAN [*Gathering up the pieces with a wail*]. O Phil! How could you! One of my most precious relics!

PHILIP [*To* MRS. JORDAN]. Is this true, or is it another of her tedious jokes?

POLLY [*Protesting*]. Oh, my dear, tedious!

MRS. JORDAN [*Wipes her eyes, after ruefully fitting the broken pieces of the knife together and laying them tenderly on the table*]. You don't deserve to have me answer you, but it is true.

PHILIP. Was this action taken with your knowledge?

MRS. JORDAN. I do not expect to be spoken to in that tone. Polly telegraphed merely the facts. He came at his own instance.

PHILIP. But you have consented to enter into relations with him?

MRS. JORDAN. I have seen him several times.

POLLY [*Triumphantly*]. And yesterday we showed him the baby! Such fun, wasn't it, Mother?

MRS. JORDAN [*Wiping her eyes, sheepishly*]. Yes, it was rather—enjoyable.

PHILIP. He can't be in this town. I should have heard of it.

POLLY. We've hid him safe.

PHILIP. Where?

POLLY. Never mind. He's on tap, and the sooner we turn on the spigot the better, is what I think. Doctor, what do you think?

DR. NEWBURY. Let me ask you again to state your view of Ruth's case. I don't think I quite grasp your view.

POLLY [*Pluming herself, doctrinaire*]. Well! Here on the one hand is the primitive, the barbaric woman, falling in love with a romantic stranger, who, like some old Viking on a harry, cuts her with his two-handed sword from the circle of her kinsmen, and bears her away on his dragon ship toward the midnight sun. Here on the other hand is the derived, the civilized woman, with a civilized nervous system, observing that the creature eats bacon with his bowie knife, knows not the manicure, has the conversation of a preoccupied walrus, the instincts of a jealous caribou, and the endearments of a dancing crab in the mating season.

MRS. JORDAN. Polly! What ideas! What language!

DR. NEWBURY. Don't be alarmed, Mrs. Jordan. The vocabulary has changed since our day, and—the point of view has shifted a little. [*To* POLLY] Well?

POLLY. Well, Ruth is one of those people who can't live in a state of divided feeling. She sits staring at this cleavage in her life, like—like that man in Dante, don't you know, who is pierced by the serpent, and who stands there in hell staring at his wound, yawning like a sleepy man.

MRS. JORDAN. Oh, Polly, do please try not to get our heads muddled up with literature!

POLLY. All I mean is that when she married her man she married him for keeps. And he did the same by her.

[PHILIP *rises, with uncontrollable impatience, and goes back to the mantelpiece, against which he leans, nervously tearing a bit of paper to pieces.*]

DR. NEWBURY. Don't you think that a mere difference of cultivation, polish —or—or something of that sort—is rather small to have led to a rupture, and so painful a one too?

POLLY [*A little nonplussed*]. Well, yes, perhaps it does *look* small. But we don't know the particulars; and men *are* such *colossal* brutes, you know, dear Doctor!

DR. NEWBURY [*Judicially*]. Yes, so they are, so they are!

POLLY. And then her pride! You know when it comes to pride, Ruth would make Lucifer look like a charity boy asking for more soup.

DR. NEWBURY. I think perhaps the plan should be tried. [*After a pause*] Yes, I think so decidedly.

PHILIP. I call this a plot against her dignity and peace of mind!

DR. NEWBURY [*Rising*]. Well, this conspirator must be going. [*He shakes hands with* POLLY *and* MRS. JORDAN, *takes his hat and stick.* PHILIP *remains plunged in angry reflection.* DR. NEWBURY *taps* PHILIP *jestingly on the shoulder with the tip of his cane.*] When you have lived as long as I have, my boy, you'll—you'll be just as old as I am! [*He goes out,* POLLY *accompanying him to the door.*]

[PHILIP, *disregarding his mother's conciliatory look and gesture as he passes her, goes out left.* POLLY *stretches her arms and draws a deep breath as the door closes after him.*]

MRS. JORDAN [*Looking at her severely*]. Pray what does that mean?

POLLY. Oh, Phil is such a walking thundercloud, these days. It's a relief to get rid of him.

MRS. JORDAN. Have you done what you could to make his life brighter?

POLLY. I never had a chance. He has always been too much wrapped up in Ruth to think of me.

MRS. JORDAN. How can you say such a thing? What do you suppose he married you for?

POLLY. Heaven knows! What do they ever do it for? It is a most curious and savage propensity. But immensely interesting to watch.

MRS. JORDAN [*With a despairing gesture*]. If you hold such heathenish views, why are you so bent on bringing those two together?

POLLY [*Soberly*]. Because they represent—what Philip and I have missed.

MRS. JORDAN. And pray what have "Philip and I" missed?

POLLY. Oh, we're all right. But we're not like those two.

MRS. JORDAN. I should hope not!

POLLY. Even I believe that now and then a marriage is made in heaven. This one was. They are predestined lovers!

MRS. JORDAN [*Mournfully, hypnotized by the evangelical note*]. I pray it may be so. [*She looks suspiciously at* POLLY.] You wretched girl! Predestined lovers and marriage made in heaven, after all you've just been saying about how impossible he is.

POLLY. He is quite impossible, but he's the kind we can't resist, any of us. He'd only have to crook his little finger at me.

MRS. JORDAN [*Lifting her hands in despair*]. What are you young women coming to! [*Pause.*] He seems to me a good man.

POLLY [*Delighted*]. Oh, he's *good!* So is a volcano between eruptions. And commonplace, too, until you happen to get a glimpse down one of the old volcanic rifts in his surface, and see—far below—underneath the cold lava-beds—fire, fire, the molten heart of a continent!

MRS. JORDAN. I only hope you have some vague general notion of what you are talking about.

POLLY. Amen.—And now let's consider when, where, and how we are to hale this dubious pair together.

MRS. JORDAN. One thing is sure, it mustn't be here.

POLLY. Why not?

MRS. JORDAN. On Philip's account.

POLLY. Oh, bother Philip!—Wasn't that the doorbell?

MRS. JORDAN. Yes. You had better go.

POLLY [*Goes out. After a moment she re-enters, excitedly*]. It's Mr. Ghent!

MRS. JORDAN [*Amazed*]. Mr. Ghent? [POLLY *nods enthusiasticallly.* GHENT *enters. He is conventionally dressed, a black string tie and the broad-brimmed hat which he carries being the only suggestions of Western costume remaining.* MRS. JORDAN *receives him in a flutter of excitement and alarm.*] Mr. Ghent——! Surely at this hour——!

GHENT. I beg your pardon. There was no other way. I am going West tonight.—Can I see you alone?

MRS. JORDAN [*Looks at* POLLY, *who goes out, pouting*]. Going West tonight?

GHENT. Yes. Trouble at the mine.

MRS. JORDAN. Isn't your business partner competent to attend to it?

GHENT. He's competent to steal the whole outfit. In fact, is doing it, or has done it already.

MRS. JORDAN [*Vaguely alarmed*]. And—my property here? Is that involved in the danger?

GHENT. Certainly not.

MRS. JORDAN [*Relieved*]. I have gone through such months of misery at the thought of losing the dear old place!—if

Ruth only knew that we owe the very roof over our heads to you——

GHENT. Well, she isn't to know, that's understood, isn't it? Besides, it's nothing to speak of. Glad if you think it a service. She wouldn't.

MRS. JORDAN. You mean——?

GHENT. I mean that if she knew about it, she wouldn't stay here overnight.

MRS. JORDAN. Sit down. [*She motions him to a seat at the table; she sits near him, speaking with nervous impulsiveness.*] Tell me what is the trouble between you! It has all been a dreadful mystery from the beginning!

GHENT. Is it a mystery that a woman like your daughter——? [*He stops and sinks into gloomy thought.*]

MRS. JORDAN. Should have chosen you?—Pardon me, I don't mean anything unkind—— [*He makes a gesture of brusque exoneration.*] But having chosen—and broken faith with her brother to do it——

GHENT [*Nervously*]. Let's drop that! [*Pause.*] Mrs. Jordan, you come of the old stock. Do you believe in the devil?

MRS. JORDAN. Perhaps not in the sense you mean.

GHENT [*Tapping his breast*]. I mean the devil inside of a man—the devil in the heart!

MRS. JORDAN. Oh, yes. We are all forced by our lives to believe in that.

GHENT. Our lives! [*He looks slowly round the room.*] How long have you lived here?

MRS. JORDAN. For thirty years, in this house. Before I was married I lived in the old house down the road yonder, opposite the church.

GHENT [*To himself*]. Think of it!

MRS. JORDAN. What did you say?

GHENT [*Gathers himself together*]. Mrs. Jordan, I want you to promise that what I put in your hands from time to time comes to your daughter as if from another source.

MRS. JORDAN. You are going away for good?

GHENT. Yes.

MRS. JORDAN. You give her up?

GHENT. A man can't give up what isn't his.

MRS. JORDAN. What isn't his? She is your wife.

GHENT. No. Never has been.

MRS. JORDAN [*Terrified*]. Oh, pitiful heavens!

GHENT. I beg your pardon.—I was only trying to say—I used to think that when a couple was married, there they were, man and wife, and that was the end of it. I used to think that when they had a child, well, sure enough it was their child, and all said.—And there's something in that, too. [*He stares before him, smiting the table and speaking with low intensity.*] Damn me if there ain't something eternal in it! [*He sits for a moment more in gloomy thought.*] Do you think she'll make up to the young one, after a bit?

MRS. JORDAN. Oh, surely! To think otherwise would be too dreadful!

GHENT. I'd give a good deal to know. —It's kind of lonesome for the little rooster, sitting out there all by himself on the world's doorstep!—I must see her for a minute before I go.—Do your best for me.

MRS. JORDAN. I will do what I can.

GHENT. You can put it as a matter of business. There is a matter of business I want to talk over with her, if I can get up the gumption.

MRS. JORDAN. Hadn't you better tell me what it is?

GHENT. Well, it's about your son Philip. That little scheme he started out in my country—the Cactus Fiber industry.

MRS. JORDAN. Yes?

GHENT. I believe he thinks his sister's going away when she did queered his game.

MRS. JORDAN. It was a severe blow

to him in every way. She was the life and soul of his enterprise.

GHENT. I want her to give him back the Cactus Fiber outfit, worth something more than when he dropped it.

MRS. JORDAN. Give it back to him? She?

GHENT [*Takes papers from his pocket*]. Yes. I happened to hear it was knocking around for nothing in the market, and I bought it—for the house, really. Hated to see that go to the dogs. Then I looked over the plant, and got a hustler to boom it. I thought as a matter of transfer, to cancel her debt, or what she thinks her debt——

[*Pause.*]

MRS. JORDAN [*Fingering the paper with hesitation*]. Mr. Ghent, we really can't accept such a thing. Your offer is quixotic.

GHENT. Quix—what?

MRS. JORDAN. Quixotic, it really is.

GHENT [*Doubtfully*]. I guess you're right. It depends on the way you look at it. One way it looks like a pure business proposition—so much lost, so much made good. The other way it looks, as you say, quix—um—. Anyway, there are the papers! Do what you think best with them. [*He lays the papers on the table, and picks up his hat.*]

MRS. JORDAN. Wait in the parlor. [*He opens the hall door.*] The second door on the left.

[*With an awkward bow to* MRS. JORDAN, *he partly closes the door after him, when the inner door opens and* RUTH *appears. She goes to the sewing table and picks up her sewing. Her mother, with a frightened glance at the half-open hall door, draws her back and kisses her.* GHENT, *unseen by* RUTH, *remains standing, with his hand on the doorknob.*]

MRS. JORDAN. Ruth, you are a brave girl, and I will treat you like one.—Your husband is here.

RUTH. Here?—Where?

[GHENT *pushes the door open, and closes it behind him.* RUTH, *sinking back against the opposite wall, stares at him blankly.*]

MRS. JORDAN. He is leaving for the West again tonight. He has asked to see you before he goes. [RUTH *covers her face with her hands, then fumbles blindly for the latch of the door. Her mother restrains her.*] It is your duty to hear what he has to say. You owe that to the love you once bore him.

RUTH. He killed my love before it was born!

MRS. JORDAN. It is your duty to hear him, and part with him in a Christian spirit, for our sakes, if not for your own.

RUTH. For whose sake?

MRS. JORDAN. For mine, and your brother's.—We owe it to him, as a family.

GHENT [*Raises his hand restrainingly*]. Mrs. Jordan—!

RUTH. Owe?

MRS. JORDAN. We owe it to him, for what he has done and wishes to do.

RUTH. What he has done?—Wishes to do?

MRS. JORDAN. Yes, don't echo me like a parrot! He has done a great deal for us, and is anxious to do more, if you will only let him.

RUTH. What is this? Explain it to me quickly.

MRS. JORDAN [*With growing impatience*]. Don't think to judge your mother!

RUTH. I demand to hear what all this is! Tell me.

MRS. JORDAN [*Losing control of herself*]. He has kept us from being turned into the street! [GHENT, *who has tried dumbly to restrain her, turns away in stoic resignation to his fate.*] He has given us the very roof over our heads!

RUTH. You said that Uncle——

MRS. JORDAN. Well, it was not your uncle! I said so to shield you in your stubborn and cold-hearted pride.

RUTH. Is there more of this?

MRS. JORDAN. Yes, there *is* more. You

wronged your brother to follow your own path of willful love, and now you wrong him again by following your own path of willful aversion. Here comes your husband, offering to make restitution——

RUTH. What restitution?

MRS. JORDAN. He has bought Philip's property out there, and wants you to give it back to him.

RUTH [*Stands motionless for a moment, then looks vacantly about, speaking in a dull voice, as at first*]. I must go away from this house.

MRS. JORDAN. You don't understand. He claims nothing. He is going away himself immediately. Whatever this dreadful trouble is between you, you are his wife, and he has a right to help you and yours.

RUTH. I am not his wife.

MRS. JORDAN. Ruth, don't frighten me. He said those same words——

RUTH. He said—what?

MRS. JORDAN. That you were not his wife.

RUTH. He said—that?

MRS. JORDAN. Yes, but afterward he explained——

RUTH [*Flaming into white wrath*]. Explained! Did he explain that when I was left alone that night at the ranch he came—with two others—and when gun and knife had failed me, and nothing stood between me and their drunken fury, I sold myself to the strongest of them, hiding my head behind the name of marriage? Did he explain that between him and the others money clinked—[*she raps on the table*] my price in hard money on the table? And now that I have run away to the only refuge I have on earth, he comes to buy the very house where I have hidden, and every miserable being within it!

[*Long pause. She looks about blankly and sinks down by the table.*]

MRS. JORDAN [*Cold and rigid*]. And you—married him—after that? [*She turns away in horror-stricken judgment.*] You ought to have—died—first! [PHILIP *opens the door and enters, staring at* GHENT *with dislike and menace.*] Oh Philip, she has told me!—You can't imagine what horrors!

[RUTH *rises, with fright in her face, and approaches her brother to restrain him.*]

PHILIP. Horrors? What horrors?

MRS. JORDAN. It was your fault! You ought never to have left her alone in that dreadful place! She—she married him—to save herself—from—Oh, horrible!

[PHILIP *waits an instant, the truth penetrating his mind slowly. Then, with mortal rage in his face, he starts toward* GHENT.]

PHILIP. You—dog!

RUTH [*Throws herself in* PHILIP'S *path*]. No, no, no!

PHILIP. Get out of my way. This is my business now.

RUTH. No, it is mine. I tell you it is mine.

PHILIP. We'll see whose it is. I said that if the truth ever came out, this man should answer to me, and now, by God, he shall answer! [*With another access of rage he tries to thrust* RUTH *from his path.* MRS. JORDAN, *terrified at the storm she has raised, clings desperately to her son's arm.*]

RUTH. I told him long ago it should be between us. Now it shall be between us.

MRS. JORDAN. Philip! For my sake, for your father's sake! Don't, don't! You will only make it worse. In pity's name, leave them alone together. Leave them alone—together!

[*They force* PHILIP *back to the door, where he stands glaring at* GHENT.]

PHILIP [*To* GHENT]. My time will come. Meanwhile, hide behind the skirts of the woman whose life you have ruined and whose heart you have broken. Hide behind her. It is the coward's privilege. Take it.

[PHILIP, *with* MRS. JORDAN *still clinging to his arm, goes out,* RUTH *closing the door after them. She and* GHENT *confront each other in silence for a moment, across the width of the room.*]

RUTH. God forgive me! You never can.

GHENT. It was a pity—but—you were in a corner. I drove you to it, by coming here.

RUTH. It was base of me—base!

GHENT. The way your mother took it showed me one thing. I've never understood you, because—I don't understand your people.

RUTH. You mean—her saying I ought to have died rather than accept life as I did?

GHENT. Yes.

RUTH. She spoke the truth. I have always seen it.

GHENT. Ruth, it's a queer thing for me to be saying, but—it seems to me, you've never seen the truth between us.

RUTH. What is the truth—between us?

GHENT. The truth is—— [*He pauses, then continues with a disconsolate gesture.*] Well, there's no use going into that. [*He fumbles in his pocket, and takes from it the nugget chain, which he looks at in silence for a time, then speaks in quiet resignation.*] I've got here the chain, that's come, one way and another, to have a meaning for us. For you it's a bitter meaning, but, all the same, I want you to keep it. Show it some day to the boy, and tell him—about me. [*He lays it on the desk and goes toward the door.*]

RUTH. What is the truth—between us?

GHENT. I guess it was only of myself I was thinking.

RUTH. What is it—about yourself?

GHENT [*After a pause*]. I drifted into one of your meeting-houses last Sunday, not knowing where else to go, and I heard a young fellow preaching about what he called "The Second Birth." A year and a half ago I should have thought it was all hocus-pocus, but you can believe me or not, the way he went on he might have been behind the door that night in that little justice den at San Jacinto, saying to the Recording Angel: "Do you see that rascal? Take notice! There ain't an ounce of bone or a drop of blood in him but what's new man!"

RUTH. You think it has been all my fault—the failure we've made of our life?

GHENT. It's been no failure. However it is, it's been our life, and in my heart I think it's been—all—right!

RUTH. All right! Oh, how can you say that? [*She repeats the words with a touch of awe and wonder.*] All right!

GHENT. Some of it has been wrong, but as a whole it has been right—right! I know that doesn't happen often, but it has happened to us, because—[*he stops, unable to find words for his idea*] because —because the first time our eyes met, they burned away all that was bad in our meeting, and left only the fact that we *had* met—pure good—pure joy—a fortune of it—for both of us. Yes, for both of us! You'll see it yourself some day.

RUTH. If you had only heard my cry to you, to wait, to cleanse yourself and me—by suffering and sacrifice—before we dared begin to live! But you wouldn't see the need!—Oh, if you could have felt for yourself what I felt for you! If you could have said, "The wages of sin is death!" and suffered the anguish of death and risen again purified! But instead of that, what you had done fell off from you like any daily trifle.

GHENT [*Steps impulsively nearer her, sweeping his hand to indicate the portraits on the walls*]. Ruth, it's these fellows are fooling you! It's they who keep your head set on the wages of sin, and all that rubbish. What have we got to do with suffering and sacrifice? That may be the law for some, and I've tried hard to see it as our law, and thought I had succeeded. But I haven't. Our law is joy, and selfishness; the curve of your shoulder and the light on your hair as you sit there says that as plain as preaching. —Does it gall you the way we came together? You asked me that night what brought me, and I told you whiskey, and sun, and the devil. Well, I tell you now I'm thankful on my knees for all three! Does it rankle in your mind that I took you when I could get you, by main strength and fraud? I guess most good women are taken that way, if they only knew it. Don't you want to be paid for? I guess every wife is paid for in some good coin or other. And as for you, I've paid for you not only with a trumpery chain, but with the heart in my breast, do you hear? That's one thing you can't throw back at me—the man you've made of me, the life and the meaning of life you've showed me the way to! [RUTH's *face is hidden in her hands, her elbows on the table. He stands over her, flushed and waiting. Gradually the light fades from his face. When he speaks again, the ring of exultation which has been in his voice is replaced by a sober intensity.*] If you can't see it my way, give me another chance to live it out in yours. [*He waits, but she does not speak or look up. He takes a package of letters and papers from his pocket, and runs them over, in deep reflection.*] During the six months I've been East——

RUTH [*Looking up*]. Six months? Mother said a week!

GHENT. Your sister-in-law's telegram was forwarded to me here. I let her think it brought me, but as a matter of fact, I came East in the next train after yours. It was rather a low-lived thing to do, I suppose, hanging about and bribing your servant for news—— [RUTH *lets her head sink in her hands. He pauses and continues ruefully*] I might have known how that would strike you! Well, it would have come out sooner or later.—That's not what I started to talk about.—You ask me to suffer for my wrong. Since you left me I *have* suffered—God knows! You ask me to make some sacrifice. Well—how would the mine do? Since I've been away they've as good as stolen it from me. I could get it back easy enough by fighting; but supposing I don't fight. Then we'll start all over again, just as we stand in our shoes, and make another fortune—for our boy. [RUTH *utters a faint moan as her head sinks in her arms on the table. With trembling hands,* GHENT *caresses her hair lightly, and speaks between a laugh and sob.*] Little mother! Little mother! What does the past matter, when we've got the future—and him? [RUTH *does not move. He remains bending over her for some moments, then straightens up, with a gesture of stoic despair.*] I know what you're saying there to yourself, and I guess you're right. Wrong is wrong, from the moment it happens till the crack of doom, and all the angels in heaven, working overtime, can't make it less or different by a hair. That seems to be the law. I've learned it hard, but I guess I've learned it. I've seen it written in mountain letters across the continent of this life.—Done is done, and lost is lost, and smashed to hell is smashed to hell. We fuss and potter and patch up. You might as well try to batter down the Rocky Mountains with a rabbit's heart-beat! [*He goes to the door, where he turns.*] You've fought hard for me, God bless you for it.—But it's been a losing game with you from the first!—You belong here, and I belong out yonder—beyond the Rockies, beyond—the Great Divide! [*He opens the door and is about to pass out.* RUTH *looks up with streaming eyes.*]

RUTH. Wait! [*He closes the door and stands waiting for her to speak.* RUTH *masters herself and goes on, her eyes shining, her face exalted.*] Tell me you know that if I could have followed you, and been your wife, without struggle and without bitterness, I would have done it.

GHENT [*Solemnly*]. I believe you would.

RUTH. Tell me you know that when I tore down with bleeding fingers the life you were trying to build for us, I did it only—because—I loved you!

GHENT [*Comes slowly to the table, looking at her with bewilderment*]. How was that?

RUTH. Oh, I don't wonder you ask! Another woman would have gone straight to her goal. You might have found such a one. But instead you found me, a woman in whose ears rang night and day the cry of an angry Heaven to us both—"Cleanse yourselves!" And I went about doing it in the only way I knew—[*she points at the portraits on the wall*] the only way my fathers knew—by wretchedness, by self-torture, by trying blindly to pierce your careless heart with pain. And all the while you—Oh, as I lay there and listened to you, I realized it for the first time—you had risen, in one hour, to a wholly new existence, which flooded the present and the future with brightness, yes, and reached back into our past, and made of it—made of all of it—something to cherish! [*She takes the chain, and comes closer.*] You have taken the good of our life and grown strong. I have taken the evil and grown weak, weak unto death. Teach me to live as you do! [*She puts the chain about her neck.*]

GHENT [*Puzzled, not yet realizing the full force of her words*]. Teach you—to live—as I do?

RUTH. And teach—*him!*

GHENT [*Unable to realize his fortune*]. You'll let me help make a kind of a happy life for—the little rooster?

RUTH [*Holds out her arms, her face flooded with happiness*]. And for us! For us!

Curtain

Eugene O'Neill

✻ 1888-1953

Eugene O'Neill, who was born in New York City, may have inherited much of his instinct for the theatrically effective from his father, James O'Neill, a celebrated hero of romantic melodramas, though the subject matter that he finally made his own and his attitude toward it would have seemed both improper and undramatic to the older star. Eugene's formal education came to an end with a year at Princeton in 1906, but the following decade was full of experiences on which he drew for his plays. During those years he filled a number of miscellaneous jobs, prospected for gold in Honduras, shipped as a seaman on a freighter to Buenos Aires, acted a minor role in one of his father's productions for fifteen weeks, worked as a cub reporter on a New London paper, and spent six months in a tuberculosis sanatorium.

This marked the turning point in his life; surrounded by death, he had for the first time to think seriously about his future, and he determined to become a playwright. When he left the sanatorium he joined the 47 Workshop at Harvard, where George Pierce Baker was training so many of the artists who were to develop the outstanding American repertory of the twenties, and then wrote a series of one-act plays based on his seagoing experiences. One of these, BOUND EAST FOR CARDIFF, *was an outstanding success of the first season of the Provincetown Players (1916), a group that had organized to revitalize the American drama. From that first production O'Neill devoted himself unswervingly to his vocation, searching for the most universal themes and the most effective techniques for their expression.*

In 1920 he was awarded the first of three Pulitzer Prizes, this for his first full-length Broadway production, BEYOND THE HORIZON. *In 1936 he was awarded the Nobel Prize for Literature. In addition to this critical and international recognition of his importance and achievement, O'Neill was also a popular success with commercial audiences. Play after play that had been produced for the coterie audience of Greenwich Village was brought uptown to compete successfully with the domestic comedies, knockabout farces, and mystery plays that had dominated the theatrical menu. Nor did he ever yield to popular taste:* ANNA CHRISTIE *proved that he could write in the conventional pattern of realism, but at the same time he was attracting audiences with a special kind of symbolic drama in* THE EMPEROR JONES *and* THE HAIRY APE. DESIRE UNDER THE ELMS *attacked the beloved myth of the farm,* MOURNING BECOMES ELECTRA *reworked a Greek myth in a modern trilogy that required the audience to attend both in the afternoon and evening, three times the length of an average play;* THE GREAT GOD BROWN *employs not only mysticism (never a popular commodity in the American theatre) but actual masks.*

O'Neill died in Boston, leaving a number of unproduced manuscripts. Three of these, LONG DAY'S JOURNEY INTO NIGHT, A TOUCH OF THE POET, *and* A MOON FOR THE MISBEGOTTEN, *were performed on Broadway and throughout the world in the seasons of 1957–1959, revealing that he never ceased to experiment with his medium or to probe deeply into the life about him.*

The Hairy Ape

A COMEDY OF ANCIENT AND MODERN LIFE

Characters

ROBERT SMITH, "YANK"
PADDY
LONG
MILDRED DOUGLAS
HER AUNT
SECOND ENGINEER
A GUARD
A SECRETARY OF AN ORGANIZATION
Stokers, Ladies, Gentlemen, etc.

Scenes

SCENE I. The firemen's forecastle of an ocean liner—an hour after sailing from New York

SCENE II. Section of promenade deck, two days out—morning

SCENE III. The stokehole. A few minutes later

SCENE IV. Same as Scene I. Half an hour later

SCENE V. Fifth Avenue, New York. Three weeks later

SCENE VI. An island near the city. The next night

SCENE VII. In the city. About a month later

SCENE VIII. In the city. Twilight of the next day

SCENE 1

Scene: The firemen's forecastle of a transatlantic liner an hour after sailing from New York for the voyage across. Tiers of narrow, steel bunks, three deep, on all sides. An entrance in rear. Benches on the floor before the bunks. The room is crowded with men, shouting, cursing, laughing, singing—a confused, inchoate uproar swelling into a sort of unity, a meaning—the bewildered, furious, baffled defiance of a beast in a cage. Nearly all the men are drunk. Many bottles are passed from hand to hand. All are dressed in dungaree pants, heavy ugly shoes. Some wear singlets, but the majority are stripped to the waist.

The treatment of this scene, or of any other scene in the play, should by no means be naturalistic. The effect sought after is a cramped space in the bowels of a ship, imprisoned by white steel. The lines of bunks, the uprights supporting them, cross each other like the steel framework of a cage. The ceiling crushes down upon the men's heads. They cannot stand upright. This accentuates the natural stooping posture which shoveling coal and the resultant over-development of back and shoulder muscles have given them. The men themselves should resemble those pictures in which the appearance of Neanderthal Man is guessed at. All are hairy-chested, with long arms of tremendous power, and low, receding brows above their small, fierce, resentful eyes. All the civilized white races are represented, but except for the slight differentiation in color of hair, skin, eyes, all these men are alike.

The curtain rises on a tumult of sound. YANK *is seated in the foreground. He seems broader, fiercer, more truculent, more powerful, more sure of himself than the rest. They respect his superior strength—the grudging respect of fear. Then, too, he represents to them a self-expression, the very last word in what they are, their most highly developed individual.*

VOICES. Gif me trink dere, you!
'Ave a wet!
Salute!
Gesundheit!
Skoal!
Drunk as a lord, God stiffen you!

Here's how!

Luck!

Pass back that bottle, damn you!

Pourin' it down his neck!

Ho, Froggy! Where the devil have you been?

La Touraine.

I hit him smash in yaw, py Gott!

Jenkins—the First—he's a rotten swine——

And the coppers nabbed him—and I run——

I like peer better. It don't pig head gif you.

A slut, I'm sayin'! She robbed me aslape——

To hell with 'em all!

You're a bloody liar!

Say dot again! [*Commotion. Two men about to fight are pulled apart.*]

No scrappin' now!

Tonight——

See who's the best man!

Bloody Dutchman!

Tonight on the for'ard square.

I'll bet on Dutchy.

He packa da wallop, I tella you!

Shut up, Wop!

No fightin', maties. We're all chums ain't we?

[*A voice starts bawling a song.*]

Beer, beer, glorious beer!
Fill yourselves right up to here.

YANK [*For the first time seeming to take notice of the uproar about him, turns around threateningly—in a tone of contemptuous authority*]. Choke off dat noise! Where d'yuh get dat beer stuff? Beer, hell! Beer's for goils—and Dutchmen. Me for somep'n wit a kick to it! Gimme a drink, one of youse guys. [*Several bottles are eagerly offered. He takes a tremendous gulp at one of them; then, keeping the bottle in his hand, glares belligerently at the owner, who hastens to acquiesce in this robbery by saying*] All righto, Yank. Keep it and have another. [YANK *contemptuously turns his back on the crowd again. For a second there is an embarrassed silence. Then* ——]

VOICES. We must be passing the Hook.

She's beginning to roll to it.

Six days in hell—and then Southampton.

Py Yesus, I vish somepody take my first vatch for me!

Gittin' seasick, Square-head?

Drink up and forget it!

What's in your bottle?

Gin.

Dot's nigger trink.

Absinthe? It's doped. You'll go off your chump, Froggy!

Cochon!

Whisky, that's the ticket!

Where's Paddy?

Going asleep.

Sing us that whisky song, Paddy.

[*They all turn to an old, wizened Irishman who is dozing, very drunk, on the benches forward. His face is extremely monkey-like with all the sad, patient pathos of that animal in his small eyes.*]

Singa da song, Caruso Pat!

He's gettin' old. The drink is too much for him.

He's too drunk.

PADDY [*Blinking about him, starts to his feet resentfully, swaying, holding on to the edge of a bunk*]. I'm never too drunk to sing. 'Tis only when I'm dead to the world I'd be wishful to sing at all. [*With a sort of sad contempt.*] "Whisky Johnny," ye want? A chanty, ye want? Now that's a queer wish from the ugly like of you, God help you. But no mather. [*He starts to sing in a thin, nasal, doleful tone.*]

Oh, whisky is the life of man!
　　Whisky! O Johnny! [*They all join in on this.*]
Oh, whisky is the life of man!
　　Whisky for my Johnny! [*Again chorus.*]
Oh, whisky drove my old man mad!
　　Whisky! O Johnny!

Oh, whisky drove my old man mad!
Whisky for my Johnny!

YANK [*Again turning around scornfully*]. Aw hell! Nix on dat old sailing ship stuff? All dat bull's dead, see? And you're dead, too, yuh damned old Harp, on'y yuh don't know it. Take it easy, see. Give us a rest. Nix on de loud noise. [*With a cynical grin.*] Can't youse see I'm tryin' to t'ink?

ALL [*Repeating the word after him as one with the same cynical amused mockery*]. Think! [*The chorused word has a brazen metallic quality as if their throats were phonograph horns. It is followed by a general uproar of hard, barking laughter.*]

VOICES. Don't be cracking your head wit ut, Yank.

You gat headache, py yingo!

One thing about it—it rhymes with drink!

Ha, ha, ha!

Drink, don't think!

Drink, don't think!

Drink, don't think! [*A whole chorus of voices has taken up this refrain, stamping on the floor, pounding on the benches with fists.*]

YANK [*Taking a gulp from his bottle—good-naturedly*]. Aw right. Can de noise. I got yuh de foist time. [*The uproar subsides. A very drunken sentimental tenor begins to sing.*]

Far away in Canada,
Far across the sea,
There's a lass who fondly waits
Making a home for me——

YANK [*Fiercely contemptuous*]. Shut up, yuh lousy boob! Where d'yuh get dat tripe? Home? Home, hell! I'll make a home for yuh! I'll knock yuh dead. Home! T'hell wit home! Where d'yuh get dat tripe? Dis is home, see? What d'yuh want wit home? [*Proudly.*] I runned away from mine when I was a kid. On'y too glad to beat it, dat was me. Home was lickings for me, dat's all. But yuh can bet your shoit no one ain't never licked me since! Wanter try it, any of youse? Huh! I guess not. [*In a more placated but still contemptuous tone.*] Goils waitin' for yuh, huh? Aw, hell! Dat's all tripe. Dey don't wait for no one. Dey'd double-cross yuh for a nickel. Dey're all tarts, get me? Treat 'em rough, dat's me. To hell wit 'em. Tarts, dat's what, de whole bunch of 'em.

LONG [*Very drunk, jumps on a bench excitedly, gesticulating with a bottle in his hand*]. Listen 'ere, Comrades. Yank 'ere is right. 'E says this 'ere stinkin' ship is our 'ome. And 'e says as 'ome is 'ell. And 'e's right! This is 'ell. We lives in 'ell, Comrades—and right enough we'll die in it. [*Raging.*] And who's ter blame, I arsks yer? We ain't. We wasn't born this rotten way. All men is born free and ekal. That's in the bleedin' Bible, maties. But what d'they care for the Bible—them lazy, bloated swine what travels first cabin? Them's the ones. They dragged us down 'til we're on'y wage slaves in the bowels of a bloody ship, sweatin', burnin' up, eatin' coal dust! Hit's them's ter blame—the damned Capitalist clarss! [*There had been a gradual murmur of contemptuous resentment rising among the men until now he is interrupted by a storm of catcalls, hisses, boos, hard laughter.*]

VOICES. Turn it off!

Shut up!

Sit down!

Closa da face!

Tamn fool! [*Etc.*]

YANK [*Standing up and glaring at* LONG]. Sit down before I knock yuh down! [LONG *makes haste to efface himself.* YANK *goes on contemptuously.*] De Bible, huh? De Cap'tlist class, huh? Aw nix on dat Salvation Army-Socialist bull. Git a soapbox! Hire a hall! Come and be saved, huh? Jerk us to Jesus, huh? Aw g'wan! I've listened to lots of guys like you, see. Yuh're all wrong. Wanter know what I t'ink? Yuh ain't no good for no one. Yuh're de bunk. Yuh ain't got no noive, get me? Yuh're yellow, dat's what. Yellow, dat's you. Say! What's dem slobs in de foist cabin got to do wit us? We're better men dan dey are, ain't we? Sure? One of us guys could clean up de whole mob wit one mit. Put one of 'em down here for one watch in de stokehole, what'd happen? Dey'd carry him off on a stretcher. Dem boids don't amount to nothin'. Dey're just baggage. Who makes dis old tub run? Ain't it us guys? Well den, we belong, don't we? We belong and dey don't. Dat's all. [*A loud chorus of approval.* YANK *goes on.*] As for dis bein' hell—aw, nuts! Yuh lost your noive, dat's what. Dis is a man's job, get me? It belongs. It runs dis tub. No stiffs need apply. But yuh're a stiff, see? Yuh're yellow, dat's you.

VOICES [*With a great hard pride in them*]. Righto!

A man's job!

Talk is cheap, Long.

He never could hold up his end.

Divil take him!

Yank's right. We make it go.

Py Gott, Yank say right ting!

We don't need no one cryin' over us.

Makin' speeches.

Throw him out!

Yellow!

Chuck him overboard!

I'll break his jaw for him!

[*They crowd around* LONG *threateningly.*]

YANK [*Half good-natured again—contemptuously*]. Aw, take it easy. Leave him alone. He ain't woith a punch. Drink up. Here's how, whoever owns dis. [*He takes a long swallow from his bottle. All drink with him. In a flash all is hilarious amiability again, back-slapping, loud talk, etc.*]

PADDY [*Who has been sitting in a blinking, melancholy daze—suddenly cries out in a voice full of old sorrow*]. We belong to this, you're saying? We make the ship to go, you're saying? Yerra then, that Almighty God have pity on us! [*His voice runs into the wail of a keen, he rocks back and forth on his bench. The men stare at him, startled and impressed in spite of themselves.*] Oh, to be back in the fine days of my youth, ochone! Oh, there was fine beautiful ships them days—clippers wid tall masts touching the sky—fine strong men in them—men that was sons of the sea as if 'twas the mother that bore them. Oh, the clean skins of them, and the clear eyes, the straight backs and full chests of them! Brave men they was, and bold men surely! We'd be sailing out, bound down round the Horn maybe. We'd be making sail in the dawn, with a fair breeze, singing a chanty song wid no care to it. And astern the land would be sinking low and dying out, but we'd give it no heed but a laugh, and never a look behind. For the day that was, was enough, for we was free men—and I'm thinking 'tis only slaves do be giving heed to the day that's gone or the day to come—until they're old like me. [*With a sort of religious exaltation.*] Oh, to be scudding south again wid the power of the Trade Wind driving her on steady through the nights and the days! Full sail on her! Nights and days! Nights when the foam of the wake would be flaming wid fire, when the sky'd be blazing and winking wid stars. Or the full of the moon maybe. Then you'd see her driving through the gray night, her sails stretching aloft all silver and white, not a sound on the deck, the lot of us dreaming dreams, till you'd believe 'twas no real ship at all you was on but a ghost ship like the *Flying Dutchman* they say does be roaming the seas forevermore widout touching a port. And there was the days, too. A warm sun on the clean decks. Sun warming the blood of you, and wind over the miles of shiny green ocean like strong drink to your lungs. Work—aye, hard work—but who'd mind that at all? Sure, you worked under the sky and 'twas work wid skill and daring to it. And wid the day done, in the dog watch, smoking me pipe at ease, the lookout would be raising land maybe, and we'd see the mountains of South Americy wid the red fire of the setting sun painting their white tops and the clouds floating by them! [*His tone of exaltation ceases. He goes on mournfully.*] Yerra, what's the use of talking? 'Tis a dead man's whisper. [*To* YANK *resentfully.*] 'Twas them days men belonged to ships, not now. 'Twas them days a ship was part of the sea, and a man was part of a ship, and the sea joined all together and made it one. [*Scornfully.*] Is it one wid this you'd be, Yank—black smoke from the funnels smudging the sea, smudging the decks—the bloody engines pounding and throbbing and shaking—wid divil a sight of sun or a breath of clean air—choking our lungs wid coal dust—breaking our backs and hearts in the hell of the stokehole—feeding the bloody furnace—feeding our lives along wid the coal, I'm thinking—caged in by steel from a sight of the sky like bloody apes in the Zoo! [*With a harsh laugh.*] Ho-ho, divil mend you! Is it to belong to that you're wishing? Is it a flesh and blood wheel of the engines you'd be?

YANK [*Who has been listening with a contemptuous sneer, barks out the answer*]. Sure ting! Dat's me. What about it?

PADDY [*As if to himself—with great sorrow*]. Me time is past due. That a great wave wid sun in the heart of it may sweep me over the side sometime I'd be dreaming of the days that's gone!

YANK. Aw, yuh crazy Mick! [*He springs to his feet and advances on Paddy threateningly—then stops, fighting some queer struggle within himself—lets his hands fall to his sides—contemptuously.*] Aw, take it easy. Yuh're aw right, at dat. Yuh're bugs, dat's all—nutty as a cuckoo. All dat tripe yuh been pullin'—Aw, dat's all right. On'y its dead, get me? Yuh don't belong no more, see. Yuh don't get de stuff. Yuh're too old. [*Disgustedly.*] But aw say, come up for air onct in a while, can't yuh? See what's happened since yuh croaked. [*He suddenly bursts forth vehemently, growing more and more excited.*] Say! Sure! Sure I meant it! What de hell— Say, lemme talk! Hey! Hey, you old Harp! Hey, youse guys! Say, listen to me—wait a moment—I gotta talk, see. I belong and he don't. He's dead but I'm livin'. Listen to me! Sure I'm part of de engines! Why de hell not? Dey move, don't dey? Dey're speed, ain't dey? Dey smash trou, don't dey? Twenty-five knots a hour! Dat's goin' some! Dat's new stuff! Dat belongs! But him, he's too old. He gets dizzy. Say, listen. All dat crazy tripe about nights and days; all dat crazy tripe about stars and moons; all dat crazy tripe about suns and winds, fresh air and de rest of it—Aw hell, dat's all a dope dream! Hittin' de pipe of de past, dat's what he's doin'. He's old and don't belong no more. But me, I'm young! I'm in de pink! I move wit it! It, get me! I mean de ting dat's de guts of all dis. It ploughs trou all de tripe he's been sayin'. It blows dat up! It knocks dat dead! It slams dat offen de face of de oith! It, get me! De engines and de coal and de smoke and all de rest of it! He can't breathe and swallow coal dust, but I kin, see? Dat's fresh air for me! Dat's food for me! I'm new, get me? Hell in de stokehole? Sure! It takes a man to work in hell. Hell, sure, dat's my fav'rite climate. I eat it up! I git fat on it! It's me makes it hot! It's me makes it roar! It's me makes it move! Sure, on'y for me everyting stops. It all goes dead, get me? De noise and smoke and all de engines movin' de woild, dey stop. Dere ain't nothin' no more! Dat's what I'm sayin'. Everyting else dat makes de woild move, somep'n makes it move. It can't move witout somep'n else, see? Den yuh get down to me. I'm at de bottom, get me! Dere ain't nothin' foither. I'm de end! I'm de start! I start somep'n and de woild moves! It—dat's me!—de new dat's moiderin' de old! I'm de ting in coal dat makes it boin; I'm steam and oil for de engines; I'm de ting in noise dat makes yuh hear it; I'm smoke and express trains and steamers and factory whistles; I'm de ting in gold dat makes money! And I'm what makes iron into steel! Steel, dat stands for de whole ting! And I'm steel—steel—steel! I'm de muscles in steel, de punch behind it! [*As he says this he pounds with his fist against the steel bunks. All the men, roused to a pitch of frenzied self-glorification by his speech, do likewise. There is a deafening metallic roar, through which* YANK's *voice can be heard bellowing.*] Slaves, hell! We run de whole woiks. All de rich guys dat tink dey're somep'n, dey ain't nothin'! Dey don't belong. But us guys, we're in de move, we're at de bottom, de whole ting is us! [PADDY *from the start of* YANK's *speech has been taking one gulp after another from his bottle, at first frightenedly, as if he were afraid to listen, then desperately, as if to drown his senses, but finally has achieved complete indifferent, even amused, drunkenness.* YANK *sees his lips moving. He quells the uproar with a shout.*] Hey, youse guys, take it easy! Wait a moment! De nutty Harp is sayin' somep'n.

PADDY [*Is heard now—throws his head back with a mocking burst of laughter*]. Ho-ho-ho-ho-ho——

YANK [*Drawing back his fist, with a snarl*]. Aw! Look out who yuh're givin' the bark!

PADDY [*Begins to sing the "Miller of Dee" with enormous good nature*].

> I care for nobody, no, not I,
> And nobody cares for me.

YANK [*Good-natured himself in a flash, interrupts* PADDY *with a slap on the bare back like a report*]. Dat's de stuff! Now yuh're gettin' wise to somep'n. Care for nobody, dat's de dope! To hell wit 'em all! And nix on nobody else carin'. I kin care for myself, get me! [*Eight bells sound, muffled, vibrating through the steel walls as if some enormous brazen gong were imbedded in the heart of the ship. All the men jump up mechanically, file through the door silently close upon each other's heels in what is very like a prisoners' lockstep.* YANK *slaps* PADDY *on the back.*] Our watch, yuh old Harp! [*Mockingly.*] Come on down in hell. Eat up de coal dust. Drink in de heat. It's it, see! Act like yuh liked it, yuh better —or croak yuhself.

PADDY [*With jovial defiance*]. To the divil wid it! I'll not report this watch. Let thim log me and be damned. I'm no slave the like of you. I'll be sittin' here at me ease, and drinking, and thinking, and dreaming dreams.

YANK [*Contemptuously*]. Tinkin' and dreamin', what'll that get yuh? What's tinkin' got to do wit it? We move, don't we? Speed, ain't it? Fog, dat's all you stand for. But we drive trou dat, don't we? We split dat up and smash trou— twenty-five knots a hour! [*Turns his back on* PADDY *scornfully.*] Aw, yuh make me sick! Yuh don't belong! [*He strides out the door in rear. Paddy hums to himself, blinking drowsily.*]

Curtain

SCENE 2

Scene: Two days out. A section of the promenade deck. MILDRED DOUGLAS *and her aunt are discovered reclining in deck chairs. The former is a girl of twenty, slender, delicate, with a pale, pretty face marred by a self-conscious expression of disdainful superiority. She looks fretful, nervous, and discontented, bored by her own anemia. Her aunt is a pompous and proud—and fat—old lady. She is a type even to the point of a double chin and lorgnettes. She is dressed pretentiously, as if afraid her face alone would never indicate her position in life.* MILDRED *is dressed all in white.*

The impression to be conveyed by this scene is one of the beautiful, vivid life of the sea all about—sunshine on the deck in a great flood, the fresh sea wind blowing across it. In the midst of this, these two incongruous, artificial figures, inert and disharmonious, the elder like a gray lump of dough touched up with rouge, the younger looking as if the vitality of her stock had been sapped before she was conceived, so that she is the expression not of its life energy but merely of the artificialities that energy had won for itself in the spending.

MILDRED [*Looking up with affected dreaminess*]. How the black smoke swirls back against the sky! Is it not beautiful?

AUNT [*Without looking up*]. I dislike smoke of any kind.

MILDRED. My great-grandmother smoked a pipe—a clay pipe.

AUNT [*Ruffling*]. Vulgar!

MILDRED. She was too distant a relative to be vulgar. Time mellows pipes.

AUNT [*Pretending boredom but irritated*]. Did the sociology you took up at college teach you that—to play the ghoul on every possible occasion, excavating old bones? Why not let your great-grandmother rest in her grave?

MILDRED [*Dreamily*]. With her pipe beside her—puffing in Paradise.

AUNT [*With spite*]. Yes, you are a natural born ghoul. You are even getting to look like one, my dear.

MILDRED [*In a passionless tone*]. I detest you, Aunt. [*Looking at her critically.*] Do you know what you remind me of? Of a cold pork pudding against a background of linoleum tablecloth in the kitchen of a—but the possibilities are wearisome. [*She closes her eyes.*]

AUNT [*With a bitter laugh*]. Merci for your candor. But since I am and must be your chaperon—in appearance—at least—let us patch up some sort of armed truce. For my part you are quite free to indulge any pose of eccentricity that beguiles you—as long as you observe the amenities——

MILDRED [*Drawling*]. The inanities?

AUNT [*Going on as if she hadn't heard*]. After exhausting the morbid thrills of social service work on New York's East Side—how they must have hated you, by the way, the poor that you made so much poorer in their own eyes! —you are now bent on making your slumming international. Well, I hope Whitechapel will provide the needed nerve tonic. Do not ask me to chaperon you there, however. I told your father I would not. I loathe deformity. We will hire an army of detectives and you may investigate everything—they allow you to see.

MILDRED [*Protesting with a trace of genuine earnestness*]. Please do not mock at my attempts to discover how the other half lives. Give me credit for some sort of groping sincerity in that at least. I would like to help them. I would like to be of some use in the world. Is it my fault I don't know how? I would like to be sincere, to touch life somewhere. [*With weary bitterness.*] But I'm afraid I have neither the vitality nor integrity. All that was burned out in our stock before I was born. Grandfather's blast furnaces, flaming to the sky, melting steel, making millions—then Father keeping those home fires burning, making more millions—and little me at the tail-end of it all. I'm a waste product in the Bessemer process—like the millions. Or, rather, I inherit the acquired trait of the by-product, wealth, but none of the energy, none of the strength of the steel that made it. I am sired by gold and damned by it, as they say at the race track—damned in more ways than one. [*She laughs mirthlessly.*]

AUNT [*Unimpressed—superciliously*].

You seem to be going in for sincerity to-day. It isn't becoming to you, really—except as an obvious pose. Be as artificial as you are, I advise. There's a sort of sincerity in that, you know. And, after all, you must confess you like that better.

MILDRED [*Again affected and bored*]. Yes, I suppose I do. Pardon me for my outburst. When a leopard complains of its spots, it must sound rather grotesque. [*In a mocking tone.*] Purr, little leopard. Purr, scratch, tear, kill, gorge yourself and be happy—only stay in the jungle where your spots are camouflage. In a cage they make you conspicuous.

AUNT. I don't know what you are talking about.

MILDRED. It would be rude to talk about anything to you. Let's just talk. [*She looks at her wrist watch.*] Well, thank goodness, it's about time for them to come for me. That ought to give me a new thrill, Aunt.

AUNT [*Affectedly troubled*]. You don't mean to say you're really going? The dirt—the heat must be frightful——

MILDRED. Grandfather started as a puddler. I should have inherited an immunity to heat that would make a salamander shiver. It will be fun to put it to the test.

AUNT. But don't you have to have the captain's—or someone's—permission to visit the stokehole?

MILDRED [*With a triumphant smile*]. I have it—both his and the chief engineer's. Oh, they didn't want to at first, in spite of my social service credentials. They didn't seem a bit anxious that I should investigate how the other half lives and works on a ship. So I had to tell them that my father, the president of Nazareth Steel, chairman of the board of directors of this line, had told me it would be all right.

AUNT. He didn't.

MILDRED. How naïve age makes one! But I said he did, Aunt. I even said he had given me a letter to them—which I had lost. And they were afraid to take the chance that I might be lying. [*Excitedly.*] So it's ho! for the stokehole. The second engineer is to escort me. [*Looking at her watch again.*] It's time. And here he comes, I think. [*The* SECOND ENGINEER *enters. He is a husky, fine-looking man of thirty-five or so. He stops before the two and tips his cap, visibly embarrassed and ill-at-ease.*]

SECOND ENGINEER. Miss Douglas?

MILDRED. Yes. [*Throwing off her rugs and getting to her feet.*] Are we all ready to start?

SECOND ENGINEER. In just a second, ma'am. I'm waiting for the Fourth. He's coming along.

MILDRED [*With a scornful smile*]. You don't care to shoulder this responsibility alone, is that it?

SECOND ENGINEER [*Forcing a smile*]. Two are better than one. [*Disturbed by her eyes, glances out to sea—blurts out.*] A fine day we're having.

MILDRED. Is it?

SECOND ENGINEER. A nice warm breeze——

MILDRED. It feels cold to me.

SECOND ENGINEER. But it's hot enough in the sun——

MILDRED. Not hot enough for me. I don't like Nature. I was never athletic.

SECOND ENGINEER [*Forcing a smile*]. Well, you'll find it hot enough where you're going.

MILDRED. Do you mean hell?

SECOND ENGINEER [*Flabbergasted, decides to laugh*]. Ho-ho! No, I mean the stokehole.

MILDRED. My grandfather was a puddler. He played with boiling steel.

SECOND ENGINEER [*All at sea—uneasily*]. Is that so? Hum, you'll excuse me, ma'am, but are you intending to wear that dress?

MILDRED. Why not?

SECOND ENGINEER. You'll likely rub against oil and dirt. It can't be helped.

MILDRED. It doesn't matter. I have lots of white dresses.

SECOND ENGINEER. I have an old coat you might throw over——

MILDRED. I have fifty dresses like this. I will throw this one into the sea when I come back. That ought to wash it clean, don't you think?

SECOND ENGINEER [*Doggedly*]. There's ladders to climb down that are none too clean—and dark alleyways——

MILDRED. I will wear this very dress and none other.

SECOND ENGINEER. No offense meant. It's none of my business. I was only warning you——

MILDRED. Warning? That sounds thrilling.

SECOND ENGINEER [*Looking down the deck—with a sigh of relief*]. There's the Fourth now. He's waiting for us. If you'll come——

MILDRED. Go on. I'll follow you. [*He goes.* MILDRED *turns a mocking smile on her aunt.*] An oaf—but a handsome, virile oaf.

AUNT [*Scornfully*]. Poser!

MILDRED. Take care. He said there were dark alleyways——

AUNT [*In the same tone*]. Poser!

MILDRED [*Biting her lips angrily*]. You are right. But would that my millions were not so anemically chaste!

AUNT. Yes, for a fresh pose I have no doubt you would drag the name of Douglas in the gutter!

MILDRED. From which it sprang. Good-by, Aunt. Don't pray too hard that I may fall into the fiery furnace.

AUNT. Poser!

MILDRED [*Viciously*]. Old hag! [*She slaps her aunt insultingly across the face and walks off, laughing gaily.*]

AUNT [*Screams after her*]. I said poser!

Curtain

SCENE 3

Scene: The stokehole. In the rear, the dimly outlined bulks of the furnaces and boilers. High overhead one hanging electric bulb sheds just enough light through the murky air laden with coal dust to pile up masses of shadows everywhere. A line of men, stripped to the waist, is before the furnace doors. They bend over, looking neither to right nor left, handling their shovels as if they were part of their bodies, with a strange, awkward, swinging rhythm. They use the shovels to throw open the furnace doors. Then from these fiery round holes in the black a flood of terrific light and heat pours full upon the men, who are outlined in silhouette in the crouching, inhuman attitudes of chained gorillas. The men shovel with a rhythmic motion, swinging as on a pivot from the coal which lies in heaps on the floor behind to hurl it into the flaming mouths before them. There is a tumult of noise—the brazen clang of the furnace doors as they are flung open or slammed shut, the grating, teeth-gritting grind of steel against steel, of crunching coal. This clash of sounds stuns one's ears with its rending dissonance. But there is order in it, rhythm, a mechanical regulated recurrence, a tempo. And rising above all, making the air hum with the quiver of liberated energy, the roar of leaping flames in the furnaces, the monotonous throbbing beat of the engines.

As the curtain rises, the furnace doors are shut. The men are taking a breathing spell. One or two are arranging the coal behind them, pulling it into more accessible heaps. The others can be dimly made out leaning on their shovels in relaxed attitudes of exhaustion.

PADDY [*From somewhere in the line—plaintively*]. Yerra, will this divil's own watch nivir end? Me back is broke. I'm destroyed entirely.

YANK [*From the center of the line—with exuberant scorn*]. Aw, yuh make me sick! Lie down and croak, why don't yuh? Always beefin', dat's you? Say, dis is a cinch! Dis was made for me! It's my meat, get me! [*A whistle is blown—a thin, shrill note from somewhere over-*

head in the darkness. YANK *curses without resentment.*] Dere's de damn engineer crackin' de whip. He tinks we're loafin'.

PADDY [*Vindictively*]. God stiffen him!

YANK [*In an exultant tone of command*]. Come on, youse guys! Git into de game! She's gittin' hungry! Pile some grub in her. Trow it into her belly. Come on now, all of youse! Open her up! [*At this last all the men, who have followed his movements of getting into position, throw open their furnace doors with a deafening clang. The fiery light floods over their shoulders as they bend round for the coal. Rivulets of sooty sweat have traced maps on their backs. The enlarged muscles form bunches of high light and shadow.*]

YANK [*Chanting a count as he shovels without seeming effort*]. One—two—tree—— [*His voice rising exultantly in the joy of battle.*] Dat's de stuff! Let her have it! All togedder now! Sling it into her! Let her ride! Shoot de piece now! Call de toin on her! Drive her into it! Feel her move! Watch her smoke! Speed, dat's her middle name! Give her coal, youse guys! Coal, dat's her booze! Drink it up, baby! Let's see yuh sprint! Dig in and gain a lap. Dere she go-o-es [*This last in the chanting formula of the gallery gods at the six-day bike race. He slams his furnace door shut. The others do likewise with as much unison as their wearied bodies will permit. The effect is of one fiery eye after another being blotted out with a series of accompanying bangs.*]

PADDY [*Groaning*]. Me back is broke. I'm bate out—bate—— [*There is a pause. Then the inexorable whistle sounds again from the dim regions above the electric light. There is a growl of cursing rage from all sides.*]

YANK [*Shaking his fist upward—contemptuously*]. Take it easy dere, you! Who d'yuh tinks runnin' dis game, me or you? When I git ready, we move. Not before! When I git ready, get me!

VOICES [*Approvingly*]. That's the stuff!

Yank tal him, py golly!
Yank ain't afeerd.
Goot poy, Yank!
Give him hell!
Tell 'im 'e's a bloody swine!
Bloody slave-driver!

YANK [*Contemptuously*]. He ain't got no noive. He's yellow, get me? All de engineers is yellow. Dey got streaks a mile wide. Aw, to hell with him! Let's move, youse guys. We had a rest. Come on, she needs it! Give her pep! It ain't for him. Him and his whistle, dey don't belong. But we belong, see! We gotter feed de baby! Come on! [*He turns and flings his furnace door open. They all follow his lead. At this instant the* SECOND *and* FOURTH ENGINEERS *enter from the darkness on the left with* MILDRED *between them. She starts, turns paler, her pose is crumbling, she shivers with fright in spite of the blazing heat, but forces herself to leave the* ENGINEERS *and take a few steps near the men. She is right behind* YANK. *All this happens quickly while the men have their backs turned.*]

YANK. Come on, youse guys! [*He is turning to get coal when the whistle sounds again in a peremptory, irritating note. This drives* YANK *into a sudden fury. While the other men have turned full around and stopped dumbfounded by the spectacle of* MILDRED *standing there in her white dress,* YANK *does not turn far enough to see her. Besides, his head is thrown back, he blinks upward through the murk trying to find the owner of the whistle, he brandishes his shovel murderously over his head in one hand, pounding on his chest, gorilla-like, with the other, shouting.*] Toin off dat whistle! Come down outa dere, yuh yellow, brass-buttoned, Belfast bum, yuh! Come down and I'll knock yer brains out! Yuh lousy, stinkin', yellow mut of a Catholic-moiderin' bastard! Come down and I'll moider yuh! Pullin' dat whistle on me, huh? I'll show yuh! I'll crash yer skull in! I'll drive yer teet' down yer troat! I'll slam yer nose trou de back of yer head! I'll cut yer guts out for a nickel, yuh lousy boob, yuh dirty, crummy, muck-eatin' son of a—— [*Suddenly he becomes conscious of all the other men staring at something directly behind his back. He whirls defensively with a snarling, murderous growl, crouching to spring, his lips drawn back over his teeth, his small eyes gleaming ferociously. He sees* MILDRED, *like a white apparition in the full light from the open furnace doors. He glares into her eyes, turned to stone. As for her, during his speech she has listened, paralyzed with horror, terror, her whole personality crushed, beaten in, collapsed, by the terrific impact of this unknown, abysmal brutality, naked and shameless. As she looks at his gorilla face, as his eyes bore into hers, she utters a low, choking cry and shrinks away from him, putting both hands up before her eyes to shut out the sight of his face, to protect her own. This startles* YANK *to a reaction. His mouth falls open, his eyes grow bewildered.*]

MILDRED [*About to faint—to the* ENGINEERS, *who now have her one by each arm—whimperingly*]. Take me away! Oh, the filthy beast! [*She faints. They carry her quickly back, disappearing in the darkness at the left, rear. An iron door clangs shut. Rage and bewildered fury rush back on* YANK. *He feels himself insulted in some unknown fashion in the very heart of his pride. He roars.*] God damn yuh! [*And hurls his shovel after them at the door which has just closed. It hits the steel bulkhead with a clang and falls clattering on the steel floor. From overhead the whistle sounds again in a long, angry, insistent command.*]

Curtain

SCENE 4

Scene: The firemen's forecastle. YANK'S *watch has just come off duty and had dinner. Their faces and bodies shine from a soap and water scrubbing but around their eyes, where a hasty dousing does not touch, the coal dust sticks like black make-up, giving them a queer, sinister expression.* YANK *has not washed either face or body. He stands out in contrast to them, a blackened, brooding figure. He is seated forward on a bench in the exact attitude of Rodin's "The Thinker." The others, most of them smoking pipes, are staring at* YANK *half-apprehensively, as if fearing an outburst; half-amusedly, as if they saw a joke somewhere that tickled them.*

VOICES. He ain't ate nothin'.

Py golly, a fallar gat to gat grub in him.

Divil a lie.

Yank feeda da fire, no feeda da face.

Ha-ha.

He ain't even washed hisself.

He's forgot.

Hey, Yank, you forgot to wash.

YANK [*Sullenly*]. Forgot nothin'! To hell wit washin'.

VOICES. It'll stick to you.

It'll get under your skin.

Give yer the bleedin' itch, that's wot.

It makes spots on you—like a leopard.

Like a piebald nigger, you mean.

Better wash up, Yank.

You sleep better.

Wash up, Yank.

Wash up! Wash up!

YANK [*Resentfully*]. Aw say, youse guys. Lemme alone. Can't youse see I'm tryin' to tink?

ALL [*Repeating the word after him as one with cynical mockery*]. Think! [*The word has a brazen, metallic quality as if their throats were phonograph horns. It is followed by a chorus of hard, barking laughter.*]

YANK [*Springing to his feet and glaring

at them belligerently]. Yes, tink! Tink, dat's what I said! What about it? [*They are silent, puzzled by his sudden resentment at what used to be one of his jokes.* YANK *sits down again in the same attitude of "The Thinker."*]

VOICES. Leave him alone.

He's got a grouch on.

Why wouldn't he?

PADDY [*With a wink at the others*]. Sure I know what's the matther. 'Tis aisy to see. He's fallen in love, I'm telling you.

ALL [*Repeating the word after him as one with cynical mockery*]. Love! [*The word has a brazen, metallic quality as if their throats were phonograph horns. It is followed by a chorus of hard, barking laughter.*]

YANK [*With a contemptuous snort*]. Love, hell! Hate, dat's what. I've fallen in hate, get me?

PADDY [*Philosophically*]. 'Twould take a wise man to tell one from the other. [*With a bitter, ironical scorn, increasing as he goes on.*] But I'm telling you it's love that's in it. Sure what else but love for us poor bastes in the stokehole would be bringing a fine lady, dressed like a white quane, down a mile of ladders and steps to be havin' a look at us? [*A growl of anger goes up from all sides.*]

LONG [*Jumping on a bench—hectically*]. Hinsultin' us! Hinsultin' us, the bloody cow! And them bloody engineers! What right 'as they got to be exhibitin' us 's if we was bleedin' monkeys in a menagerie? Did we sign for hinsults to our dignity as 'onest workers? Is that in the ship's articles? You kin bloody well bet it ain't! But I knows why they done it. I arsked a deck steward 'o she was and 'e told me. 'Er old man's a bleedin' millionaire, a bloody Capitalist! 'E's got enuf bloody gold to sink this bleedin' ship! 'E makes arf the bloody steel in the world! 'E owns this bloody boat! And you and me, Comrades, we're 'is slaves! And the skipper and mates and engineers, they're 'is slaves! And she's 'is bloody daughter and we're all 'er slaves, too! And she gives 'er orders as 'ow she wants to see the bloody animals below decks and down they takes 'er! [*There is a roar of rage from all sides.*]

YANK [*Blinking at him bewilderingly*]. Say! Wait a moment! Is all dat straight goods?

LONG. Straight as string! The bleedin' steward as waits on 'em, 'e told me about 'er. And what're we goin' ter do, I arsks yer? 'Ave we got ter swaller 'er hinsults like dogs? It ain't in the ship's article. I tell yer we got a case. We kin go to law——

YANK [*With abysmal contempt*]. Hell! Law!

ALL [*Repeating the word after him as one with cynical mockery*]. Law! [*The word has a brazen metallic quality as if their throats were phonograph horns. It is followed by a chorus of hard, barking laughter.*]

LONG [*Feeling the ground slipping from under his feet—desperately*]. As voters and citizens we kin force the bloody governments——

YANK [*With abysmal contempt*]. Hell! Governments!

ALL [*Repeating the word after him as one with cynical mockery*]. Governments! [*The word has a brazen metallic quality as if their throats were phonograph horns. It is followed by a chorus of hard, barking laughter.*]

LONG [*Hysterically*]. We're free and equal in the sight of God——

YANK [*With abysmal contempt*]. Hell! God!

ALL [*Repeating the word after him as one with cynical mockery*]. God! [*The word has a brazen metallic quality as if their throats were phonograph horns. It is followed by a chorus of hard, barking laughter.*]

YANK [*Witheringly*]. Aw, join de Salvation Army!

ALL. Sit down! Shut up! Damn fool!

Sea-lawyer! [LONG *slinks back out of sight.*]

PADDY [*Continuing the trend of his thoughts as if he had never been interrupted—bitterly*]. And there she was standing behind us, and the Second pointing at us like a man you'd hear in a circus would be saying: In this cage is a queerer kind of baboon than ever you'd find in darkest Africy. We roast them in their own sweat—and be damned if you won't hear some of thim saying they like it! [*He glances scornfully at* YANK].

YANK [*With a bewildered uncertain growl*]. Aw!

PADDY. And there was Yank roarin' curses and turning round wid his shovel to brain her—and she looked at him, and him at her——

YANK [*Slowly*]. She was all white. I tought she was a ghost. Sure.

PADDY [*With heavy, biting sarcasm*]. 'Twas love at first sight, divil a doubt of it! If you'd seen the endearin' look on her pale mug when she shriveled away with her hands over her eyes to shut out the sight of him! Sure, 'twas as if she'd seen a great hairy ape escaped from the Zoo!

YANK [*Stung—with a growl of rage*]. Aw!

PADDY. And the loving way Yank heaved his shovel at the skull of her, only she was out the door! [*A grin breaking over his face.*] 'Twas touching, I'm telling you! It put the touch of home, swate home in the stokehole. [*There is a roar of laughter from all.*]

YANK [*Glaring at* PADDY *menacingly*]. Aw, choke dat off, see!

PADDY [*Not heeding him—to the others*]. And her grabbin' at the Second's arm for protection. [*With a grotesque imitation of a woman's voice.*] Kiss me, Engineer dear, for it's dark down here and me old man's in Wall Street making money! Hug me tight, darlin', for I'm afeerd in the dark and me mother's on deck makin' eyes at the skipper! [*Another roar of laughter.*]

YANK [*Threateningly*]. Say! What yuh tryin' to do, kid me, yuh old Harp?

PADDY. Divil a bit! Ain't I wishin' myself you'd brained her?

YANK [*Fiercely*]. I'll brain her! I'll brain her yet, wait 'n' see! [*Coming over to* PADDY *slowly.*] Say, is dat what she called me—a hairy ape?

PADDY. She looked it at you if she didn't say the word itself.

YANK [*Grinning horribly*]. Hairy ape, huh? Sure! Dat's de way she looked at me, aw right. Hairy ape! So dat's me, huh? [*Bursting into rage—as if she were still in front of him.*] Yuh skinny tart! Yuh white-faced bum, yuh! I'll show yuh who's a ape! [*Turning to the others, bewilderment seizing him again.*] Say, youse guys. I was bawlin' him out for pullin' de whistle on us. You heard me. And den I seen youse lookin' at somep'n and I tought he'd sneaked down to come up in back of me, and I hopped round to knock him dead wit de shovel. And dere she was wit de light on her! Christ, yuh coulda pushed me over with a finger! I was scared, get me? Sure! I tought she was a ghost, see? She was all in white like dey wrap around stiffs. You seen her. Kin yuh blame me? She didn't belong, dat's what. And den when I come to and seen it was a real skoit and seen de way she was lookin' at me—like Paddy said—Christ, I was sore, get me? I don't stand for dat stuff from nobody. And I flung de shovel—on'y she'd beat it. [*Furiously.*] I wished it'd banged her! I wished it'd knocked her block off!

LONG. And be 'anged for murder or 'lectrocuted? She ain't bleedin' well worth it.

YANK. I don't give a damn what! I'd be square wit her, wouldn't I? Tink I wanter let her put somep'n over on me? Tink I'm goin' to let her git away wit dat stuff? Yuh don't know me! No one ain't never put nothin' over on me and got away wit it, see!—not dat kind of stuff—

no guy and no skoit neither! I'll fix her! Maybe she'll come down again——

VOICE. No chance, Yank. You scared her out of a year's growth.

YANK. I scared her? Why de hell should I scare her? Who de hell is she? Ain't she de same as me? Hairy ape, huh? [*With his old confident bravado.*] I'll show her I'm better'n her, if she on'y knew it. I belong and she don't, see! I move and she's dead! Twenty-five knots a hour, dat's me! Dat carries her but I make dat. She's on'y baggage. Sure! [*Again bewilderedly.*] But, Christ, she was funny lookin'! Did yuh pipe her hands? White and skinny. Yuh could see de bones through 'em. And her mush, dat was dead white, too. And her eyes, dey was like dey'd seen a ghost. Me, dat was! Sure! Hairy ape! Ghost, huh? Look at dat arm! [*He extends his right arm, swelling out the great muscles.*] I coulda took her wit dat, wit' just my little finger even, and broke her in two. [*Again bewilderedly.*] Say, who is dat skoit, huh? What is she? What's she come from? Who made her? Who give her de noive to look at me like dat? Dis ting's got my goat right. I don't get her. She's new to me. What does a skoit like her mean, huh? She don't belong, get me! I can't see her. [*With growing anger.*] But one ting I'm wise to, aw right, aw right! Youse all kin bet your shoits I'll git even wit her. I'll show her if she tinks she— She grinds de organ and I'm on de string, huh? I'll fix her! Let her come down again and I'll fling her in de furnace! She'll move den! She won't shiver at nothin', den! Speed, dat'll be her! She'll belong den! [*He grins horribly.*]

PADDY. She'll never come. She's had her belly-full, I'm telling you. She'll be in bed now, I'm thinking, wid ten doctors and nurses feedin' her salts to clean the fear out of her.

YANK [*Enraged*]. Yuh tink I made her sick, too, do yuh? Just lookin' at me, huh? Hairy ape, huh? [*In a frenzy of rage.*] I'll fix her! I'll tell her where to git off! She'll git down on her knees and take it back or I'll bust de face offen her! [*Shaking one fist upward and beating on his chest with the other.*] I'll find yuh! I'm comin,' d'yuh hear? I'll fix yuh, God damn yuh! [*He makes a rush for the door.*]

VOICES. Stop him!
He'll get shot!
He'll murder her!
Trip him up!
Hold him!
He's gone crazy!
Gott, he's strong!
Hold him down!
Look out for a kick!
Pin his arms!

[*They have all piled on him and, after a fierce struggle, by sheer weight of numbers have borne him to the floor just inside the door.*]

PADDY [*Who has remained detached*]. Kape him down till he's cooled off. [*Scornfully.*] Yerra, Yank, you're a great fool. Is it payin' attention at all you are to the like of that skinny sow without one drop of rale blood in her?

YANK [*Frenziedly, from the bottom of the heap*]. She done me doit! She done me doit, didn't she? I'll git square wit her! I'll get her some way! Git offen me, youse guys! Lemme up! I'll show her who's a ape!

Curtain

SCENE 5

Scene: Three weeks later. A corner of Fifth Avenue in the Fifties on a fine Sunday morning. A general atmosphere of clean well-tidied, wide street; a flood of mellow, tempered sunshine; gentle, genteel breezes. In the rear, the show windows of two shops, a jewelry establishment on the corner, a furrier's next to it. Here the adornments of extreme wealth are tantalizingly displayed. The jeweler's window is gaudy with glittering diamonds, emeralds, rubies, pearls, etc., fashioned in ornate tiaras, crowns, necklaces, collars, etc. From each piece hangs an enormous tag from which a dollar sign and numerals in intermittent electric lights wink out the incredible prices. The same in the furrier's. Rich furs of all varieties hang there bathed in a downpour of artificial light. The general effect is of a background of magnificence cheapened and made grotesque by commercialism, a background in tawdry disharmony with the clear light and sunshine on the street itself.

Up the side street YANK *and* LONG *come swaggering.* LONG *is dressed in shore clothes, wears a black Windsor tie, cloth cap.* YANK *is in his dirty dungarees. A fireman's cap with black peak is cocked defiantly on the side of his head. He has not shaved for days and around his fierce, resentful eyes—as around those of* LONG *to a lesser degree—the black smudge of coal dust still sticks like make-up. They hesitate and stand together at the corner, swaggering, looking about them with a forced, defiant contempt.*

LONG [*Indicating it all with an oratorical gesture*]. Well, 'ere we are. Fif' Avenoo. This 'ere's their bleedin' private lane, as yer might say. [*Bitterly.*] We're trespassers 'ere. Proletarians keep orf the grass!

YANK [*Dully*]. I don't see no grass, yuh boob. [*Staring at the sidewalk.*] Clean, ain't it? Yuh could eat a fried egg offen it. The white wings got some job sweepin' dis up. [*Looking up and down the avenue—surlily.*] Where's all de white-collar stiffs yuh said was here—and de skoits—*her* kind?

LONG. In church, blarst 'em! Arskin' Jesus to give 'em more money.

YANK. Choich, huh? I useter go to choich onct—sure—when I was a kid. Me old man and woman, dey made me. Dey never went demselves, dough. Always got too big a head on Sunday mornin,' dat was dem. [*With a grin.*] Dey was scrappers for fair, bot' of dem. On Satiday nights when dey bot' got a skinful dey could put up a bout oughter been staged at de Garden. When dey got trough dere wasn't a chair or table wit a leg under it. Or else dey bot' jumped on me for somep'n. Dat was where I loined to take punishment. [*With a grin and a swagger.*] I'm a chip offen de old block, get me?

LONG. Did yer old man follow the sea?

YANK. Naw. Worked along shore. I runned away when me old lady croaked wit de tremens. I helped at truckin' and in de market. Den I shipped in de stokehole. Sure. Dat belongs. De rest was nothin.' [*Looking around him.*] I ain't never seen dis before. De Brooklyn waterfront, dat was where I was dragged up. [*Taking a deep breath.*] Dis ain't so bad at dat, huh?

LONG. Not bad? Well, we pays for it wiv our bloody sweat, if yer wants to know!

YANK [*With sudden angry disgust*]. Aw, hell! I don't see no one, see—like her. All dis gives me a pain. It don't belong. Say, ain't dere a back room around dis dump? Let's go shoot a ball. All dis is too clean and quiet and dolled-up, get me? It gives me a pain.

LONG. Wait and yer'll bloody well see——

YANK. I don't wait for no one I keep on de move. Say, what yuh drag me up here for, anyway? Trying' to kid me, yuh simp, yuh?

LONG. Yer wants to get back at 'er, don't yer? That's what yer been sayin' every bloomin' hour since she hinsulted yer.

YANK [*Vehemently*]. Sure ting I do! Didn't I try to get even wit her in Southampton? Didn't I sneak on de dock and wait for her by de gangplank? I was goin' to spit in her pale mug, see! Sure, right in her pop-eyes! Dat woulda made me even, see? But no chanct. Dere was a whole army of plainclothes bulls around. Dey spotted me and gimme de bum's rush. I never seen her. But I'll git square wit her yet, you watch! [*Furiously.*] De lousy tart! She tinks she kin get away with moider—but not wit me! I'll fix her! I'll tink of a way!

LONG [*As disgusted as he dares to be*]. Ain't that why I brought yer up 'ere—to show yer? Yer been lookin, at this 'ere 'ole affair wrong. Yer been actin' an' talkin' 's if it was all a bleedin' personal matter between yer and that bloody cow. I wants to convince yer she was on'y a representative of 'er clarss. I wants to awaken yer bloody clarss consciousness. Then yer'll see it's 'er clarss you've got to fight, not 'er alone. There's a 'ole mob of 'em like 'er, Gawd blind 'em!

YANK [*Spitting on his hands—belligerently*]. De more de merrier when I gits started. Bring on de gang!

LONG. Yer'll see 'em in arf a mo', when that church lets out. [*He turns and sees the window display in the two stores for the first time.*] Blimey! Look at that, will yer? [*They both walk back and stand looking in the jeweler's.* LONG *flies into a fury.*] Just look at this 'ere bloomin' mess! Just look at it! Look at the bleedin' prices on 'em—more'n our 'ole bloody stokehole makes in ten voyages sweatin' in 'ell! And they—'er and 'er bloody clarss—buys 'em for toys to dangle on 'em! One of these 'ere would buy scoff for a starvin' family for a year!

YANK. Aw, cut de sob stuff! T' hell wit de starvin' family! Yuh'll be passin' de hat to me next. [*With naïve admiration.*] Say, dem tings is pretty, huh? Bet yuh dey'd hock for a piece of change aw right. [*Then turning away, bored.*] But, aw hell, what good are dey? Let 'er have 'em. Dey don't belong no more'n she does. [*With a gesture of sweeping the jewelers into oblivion.*] All dat don't count, get me?

LONG [*Who has moved to the furrier's —indignantly*]. And I s'pose this 'ere don't count neither—skins of poor, 'armless animals slaughtered so as 'er and 'ers can keep their bleedin' noses warm!

YANK [*Who has been staring at something inside—with queer excitement*]. Take a slant at dat! Give it de once-over! Monkey fur—two t'ousand bucks! [*Bewilderedly.*] Is dat straight goods—monkey fur? What de hell——?

LONG [*Bitterly*]. It's straight enuf. [*With grim humor.*] They wouldn't bloody well pay that for a 'airy ape's skin—no, nor for the 'ole livin' ape with all 'is 'ead, and body, and soul thrown in!

YANK [*Clenching his fists, his face growing pale with rage as if the skin in the window were a personal insult*]. Trowin' it up in my face! Christ! I'll fix her!

LONG [*Excitedly*]. Church is out. 'Ere they come, the bleedin' swine. [*After a glance at* YANK'*s lowering face —uneasily.*] Easy goes, Comrade. Keep yer bloomin' temper. Remember force defeats itself. It ain't our weapon. We must impress our demands through peaceful means—the votes of the on-marching proletarians of the bloody world!

YANK [*With abysmal contempt*]. Votes hell! Votes is a joke, see. Votes for women! Let dem do it!

LONG [*Still more uneasily*]. Calm, now. Treat 'em wiv the proper contempt. Observe the bleedin' parasites but 'old yer 'orses.

YANK [*Angrily*]. Git away from me! Yuh're yellow, dat's what. Force, dat's me! De punch, dat's me every time, see! [*The crowd from church enter from the right, sauntering slowly and affectedly, their heads held stiffly up, looking neither to right nor left, talking in toneless simpering voices. The women are rouged, calcimined, dyed, overdressed to the nth degree. The men are in Prince Alberts, high hats, spats, canes, etc. A procession of gaudy marionettes, yet with some-*

thing of the relentless horror of Frankenstein monsters in their detached, mechanical unawareness.]

VOICES. Dear Doctor Caiaphas! He is so sincere!

What was the sermon? I dozed off.

About the radicals, my dear—and the false doctrines that are being preached.

We must organize a hundred per cent American bazaar.

And let everyone contribute one one-hundredth per cent of their income tax.

What an original idea!

We can devote the proceeds to rehabilitating the veil of the temple.

But that has been done so many times.

YANK [*Glaring from one to the other of them—with an insulting snort of scorn*]. Huh! Huh! [*Without seeming to see him, they make wide detours to avoid the spot where he stands in the middle of the sidewalk.*]

LONG [*Frightenedly*]. Keep yer bloomin' mouth shut, I tells yer.

YANK [*Viciously*]. G'wan! Tell it to Sweeney! [*He swaggers away and deliberately lurches into a top-hatted gentleman, then glares at him pugnaciously.*] Say, who d'yuh tink you're bumpin'? Tink yuh own de oith?

GENTLEMAN [*Coldly and affectedly*]. I beg your pardon. [*He has not looked at* YANK *and passes on without a glance, leaving him bewildered.*]

LONG [*Rushing up and grabbing* YANK'S *arm*]. 'Ere! Come away! This wasn't what I meant. Yer'll 'ave the bloody coppers down on us.

YANK [*Savagely—giving him a push that sends him sprawling*]. G'wan!

LONG [*Picks himself up—hysterically*]. I'll pop orf then. This ain't what I meant. And whatever 'appens, yer can't blame me. [*He slinks off left.*]

YANK. T' hell wit youse! [*He approaches a lady—with a vicious grin and a smirking wink.*] Hello, Kiddo. How's every little ting? Got anyting on for tonight? I know an old boiler down to de docks we kin crawl into. [*The lady stalks by without a look, without a change of pace.* YANK *turns to others—insultingly.*] Holy smokes, what a mug! Go hide yuhself before de horses shy at yuh. Gee, pipe de heine on dat one! Say, youse, yuh look like de stoin of a ferryboat. Paint and powder! All dolled up to kill! Yuh look like stiffs laid out for de boneyard! Aw, g'wan, de lot of youse! Yuh give me de eye-ache. Yuh don't belong, get me! Look at me, why don't youse dare? I belong, dat's me! [*Pointing to a skyscraper across the street which is in process of construction—with bravado.*] See dat building goin' up dere? See de steel work? Steel, dat's me! Youse guys live on it and tink yuh're somep'n. But I'm *in* it, see! I'm de hoistin' engine dat makes it go up! I'm it—de inside and bottom of it! Sure! I'm steel and steam and smoke and de rest of it! It moves—speed—twenty-five stories up—and me at de top and bottom—movin'! Youse simps don't move. Yuh're on'y dolls I winds up to see 'm spin. Yuh're de garbage, get me—de leavins—de ashes we dump over de side! Now, what 'a' yuh gotta say? [*But as they seem neither to see nor hear him, he flies into a fury.*] Bums! Pigs! Tarts! Bitches! [*He turns in a rage on the men, bumping viciously into them but not jarring them the least bit. Rather it is he who recoils after each collision. He keeps growling.*] Git off de oith! G'wan, yuh bum! Look where yuh're goin', can't yuh? Git outa here! Fight, why don't yuh? Put up yer mits! Don't be a dog! Fight or I'll knock yuh dead! [*But, without seeming to see him, they all answer with mechanical affected politeness.*] I beg your pardon. [*Then at a cry from one of the women, they all scurry to the furrier's window.*]

THE WOMAN [*Ecstatically, with a gasp of delight*]. Monkey fur! [*The whole crowd of men and women chorus after her in the same tone of affected delight.*] Monkey fur!

YANK [*With a jerk of his head back on his shoulders, as if he had received a punch full in the face—raging*]. I see yuh, all in white! I see yuh, yuh white-faced tart, yuh! Hairy ape, huh? I'll hairy ape yuh! [*He bends down and grips at the street curbing as if to pluck it out and hurl it. Foiled in this, snarling with passion, he leaps to the lamp-post on the corner and tries to pull it up for a club. Just at that moment a bus is heard rumbling up. A fat, high-hatted, spatted gentleman runs out from the side street. He calls out plaintively.*] Bus! Bus! Stop there! [*And runs full tilt into the bending, straining* YANK, *who is bowled off his balance.*]

YANK [*Seeing a fight—with a roar of joy as he springs to his feet*]. At last! Bus, huh! I'll bust yuh! [*He lets drive a terrific swing, his fist landing full on the fat gentleman's face. But the gentleman stands unmoved as if nothing had happened.*]

GENTLEMAN. I beg your pardon. [*Then irritably.*] You have made me lose my bus. [*He claps his hands and begins to scream.*] Officer! Officer! [*Many police whistles shrill out on the instant and a whole platoon of policemen rush in on* YANK *from all sides. He tries to fight but is clubbed to the pavement and fallen upon. The crowd at the window have not moved or noticed this disturbance. The clanging gong of the patrol wagon approaches with a clamoring din.*]

Curtain

SCENE 6

Scene: Night of the following day. A row of cells in the prison on Blackwell's Island. The cells extend back diagonally from right front to left rear. They do not stop, but disappear in the dark background as if they ran on, numberless, into infinity. One electric bulb from the low ceiling of the narrow corridor sheds its light through the heavy steel bars of the cell at the extreme front and reveals part of the interior. YANK *can be seen within, crouched on the edge of his cot in the attitude of Rodin's "The Thinker." His face is spotted with black and blue bruises. A blood-stained bandage is wrapped around his head.*

YANK [*Suddenly starting as if awakening from a dream, reaches out and shakes the bars—aloud to himself, wonderingly*]. Steel. Dis is de Zoo, huh? [*A burst of hard, barking laughing comes from the unseen occupants of the cells, runs back down the tier, and abruptly ceases.*]

VOICES [*Mockingly*]. The Zoo? That's a new name for this coop—a damn good name!

Steel, eh? You said a mouthful. This is the old iron house.

Who is that boob talkin'?

He's the bloke they brung in out of his head. The bulls had beat him up fierce.

YANK [*Dully*]. I musta been dreamin'. I tought I was in a cage at de Zoo—but de apes don't talk, do dey?

VOICES [*With mocking laughter*]. You're in a cage aw right.

A coop!

A pen!

A sty!

A kennel! [*Hard laughter—a pause.*]

Say, guy! Who are you? No, never mind lying. What are you?

Yes, tell us your sad story. What's your game?

What did they jug yuh for?

YANK [*Dully*]. I was a fireman—stokin' on de liners. [*Then with sudden rage, rattling his cell bars.*] I'm a hairy ape, get me? And I'll bust youse all in de jaw if yuh don't lay off kiddin' me.

VOICES. Huh! You're a hard boiled duck, ain't you!

When you spit, it bounces! [*Laughter.*]

Aw, can it. He's a regular guy. Ain't you?

What did he say he was—a ape?

YANK [*Defiantly*]. Sure ting! Ain't dat what youse all are—apes? [*A silence. Then a furious rattling of bars from down the corridor.*]

A VOICE [*Thick with rage*]. I'll show yuh who's a ape, yuh bum!

VOICES. Ssshh! Nix!

Can de noise!

Piano!

You'll have the guard down on us!

YANK [*Scornfully*]. De guard? Yuh mean de keeper, don't yuh? [*Angry exclamations from all the cells.*]

VOICE [*Placatingly*]. Aw, don't pay no attention to him. He's off his nut from the beatin'-up he got. Say, you guy! We're waitin' to hear what they landed you for—or ain't yuh tellin'?

YANK. Sure, I'll tell youse. Sure! Why de hell not? On'y—youse won't get me. Nobody gets me but me, see? I started to tell de Judge and all he says was: "Toity days to tink it over." Tink it over! Christ, dat's all I been doin' for weeks! [*After a pause.*] I was tryin' to git even wit someone, see?—someone dat done me doit.

VOICES [*Cynically*]. De old stuff, I bet.Your goil, huh?

Give yuh the double-cross, huh?

That's them every time!

Did yuh beat up de odder guy?

YANK [*Disgustedly*]. Aw, yuh're all wrong! Sure dere was a skoit in it—but not what youse mean, not dat old tripe. Dis was a new kind of skoit. She was dolled up all in white—in de stokehole. I tought she was a ghost. Sure. [*A pause.*]

VOICES [*Whispering*]. Gee, he's still nutty.

Let him rave. It's fun listenin'.

YANK [*Unheeding—groping in his thoughts*]. Her hands—dey was skinny and white like dey wasn't real but painted on somep'n. Dere was a million miles from me to her—twenty-five knots a hour. She was like some dead ting de cat brung in. Sure, dat's what. She didn't belong. She belonged in de window of a toy store, or on de top of a garbage can, see! Sure! [*He breaks out angrily.*] But would yuh believe it, she had de noive to do me doit. She lamped me like she was seein' somep'n broke loose from de menagerie. Christ, yuh'd oughter seen her eyes! [*He rattles the bars of his cell furiously.*] But I'll get back at her yet, you watch! And if I can't find her I'll take it out on de gang she runs wit. I'm wise to where dey hangs out now. I'll show her who belongs! I'll show her who's in de move and who ain't. You watch my smoke!

VOICES [*Serious and joking*]. Dat's de talkin'!

Take her for all she's got!

What was this dame, anyway? Who was she, eh?

YANK. I dunno. First cabin stiff. Her old man's a millionaire, dey says—name of Douglas.

VOICES. Douglas? That's the president of the Steel Trust, I bet.

Sure. I seen his mug in de papers.

He's filthy with dough.

VOICE. Hey, feller, take a tip from me. If you want to get back at that dame, you better join the Wobblies. You'll get some action then.

YANK. Wobblies? What de hell's dat?

VOICE. Ain't you ever heard of the I.W.W.?

YANK. Naw. What is it?

VOICE. A gang of blokes—a tough gang. I been readin' about 'em today in the paper. The guard give me the *Sunday Times*. There's a long spiel about 'em. It's from a speech made in the Senate by a guy named Senator Queen. [*He is in the cell next to* YANK'S. *There is a rustling of paper.*] Wait'll I see if I got light enough and I'll read you. Listen. [*He reads.*] "There is a menace existing in this country today which threatens the vitals of our fair Republic—as foul a menace against the very life-blood of the American Eagle as was the foul conspiracy of Cataline against the eagles of ancient Rome!"

VOICE [*Disgustedly*]. Aw, hell! Tell him to salt de tail of dat eagle!

VOICE [*Reading*]. "I refer to that devil's brew of rascals, jailbirds, murderers and cutthroats who libel all honest working men by calling themselves the Industrial Workers of the World; but in the light of their nefarious plots, I call them the Industrious *Wreckers* of the World!"

YANK [*With vengeful satisfaction*]. Wreckers, dat's de right dope! Dat belongs! Me for dem!

VOICE. Ssshh! [*Reading.*] "This fiendish organization is a foul ulcer on the fair body of our Democracy——"

VOICE. Democracy, hell! Give him the boid, fellers—the raspberry! [*They do.*]

VOICE. Ssshh! [*Reading.*] "Like Cato I say to this Senate, the I.W.W. must be destroyed! For they represent an ever-present dagger pointed at the heart of the greatest nation the world has ever known, where all men are born free and equal, with equal opportunities to all, where the Founding Fathers have guaranteed to each one happiness, where Truth, Honor, Liberty, Justice, and the Brotherhood of Man are a religion absorbed with one's mother's milk, taught at our father's knee, sealed, signed, and stamped upon in the glorious Constitution of these United States!" [*A perfect storm of hisses, catcalls, boos, and hard laughter.*]

VOICES [*Scornfully*]. Hurrah for de Fort' of July!

Pass de hat!

Liberty!

Justice!

Honor!

Opportunity!

Brotherhood!

ALL [*With abysmal scorn*]. Aw, hell!

VOICE. Give that Queen Senator guy the bark! All togedder now—one—two—tree—— [*A terrific chorus of barking and yapping.*]

GUARD [*From a distance*]. Quiet there, youse—or I'll git the hose. [*The noise subsides.*]

YANK [*With growling rage*]. I'd like to catch dat senator guy alone for a second. I'd loin him some trute!

VOICE. Ssshh! Here's where he gits down to cases on the Wobblies. [*Reads.*] "They plot with fire in one hand and dynamite in the other. They stop not before murder to gain their ends, nor at the outraging of defenseless womanhood. They would tear down society, put the lowest scum in the seats of the mighty, turn Almighty God's revealed plan for the world topsy-turvy, and make of our sweet and lovely civilization a shambles, a desolation where man, God's masterpiece, would soon degenerate back to the ape!"

VOICE [*To* YANK]. Hey, you guy. There's your ape stuff again.

YANK [*With a growl of fury*]. I got him. So dey blow up tings, do dey? Dey turn tings round, do dey? Hey, lend me dat paper, will yuh?

VOICE. Sure. Give it to him. On'y keep it to yourself, see. We don't wanter listen to no more of that slop.

VOICE. Here you are. Hide it under your mattress.

YANK [*Reaching out*]. Tanks. I can't read much but I kin manage. [*He sits, the paper in the hand at his side, in the attitude of Rodin's "The Thinker." A pause. Several snores from down the corridor. Suddenly* YANK *jumps to his feet with a furious groan as if some appalling thought had crashed on him—bewilderedly.*] Sure—her old man—president of de Steel Trust—makes half de steel in de world—steel—where I tought I belonged

—drivin' trou—movin'—in dat—to make *her*—and cage me in for her to spit on! Christ— [*He shakes the bars of his cell door till the whole tier trembles. Irritated, protesting exclamations from those awakened or trying to get to sleep.*] He made dis—dis cage! Steel! *It* don't belong, dat's what! Cages, cells, locks, bolts, bars —dat's what it means!—holdin' me down wit him at de top! But I'll drive trou! Fire, dat melts it! I'll be fire—under de heap—fire dat never goes out—hot as hell—breakin' out in de night—— [*While he has been saying this last he has shaken his cell door to a clanging accompaniment. As he comes to the "breakin' out" he seizes one bar with both hands and, putting his two feet up against the others so that his position is parallel to the floor like a monkey's, he gives a great wrench backward. The bar bends like a licorice stick under his tremendous strength. Just at this moment the* PRISON GUARD *rushes in, dragging a hose behind him.*]

GUARD [*Angrily*]. I'll loin youse bums to wake me up! [*Sees* YANK.] Hello, it's you, huh? Got the D.Ts., hey? Well, I'll cure 'em. I'll drown your snakes for yuh! [*Noticing the bar.*] Hell, look at dat bar bended! On'y a bug is strong enough for dat!

YANK [*Glaring at him*]. Or a hairy ape, yuh big yellow bum! Look out! Here I come! [*He grabs another bar.*]

GUARD [*Scared now—yelling off left*]. Toin de hose on, Ben!—full pressure! And call de others—and a straitjacket! [*The curtain is falling. As it hides* YANK *from view, there is a splattering smash as the stream of water hits the steel of* YANK'S *cell.*]

Curtain

SCENE 7

Scene: Nearly a month later. An I.W.W. local near the waterfront, showing the interior of a front room on the ground floor, and the street outside. Moonlight on the narrow street, buildings massed in black shadows. The interior of the room, which is general assembly room, office, and reading room, resembles some dingy settlement boys' club. A desk and high stool are in one corner. A table with papers, stacks of pamphlets, chairs about it, is at center. The whole is decidedly cheap, banal, commonplace and unmysterious as a room could well be. The SECRETARY *is perched on the stool making entries in a large ledger. An eye shade casts his face into shadows. Eight or ten men, longshoremen, iron workers, and the like are grouped about the table. Two are playing checkers. One is writing a letter. Most of them are smoking pipes. A big signboard is on the wall at the rear, "Industrial Workers of the World—Local No. 57."*

[YANK *comes down the street outside. He is dressed as in Scene 5. He moves cautiously, mysteriously. He comes to a point opposite the door, tiptoes softly up to it, listens, is impressed by the silence within, knocks carefully, as if he were guessing at the password to some secret rite. Listens. No answer. Knocks again a bit louder. No answer. Knocks impatiently, much louder.*]

SECRETARY [*Turning around on his stool*]. What the hell is that—someone knocking? [*Shouts.*] Come in, why don't you? [*All the men in the room look up.* YANK *opens the door slowly, gingerly, as if afraid of an ambush. He looks around for secret doors, mystery, is taken aback by the commonplaceness of the room and the men in it, thinks he may have gotten in the wrong place, then sees the signboard on the wall and is reassured.*]

YANK [*Blurts out*]. Hello.

MEN [*Reservedly*]. Hello.

YANK [*More easily*]. I tought I'd bumped into de wrong dump.

SECRETARY [*Scrutinizing him carefully*]. Maybe you have. Are you a member?

YANK. Naw, not yet. Dat's what I come for—to join.

SECRETARY. That's easy. What's your job—longshore?

YANK. Naw. Fireman—stoker on de liners.

SECRETARY [*With satisfaction*]. Welcome to our city. Glad to know you people are waking up at last. We haven't got many members in your line.

YANK. Naw. Dey're all dead to de woild.

SECRETARY. Well, you can help to wake 'em. What's your name? I'll make out your card.

YANK [*Confused*]. Name? Lemme tink.

SECRETARY [*Sharply*]. Don't you know your own name?

YANK. Sure; but I been just Yank for so long—Bob, dat's it—Bob Smith.

SECRETARY [*Writing*]. Robert Smith. [*Fills out the rest of card.*] Here you are. Cost you half a dollar.

YANK. Is dat all—four bits? Dat's easy. [*Gives the* SECRETARY *the money.*]

SECRETARY [*Throwing it in drawer*]. Thanks. Well, make yourself at home. No introductions needed. There's literature on the table. Take some of those pamphlets with you to distribute aboard ship. They may bring results. Sow the seed, only go about it right. Don't get caught and fired. We got plenty out of work. What we need is men who can hold their jobs—and work for us at the same time.

YANK. Sure. [*But he still stands, embarrassed and uneasy.*]

SECRETARY [*Looking at him—curiously*]. What did you knock for? Think we had a coon in uniform to open doors?

YANK. Naw. I tought it was locked—and dat yuh'd wanter give me the once-over trou a peep-hole or somep'n to see if I was right.

SECRETARY [*Alert and suspicious but with an easy laugh*]. Think we were running a crap game? That door is never locked. What put that in your nut?

YANK [*With a knowing grin, convinced that this is all camouflage, a part of the secrecy*]. Dis burg is full of bulls, ain't it?

SECRETARY [*Sharply*]. What have the cops got to do with us? We're breaking no laws.

YANK [*With a knowing wink*]. Sure. Youse wouldn't for woilds. Sure. I'm wise to dat.

SECRETARY. You seem to be wise to a lot of stuff none of us knows about.

YANK [*With another wink*]. Aw, dat's aw right, see. [*Then made a bit resentful by the suspicious glances from all sides.*] Aw, can it! Youse needn't put me trou de toid degree. Can't youse see I belong? Sure! I'm reg'lar. I'll stick, get me? I'll shoot de woiks for youse. Dat's why I wanted to join in.

SECRETARY [*Breezily, feeling him out*]. That's the right spirit. Only are you sure you understand what you've joined? It's all plain and aboveboard; still, some guys get a wrong slant on us. [*Sharply.*] What's your notion of the purpose of the I.W.W.?

YANK. Aw, I know all about it.

SECRETARY [*Sarcastically*]. Well, give us some of your valuable information.

YANK [*Cunningly*]. I know enough not to speak outa my toin. [*Then resentfully again.*] Aw, say? I'm reg'lar. I'm wise to de game. I know yuh got to watch your step wit a stranger. For all youse know, I might be a plain-clothes dick, or somep'n, dat's what yuh're tinkin', huh? Aw, forget it! I belong, see? Ask any guy down to de docks if I don't.

SECRETARY. Who said you didn't?

YANK. After I'm 'nitiated, I'll show yuh.

SECRETARY [*Astounded*]. Initiated? There's no initiation.

YANK [*Disappointed*]. Ain't there no password—no grip nor nothin'?

SECRETARY. What'd you think this is —the Elks—or the Black Hand?

YANK. De Elks, hell! De Black Hand, dey're a lot of yellow backstickin' Ginees. Naw. Dis is a man's gang, ain't it?

SECRETARY. You said it! That's why we stand on our two feet in the open. We got no secrets.

YANK [*Surprised but admiringly*]. Yuh mean to say yuh always run wide open—like dis?

SECRETARY. Exactly.

YANK. Den yuh sure got your noive wit youse!

SECRETARY [*Sharply*]. Just what was it made you want to join us? Come out with that straight.

YANK. Yuh call me? Well, I got noive, too! Here's my hand. Yuh wanter blow tings up, don't yuh? Well, dat's me! I belong!

SECRETARY [*With pretended carelessness*]. You mean change the unequal conditions of society by legitimate direct action—or with dynamite?

YANK. Dynamite! Blow it offen de oith—steel—all de cages—all de factories, steamers, buildings, jails—de Steel Trust and all dat makes it go.

SECRETARY. So—that's your idea, eh? And did you have any special job in that line you wanted to propose to us? [*He makes a sign to the men, who get up cautiously one by one and group behind* YANK.]

YANK [*Boldly*]. Sure, I'll come out wit it. I'll show youse I'm one of de gang. Dere's dat millionaire guy, Douglas——

SECRETARY. President of the Steel Trust, you mean? Do you want to assassinate him?

YANK. Naw, dat don't get yuh nothin'. I mean blow up de factory, de woiks, where he makes de steel. Dat's what I'm after—to blow up de steel, knock all de steel in de woild up to de moon. Dat'll fix tings! [*Eagerly, with a touch of bravado.*] I'll do it by me lonesome! I'll show yuh! Tell me where his woiks is, how to git there, all de dope. Gimme de stuff, de old butter—and watch me do de rest! Watch de smoke and see it move! I don't give a damn if dey nab me—long as it's done! I'll soive life for it—and give 'em de laugh! [*Half to himself.*] And I'll write her a letter and tell her de hairy ape done it. Dat'll square tings.

SECRETARY [*Stepping away from* YANK]. Very interesting. [*He gives a signal. The men, huskies all, throw themselves on* YANK *and before he knows it they have his legs and arms pinioned. But he is too flabbergasted to make a struggle, anyway. They feel him over for weapons.*]

MAN. No gat, no knife. Shall we give him what's what and put the boots to him?

SECRETARY. No. He isn't worth the trouble we'd get into. He's too stupid. [*He comes closer and laughs mockingly in* YANK'S *face.*] Ho-ho! By God, this is the biggest joke they've put up on us yet. Hey, you Joke! Who sent you—Burns or Pinkerton? No, by God, you're such a bonehead I'll bet you're in the Secret Service! Well, you dirty spy, you rotten agent provocator, you can go back and tell whatever skunk is paying you blood-money for betraying your brothers that he's wasting his coin. You couldn't catch a cold. And tell him that all he'll ever get on us, or ever has got, is just his own sneaking plots that he's framed up to put us in jail. We are what our manifesto says we are, neither more nor less—and we'll give him a copy of that any time he calls. And as for you—— [*He glares scornfully at* YANK, *who is sunk in an oblivious stupor.*] Oh, hell, what's the use of talking? You're a brainless ape.

YANK [*Aroused by the word to fierce but futile struggles*]. What's dat, yuh Sheeny bum, yuh!

SECRETARY. Throw him out, boys. [*In*

spite of his struggles, this is done with gusto and éclat. Propelled by several parting kicks, YANK *lands sprawling in the middle of the narrow cobbled street. With a growl he starts to get up and storm the closed door, but stops bewildered by the confusion in his brain, pathetically impotent. He sits there, brooding, in as near to the attitude of Rodin's "Thinker" as he can get in his position.*]

YANK [*Bitterly*]. So dem boids don't tink I belong, neider. Aw, to hell wit 'em! Dey're in de wrong pew—de same old bull—soapboxes and Salvation Army—no guts! Cut out an hour offen de job a day and make me happy! Gimme a dollar more a day and make me happy! Tree square a day, and cauliflowers in de front yard—ekal rights—a woman and kids—a lousy vote—and I'm all fixed for Jesus, huh? Aw, hell! What does dat get yuh? Dis ting's in your inside, but it ain't your belly. Feedin' your face—sinkers and coffee—dat don't touch it. It's way down—at de bottom. Yuh can't grab it, and yuh can't stop it. It moves, and everything moves. It stops and de whole woild stops. Dat's me now—I don't tick, see?—I'm a busted Ingersoll,[1] dat's what. Steel was me, and I owned de woild. Now I ain't steel, and de woild owns me. Aw, hell! I can't see—it's all dark, get me? It's all wrong! [*He turns a bitter mocking face up like an ape gibbering at the moon.*] Say, youse up dere, Man in de Moon, yuh look so wise, gimme de answer, huh? Slip me de inside dope, de information right from de stable—where do I get off at, huh?

A POLICEMAN [*Who has come up the street in time to hear this last—with grim humor*]. You'll get off at the station, you boob, if you don't get up out of that and keep movin'.

YANK [*Looking up at him—with a hard, bitter laugh*]. Sure! Lock me up! Put me in a cage! Dat's de on'y answer yuh know. G'wan, lock me up!

POLICEMAN. What you been doin'?

YANK. Enuf to gimme life for! I was born, see? Sure, dat's de charge. Write it in de blotter. I was born, get me!

POLICEMAN [*Jocosely*]. God pity your old woman! [*Then matter-of-fact.*] But I've no time for kidding. You're soused. I'd run you in but it's too long a walk to the station. Come on now, get up, or I'll fan your ears with this club. Beat it now! [*He hauls* YANK *to his feet.*]

YANK [*In a vague mocking tone*]. Say, where do I go from here?

POLICEMAN [*Giving him a push—with a grin, indifferently*]. Go to hell.

Curtain

SCENE 8

Scene: Twilight of the next day. The monkey house at the Zoo. One spot of clear gray light falls on the front of one cage so that the interior can be seen. The other cages are vague, shrouded in shadow from which chatterings pitched in a conversational tone can be heard. On the one cage a sign from which the word "gorilla" stands out. The gigantic animal himself is seen squatting on his haunches on a bench in much the same attitude as Rodin's "Thinker." YANK *enters from the left. Immediately a chorus of angry chattering and screeching breaks out. The gorilla turns his eyes but makes no sound or move.*

YANK [*With a hard, bitter laugh*]. Welcome to your city, huh? Hail, hail, de gang's all here! [*At the sound of his voice the chattering dies away into an attentive silence.* YANK *walks up to the gorilla's cage and, leaning over the railing, stares in at its occupant, who stares back at him, silent and motionless. There is a pause of dead stillness. Then* YANK *begins to talk in a friendly confidential tone, half-mockingly, but with a deep undercurrent of sympathy.*] Say, yuh're

[1] A "dollar watch."

some hard-lookin' guy, ain't yuh? I seen lots of tough nuts dat de gang called gorillas, but yuh're de foist real one I ever seen. Some chest yuh got, and shoulders, and dem arms and mits! I bet yuh got a punch in eider fist dat'd knock 'em all silly! [*This with genuine admiration. The gorilla, as if he understood, stands upright, swelling out his chest and pounding on it with his fist.* YANK *grins sympathetically.*] Sure, I get yuh. Yuh challenge de whole woild, huh? Yuh got what I was sayin' even if yuh muffed de woids. [*Then bitterness creeping in.*] And why wouldn't yuh get me? Ain't we both members of de same club—de Hairy Apes? [*They stare at each other—a pause—then* YANK *goes on slowly and bitterly.*] So yuh're what she seen when she looked at me, de white-faced tart! I was you to her, get me? On'y outa de cage—broke out—free to moider her, see? Sure! Dat's what she tought. She wasn't wise dat I was in a cage, too—worser'n yours—sure—a damn sight—'cause you got some chanct to bust loose—but me——[*He grows confused.*] Aw, hell! It's all wrong, ain't it? [*A pause.*] I s'pose yuh wanter know what I'm doin' here, huh? I been warmin' a bench down to de Battery—ever since last night. Sure. I seen de sun come up. Dat was pretty, too—all red and pink and green. I was lookin' at de skyscrapers—steel—and all de ships comin' in, sailin' out, all over de oith—and dey was steel, too. De sun was warm, dey wasn't no clouds, and dere was a breeze blowin'. Sure, it was great stuff. I got it aw right—what Paddy said about dat bein' de right dope—on'y I couldn't get *in* it, see? I couldn't belong in dat. It was over my head. And I kept tinkin'—and den I beat it up here to see what youse was like. And I waited till dey was all gone to git yuh alone. Say, how d'yuh feel sittin' in dat pen all de time, havin' to stand for 'em comin' and starin' at yuh—de white-faced, skinny tarts and de boobs what marry 'em—makin' fun of yuh, laughin' at yuh, gittin' scared of yuh—damn 'em! [*He pounds on the rail with his fist. The gorilla rattles the bars of his cage and snarls. All the other monkeys set up an angry chattering in the darkness.* YANK *goes on excitedly.*] Sure! Dat's de way it hits me, too. On'y yuh're lucky, see? Yuh don't belong wit 'em and yuh know it. But me, I belong wit 'em—but I don't, see? Dey don't belong wit me, dat's what. Get me? Tinkin' is hard——[*He passes one hand across his forehead with a painful gesture. The gorilla growls impatiently.* YANK *goes on gropingly.*] It's dis way, what I'm drivin' at. Youse can sit and dope dream in de past, green woods, de jungle and de rest of it. Den yuh belong and dey don't. Den yuh kin laugh at 'em, see? Yuh're de champ of de woild. But me—I ain't got no past to tink in, nor nothin' dat's comin', on'y what's now—and dat don't belong. Sure, you're de best off! Yuh can't tink, can yuh? Yuh can't talk neider. But I kin make a bluff at talkin' and tinkin'—a'most git away wit it—a'most!—and dat's where de joker comes in. [*He laughs.*] I ain't on oith and I ain't in heaven, get me? I'm in de middle tryin' to separate 'em, takin' all de woist punches from bot' of 'em. Maybe dat's what dey call hell, huh? But you, yuh're at de bottom. You belong! Sure! Yuh're de on'y one in de woild dat does, yuh lucky stiff! [*The gorilla growls proudly.*] And dat's why dey gotter put yuh in a cage, see? [*The gorilla roars angrily.*] Sure! Yuh get me. It beats it when you try to tink it or talk it—it's way down—deep—behind—you 'n' me we feel it. Sure! Bot' members of dis club! [*He laughs—then in a savage tone.*] What de hell! T' hell wit it! A little action, dat's our meat! Dat belongs! Knock 'em down and keep bustin' 'em till dey croaks yuh wit a gat—wit steel! Sure! Are yuh game? Dey've looked at youse, ain't dey—in a cage? Wanter get even? Wanter wind up like a sport 'stead of croakin' slow in dere? [*The gorilla roars an emphatic affirmative.* YANK *goes on with a sort of furious exaltation.*] Sure! Yuh're reg'lar! Yuh'll stick to de finish! Me 'n' you, huh?—bot' members of this club! We'll put up one last star bout dat'll knock 'em offen deir seats! Dey'll have to make de cages stronger after we're trou! [*The gorilla is straining at his bars, growling, hopping from one foot to the other.* YANK *takes a jimmy from under his coat and forces the lock on the cage door. He throws this open.*] Pardon from de governor! Step out and shake hands! I'll take yuh for a walk down Fif' Avenoo. We'll knock 'em offen de oith and croak wit de band playin'. Come on, Brother. [*The gorilla scrambles gingerly out of his cage. Goes to* YANK *and stands looking at him.* YANK *keeps his mocking tone—holds out his hand.*] Shake—de secret grip of our order. [*Something, the tone of mockery, perhaps, suddenly enrages the animal. With a spring he wraps his huge arms around* YANK *in a murderous hug. There is a crackling snap of crushed ribs—a gasping cry, still mocking, from* YANK.] Hey, I didn't say kiss me! [*The gorilla lets the crushed body slip to the floor; stands over it uncertainly, considering; then picks it up, throws it in the cage, shuts the door, and shuffles off menacingly into the darkness at left. A great uproar of frightened chattering and whimpering comes from the other cages. Then* YANK *moves, groaning, opening his eyes, and there is silence. He mutters painfully.*] Say—dey oughter match him—wit Zybszko.[2] He got me, aw right. I'm trou. Even him didn't tink I belonged. [*Then, with sudden passionate despair.*] Christ, where do I get off at? Where do I fit in? [*Checking himself as suddenly.*] Aw, what de hell! No squawkin', see! No quittin', get me! Croak with your boots on! [*He grabs hold of the bars of the cage and hauls himself painfully to his feet—looks around him bewilderedly—forces a mocking laugh.*] In de cage, huh? [*In the strident tones of a circus barker.*] Ladies and gents, step forward and take a slant at de one and only—[*His voice weakened*]—one and original—Hairy Ape from de wilds of——[*He slips in a heap on the floor and dies. The monkeys set up a chattering, whimpering wail. And, perhaps, the Hairy Ape at last belongs.*]

Curtain

[2] Stanislaus Zybszko, wrestling champion.

Robert Emmet Sherwood

❋ 1896-1955

Robert E. Sherwood, who moved from critic to playwright to screenwright to presidential adviser, was born in New Rochelle, New York, in 1896. In 1917 he interrupted his college career at Harvard to join the Canadian Black Watch for service in the First World War, an early instance of his concern for non-literary affairs. After the war he became first the motion picture critic of Vanity Fair, *then of* Life, *the old humorous magazine, where he remained to become editor-in-chief in 1927–1928. His first plays were comedies with slightly satiric overtones:* THE ROAD TO ROME *(1927) dealing with the defeat of Hannibal, and* THE QUEEN'S HUSBAND *(1928) whose chief character was drawn from Queen Marie of Rumania, then much in the headlines.*

These were followed by several lesser pieces until, in REUNION IN VIENNA *(1931), he found the combination of comedy and social commentary that established his reputation. His later plays reflect very precisely the changing moods of the thirties as sensed by a liberal and intellectual mind: the despair of* THE PETRIFIED FOREST *(1934), the angry irony of* IDIOT'S DELIGHT *(1936), the rediscovery of a foundation for idealism in* ABE LINCOLN IN ILLINOIS *(1938), the resolve to act in* THERE SHALL BE NO NIGHT *(1940). The last three plays were awarded the Pulitzer Prize for the outstanding American drama of their seasons. As a screenwright his* THE BEST YEARS OF THEIR LIVES *(1946) was given seven Academy Awards.*

An early advocate of American intervention in the Second World War, he became an adviser to Franklin D. Roosevelt and assisted in drafting many of his speeches. During the war he was overseas director of the Office of War Information and later edited the papers of Roosevelt and Hopkins, for which he received the Pulitzer award in history in 1949. Although he had been a founder and continuing member of the Playwrights' Company since 1938, his own dramatic activity suffered from his non-theatrical concerns. He experimented unsuccessfully with television scriptwriting, revised for production SECOND THRESHOLD, *a posthumous play by Philip Barry, and at the time of his death was working on an original comedy,* SMALL WAR ON MURRAY HILL.

Unlike many of his successful contemporaries, Sherwood was not an experimenter in dramatic technique. His importance is in the precision with which he reflects the moods and concerns of his time, yet always with the full concern of the artist, never with the deliberately limited vision of the journalist.

The Petrified Forest

A PLAY IN TWO ACTS

Characters

GRAMP MAPLE	ANOTHER LINEMAN
BOZE HERTZLINGER	JASON MAPLE
A TELEGRAPH LINEMAN	GABBY MAPLE
	PAULA

ALAN SQUIER	PYLES
HERB	LEGION COMMANDER
MR. CHISHOLM	ANOTHER LEGIONNAIRE
MRS. CHISHOLM	SHERIFF
JOSEPH	A DEPUTY
JACKIE	ANOTHER DEPUTY
DUKE MANTEE	
RUBY	

ACT I

The scene of the entire play is the lunch room of the Black Mesa Filling Station and Bar-B-Q on the desert in eastern Arizona.

There is an atmosphere about the place of strenuous if not hearty welcome.

At the upper right are double doors, with glass panels leading out to a covered porch. Off to the right, barely visible through these doors, are the red pumps of the filling station.

Downstage left is a door leading to the bedrooms of the MAPLE *family, who own this establishment. Upstage left is a swinging door leading to the kitchen. Upstage is a lunch counter, with cash register, ketchup bottles, paper napkins, toothpicks, chewing-gum and Life-Saver rack, cigars, cigarettes, etc.*

In the right wall are wide windows, through which may be seen the porch and, beyond it, the desert purpling in the sunset. At the left is a stove, with a high-backed rocking chair beside it.

There are three small square tables—downstage left, downstage right and center. There are three chairs at each table. At the right, along the wall, is a wooden bench.

The walls are of phony adobe. The window and door trimmings are painted a dark, burnt red. Above the windows is a sign, with the words, "Black Mesa Bar-B-Q" *worked in rustic letters. This formerly hung outside, but was replaced by a neon sign, the green gleam of which will be evident later on when darkness descends.*

The walls are decorated with advertisements of Rye Whisky, Gas and Oil, the NRA, the TVA, the Red Cross, the American Legion, the Santa Fé R. R., Apache Beer, etc. On the wall is a framed photograph of General Pershing and below it an old service flag with one star. Prominently displayed is a crudely lettered sign that shouts: "Tipping Is Un-American—Keep Your Change!"

At the table downstage right are two TELEGRAPH LINEMEN, *eating hamburger and drinking coffee. Both are young. The* FIRST *is thin and explosive in speech, the* SECOND *beefy and calm.*

Between them, and drawn back from the table, sits BOZE HERTZLINGER, *a stalwart, bronzed young man, who wears dirty white canvas pants and a filthy football jersey, on the back of which is a patch with the number 42. He is lighting a cigarette.*

At left in the rocking chair, sits GRAMP MAPLE—*an old, old man. His eyes are watery and his vision blurred. His skin is like leather that has been dried by a lifetime under the desert sun and worn thin by constant rough usage. He holds a tattered pink copy of the* Denver Post, *but he is paying more attention to the talk of the* LINEMEN *than to the screaming headlines.*

FIRST LINEMAN [*Swallowing*]. Certainly it's Revolution! And that's exactly what we got to come to, whether a lot of old fluffs back east like it or not——

SECOND LINEMAN. Yeah—and when it comes—how are *you* going to——

FIRST LINEMAN. When it comes, we're going to finally get some of that equality they talked about in the Declaration of Independence.

SECOND LINEMAN. Equality—hell! It's slavery. And how will you like that?

FIRST LINEMAN. What have we got *now*, I'd like to know? Do you call *this* freedom? [*He stows more food into his nimble mouth.*]

BOZE. Listen to me, kid. In school we

had to read up a lot on that cock-eyed system they got in Russia—and I'm here to tell you that if you were living over there you wouldn't be able to call your soul your own.

FIRST LINEMAN. And how do I know I've *got* a soul?

BOZE. You're alive, aren't you?

FIRST LINEMAN. Oh, sure—I'm alive. I got a heart—I can hear it beating. I got a stomach—I can hear it growling. I got blood—I can see it, when I stick myself with one of them God-damn splinters. But where's this soul that everybody hollers about?

BOZE. Its in your tongue, I guess. [*He winks broadly at* SECOND LINEMAN. *A car is heard stopping off at right.*]

FIRST LINEMAN. Yeah—and maybe they got it locked up in the safe at the Postal Telegraph Company, along with the rest of their doubtful assets.

[JASON MAPLE *has come in from upper right. He is a dull, defeated man, of about forty, solemn, bespectacled, paunchy. He wears a gray alpaca cap, and a gray suit. In his lapel is an American Legion button.*]

JASON [*To* BOZE]. Lady wants five gallons. Get going.

BOZE. O.K., boss. [*He pinches out the coal of his cigarette and places the butt behind his ear.*]

JASON. And you better keep on the alert out there so's customers don't have to wait. See?

BOZE. O.K., boss. [*He goes out.* FIRST LINEMAN *laughs.*]

FIRST LINEMAN. And there's the guy who's here to tell me that in Russia you can't even call your soul your own.

JASON. You fellers want pie? [*His attitude toward* FIRST LINEMAN *is not conspicuously amiable.*]

SECOND LINEMAN. Yeah.

FIRST LINEMAN. And another cuppa coffee. [JASON *picks up their cups and goes to door at left.*] Rugged individualism! Every man for himself! That's the kind of liberty we've been getting.

JASON [*Through door at the left*]. A couple of pies. [*He goes to coffee boiler on counter to refill the two cups.*]

SECOND LINEMAN. What are you complaining about? You're eating.

FIRST LINEMAN [*Significantly*]. "Man cannot live by bread alone."

SECOND LINEMAN. Who says he can't?

FIRST LINEMAN. God says so! That's who.

SECOND LINEMAN. Oh—is God a Russian?

FIRST LINEMAN. He certainly ain't with the Postal Telegraph.

[PAULA, *the Mexican cook, comes in, bearing the pie.* JASON *lights a cigar.*]

JASON. Take these. [JASON *gives cups to* PAULA *as she passes.*]

FIRST LINEMAN. Why do you suppose it is that Russia's got the whole world scared? It's because they're pushing ahead. They're pioneering!

GRAMP. They're what?

FIRST LINEMAN. I said, they're pioneering. They're opening up new territory—and for the benefit of all, not so's a few land grabbers can step in and take the profits after somebody else has done the real work. Gracias. [*This is addressed to* PAULA, *who has delivered pie and is now removing remnants of the hamburger.*] Those engineers in Russia are building something new! That's where they've got it on us. We ain't building—we're *repairing*. Just like you and me. What do we do—day after day? We climb up poles, and fix the wires, so that some broker in New York can telegraph in a split second to some guy in Los Angeles to tell him he's ruined.

GRAMP. Well, my friend—when you talk about pioneering—you're talking about something I can tell *you* a few things about. [*He has risen and is crossing to occupy chair vacated by* BOZE.]

JASON. Shut up, Gramp.

GRAMP. I won't shut up.

JASON. I told you not to get into arguments with the guests.

GRAMP. Listen—I can tell these boys some things they'd be glad to hear. Wouldn't you, boys?

SECOND LINEMAN. Sure! Go ahead, Pop. Change the subject. [*Both* LINEMEN *are devouring the pie.*]

GRAMP. Listen, my friend. I come down into this desert fifty-six years ago. I come down from Virginia City by way of Salt Lake and Mesa Verde. You had to be tough to cross this country in them days—Piyutes—Apaches—and plenty of white men with no love for their neighbors. Yes, *sir!* I was in your same line of business—wire-stringing. I helped string the first line that run west out of Albuquerque, and we had one hell of a time doing it, too.

BOZE [*Comes in*]. Lady wants a pack of Camels.

GRAMP. Do you want to know who was the governor of this territory in them days? Well, I'll tell you. General Lew Wallace. He wrote "Ben Hur" right there in the palace in Santa Fé. He was a brave man and he had to be, because governing around here was dangerous work. It meant killing or being killed.

BOZE. Attaboy, Mr. Maple. Tell 'em about the time you took a shot at Billy the Kid.

[JASON *hands* BOZE *Camels and change.*]

GRAMP. I didn't take no shots at the Kid. I had too God-damn much sense. But he took a couple at me. I'm practically the only man he ever missed; but he was only doing it in fun, so it couldn't hardly count.

[GABBY MAPLE *comes in from left on the cue "he ever missed." She is young and pretty, with a certain amount of style about her. Her principal distinguishing feature is an odd look of resentment in her large, dark eyes. She carries a thin book, her forefinger marking the place. She sits down at table at left and starts to read.*]

JASON. Get on out with those Camels.

BOZE. O.K., boss. [*He goes out, with a knowing look at* GABBY *which she ignores.*]

FIRST LINEMAN. Well, Pop, it's been interesting, but I've got to be——

GRAMP. Wait a minute. I was just going to tell you about the first message we ever sent over that line. General Wallace dictated it and we sent it all the way through to Washington to President Hayes. And do you want to know what it said? It said, "God Save the Republic!" That's what General Wallace told us to say—and he was a great author.

FIRST LINEMAN [*Who has risen*]. You better send that same message through again, Pop—because the old republic's badly in need of assistance. How much do we owe? [*He has crossed to lunch counter, the* SECOND LINEMAN *following.*]

JASON. That'll be fifty-five cents apiece.

GABBY. What did they have?

JASON. Hamburger special, pie, and two cups of coffee.

GABBY. All right. [*She puts down book and picks up pie plates and coffee mugs and goes out into kitchen at left.* LINEMEN *are paying at counter.*]

GRAMP. Hope you'll call in again, boys. I always enjoy talking to anybody in the telegraphing business.

SECOND LINEMAN. Maybe we will, Pop. Never can tell where we'll be sent next.

GRAMP. That's right—you can't.

JASON [*As he shoves change across counter*]. There's just one remark I'd like to pass to you, brother. Just watch out how you talk about the United States of America.

FIRST LINEMAN. What do you mean?

JASON. I mean simply this: belittling our system of government, preaching revolution and destruction, and red propaganda—well, it isn't a very healthy occupation. That's all.

GRAMP. I thought you said not to argue with the guests.

JASON. I'm only telling you, brother —for the sake of your own good.

FIRST LINEMAN. So it's unhealthy, eh! How do you think this government was started if it wasn't by revolution?

SECOND LINEMAN. Come on, Nick. We got to get going.

FIRST LINEMAN. Wait till he answers my question.

JASON. The American Revolution was fought to establish law and order. But the object of your dirty red propaganda is to destroy it——

FIRST LINEMAN. And how much law and order have *we* got? Did you read about that massacre yesterday in Oklahoma City? What kind of law and order is that?

SECOND LINEMAN. Listen, Nick. I got a dame waiting up for me in Gallup and I——

JASON. If some of you Bolsheviks would quit preaching disrespect for law, it wouldn't be possible for criminals to——

FIRST LINEMAN. Yeah? Do you want to know something? They don't have crime in Russia. And why? Because they've abolished the cause of crime. They've abolished greed! And I'll tell you something else——

SECOND LINEMAN. I'm going. [*He starts out.*]

JASON. You got your eats and there's your change. Now kindly get out.

FIRST LINEMAN [*Pocketing his change*]. O.K., Mr. Tin-horn Patriot. I only hope I'm around here when it happens. I want to see you when you've joined the mob and started waving the red flag. [*He turns and starts out.*]

GRAMP. 'By, boys.

FIRST LINEMAN. Good-by, Pop. [LINEMEN *go out.*]

GRAMP. You never should get into arguments with a boy like that, Jason. You only make a fool out of yourself.

JASON. [*Back of counter*]. I'm sorry I didn't get his name, so's I could report him.

GRAMP. You tend to your own business, son, and stop fussing about other——

JASON [*With surprising vehemence*]. My own business! That's a fine thing to say to me. What business have *I* got? Miserable little service station on the edge of nowheres.

GRAMP. It's a living, ain't it?

JASON. A living—yes—just barely. But it's one hell of a life for a man that ought to be getting some place in the world.

GRAMP. Maybe it's all you're good for.

JASON. I know—that's what *you* think. It's what you've always thought, since I was a boy. What chance have I ever had to prove what I can do?

GRAMP. You had a war, didn't you? Biggest war yet.

JASON. Yes—and you think I failed in that because I didn't come home with a lot of medals, and some German scalps hanging on my belt. Well, they didn't hand out medals to us soldiers that drove trucks—even if we did get right up into the danger zone time and again.

GRAMP. All right, son—all right! You could have enlisted in the infantry if you'd had a mind to.

JASON [*Hotly*]. I enlisted in the branch of the service where my knowledge of mechanics could do the most good to my country. And I've still got that knowledge. And you know damned well it's your fault I don't get more scope for using it. [*He has come out from behind counter.*]

GRAMP. My fault?

JASON. That's what I said. Hanging on to this place when you can sell it for good money.

GRAMP. I don't have to sell if I don't want to.

JASON. Dana Trimble's renewed his offer. Seven thousand dollars, and I know I can get him up to nine, maybe ten.

GRAMP. What makes him think this property's worth that much?

JASON. He knows perfectly well they're going to make this an interstate highway and run the bus route to El Paso through here.

GRAMP. All right—if it's good for him, it's good for us.

JASON. With seven thousand dollars I could buy a big piece of an auto camp on Redondo Boulevard in one of the best districts of Los Angeles. I'd put in a Bar-B-Q service and in a couple of years we'd *have* something——

GRAMP. Los Angeles! My God! You want to go to Los Angeles and Gabby wants to go to Europe. Ain't they nobody around here that's satisfied to stay put?

JASON. How about yourself? Were you ever satisfied to stay put, until you got so damned old you didn't have enough energy to move?

GRAMP. Listen to me, son. In my day, we had places to go—*new* places. But, my God—Los Angeles——[GABBY *comes in from kitchen.*]

GABBY. Paula's scared.

GRAMP. What's she scared of?

GABBY. The Mexicans are saying that Mantee is headed this way.

JASON. He was headed for the border and he's over it by now—if the Texas Rangers haven't got him.

GRAMP. They won't get him. Have you seen his picture? Straight black hair. Got Injun blood. He'll fool 'em.

JASON [*Importantly*]. You can't fool all the people all the time. [*He turns to go.*] Watch the counter, will you, Gabby? I got to get dressed.

GRAMP. Dressed? For what?

JASON. Legion meeting.

GABBY. What time will you be home, Dad?

JASON. About ten, I guess—maybe later. There's a lot of important business coming up. [*He addresses* GRAMP, *with some defiance.*] And I'm going to make some inquiries about those telegraph men. And if I can locate 'em, that Bolshevik will be out of a job and then he can go look for work pioneering in Russia.

GABBY. What'll you do—blow a bugle and turn the whole God-damn Legion loose on him?

JASON. Will you kindly control your language?

GABBY. I'll talk the only language I understand.

GRAMP. You'll never get Gabby to talk respectable. Never in all this world.

JASON. Well, I only hope some day my own daughter will learn to cultivate a little respect for the things I stand for. Maybe the time will come when you'll be thankful your father fought for his country. [*He goes out at left.*]

GABBY. [*Going behind counter*]. What did that telegraph man say that got Dad in such a stew?

GRAMP. I don't know what he said—something about Russia and pioneering. But there's a lot in it, whatever it was. The trouble with this country is, it's got settled. It's camped down in the bed of a dried-up river, and whenever anybody says, "Let's get the hell out of here," all the rest start to holler, "If we move a step the Injuns'll get us." Well—say—if we'd been that way in my time, I'd like to know how this country'd ever have got rich enough to be able to support the American Legion. [*Two toots from an auto horn are heard.*] Say! There's the mail. [*With surprising alacrity,* GRAMP *jumps up and hurries out.* GABBY *has poured herself a cup of coffee and brought it down to table at left. She sits down, sips coffee, opens her book, and reads. After a moment* BOZE *comes in, sees that she is alone, and closes door behind him.* GABBY *looks up, sees who it is, indicates indifference, and resumes reading.* BOZE *comes up behind her, leans over and kisses the back of her neck. She brushes him off as though he were a fly.*]

GABBY [*Without vehemence*]. Cut it out. [BOZE *grins, draws up a chair, and sits down close to her, his hefty forearms resting on table.*]

BOZE. Not mad, are you, Gabby?

GABBY. Where's Gramp?

BOZE. He's out talking to the postman. Don't worry about him.

GABBY. I wasn't worrying.

BOZE. Don't you like me, honey sweet?

GABBY. No—not very much.

BOZE. O.K. I'll forgive you—seeing as I've been here only a little while and I haven't had much chance to go into my act. But when I do—you're going to change your attitude awful fast. [*She fails to comment on his threat. He is silent for a moment, his jaws confidently chewing on a small piece of gum.*] What's that you're reading?

GABBY. You wouldn't like it.

BOZE. How do *you* know how I feel about things? Can I look?

GABBY. Sure. Go ahead and look. [*He takes opened book and examines it.*]

BOZE. Hah—Poems. [*He reads.*]

The shapely slender shoulders small,
Long arms, hands wrought in glorious wise,
Round little breasts, the hips withal
High, full of flesh, not scant of size,
Fit for all amorous masteries——

[*He whistles through his teeth.*] Say! That's kind of pash! [*She snatches book away from him.*] So that's the kind of stuff you read. . . . Well, honey, I'm not a bit surprised. I've been suspecting all along that all you needed was a little encouragement. [*She looks at him, curiously, with a mixture of contempt and some slight interest.*] And I don't wonder that in a God-forsaken place like this you'd have to get it out of poetry.

GABBY. [*Defensive*]. It's great poetry!

BOZE. Certainly it's great. But I can think of something a whole lot better. . . . Look at me, honey. [*She looks at him.*] I'm not so terrible-looking, am I?

GABBY. Why do you wear that locket around your neck?

BOZE [*Laughing*]. Locket!

GABBY. It makes you look like a sissy.

BOZE. I've been waiting for you to notice that. That was my father's watch chain. My mother gave it to me when I graduated. I'd like you to know my mother. She lives in Grants Pass, Oregon, and she could tell you some pretty nice things about me. But wait till you see what's on the end. [*He draws chain out and displays a gold football.*] It's a gold football—solid gold! I got that for intercepting a pass and running sixty-eight yards for a touchdown.

GABBY. What was your school?

BOZE. Nevada Tech. If I'd been with Princeton or Minnesota or any of those big clubs, I'd have been All-American. Wait till I show you something. [*He produces a billfold from his hip pocket and extracts therefrom a frequently folded clipping.*] That's from Sid Ziff's column in the *Los Angeles Herald.* He saw me play against Loyola. Listen to what he says: "Tip to the pigskin fraternity: When pondering your All-American selections for this current Anno Domini, just mull over the name of Boze Hertzlinger of Nevada Tech. Playing with an admittedly minor league club, and protected by interference of cellophane strength, Hertzlinger managed to remind some of us observers of the Illini Phantom himself." Do you know who the Illini Phantom was? Red Grange! [*He folds up clipping and restores it to his pocket.*] That's just a sample of the kind of notices I got. I could show you dozens more like it.

GABBY. You think a hell of a lot of yourself, don't you?

BOZE [*Disarmingly*]. Who wouldn't, in my position?

GABBY. Why do you have to work in a filling station?

BOZE. Well—that's a point that I don't know if I could explain so's you'd understand it. I could be making good money in a lot of ways right now—engineering, coaching, the insurance game—lots of ways. But—I just can't be tied down—not yet. I've got an itch inside here that keeps me on the move—chasing the rainbow.

GABBY. Do you ever expect to catch it?

BOZE. I'll catch it all right. I'll twist its tail, and make it do tricks. . . . Maybe I'm kind of close to it right now.

GABBY. You'd better look some place else. There aren't any rainbows around Black Mesa.

BOZE. I wouldn't bet on that. . . . You know, Gabby—you're a queer kid. Sometimes you seem too young to know anything. And then—sometimes—you seem like God's grandmother. And reading that pash poetry. That gives me an idea.

GABBY. An idea of what?

BOZE. Oh—it's easy to tell when a girl's ready for love.

GABBY. How do you tell that, Boze?

BOZE. Well—one pretty sure way is when she starts calling me by my own name for the first time. And another way is how I feel myself. It takes two to make a radio program, you know—the one that's sending, and the one that's receiving. And when I'm with a girl that's cute and appealing, with big, soft eyes—well—I can feel sort of electric waves running all through me—and I can be pretty sure she's doing some broadcasting, whether she knows it or not.

GABBY. Have you got a program coming in now?

BOZE. Listen—It's like the hottest torch song that ever was sung. Can't you kind of hear it, honey? [*She looks away from him, but says nothing. He reaches out and takes hold of her hand, entwining his fingers with hers.*] You can call me a sap if you want to, Gabby—but I guess I'm falling in love with you. I'm getting so I want you more than is good for me.

GABBY [*Looking at him, levelly*]. Have you ever been in love before?

BOZE [*Scornfully*]. No!

GABBY. Have you ever *said* you were?

BOZE. Sure—plenty of times.

GABBY. Did they believe you?

BOZE [*Amused*]. Certainly they did. And I'll tell you why: it's because they were all dumb! But that's just where you're different. I couldn't fool you, Gabby.

GABBY. I'm smart, am I?

BOZE. Too smart—for most men. You'd catch on to 'em. But that's what I want. Because the more you see into me, the better you're going to like me. [*With his free hand, he takes hold of her chin.*]

GABBY. You'd better look out, if you want to hold on to your job. Dad might come in and he doesn't like to have the help making passes at me.

BOZE. That wouldn't bother me, honey sweet. There are plenty more jobs for anyone with the ambition I've got. But there aren't plenty more girls like you. [*He leans over and kisses her.*] You're going to love me, Gabby. You're going to love me a lot.

GABBY. Look out! There's someone——

BOZE [*Unconcerned*]. We'll talk about it some more later.

[ALAN SQUIER *has appeared in doorway, and, seeing that he has interrupted some amour, has paused to give them time to break. He is a thin, wan, vague man of about thirty-five. He wears a brown felt hat, brown tweed coat and gray flannel trousers—which came originally but much too long ago from the best Saville Row tailors. He is shabby and dusty but there is about him a sort of afterglow of elegance. There is something about him and it is impossible in a stage direction to say just what it is—that brings to mind the ugly word "condemned." He carries a heavy walking stick and a rucksack is slung over his shoulders. He is diffident in manner, ultra-polite and soft spoken, his accent is that of an Anglicized American.*]

SQUIER. Good evening.

BOZE [*Cordially*]. Good evening! What can we do for you?

SQUIER. Can I order something to eat?

BOZE. Why, certainly. Miss Maple will take care of you. [*While* SQUIER *is taking off his rucksack and hat, and putting them on bench at right,* BOZE *turns to* GABBY *and speaks in a low tone.*] Your father going into town?

GABBY. Yes. [*She is taking a menu card to table at center.*]

BOZE [*Significantly*]. O.K. [*He goes out.*]

GABBY. Will you sit down here, sir?

SQUIER. Thanks. [*He sits. She hands him menu card.*]

GABBY. Driven far?

SQUIER. I've been walking.

GABBY. Do you live around here?

SQUIER. No. My last host of the road reached his own ranch, about ten miles back, and didn't ask me in. I had to continue on foot. It's wonderful what progress you can make just by doing this. [*He jerks his thumb and looks at menu.*] "Today's Special." . . . Just what is a Bar-B-Q?

GABBY. Well—here it's hamburger sandwich with vegetables on the side. It's always "Today's Special." But it's pretty good.

SQUIER. I want it. But first I'd like some of that cream of corn soup, and some beer, and—I'll order the dessert later.

GABBY. O.K. [*She takes menu.*]

SQUIER. Another question. Where am I?

GABBY. This place is called Black Mesa, but there's nothing else here. Where were you planning to go?

SQUIER. My plans have been uncertain.

GABBY. You mean, you were just bumming along?

SQUIER. Call it gipsying. I had a vague idea that I'd like to see the Pacific Ocean, and perhaps drown in it. But that depends——

GABBY. Where did you come from?

SQUIER. Quite a long way, Miss Maple. Is that the name?

GABBY [*Smiling*]. Yes—that's it. Are you English?

SQUIER. No. You might call me an American once removed. . . . But—if you don't mind——

GABBY. The soup'll be right in. The washroom's through there, on your left, if you want it. [*She indicates door at left.*]

SQUIER. Thank you. [GABBY *goes out* at left. SQUIER *rises. He sees book of verse, picks it up and looks at it, wonderingly. The door at left opens and* JASON *comes out resplendent in the uniform of his Legion post. It is horizon blue, with white Sam Browne belt and pistol holster.* SQUIER *looks at* JASON *with amazement.*]

JASON. Good evening.

SQUIER. Good evening.

JASON. Anyone take your order?

SQUIER. Yes—a charming young lady——

JASON. That's my daughter. [*He says this with a note of warning, as much as to add: "And don't try to get fresh."* JASON *crosses to cash register, punches the "No Sale," and extracts five silver dollars from till. He then reaches under counter, takes out a revolver, breaks it to make sure it's loaded, and rubs it with a cloth.* SQUIER *has one more puzzled look at him, then goes out at left.* GRAMP *comes in from upper right, bearing a fresh copy of the* Denver Post.]

GRAMP [*At end of counter*]. I was just talking to Roy Greeley and he says in town they're all certain that Mantee outfit is headed here. Look! They got the whole story here in the *Post*. Oklahoma City Massacre! Six killed—four wounded—two not expected to live. [JASON *glances at paper.*] The sheriff's got all his deputies out patrolling the roads. They think there's sure going to be some killing around here.

JASON. Well—if there is—we can't trust that sheriff to do a damn thing. We'll turn out the Legion.

GRAMP. You *would?*

JASON. Certainly! That's what we're there for. [*He thrusts revolver in holster of his Sam Browne belt, goes to kitchen door, and calls through it: "Gabby!"*]

GABBY'S VOICE. Yes?

JASON. I'm leaving now. And I—I took five bucks. If anything delays me getting back, I'll phone.

GABBY'S VOICE. O.K.

JASON. Don't forget to light the neon sign when it gets dark.

GABBY'S VOICE. I won't. [*He shuts kitchen door and crosses up front of counter.*]

GRAMP. Well, by God, you'd better not try to do any shooting in that get-up. I never seed a better target.

JASON. You needn't be afraid about me. [GABBY *comes in with soup.*]

GRAMP. *I* ain't afraid. But I would be if I was you.

GABBY. How much did you say you took?

JASON. Five bucks.

GABBY. What do you need all that for?

JASON. Just in case of emergency. [*He decides to resent all this interference.*] By God, between the two of you, you'd think I wasn't fit to be trusted with money or ideas or anything. But I'm here to tell you, both of you——

GABBY [*Putting soup on table*]. What, Dad?

JASON. Oh, never mind. [*He goes out.* GABBY *goes to counter, opens a bottle of beer, and takes it to center table.*]

GRAMP [*While she is about this*]. It's too bad they didn't wear a uniform like that when they fit the Germans. They wouldn't none of 'em have come home. . . . Who's that food for?

GABBY. Customer. He's in the washroom, I guess.

GRAMP. Is it that young feller that walked in with a little pack on his back? [*He goes to his rocking chair at left.*]

GABBY. Yes—that's the one.

GRAMP. Looked to me like one of them things you see up around Taos. [*He sits down.*] Hey, Gabby, how about letting your poor, weary old grandfather have a little drink now?

GABBY. No.

GRAMP. Aw—come on. I ain't got so long to live. [SQUIER *comes in from left.*]

GABBY. You can have one before you go to bed, and that's all. [*She goes out through kitchen door.*]

GRAMP. Your soup's waiting for you, my friend.

SQUIER. Thank you.

GRAMP. Looks good, too.

SQUIER. Yes. It looks fine. [SQUIER *sits down and starts to eat, ravenously.* GRAMP *decides that the* Denver Post *will serve as a conversation opener. He crosses to* SQUIER'S *table.*]

GRAMP. Like to see a picture of that Duke Mantee? [*He holds out newspaper.* SQUIER *looks at clamorous headlines.*]

SQUIER. My God! Six killed. Did *he* do all that?

GRAMP. Him and his friends did, when they sprung him from the law. Fine lot of sheriffs they must have there in Oklahoma City—letting themselves get knocked over right out in front of the Court House.

SQUIER [*Still eating*]. He doesn't look very vicious, does he?

GRAMP [*Sitting down*]. Well—I'll tell you; you can't tell a killer from his picture, except by his chin. That's a funny thing about a killer—always holds his chin in. Ever notice that?

SQUIER [*Buttering some bread*]. I don't think I've ever seen a killer.

GRAMP. I have. Plenty of 'em. Ever hear of Billy the Kid?

SQUIER. Yes, indeed.

GRAMP. I knowed him well, down in the Pecos country. [*Proudly.*] He took a couple of shots at me, once.

SQUIER. I congratulate you on still being with us.

GRAMP. Well—it was kind of dark, and he'd had a few—and, besides, I don't think he really meant to do me any real harm. Just wanted to scare the pants off of me.

SQUIER. Did he do it?

GRAMP. Naw—I seed he was just having some fun. So I said to him: "Kid you're drunk!" And he said, "What makes you think that?" He was always soft-spoken. And I said: "Because you missed me!" Well, sir—he had to laugh. . . . You're kind of hongry, aren't you?

SQUIER. Yes. You can go just so long without food——

GRAMP. Been having some bad luck?

SQUIER. Yes.

GRAMP. Well—no disgrace in that these days. What line of work you in?

SQUIER. None, just now. I have been, at times, a writer.

GRAMP. A writer, eh? That's a funny thing——

SQUIER [*Laughing silently*]. Yes—it is.

GRAMP. I knew the greatest writer that ever lived. Sam Clemens. Ever hear of him?

SQUIER [*Trying hard to think*]. Let me see——

GRAMP. Well, did you ever hear of Mark Twain?

SQUIER. Oh, *yes!*

GRAMP. Same feller!

SQUIER. Really? [GABBY *comes in with "Today's Special," which she puts on table.*]

GRAMP. Yes, sir. I knew him when I was a boy up in Virginia City. He was writing comical pieces for the paper there —the *Enterprise*—and he was the best God-damn liar I ever seed, and I've seed plenty. He used to say he did his writing on the principle that his readers wanted everything but the truth, so that's what he give 'em. [GABBY *is on the way out.*] Are you a famous writer? [*At kitchen door,* GABBY *turns to look at* SQUIER, *then goes out.*]

SQUIER. No.

GRAMP. Maybe you're just modest. What's your name?

SQUIER. Alan Squier.

GRAMP. Well, maybe you are famous, for all I'd know. I don't get to do much reading, outside of the headlines. Eyes have gone back on me. But when I was your age, I could hit a running jack rabbit at fifty paces——

GABBY [*Coming in*]. Your supper's ready, Gramp.

GRAMP. And I'm ready for it. Got *me* hongry, watching him eat. [*He has risen.*] Pleased to have met you, Mr. Squier.

SQUIER. Pleased to have met *you,* sir.

GRAMP. Yes, sir. Thank you, sir. [*He goes out.*]

GABBY. Like the soup?

SQUIER [*From the heart*]. It was glorious!

GABBY. Want some coffee?

SQUIER. Will it mix with the beer?

GABBY. Oh, sure. Coffee will mix with anything. [*She goes to counter to get his coffee.*]

SQUIER. That's a charming old gentleman. Your grandfather?

GABBY. Yes.

SQUIER. He told me he'd been missed by Billy the Kid.

GABBY. He tells everybody about that. Poor Gramp. You get terribly sick of him after a while. [*She has brought down coffee.*] Did I hear him say you're a writer?

SQUIER [*Humbly*]. Yes.

GABBY. I haven't met many writers—except Sidney Wenzell. Ever heard of him?

SQUIER. That's not Mark Twain, is it?

GABBY. No! Sidney Wenzell—he's with Warner Brothers. He stopped here once, when he was driving out to the Coast. He said I ought to go to Hollywood, and to be sure and look him up. But—what the hell! They never mean it.

SQUIER. No! They never mean a thing. [*She has picked up her book and started to go.*] Please don't go. [*She pauses and turns.*]

GABBY. Something else you want? We got pie and layer cake.

SQUIER. No. I—I'd like to talk to you. Please sit down.

GABBY. All right. [*She sits down, across from him, at center table.* SQUIER *eats rapidly, mechanically, during the subsequent dialogue, stowing food away as he talks and listens.*]

SQUIER. I suppose you want to go into the movies?

GABBY [*Scornfully*]. God, *no!*

SQUIER. But—I thought every beautiful girl had her heart set on Hollywood.

GABBY. That's just it. It's too common. I want to go to Bourges. [*She fails to soften the "G."*]

SQUIER. Where?

GABBY. Bourges—in France. You'd never guess it, but that's where I came from.

SQUIER. You're not French?

GABBY. Partly. I was born in Bourges—but I left it almost before I was able to walk, so all I know about it is from the picture postcards my mother sends me. They got a cathedral there.

SQUIER. Your mother still lives there?

GABBY. Yes. Dad brought us back here after the war. Mother stuck it out in this desert for a couple of years, and then she packed up and went back to Bourges. We've never seen her since. Some people seem to think it was cruel of her to leave me. But what could she do? She didn't have any money to bring me up. She just couldn't *live* here—and you can't blame her for that. Do you think she was cruel?

SQUIER. Not if you don't, Miss Maple.

GABBY. Well—I *don't.* She's tried lots of times to get me over there to see her—but Dad won't allow it. She got a divorce and married a Frenchman that's got a bookstore. Mother was always a great reader, so I guess it's nice for her. She's got three more kids. Just think of that! I've got a half-brother and half-sisters that can't speak a word of English. I'd sure like to see them.

SQUIER. Can you speak French?

GABBY. Only what you learn in high school—like *table* for "table." [*She takes photograph from book.*] Look—there's my mother's picture. That was just before she married Dad. She had her picture taken smelling a rose.

SQUIER. She's lovely! And I can see the resemblance.

GABBY. It's hard to imagine her being married to Dad, isn't it? But I guess he looked all right in his American uniform. Mother used to send me a book every year for my birthday, but they were all in French and I couldn't read them. So last year I wrote and asked if she'd mind sending me one in English, and she sent me this one. It's the Poems of François Villon. Ever read it?

SQUIER. Yes.

GABBY. It's wonderful poetry. She wrote in it: *"à ma chère petite Gabrielle."* That means "to my dear little Gabrielle." She gave me that name. It's about the only French thing I've got.

SQUIER. Gabrielle. It's a beautiful name.

GABBY. Wouldn't you know it would get changed into "Gabby" by these ignorant bastards around here? I guess you think I use terrible language.

SQUIER. Oh, no! It—it's picturesque.

GABBY. Well—it suits this kind of country.

SQUIER. You share your mother's opinion of the desert? [*She nods.*] But you can find solace in the Poems of François Villon.

GABBY. Yes. They get the stink of the gasoline and the hamburger out of my system.

SQUIER. Would you like to read me one of those poems, Gabrielle?

GABBY. You mean now?

SQUIER. Yes. While I'm finishing "Today's Special."

GABBY. O.K. I'll read you the one I like best. He wrote it about a friend of his who was getting married. [*She reads, with marked but inexpert emphasis.*]

At daybreak, when the falcon claps his wings
No whit for grief, but noble heart held high
With loud glad noise he stirs himself and springs,
And takes his meat and toward his lure draws nigh;
Such good I wish you! Yea, and heartily
I'm fired with hope of true love's meed to get;
Knowing Love writes it in his book; for why,
This is the end for which we twain are met.

Did you ever see a falcon?

SQUIER. Yes.

GABBY. What does it look like?

SQUIER. Not very pleasant. Like a hawk. Go on, Gabrielle.

GABBY [*Resuming reading*]

Mine own heart's lady with no gain-sayings
You shall be always till I die;
And in my right against all bitter things
Sweet laurel with fresh rose its force shall try;
Seeing reason wills not that I cast love by
Nor here with reason shall I chide and fret

[*She closes book and recites*]

Nor cease to serve, but serve more constantly;
This is the end for which we twain are met.

[*She looks at him, and he at her. Then he resumes his attack on hamburger.*] You know—that's wonderful stuff. But that's the way the French people are: they can understand everything—like life, and love—and death—and they can enjoy it, or laugh at it, depending on how they feel.

SQUIER. And that's why you want to go to France—for understanding.

GABBY. I *will* go there! When Gramp dies, we can sell this place. Dad's going to take his share and move to Los Angeles, so that he can join a really big Legion post and get to be a political power. But I'm going to spend my part of the money on a trip to Bourges, where there's something beautiful to look at, and wine, and dancing in the streets.

SQUIER. If I were you—I'd stay here, Gabrielle, and avoid disappointment.

GABBY. What makes you think I'd be disappointed?

SQUIER. I've been to France.

GABBY. You were there in the war?

SQUIER. No, I missed that. But I lived there for eight years, through seventeen changes of government.

GABBY. What were you doing—writing books?

SQUIER. No—planning to write books. You know what a gigolo is?

GABBY. Were *you* one of those? [*He nods.*] You danced with women for money?

SQUIER. Oh lord, no! I never was a good enough dancer for that. I—I married.

GABBY. Oh.

SQUIER. Please don't think too ill of me. I once actually wrote a book.

GABBY. What was it—fiction?

SQUIER. In a sense. It was a novel about the bleak, glacier-stripped hills of my native New England. I was twenty-two when I wrote it, and it was very, very stark. It sold slightly over six hundred copies. It cost the publisher quite a lot of money, and it also cost him his wife. You see, she divorced him and married me. She had faith in me, and she had the chance to display it, because her husband was very generous in the financial settlement. I suppose he had faith in me, too. She saw in me a major artist, profound, but inarticulate. She believed that all I needed was background, and she gave it to me—with southern exposure and a fine view of the Mediterranean. That was considered the thing to do in the period that followed Scott Fitzgerald. For eight years I reclined there, on the Riviera, on my background—and I waited for the major artist to step forth and say something of enduring importance. He preferred to remain inarticulate.

GABBY. And you've left your wife, now?

SQUIER. Yes.

GABBY. I'm glad you did.

SQUIER. I left her at her suggestion. She has taken up with a Brazilian painter—also a major artist. There was nothing for me to do but travel. I decided to go forth and discover America—and I've gone this far on my journey, thanks to the power of the thumb. [*He gestures with his thumb.*]

GABBY. What were you looking for?

SQUIER. Well—that's rather hard to say. I—I suppose I've been looking for something to believe in. I've been hoping to find something that's worth living for—and dying for.

GABBY. What have you found?

SQUIER. Nothing so interesting as an old man who was missed by Billy the Kid, and a fair young lady who reads Villon.

GABBY [*After a pause*]. Well—I do other things that'd surprise you.

SQUIER. I'm sure you do.

GABBY. I wouldn't tell this to everybody—but you—well, you're kind of——

SQUIER. I'm kind of nobody. What is it, Gabrielle?

GABBY. I paint pictures.

SQUIER. Are they any good?

GABBY. Hell, *no!*

SQUIER. Could I see them?

GABBY. Oh—I never let people look at them. I'd only get kidded. They're kind of crazy pictures.

SQUIER. All the better. Please let me see them.

GABBY. You know anything about art?

SQUIER. Oh—I've studied the whole cycle—right from El Greco through Burne Jones and back to El Greco again. Perhaps you're another genius. Perhaps it's my mission to introduce you to posterity.

GABBY. Are you kidding me?

SQUIER. No, Gabrielle. I've never kidded anybody outside of myself. [*The voice of* HERB, *a cowboy, is heard offstage.*]

GABBY. All right. But you've got to promise not to tell anybody.

SQUIER. My word of honor—for all it's worth. [GABBY *goes out.*]

HERB'S VOICE. Sure, Boze. I know you've got all the inside dope. But I'll bet you four bits he flattens him inside of five rounds.

BOZE. Four bits to what?

HERB. No—I ain't giving you no odds.

BOZE. All *right!*

HERB. All *right!* [HERB *has come in during this cheerful challenge. He wears a big black hat, gray shirt and blue overalls, and carries a gunny sack. Genially, to* SQUIER.] How de do.

SQUIER [*Still eating*]. Good evening.

HERB. Where's Gab?

SQUIER. She'll be back in a moment. [HERB *has crossed to counter.*]

HERB. They sure give you a good meal here, don't they?

SQUIER. Superb!

HERB. Well—I'll tell you. Jason Maple's got a natural-born gift for hotel keeping, and by God I think Gabby's better at it than he is. The only trouble with 'em is, they ain't got a hotel. [*He has to laugh at that.*]

SQUIER. Yes—that does restrict the full play of their talents. [GABBY *comes in with a sheaf of water color paintings of comparatively small size but of virulent color.*]

HERB. Hi, Gab.

GABBY. Hi, Herb. [*Nervously she puts pictures face down on table by* SQUIER. *She cautions him with a look not to display them to* HERB. *But during subsequent dialogue,* SQUIER *peeks at them with a certain amount of neck-stroking bewilderment.*]

HERB. Got any moon?

GABBY. Sure.

HERB. How much you asking for it?

GABBY. A dollar fifty a bottle.

HERB. *Holy* Cow! Well—give us a bottle, and half a dozen bottles of beer.

GABBY. You fellers going to get drunk tonight? [*She has gone to counter to fill order.*]

HERB [*Leaning on counter*]. By God —that's the way it looks. Sheriff called up the old man and asked if we could be spared for patrolling the roads and the old man says sure and the sheriff says he'll come out and swear us in, but he ain't come yet, so we got a poker game started up the road a piece and thought we might as well have something to go along with it.

GABBY. There you are, Herb. That'll be two thirty.

HERB. All I got's two bucks. [*He tenders it.*] Will you trust me for the thirty cents?

GABBY. I'll take back two bottles of beer. That'll make it even.

HERB [*As he dumps bottles into gunnysack*]. Gosh—liquor sure is getting expensive these days. Well—I guess we got enough here seeing as there's only three of us.

GABBY. How you going to play poker if you haven't got any more money?

HERB. Oh, we got a book. So long, Gabby.

GABBY. So long, Herb. [*He goes out.* GABBY *rings up the two dollars in cash register and comes down. She is eager to know how* SQUIER *feels about her paintings, but she is trying desperately hard to be offhand about it.*] They're terrible, aren't they? [SQUIER *is now examining pictures with rapt attention.*]

SQUIER. I—I don't know. Is—this a portrait of someone?

GABBY. That's Paula, our Mexican cook. She's the only one knows I ever try to do that junk. It isn't much of a likeness.

SQUIER. I'm sure it wasn't intended to be. [*He picks up another picture.*] Certainly no critic could condemn you for being photographic.

GABBY. This is the one I like best. [SQUIER *looks at it.*] I wanted to show how the storm clouds look when they roll down from the mountains.

SQUIER. What made you paint in this strange manner?

GABBY. It's—just the way I feel.

SQUIER. You're a product of the ultimate French school, all right.

GABBY [*Pleased*]. You think so?

SQUIER. These are somewhat in the Dufy manner—and yet—a lot less conventional.

GABBY. But are they any *good?*

SQUIER. I tell you, Gabrielle—I can't say. I'm tremendously impressed and, also, bewildered.

GABBY. I'll bet I could improve if I could get to France. You know, they've got some of the finest art schools in the world there. And they've got beautiful things to paint, too—flowers, and castles and rivers. But here in this desert—it's just the same thing over and over again.

SQUIER. Don't you realize—there are probably thousands of artists in France today who are saying, "I'd find a really big theme for my canvas if I could only get out to Arizona."

GABBY. I know. A lot of people come out here and go crazy about the desert. They say it's full of mystery, and it's haunted, and all that. Well—maybe it is. But there's something in me that makes me want something different.

SQUIER [*Looking at her*]. I know there's something in you. I wish I could figure out what it is.

GABBY. Listen—you've been in France. What are they like there?

SQUIER. Well—it's rather difficult to render a sweeping judgment.

GABBY. I've always imagined they must all be like Villon—gay, reckless, poetic.

SQUIER. No—I shouldn't call them any of those things. Especially not reckless!

GABBY. But they're always having a good time, aren't they?

SQUIER. Not invariably.

GABBY. Maybe I know them better than you do, because it's in my blood. Sometimes I can feel as though I were sparkling all over, and I don't care what happens—I want to go out and do something that's absolutely crazy—and marvelous. But then the American part of me speaks up and spoils everything. It makes me go to work and figure out a lot of dull accounts; so many pounds of coffee, so many frankfurters, so many rolls——

SQUIER. You keep the accounts correctly?

GABBY. If I didn't, this place would be bankrupt.

SQUIER. Then that's the French part of you. The sparkle must be one hundred per cent American. Would you like to marry a Frenchman?

GABBY. I don't want to marry anybody. I want to always be free!

SQUIER. How about that stalwart youth out there in the football jersey?

GABBY. What makes you think I'd take any notice of him?

SQUIER. Well—when I came in here——

GABBY. Oh, sure. He was kissing me. That's nothing.

SQUIER. Perhaps. But there's always the chance of development.

GABBY. He's trying to make me. That's all he wants.

SQUIER. Do you think he'll succeed?

GABBY. I haven't decided yet. It would be experience, and that's what I need. Do you think I ought to give in?

SQUIER. Don't ask me, Gabrielle. Let your French blood guide you. It's infallible, in matters like that.

GABBY. But you ought to know *something*. You've seen a lot, and you've written a book, and you've been married——

SQUIER. I don't know anything. You see—the trouble with me is, I belong to a vanishing race. I'm one of the intellectuals.

GABBY. That means you've got brains. I can see you have.

SQUIER. Yes—brains without purpose. Noise without sound. Shape without substance. Have you ever read "The Hollow Men"? [*She shakes her head.*] Don't. It's discouraging, because it's true. It refers to the intellectuals, who thought they'd conquered Nature. They dammed it up, and used its waters to irrigate the wastelands. They built streamlined monstrosities to penetrate its resistance. They wrapped it up in cellophane and sold it to drugstores. They were so certain they had it subdued. And now—do you realize what it is that is causing world chaos?

GABBY. No.

SQUIER. Well, I'm probably the only living person who can tell you. . . . It's Nature hitting back. Not with the old weapons—floods, plagues, holocausts. We can neutralize them. She's fighting back with strange instruments called neuroses. She's deliberately afflicting mankind with the jitters. Nature is proving that she can't be beaten—not by the likes of us. She's taking the world away from the intellectuals and giving it back to the apes. . . . Forgive me, Gabrielle . . . I can't tell you what a luxury it is to have someone to talk to. . . . But don't listen to me. I was born in 1901, the year Victoria died. I was just too late for the Great War—and too soon for the revolution. You're a war baby. You may be an entirely different species, for all I know. You can easily be one of Nature's own children, and therefore able to understand her, and laugh at her—or enjoy her—depending on how you feel. You're the only one who can say whether or not you should yield to the ardors of Number 42 out there. [*He finishes his glass of beer.*] That beer is excellent.

GABBY. It's made in Phoenix. [*She is looking at him intently.*] You know—you talk like a God-damn fool.

SQUIER. I know it. [*He is taking out the last of his cigarettes.*]

GABBY. No wonder your wife kicked you out. . . . And no wonder she fell for you in the first place. [*He pauses in act of lighting his cigarette.*]

SQUIER. That sounds alarmingly like a compliment.

GABBY. It is a compliment. What did you say your name was?

SQUIER. Alan Squier. I've been calling you Gabrielle, so you'd better——

GABBY. Where are you going from here, Alan?

SQUIER. That depends on where this road leads.

GABBY. It leads to the petrified forest.

SQUIER. What's that?

GABBY. Oh—just a lot of dead old trees in the desert, that have turned to stone.

SQUIER. The petrified forest! A suitable haven for me. Perhaps that's what I'm destined for—to make an interesting fossil for future study. Homo Semi-Americanus—a specimen of the in-between age.

GABBY. I was just thinking—I'd like to go to France with you. [*He looks at her, sharply—then looks sharply away.*]

SQUIER. Oh, no, Gabrielle! I could never retrace my footsteps.

GABBY. You mean you haven't enough money?

SQUIER. Even that is an understatement.

GABBY. I haven't enough, either—yet. But I can do this as well as you can. [*She gestures with her thumb.*]

SQUIER. We'd reach a point, on the Atlantic Coast, where even that gesture would be unavailing.

GABBY. You know, Alan—there's something about you that's very appealing.

SQUIER. Appealing! Yes—that's been my downfall. It was that very quality which led me into the gigolo trade.

GABBY. Why wouldn't you like to be a gigolo for me?

SQUIER. For one very good reason: you couldn't afford it.

GABBY. But I *will* be able to afford it.

SQUIER. On your share of this property? [*He shakes his head.*]

GABBY. Listen—I've got more than that coming to me. Do you know how much Gramp has got salted away in the bank in Santa Fé? Twenty-two thousand dollars! He had every cent of it in gold and silver in the safety vaults. Why—we didn't even know about it until the government passed a law against hoarding and they printed his name in the papers. It's in Liberty Bonds now, and it's all willed to me. I guess we could travel pretty far on that, couldn't we?

SQUIER. Too far.

GABBY. We could go to France, and you'd show me everything, all the cathedrals and the art—and explain everything. And you wouldn't have to marry me, Alan. We'd just live in sin and have one hell of a time.

SQUIER. That's a startling proposal, Gabrielle. I hadn't expected to receive anything like that in *this* desert.

GABBY. We'd have to wait—maybe

years. But I could have Boze fired and give you the job tending the gas station.

SQUIER. You think you'd like to have me for a companion?

GABBY. I know I would. And I don't make mistakes. You're no ape-man, Alan—but you're lovable.

SQUIER. Lovable! The next grade below appealing.

GABBY. Wouldn't you like to be loved by me?

SQUIER [*Looking at her intently*]. Yes, Gabrielle . . . I should like to be loved by you.

GABBY. You think I'm attractive?

SQUIER. There are better words than that for what you are.

GABBY. Then why don't we at least make a start at it? You haven't got anything else to do.

SQUIER [*Smiling*]. No—that's just it. You couldn't live very long with a man who had nothing else to do but worship you. That's a dull kind of love, Gabrielle. It's the kind of love that makes people old, too soon. [*He rises.*] But—I thank you for the suggestion. You've opened up a new channel of my imagination which will be pleasant to explore during my lonely wanderings. I'll think of the chimes of Bourges—and you—and sin.

GABBY. You're going now?

SQUIER. Yes. And I shall continue going until either I drop or that major artist emerges to announce his message to posterity.

GABBY. [*Rising*]. Well—I can't stop you.

SQUIER. No, Gabrielle, you can't. But you can do me one great favor, before I go. . . . Would you mind very much if I kissed you good-by? [GABBY *looks at him levelly.*]

GABBY. No. I wouldn't mind.

SQUIER. You'd understand that it would be nothing more——

GABBY. I'd understand. It'd be just a kiss—that's all.

SQUIER. That's absolutely all. [*He kisses her.* BOZE *is seen through glass of doorway. He bursts door open.*]

BOZE. Ah-hah! So that's what's been going on in here! Necking, huh! [*He strides up to* SQUIER *and seizes him by shoulder.*] Who the hell are you?

GABBY. Lay off him, Boze. [*She has seized her paintings.*]

BOZE. Just because she's cute and sweet you thought you could get fresh, huh!

GABBY. He didn't get fresh! He only wanted to kiss me good-by.

SQUIER. Yes—the impulse is rather hard to explain—but I——

BOZE. You needn't wait to explain it. Pay your check and get out.

SQUIER. Very well. How much do I owe, Miss Maple?

GABBY. Thirty cents.

BOZE. Is that all he ate? [*He looks down at table at remains of* SQUIER'S *meal.*]

GABBY. Yes! Shut up!

SQUIER. Thirty cents, eh. Very reasonable. Very reasonable indeed! But—that brings us to another embarrassment. I—I haven't got thirty cents. I haven't anything.

BOZE. Well—by God—I didn't expect to find such nerve in anybody that looked like you. What are you going to do about it?

SQUIER. I haven't the remotest——

BOZE. What have you got in your pack there?

SQUIER. Shirt, underwear, socks, toothbrush, passport, an insurance policy, and a copy of "Modern Man in Search of a Soul," by Dr. Jung.

BOZE. You thought you could pay with a kiss, did you? [*He seizes* SQUIER *again. A car is heard stopping.*] Thought if you brought a little romance into her poor, starved life the check'd be forgotten, did you?

GABBY. Take your hands off him, Boze. Go on, Alan, beat it!

SQUIER. I'll go.

BOZE. I'll just give you a little head start. [*He has* SQUIER *by the collar and is about to propel him out door, when* MR. *and* MRS. CHISHOLM *come in.* MR. CHISHOLM *is about forty-five—thin, dry, sharp, persnickety, with pince-nez eyeglasses.* MRS. CHISHOLM *is about ten years younger—rather attractive, rather chic, very world-weary. The* CHISHOLMS *belong to the topmost layer of society in Dayton, Ohio.*]

MRS. CHISHOLM [*In an undertone to* GABBY]. Where is the Ladies' Room, please?

GABBY. This way, madam. [*She directs* MRS. CHISHOLM *to door at left and points off.*] That door there, on your left.

MRS. CHISHOLM. Thank you. [JOSEPH, *the* CHISHOLMS' *Negro chauffeur, appears in doorway. He is short, elegant, wears a neat uniform and yellow glasses.*]

JOSEPH. We want fifteen gallons and a quart of oil.

BOZE. Be right with you. [*In an undertone to* SQUIER.] You ready to leave?

SQUIER. Just a moment—my rucksack.

GABBY. Get on the job, Boze. [*She goes up to lunch counter and hides her paintings.* BOZE *mutters something unpleasant to* SQUIER *and goes out.* SQUIER *is putting on his rucksack.*]

CHISHOLM. What kind of cigars have you?

GABBY. Admiration, White Owl, and Texas Dandies.

CHISHOLM. How much are the Texas Dandies.

GABBY. Three for a dime.

CHISHOLM. Let me have an Admiration.

GABBY. [*Offering him box*]. Come far?

CHISHOLM [*Selecting one*]. Yes. We've driven from Dayton, Ohio. We're on our way out to Santa Barbara for the winter. [*As he pays for cigar.*] We lost a great deal of time today as I wanted Mrs. Chisholm to see the Gila cliff dwellings. She was rather disappointed. How far is it to the Phoenix Biltmore?

GABBY. It's a good two hundred miles from here. [*She hands him his change.*]

CHISHOLM [*Consulting his watch*]. I imagine we can make it by midnight.

GABBY. You'll have to step. What kind of car you driving?

CHISHOLM [*Lighting cigar*]. Dusenberg.

SQUIER. Good-by Miss Maple.

GABBY. Just a minute, Alan. [*She turns again to* CHISHOLM.] Excuse me, sir.

CHISHOLM. What?

GABBY. Would you have room in your car for another party? [SQUIER *signals to her not to bother.*]

CHISHOLM [*Suspicious*]. Who is it?

GABBY. This friend of mine, Mr. Squier. He's on his way to the coast and he—he hasn't got a car just now. He's an author.

CHISHOLM [*To* SQUIER]. Have you any luggage?

SQUIER. Just this, sir—on my back. [CHISHOLM *looks him over, goes to open door, and calls "Joseph."*]

CHISHOLM. Where'd you come from?

SQUIER. From Saint Tropez. That's on the Riviera. [*Joseph comes in.*]

CHISHOLM. I know where it is. Do you think it's all right to give this man a lift to Phoenix? [JOSEPH *subjects* SQUIER *to extremely critical inspection.*]

SQUIER. You've been there?

CHISHOLM. Yes . . . [JOSEPH *taps* SQUIER *all over for concealed weapons.*]

SQUIER. It's a lovely spot, Saint Tropez.

CHISHOLM [*Without enthusiasm*]. Yes.

JOSEPH. I guess he's all right, Mr. Chisholm.

CHISHOLM. Very well. [JOSEPH *touches his cap and goes out.*] Glad to have you with us.

SQUIER. Thank you very much, Mr.

Chisholm. [GABBY *punches "No Sale" key and takes out a silver dollar.* SQUIER *crosses to her.*] And thank you, Miss Maple. I'll remember your kindness.

GABBY. I forgot to give you your change. [*She offers him the dollar.*]

SQUIER. Oh, no—I wanted you to keep that.

GABBY [*Pointing to a sign*]. Tipping is un-American and we don't allow it. Here—take it.

SQUIER. I—I can't very well pretend that I don't need——

GABBY. Perhaps Mr. Chisholm will take you all the way to the coast. When you get there, send me a postcard, with a view of the Pacific Ocean. I like pictures of the sea. [*She has forced coin into his hand.* MRS. CHISHOLM *emerges.*]

CHISHOLM. This is Mr.—er——

GABBY. Squier.

CHISHOLM. Mr. Squier, darling. We're giving him a lift as far as the Phoenix Biltmore. [MRS. CHISHOLM *frowns.*] It's all right; Joseph went over him.

SQUIER. How do you do, Mrs. Chisholm?

MRS. CHISHOLM. How do you do? Are we ready to start? [*She crosses toward door.*]

CHISHOLM. Just been waiting for you. Come along, Mr. Squier. [*The* CHISHOLMS *have gone out.*]

SQUIER. I suppose I'll never see you again.

GABBY. No. That's the way it is in a gas station. They come and they go.

SQUIER. But, somehow or other, I'll repay that dollar. God knows when.

GABBY. Perhaps we'll run into each other some day in Bourges. [*The horn of the Dusenberg is heard summoning, shrilly.*]

SQUIER. Good-by, Gabrielle.

GABBY [*Shaking hands*]. Good-by, Alan. [*He goes out. After a moment, she comes down and picks up the Poems of François Villon. Car is heard starting and charging off into the night.* GABBY *suddenly remembers neon sign, goes to a switch by door and turns it on.* BOZE *comes in.*]

BOZE. Well—I took pity on that poor panhandler. I slipped him a dime.

GABBY. You *did?*

BOZE. I tried to—but he wouldn't take it. He said, "I don't deserve your kindness," and handed it back. It's a funny thing about a guy like that: he'll hold you up for a meal and think nothing of it. But when it comes to taking money, they suddenly discover they've got some pride.

GABBY. I appreciate that very much, Boze.

BOZE. Appreciate what, honey?

GABBY. Your wanting to help him. That was very kind.

BOZE. Why, say—you talk as if you were nuts about him.

GABBY. I'm not nuts about him. But now and then you see somebody that's just a natural object of charity.

BOZE [*Pleased*]. Well! If you appreciate it so much—how about being a little nice to me for a change? [*He goes to her and takes hold of her arms.*]

GABBY. I'd like to be nice to you . . . I'd like to be nice to everybody.

BOZE. You can be, Gabby. Listen—how about us taking a little walk around the Mesa? It's warm out and the moon's just coming up. How about it, sweetheart?

GABBY. But supposing a car came along wanting something?

BOZE. You know there's practically no traffic at this time of night.

GABBY. But suppose someone *did* come——

BOZE. Well—what if they did? In a pinch, the old man and that Mexican woman could take care of 'em. And you know how your grandfather is—he'd never notice anything peculiar about us being out for a while. . . . [*He goes after her.*] Listen, honey sweet. You've got to grow up sometime. And before you can grow up, you've got to stop being afraid.

GABBY. I'm not afraid!

BOZE. Oh, yes, you are. You think I'm something terrible and you've got to keep away from me. But I'm not so bad, Gabby. I'm just a big guy with a good heart and plenty of hot blood. And I'm full of love, honey. [*He takes her in his arms.*] And so are you. You don't know it yet—but you are. And when we get out there in the moonlight, you'll be glad I suggested it. Honestly you will, honey sweet. [*He kisses her lips passionately. After a moment, she struggles a little. He relaxes his hold on her. He is confident of progress.*] All right—I'm not holding you against your will. I'm not trying to force you into anything that's wrong.

GABBY. I didn't say you were.

BOZE [*Follows her*]. It *isn't* wrong—except in the minds of old cranks that have forgotten how to love—if they ever knew. My God! It's the most natural thing in the world, for two people, like us, that are young, and clean, and . . . Why, it'd be wrong if we *didn't* take the chance when we've got it.

GABBY. Do you know what he said?

BOZE. What who said?

GABBY. He said we'd been trying to fight Nature, and we thought we'd licked it, because we've built a lot of dams, and cellophane and things like that. But that's where we're wrong, and that's what's the matter with the world. We've got to admit that Nature can't be beaten!

BOZE. Well—isn't that exactly what I've been trying to tell you all along?

GABBY. I guess it is, Boze. [*He takes her in his arms again.*]

BOZE. You're coming with me, aren't you, sweetheart? You're going to find out things about Nature more wonderful and exciting than anything you ever dreamed of. Aren't you, honey sweet?

GABBY. Oh, well—what the hell! I'll go out with you, Boze. [*He kisses her.*] We'd better go now.

BOZE. Yes, Gabby. Oh, God—you're a beautiful kid! [*He kisses her again, passionately. A car is heard stopping. They break apart, quickly.*] I'll get rid of 'em fast. [*He starts toward door, but stops short when it opens and* JACKIE *appears. He is a short, chubby, cherubic gangster. He carries a sub-machine gun and wears a cheery smile.*]

JACKIE. Now—just behave yourselves folks, and nobody'll get hurt. Who's the boss here?

BOZE. He's out.

JACKIE. Got any guns with you? [*He searches* BOZE *with practiced speed.*]

BOZE. No. [*He and* GABBY *have been retreating into the room as* JACKIE *has advanced. Following* JACKIE *has come* RUBY, *thin, sallow, adenoidal—and after him has come* DUKE MANTEE—*well-built but stoop-shouldered, with a vaguely thoughtful, saturnine face. He is about thirty-five and, if he hadn't elected to take up banditry, might have been a fine leftfielder. There is, about him, one quality of resemblance to* ALAN SQUIER; *he too is unmistakably condemned. He is hatless and unshaven and wears an ill-fitting suit with a gray prison shirt.* MANTEE *carries no visible arms, but* RUBY *has another machine gun and a sawed-off shotgun.*]

JACKIE. This is Duke Mantee, folks. He's the world-famous killer and he's hungry. [DUKE *looks around.*]

DUKE. What's in there and in there? [*He speaks quietly, even gently, with an effortless ferocity.*]

GABBY. That's the kitchen, and in there's our bedrooms.

DUKE. You two married?

GABBY. No. He just works here.

JACKIE. Anybody else in?

BOZE. Only one old man and——

GABBY. My grandfather's in there and the cook. There's nobody in there.

DUKE. Bring 'em in, Jackie.

JACKIE. O.K., Duke. [*He goes out at upper left.* DUKE *goes to front door and calls out.*]

DUKE. Hey, Pyles. [PYLES' *voice is heard to reply: "Yeah, boss."*] Back that car into the shadow and stay with it.

PYLES' VOICE. Do I get to eat?

DUKE. You'll eat. [DUKE *goes to table, downstage right, and takes his coat off, revealing a harness over his waistcoat with two revolvers in holsters under either armpit. He folds his coat neatly and lays it on bench, then turns to* RUBY.] Hey, Ruby—pull that table over here. [RUBY *moves table to right as directed.* BOZE *lowers his hands.*] Keep 'em up. [*The hands go up promptly.* RUBY *picks up his machine gun.*] Take a look around in there.

RUBY. How long do we stay here?

DUKE. Until they get here.

RUBY. You're going to wait for that blonde?

DUKE. Get out!

RUBY. O.K. [*He goes out at lower left.*]

DUKE. You sit down there. [BOZE *sits down as directed at center table.*] What have you got to eat, sister? [GABBY *produces menu card.* DUKE *addresses* BOZE.] Football player, eh?

BOZE. Yes. And you better not let me get close enough to take a sock at you.

DUKE [*Unconcerned*]. I used to be quite a fan. What's your school?

BOZE. Nevada Tech.

DUKE. Never heard of it. [GRAMP *and* PAULA *the cook come in from kitchen, followed by* JACKIE.]

PAULA. Don't shoot me, mister. Don't kill me, mister. In the name of the Holy Mother of God, don't kill me, mister. [JACKIE *prods her with machine gun. She screams lustily.*]

JACKIE. Quiet, Pepita—quiet. We aren't going to do you any harm. [*In a ludicrously soothing voice.*] All we're going to do is ask you to cook something. You wouldn't mind that, would you, Pepita?

PAULA. No, mister. I swear to God, I cook anything. You just tell me——

JACKIE. All right, Pepita. We got that settled.

GRAMP [*Staring admiringly at* DUKE]. So you're Mantee, are you? You're the killer!

DUKE. Would you mind sitting down over there, Pop? Take a look around that counter, Jackie. [GRAMP *sits down at left.* JACKIE *searches counter.*]

JACKIE. Yes, Pop. That's the greatest killer alive today. Did you hear what happened in Oklahoma City? [DUKE *inspects menu.*]

GRAMP. Yes—I heard. You pulled off a massacre.

JACKIE. Who said it was a massacre? [*He comes down from counter.*]

GRAMP. The *Denver Post.* [*He holds up paper.*]

JACKIE [*Snatching it*]. Let me see it!

DUKE. Put that paper down! [JACKIE *drops paper.*]

JACKIE. Did it say how many we killed?

GRAMP. Six killed and four wounded.

JACKIE. Did you hear that, Duke? We killed six and wounded four. [*He returns to counter to empty cash register.*]

DUKE [*To* GABBY]. Got any steak?

GABBY. Only hamburger.

PAULA. And we got chicken, mister.

GRAMP. Two of the wounded's not expected to live.

DUKE. All right. Cook the chicken and four hamburgers. And plenty of onions.

JACKIE. Boy! That was some massacre!

GABBY. Anything else? [RUBY *comes in from lower left.*]

RUBY. Nobody in there, boss. There's a good window at the end of the hall with a four-foot drop to the ground, right by where the car is.

DUKE. Take a look around outside. Tell Pyles not to hit that horn unless somebody comes up that really looks like trouble, and then to hit it plenty. [RUBY *goes out.*] Bring us beer for the bunch, sister. [*He addresses* BOZE *and* GRAMP.] You fellers like to join us?

BOZE. I never touch it.

GRAMP. I guess I'll have whisky.

GABBY [*To* GRAMP]. No, none for you, Gramp.

GRAMP [*Disconsolate*]. She says I can't have even a little one.

DUKE. Let him have it, sister.

JACKIE. Sure! He can only be young once.

PAULA. Can I begin cooking now, mister?

DUKE. Yeh. Go with her, Jackie. [RUBY *returns.*]

JACKIE. Come on, Pepita. And while the chicken's in the oven, you and me'll have a little fun, eh, kid? [*They go out into kitchen.*]

DUKE. Hey, Ruby. Sit dcwn there. [RUBY *sits down between counter and front door.*] And keep that gun in your lap. [RUBY *obeys, and from now on his eyes ceaselessly patrol the area from front door to kitchen door.* DUKE *crosses with a convict's gait and goes out at the left.* GABBY *is behind counter getting out the beer.* GRAMP *rises and starts to cross to his rocking chair.*]

RUBY. Sit down!

GRAMP [*Sitting down hastily*]. You needn't think I'm scared of you. I've known *real* killers in my time. And they knew how to make a six-shooter act like a machine gun. Did you ever hear of fanning?

RUBY. No.

GRAMP. Well—you'd file down the trigger catch so that the hammer worked free, and then you'd fan it like this. [*He points his forefinger at* RUBY *and wiggles his thumb.*] Wild Bill Hickok once knocked over five men that way. They was lined up at a bar and . . . [SQUIER *comes in, hatless and breathless.* GABBY *is in center of stage, with tray of bottles and glasses of beer.*]

GABBY. Alan! What did you come back for?

SQUIER [*Panting*]. There are some bandits around here.

BOZE. Yes. So we heard.

SQUIER. They cut in ahead of us about a mile down the road, and made us stop and get out, and then they got into Mr. Chisholm's car and drove off. They said we could take their car, but they'd left it locked. They were terrible-looking cutthroats, with a lot of guns and ammunition. [*He addresses* BOZE.] Could you come with me back there and see if you can unlock that——

[DUKE *comes in from left.*]

GABBY. Look out, Alan! [SQUIER *turns and sees* DUKE. *Then he looks around and sees* RUBY *who has raised his machine gun.*]

SQUIER [*Lamely*]. Oh—so we—meet again.

DUKE. Sit down, pal. Down there.

SQUIER. Why, thanks, I'd be delighted to.

DUKE. Wait a minute. [*He takes the rucksack from* SQUIER, *who then sits down opposite* BOZE *at center table.*]

GRAMP [*Proudly*]. That's Duke Mantee. We were looking at his picture. Remember?

SQUIER. Yes—I remember. [DUKE *goes to extreme right and sits down, his back to wall.*]

DUKE. Join us in a glass of beer?

SQUIER. Why—thank you—but might I have some whisky, instead?

DUKE. Certainly. Give him a drink, sister. And how about turning on the radio? [GABBY *puts bottle and a glass before* SQUIER. *He pours himself a stiff one.*]

GRAMP. What did I tell you? Look at that chin. He's a killer, all right!

BOZE. He's a gangster and a rat!

SQUIER. Sh!

GRAMP. *He* ain't a gangster! He's a real old-time desperado. Gangsters is foreigners. He's an American! And if the sheriffs find out he's here, we'll see some real killing—*won't* we? [GABBY *turns on radio. Soft, sticky music emerges.*]

DUKE. The cops ain't likely to catch up with us—not tonight. So we can all be quiet and peaceable, and have a few beers together, and listen to the music—and not make any wrong moves. Because—I may as well tell you, folks—old Ruby there, with the machine gun—he's pretty nervous and jumpy and he's got the itch between his fingers. So let's everybody stay where they are.

SQUIER. Let there be killing! All evening long, I've had a feeling of Destiny closing in. [*To* DUKE.] Do you believe in astrology?

DUKE. I couldn't say, pal.

SQUIER. I don't—normally. But just now, as I was walking along that road, I began to feel the enchantment of this desert. I looked up at the sky and the stars seemed to be reproving me, mocking me. They were pointing the way to that gleaming sign, and saying, "There's the end of your tether! You thought you could escape it, and skip off to the Phoenix Biltmore. But we know better." That's what the stars told me, and perhaps they know that carnage is imminent, and that I'm due to be among the fallen. . . . It's a fascinating thought.

DUKE. Let's skip it. [*He lifts his glass.*] Here's happy days.

GRAMP. Yes, *sir*—it sure is pleasant to have a killer around here again.

SQUIER. Yes. It's pleasant to be back again—among the living. [*He raises his glass.*] Hooray! [*He drinks.*]

Curtain

ACT II

About half an hour has elapsed since the end of Act I. DUKE *and* JACKIE *are finishing their meal at right table.* RUBY *is sitting on a stool at counter, drinking coffee, watching everything.* GRAMP *and* PAULA *are sitting at table at left.* BOZE *and* SQUIER *are at center. The radio is murmuring faintly.*

GABBY *alone is permitted to move about—removing dishes, refilling coffee cups.*

GRAMP. That old Andy Anderson I was telling you about, he was a great character. He didn't kill for business reasons, like you fellers. He killed just for the fun of it. He was born somewheres up in Nova Scotia and come down to the State of Maine so's he could get into the Civil War and he fit all through it. And he never stopped talking about it as long as he lived. He always said that was a regular paradise for killing. He'd stick a Johnny Reb with his bayonet, throw him over his shoulder and then stick another. And he always said that the beauty of it was there was no sheriffs around to reprove him for it.

JACKIE. Say, Pop—I wish you wouldn't talk so much about blood while we're eating.

BOZE. Got it on your conscience, eh?

JACKIE. On my *what?*

BOZE. Yes—I thought so. A punk like you hasn't got any more conscience than a coyote.

JACKIE. Hmm! Listen to the halfback. How much did *you* get for playing on the team?

BOZE. I worked my way through college!

JACKIE. What were you doing? Peddling subscriptions to the *American Boy?*

BOZE. I worked for three whole years in the Student Laundry.

JACKIE. Oh—how nice! [*He lifts his coffee cup.*]

BOZE. Wait a minute—smart guy. I got something to show you. [*He reaches for his wallet.*]

RUBY. Keep your hand off your hip!

BOZE. I was only going to show him a newspaper clipping that said I ought to be All-American. . . . I scared you, did I? I know it. You're all yellow.

[*A none too pleasant expression appears in* JACKIE'*s eyes over the rim of his coffee cup.*]

SQUIER. I'd be a little tactful, Boze. Remember—they're your guests.

[GABBY *has sat down at center table between* SQUIER *and* BOZE.]

BOZE. They're a bunch of yellow dogs. That's what made 'em turn crooked in the first place.

SQUIER. No—no. Cowardice isn't the cause of crime. It has something to do with glands.

BOZE. They just haven't got the guts to face the bigger problems of life. They've got to fight their way with guns instead of with *principles.* [SQUIER *is by now slightly tight and is to become more so, by imperceptible degrees, as the Act proceeds.* JACKIE *sets down his coffee cup with ominous deliberateness and rises, picking up a sawed-off shotgun.*]

JACKIE. Step over to that side of the room, halfback.

GRAMP. You're going to kill him?

BOZE [*Scared*]. It's just what I said——

JACKIE. Come on. This shotgun scatters, and you wouldn't want me to hurt that cute dame, would you?

[*The dulcet chimes of the radio are heard.* BOZE *slowly rises.*]

SQUIER [*To* JACKIE]. You know—you're taking this much too seriously.

[*The radio announcer's voice can be heard introducing the nightly news broadcast.*]

BOZE. I'm not afraid to die. [*But his voice is strained.*]

JACKIE. Come on! Move!

DUKE. Step up that radio—will you, sister? [*To* JACKIE.] Sit down, Jackie Cooper.

JACKIE. Did you hear what he——?

DUKE [*Grinning*]. Sit down! [*To* BOZE.] You too. [*They both sit down.* GABBY *has turned up volume control dial.*]

RADIO VOICE [*Very brisk*]. . . . all anxious first off to hear latest bulletins concerning the greatest manhunt in human history. A monster dragnet has been cast over the entire southwest from St. Louis to the Pacific Coast. National Guardsmen are co-operating with state police and the famed Texas Rangers as well as countless local posses and Legion posts in a determined effort to apprehend the members of the notorious Mantee gang—to bring to justice this fierce, colorful band of murderers, kidnappers, bank-robbers, perpetrators of the shocking massacre in Oklahoma City——

JACKIE. Take a bow, Duke.

RADIO VOICE. The gang made its escape in two cars, one of which contained Mantee and three other men, the other car containing three men and *one woman.* The Mantee car was seen early this morning at Tularosa and later at Hillsboro in New Mexico. The second car was positively identified at Estelline in the Texas Panhandle when it stopped at the local police station, held it up, and departed with a large supply of guns and ammunition.

JACKIE. Nice going, boys! I don't see how they did it with Doris along to——

DUKE. Shut up!

RADIO VOICE. Both cars are undoubtedly headed for the border, but it is considered certain they haven't reached it, due to the number and vigilance of the patrols. Wartime conditions prevail on all the roads of Western Texas, New Mexico, and Arizona and you know how the officers of the law are in this red-blooded frontier region: they shoot first and ask questions afterward. [JACKIE *indicates his scorn, but* DUKE *withers him with a look.*] The Governor of Arizona has issued the following statement: "As long as Mantee and his followers are at large a blot of shame will mar the proud scutcheon of these United States. Any citizen who knowingly gives aid or comfort to these public enemies is a traitor to his country and will be answerable before the great bar of public opinion." . . . I'll now give you the scores of the leading football games of the day. Carnegie Tech—13, Miami—7; Washington State—19——

DUKE. Turn it off, sister.

RADIO VOICE. U.S.C.—0; Navy—21, Virginia—6——[GABBY *switches off radio.*]

JACKIE [*To* PAULA]. Did you hear that, Pepita? You're a traitor for cooking for us. They'll string you up for that—if they can find a tree around here.

PAULA. The Holy Mother of God knows they put a gun in my stomach and said *you cook*——

JACKIE. Sure *she* knows. But that don't count with the Governor. We're Public Enemies.

DUKE [*To* RUBY]. Go on out to the car, Ruby, and tell Pyles to come in and get his supper. And tell him to bring in that sack of ammunition and the road map. And you stay there and keep awake.

RUBY. Yeah. O.K. [*He goes out.*]

GRAMP. Are you going to make a run for the border, boys?

JACKIE. Oh, sure! We'll give you our whole route before we leave, so's you can tell the hick cops and have 'em give us a motorcycle escort.

SQUIER. I think I'm about ready for another whisky, Gabrielle, if I may. [GABBY *goes behind counter and brings forth a quart bottle and a bottle of drinking water, which she places on table.*]

BOZE. Listen, panhandler! Who told you you could call her by her first name?

SQUIER. Now, please, Boze—you and I must be friends, as long as they'll let us.

JACKIE. Why don't you take a sock at *him,* halfback? He hasn't got a gun. [PYLES *comes in. He is a lean, lithe Negro, who carries a machine gun and a bulging gunny sack.*]

PYLES. Hi, everybody! 'Bout time you got around to asking me in. Here's your map, boss. [*He puts sack full of ammunition down on a bench at back, and tosses map down on the table before* DUKE.] Lord, God! Look what you done to that chicken!

DUKE [*To* PAULA]. Cook him some hamburger, sister.

PAULA. All right, mister. [*She rises.*] But you people better tell that mister Governor I didn't——

DUKE. Go with her, Pyles.

PYLES. O.K., boss. I guess I don't get to eat with the white folks. [*He picks up carcass of the chicken and starts to gnaw it as he crosses to kitchen.*]

DUKE. Look around in there and see if you can find any rope.

PYLES. O.K., boss. [*He turns quickly to* DUKE.] When we going to lam out of here?

DUKE. When it's time.

JACKIE. Sure—as soon as the Duke connects with that heavy date. [*He winks broadly at* PYLES.]

PYLES [*As he goes*]. Well—I don't like that dame stuff. I like to get out of range. [*He has gone out at left after* PAULA. DUKE *has opened road atlas to Arizona and New Mexico, and from now on he and* JACKIE *are studying it and murmuring to each other in inaudible tones.*]

GRAMP. How about passing that bottle over this way?

SQUIER. Why, certainly. Forgive me—— [*He is reaching for bottle, but* GABBY *stops him.*]

GABBY. No! [*To* GRAMP.] You've had all you're going to get.

SQUIER [*To* GRAMP]. I'm very sorry.

GRAMP. Oh—that's all right. [*He reaches in his pocket for his pipe.*]

JACKIE. What are you doing?

GRAMP. Going to smoke my pipe.

DUKE. Go ahead, Pop. [GRAMP *takes out pipe, fills it with great care, lights it, and lapses into silence as he sits in his rocking chair.*]

BOZE. How long are you yeggs going to stick around here?

JACKIE. Keep quiet, halfback.

BOZE. The longer the better, to suit me. Because the U.S. Government is after you and pretty soon they'll be sending for your relatives to identify the bodies and it will probably be the first good look at you they've had in years.

GABBY. You'd better do what you're told and keep your trap shut.

SQUIER. That's good advice, Boze. Because those glandular phenomena I was talking about manifest themselves in sudden and violent ways.

BOZE [*Savagely*]. How are you going to pay for all that liquor you're drinking? [BOZE *is in an ugly mood, the result of humiliating frustration, and he is taking it out on the one completely defenseless person present.*]

SQUIER. I can pay, and will pay, Boze. For every drop! I have a dollar.

BOZE. Oh, you *have!* So you were holding out on us when you——

SQUIER. No—No. I've acquired it since then.

BOZE. Where did you get it?

GABBY. Probably those rich people gave it to him. Now lay off!

[*Kitchen door opens and* PYLES *appears.*]

PYLES. Here's some clothesline, boss.

DUKE. Throw it down. [PYLES *tosses coil on floor and vanishes into kitchen.*]

BOZE. So you turned down my dime and accepted their dollar. Your pride has its price, eh?

SQUIER. If you must know—I'll tell you the extent of my pride. Gabrielle gave me the dollar.

BOZE [*To* GABBY]. You *did?*

GABBY. It's none of your God-damn business what I do.

BOZE. You were feeling kind of generous tonight, weren't you? [*He turns to* SQUIER.] Would you like to know what she was just going to give me when those rats showed up? Would you like to know?

GABBY. Well—speaking of rats! Of all the low, slimy, stinking——

SQUIER. No, Gabby. You mustn't blame Boze for anything he says now. He's a man of muscle, and he's suffering from the pangs of frustration.

GABBY. I say, you're a dirty, low, stinking——

BOZE. I didn't mean it, Gabby.

GABBY. Then why the hell did you start——

BOZE. I'm terrible sorry, honey sweet. They've got me absolutely crazy mad, with those shotguns and machine guns staring me in the face.

SQUIER. That's all it is.

BOZE. I didn't know what I was saying. Will you please forgive me, Gabby?

GABBY. No! Never!

BOZE [*Humbly*]. All right.

SQUIER. I sympathize with you utterly, Boze. Did you ever read "All Quiet on the Western Front"?

BOZE. No.

SQUIER. Well—all of us here tonight are under very much the same tension. You'd better have a drink, old man. [*He has one himself.*]

BOZE [*Ignoring* SQUIER]. I love you, Gabby. [*Startled by this sudden declaration* SQUIER *sets down his glass.*] I love you, sweetheart—and if I thought I'd done or said anything to hurt you, I'd go over and I'd hang one on those yeggs and die for it, gladly. *Please* tell me you forgive me, honey sweet.

SQUIER. Excuse me. [*He stands up.*] Would you rather I left?

JACKIE. Stay where you are!

SQUIER. But I'm intruding.

JACKIE. Sit down. [SQUIER *sits.*]

GABBY. That's all right, Alan. We've got nothing to hide. Have we, Boze?

BOZE. No—worse luck.

GABBY [*To* SQUIER]. I told you he'd been trying to make me.

BOZE. Now, listen——

GABBY. And tonight, just after you left, he went at it again. And I decided I was ready to give in to him, and find out what it's like.

BOZE. That's a dirty trick—telling that, before a total stranger.

SQUIER [*To* BOZE]. Honestly, Boze—I'm not blaming you—not for an instant.

GABBY [*To* BOZE]. I'll say this much for you: you're a pretty good lovemaker when you get going.

BOZE. I wasn't turning on any act. I told you I was full of love, and I was telling the truth, and I don't care who knows it.

JACKIE [*Has risen and started to cross toward left with map*]. Full of love, are you, halfback?

DUKE. And don't let that Mexican hear you mention the names of any of those towns.

JACKIE. I'll be careful, Duke. I don't want to die. I got a dame, too. [*To* BOZE.] Keep it up, halfback. I'm rooting for you. *Touchdown!* [*He goes into kitchen.*]

BOZE [*To* GABBY]. It doesn't make any difference to you what I'm trying to tell you—because you don't know what it means to be really crazy about somebody. [*She looks at him, through him, for a moment.*]

GABBY. For all you know, maybe I do.

BOZE. I don't believe it. Who have you ever——?

DUKE. Get me a cigar, will you, sister?

GABBY [*Rising*]. We've got Admiration, White Owl, and Texas Dandies.

DUKE. Whatever costs the most. [GABBY *has gone back of counter to get a cigar box, which she takes down to* DUKE.]

GRAMP. You fellers going to spend the night here?

DUKE. Can't say, Pop. Maybe we'll decide to get buried here. [GABBY *hands him box of cigars and he takes a fistful.*] Thanks.

SQUIER. You'd better come with me, Duke. I'm planning to be buried in the Petrified Forest. I've been evolving a theory about that that would interest you. It's the graveyard of the civilization that's been shot from under us. It's the world of outmoded ideas. Platonism—patriotism—Christianity—romance—the economics of Adam Smith—they're all so many dead stumps in the desert. That's where I belong—and so do you, Duke. For you're the last great apostle of rugged individualism. Aren't you?

DUKE [*Has been calmly defoiling a cigar, biting the end off, and lighting it*]. Maybe you're right, pal.

SQUIER [*Returning to his drink*]. I'm eternally right. But what use do I make of it?

DUKE. I couldn't say.

BOZE [*To* GABBY, *who is resuming her seat*]. Who were you ever crazy about?

GABBY. Is it any of your business?

BOZE. Everything about you is my business!

GABBY. Well—if you've got to know—it's him.

SQUIER [*Startled*]. What?

GABBY. I was just telling Boze that I'm crazy about you.

BOZE. That panhandler?

GABBY. You don't know the worst of him. He's more than a panhandler. He's a gigolo.

BOZE. Did you ever see him before?

GABBY. No. But that doesn't matter. I love him. I don't think I'll ever love anybody else.

SQUIER. Can I possibly be drunk?

GABBY. You will be if you keep hitting that rye.

BOZE. How did you happen to get that way, Gabby?

GABBY. I don't know. Just something.

SQUIER. I swear before God, Boze—I wasn't trying to be seductive.

BOZE [*Scornfully*]. No—I don't believe you could even try.

GABBY. After you left, Alan—I felt as if something had been taken out of me—or sort of as if I'd come out of a dream. I caught on to myself, and I knew I'm just another desert rat, and I'll never be anything else. I'd better get rid of all the girlish bunk that was in me, like thinking so much about going to France, and Art, and dancing in the streets. And I'd better make the most of what I can find right here—and it happened to be you, Boze. Do you know what I asked him? I asked him to let me go away with him, and live in sin. [*She turns again to* SQUIER.] But you wouldn't have done it, even if we'd had the money—would you, Alan? [SQUIER *is looking straight into her eyes.*] Would you?

SQUIER. No, Gabrielle.

GABBY [*To* BOZE]. You see—he doesn't give a hoot in hell for me. I saw that, plainly enough. And it only made me love him all the more. And that's why I was willing to go out into the moonlight with you, when Duke Mantee came in.

DUKE. I'm sorry, sister. I don't like to interfere with anybody's fun.

BOZE [*With labored insincerity*]. Oh—that's all right. It was probably all for the best.

DUKE. Yes. When I look at you, I guess it was. [DUKE *turns and opens window at his side about three inches.*]

SQUIER [*Still looking at* GABBY]. I'm sorry now that I came back.

[BOZE *has darted a look at* DUKE, *and there is born in his mind an idea: by a sudden, tiger-like leap, he might get possession of shotgun which is lying on table.*]

BOZE. I'll take a drink of that stuff. [GABBY *passes him bottle which has remained on table.* BOZE *pours himself a stiff one, drinks it—and a moment later pours and consumes another. But he is constantly, furiously watching* DUKE.]

SQUIER [*Still looking at* GABBY]. When I went out before—it was the poignant ending to a—an idyllic interlude. But now it's spoiled. I can't go forth quite so gracefully again.

GABBY. You're sorry you heard the real truth?

SQUIER. I told you that I'm the type of person to whom the truth is always distasteful.

GABBY. That wife of yours must have been terrible.

SQUIER. Why do you think so?

GABBY. Because she's talked all the heart out of you. I could put it back, Alan.

SQUIER [*With sudden irritability*]. No! Don't delude yourself. If you have love, and don't know what to do with it, why don't you lavish it on Duke Mantee? There's your real mate—another child of Nature.

GABBY. You'd better not drink any more of that rye.

SQUIER. It's not the rye! It's the same disease that's afflicting Boze! Impotence! [*He stands up.*]

DUKE. Sit down, pal.

SQUIER. What do you care whether I sit or stand? What can *I* do to assail your superiority?

DUKE. I got to think about my health, pal.

SQUIER. If I had a machine gun, I wouldn't know what to do with it. . . . I want to talk to him. [*Indicating* GRAMP.]

GRAMP. Me?

DUKE. You can talk sitting down. I heard you doing it.

SQUIER [*Sitting down*]. Very well ——

GRAMP. What's on your mind?

SQUIER. Those Liberty Bonds of yours, buried in Santa Fé.

GRAMP [*Sharply*]. How do *you* know about them?

SQUIER. What are you going to do with them?

GRAMP. Going to leave 'em where they are!

SQUIER. Yes—leave them where they are! Your granddaughter is stifling and suffocating in this desert when a few of your thousands would give her the chance to claim her birthright.

GRAMP. Yes—and maybe give *you*

the chance to steal it. I've heard what you've been saying.

SQUIER. That's a low way to justify your stinginess. Oh—I know you were a pioneer once. But what are you now? A mean old miser, hanging on to that money as though it meant something. Why in God's name don't you die and do the world some good?

GRAMP. Must be drunk.

DUKE [*Rising menacingly*]. Yes—drunk—or just about the lowest grade son of a bitch I ever run across. What do you mean talking to an old man like that? [RUBY *appears in door.*]

RUBY. Say—there's three people coming down the road. Two men and a woman. Look to me like the owners of that Duesenberg.

DUKE. O.K. Keep quiet when they get here.

RUBY. It's all right out here. You can see plain in the moonlight. It's kind of nice to look at, too. [*He goes out.*]

SQUIER. I admit it, Duke. I was guilty of bad taste—and I apologize, Mr. Maple.

GRAMP. Sure.

DUKE. You'd better crawl, or I might have to put the lug on you. Talking to an old man like that——

SQUIER. Listen, Duke. If you had any of Robin Hood in you you'd go to Santa Fé, and rob that bank, and give it to her, before it's too late for her to use it as it should be used——

GRAMP. She'll get it when she needs it—when she has a family of her own to support—and probably a good-for-nothing unemployed husband . . .

[DUKE *turns to look out window.* BOZE *sees his chance. He effects the tiger-like leap, seizes shotgun and wrests it from* DUKE'S *frantic grasp.* BOZE *backs away quickly, covering* DUKE.]

BOZE [*Breathless with excitement*]. Put 'em up! Now I've got you. I've been waiting for this chance. I've been watching every move you—— [MR. *and* MRS. CHISHOLM *appear in doorway, followed by* JOSEPH. *Seeing* BOZE *with shotgun, and* DUKE *with hands up,* MRS. CHISHOLM *screams.* BOZE *whirls to cover them. As he does so,* DUKE *whips out one of his revolvers and fires.* BOZE *drops shotgun and grabs his left hand with his right. Kitchen door flies open and* JACKIE *hurtles out.*]

DUKE. Get that gun. [*As* JACKIE *dives for shotgun, the* CHISHOLMS *turn to rush into the night.* PYLES *has followed* JACKIE *out of kitchen, his machine gun at the alert, his mouth full.*]

RUBY'S VOICE [*From off right*]. Get back there or I'll shoot you dead!

GABBY. Are you hurt, Boze?

DUKE [*To* JACKIE]. Give me that Tommy. [JACKIE *gives his machine gun to* DUKE. MR *and* MRS. CHISHOLM *and* JOSEPH *return, followed by* RUBY.]

BOZE. He got me in the hand. [*His left hand is seen to be covered with blood.*]

JACKIE. So you tried to be brave, did you?

DUKE. Frisk 'em, Ruby. [RUBY *hurriedly taps the* CHISHOLMS *all over.*]

MRS. CHISHOLM. Let us out of here! We didn't have anything to do with this.

JACKIE. Shut up.

MRS. CHISHOLM. I *won't* have that man pawing me.

DUKE. Get back to the car, Ruby.

RUBY. They're harmless, Duke. [*He goes.*]

DUKE. Sit down over there. Come on! Step! You down there. [*The* CHISHOLMS *sit at the center table, with* SQUIER. JOSEPH *sits upstage by the counter.*] Take him in and bandage him, sister. He'll be all right. Go with 'em, Jackie—and you better take that line and tie him up and leave him in there.

[GABBY *and* BOZE *cross toward the left.*]

JACKIE [*Picking up the clothesline*]. I'll tie him.

BOZE [*To the* CHISHOLMS]. God damn

you! Why did you have to pick that moment to come in here?

CHISHOLM. Why indeed!

GABBY. Come on, Boze.

BOZE. Oh, God! I had the chance and I muffed it. I could have got Mantee and got him good.

JACKIE. Tough luck, halfback. You made a nice try.

[GABBY *and* BOZE *go out at the left followed by* JACKIE.]

PYLES. Say, boss—we better lam out of here.

DUKE. We go when I say so.

PYLES [*Contemplating the* CHISHOLMS]. But if any more people come in here we'll have to be sending out for recruits. [*Turns to* JOSEPH.] Hi-yah, colored brother!

JOSEPH [*With dignified asperity*]. Good evening.

DUKE. Finish your supper, Pyles.

PYLES. Sure you don't need me? They almost got you that time.

DUKE. Almost ain't good enough. Go on.

PYLES. O.K., boss. [*He goes out into kitchen.*]

GRAMP. Say, Mantee—did you mean to hit him in the hand or was that a bad shot?

DUKE [*Quietly*]. It was a bad shot, Pop. But I had to get it off fast. Now, listen—I let that mugg make a mugg out of me. But—don't anybody try that again. Just keep in mind that I and the boys are candidates for hanging, and the minute anybody makes the wrong move, I'm going to kill the whole lot of you. So keep your seats. [*He returns his revolver to its holster, picks up tommy gun and sits down at right. There is a dead pause.*]

CHISHOLM. Are *you* Mantee?

DUKE. Yes, pal.

MRS. CHISHOLM. I *knew* it was a mistake to take that hitchhiker into the car.

CHISHOLM. I don't see what *he* had to do with it.

MRS. CHISHOLM. He certainly didn't help matters much. [SQUIER *was at first stunned by* BOZE's *spectacular action—then, as he thought it over, resentful—and then, as he thought still more, determined to do something spectacular himself. He has helped himself to another stiff slug of rye.*]

SQUIER [*Gravely*]. I'm afraid that's unanswerable, Mr. Chisholm. I have not helped matters at all—up to now. [*He finishes his drink and turns to* DUKE.] Would you mind passing me that rucksack that's on the bench beside you?

DUKE. What do you want with it?

SQUIER. I want to get out my life-insurance policy. If you reach in there, you'll find it, in a bundle of papers. [DUKE *reaches with his left hand and extracts the papers.*]

GRAMP. What do you want with your insurance? Expecting to die?

SQUIER. You've guessed it, Mr. Maple. [DUKE *tosses bundle to* SQUIER.] Thank you. Now can I take out my fountain pen? Here it is. [*He points to his breast pocket.* DUKE *nods.* SQUIER *takes out his pen, and starts to write on policy.*]

CHISHOLM [*To* DUKE]. What about my car?

DUKE. That's a nice bus you got there.

CHISHOLM. Are you going to restore it to me? And my luggage——

DUKE. You're likely to get the car back. Let's hope it won't be all full of bullet holes and blood.

MRS. CHISHOLM. There's one little traveling case with some—some things I need. Can I please have that?

DUKE. I took a look in that case.

MRS. CHISHOLM. You're going to steal it?

DUKE. Yes, ma'am. I got a friend that likes rubies.

MRS. CHISHOLM. You're a filthy *thief!*

DUKE. Yes, ma'am.

CHISHOLM. Look here, old man. How much will you take to let us out of here?

DUKE. How much have you got?

CHISHOLM. I could let you have—say—two hundred dollars in cash.

DUKE. Bring it here. [CHISHOLM *walks timorously over to* DUKE, *produces his wallet, and starts to take out some bills.*] Just put down the whole wallet. [CHISHOLM *does so, with trembling hands.*] Got any more?

CHISHOLM [*Patting his pants pockets*]. Only some small change.

DUKE. Keep it.

MRS. CHISHOLM [*Rising*]. Now can we go?

DUKE. No.

CHISHOLM. But I understood that you——

DUKE. Sit down where you were.

MRS. CHISHOLM. You are a cheap, contemptible, crooked thief——

CHISHOLM. Be quiet, Edith. [*He resumes his seat.*] We're in his hands. There's nothing we can do—but hope that some day the United States Government will take some measures to protect the lives and property of its citizens. [DUKE *has been calmly taking all the money from wallet.*]

DUKE. Here's your wallet, pal. [*He tosses it to* CHISHOLM, *who stoops to pick it up.* SQUIER *has finished writing. He turns to* DUKE *and from now on speaks rapidly and with a peculiar earnestness.*]

SQUIER. Duke—I have a great favor to ask of you.

DUKE. Yeah?

SQUIER. I don't think you'll refuse it. Because—you're a man of imagination. You're not afraid to do—rather outlandish things——

DUKE. What are you getting at?

SQUIER. This insurance policy—it's my only asset. It's for five thousand dollars—and it was made out in favor of my wife. She's a rich woman, and she doesn't need that money—and I know she doesn't *want* it, from me. I've written on the policy that I want the money paid to Miss Maple—that young lady in there. If Mr. and Mrs. Chisholm will witness my signature, I'm sure it will be all right. My wife would never contest it. She's a good sort—really she is. Well—what I'm getting at is this, Duke: after they've signed, I wish—I'd be much obliged if you'd just—kill me. [DUKE *looks at him levelly.*] It couldn't make any difference to you, Duke. After all, if they catch you they can hang you only once—and you know better than anyone else they already have more than they need against you. And you can't be bothered by any humane considerations. You'd have a hard time finding a more suitable candidate for extermination. I'll be mourned by no one. In fact, my passing will evoke sighs of relief in certain quarters. You see, Duke—in killing me—you'd only be executing the sentence of the law—I mean, natural law—survival of the fittest——

GRAMP. My God—he *is* drunk!

DUKE. Sure—and having a fine time showing off.

SQUIER. Of course I'm showing off. I'm trying to outdo Boze in gallantry. But is there anything unnatural in that? Boze was ready to sacrifice his life to become an All-American star. And I'm ready to do likewise. [*He addresses the* CHISHOLMS.] Can't you see I mean it?

CHISHOLM. I'm afraid I'm not greatly interested in your whimsicalities.

SQUIER. I don't blame you. But you must remember that this is a weird country we're in. These Mesas are enchanted—and you have to be prepared for the improbable. I'm only asking that you attest to my signature on this——

MRS. CHISHOLM. I believe you *do* mean it!

SQUIER. Good for you, Mrs. Chisholm! You're a kindred spirit! I'll bet that you, too, have been thrilled by "A Tale of Two Cities."

MRS. CHISHOLM. You're in love with her, aren't you?

SQUIER. Yes—yes, I suppose I am.

And not unreasonably. She has heroic stuff in her. She may be one of the immortal women of France—another Joan of Arc, or George Sand, or Madame Curie. I want to show her that I believe in her—and how else can I do it? Living, I'm worth nothing to her. Dead—I can buy her the tallest cathedrals, and golden vineyards, and dancing in the streets. One well-directed bullet will accomplish that. And it will gain a measure of reflected glory for him who fired it and him who stopped it. [*He holds up insurance policy.*] This document will be my ticket to immortality. It will inspire people to say of me: "*There* was an artist, who died before his time!" Will you do it, Duke?

DUKE [*Quietly*]. I'll be glad to.

SQUIER. Then can I have this signed?

DUKE. Sure.

CHISHOLM [*To* GRAMP]. Is he by any chance insane?

GRAMP. Don't ask *me*. He's no friend of mine.

MRS. CHISHOLM. Of *course* he's insane. But what of it? [SQUIER *gives her policy and pen.*]

SQUIER. Thank you, Mrs. Chisholm. Please sign where I've written, "Witness this day." [*They start to sign.*] I'm going to entrust this to you, Mr. Maple. And after I—after the Duke has obliged, put it in the hands of some good lawyer for collection. My passport is on that table for identification purposes. Thank you very much. [*As they hand him back policy.*] Here, Mr. Maple. [*He rises and hands policy to* GRAMP.]

DUKE. Let me know when you want to be killed.

SQUIER. Pick your own moment, Duke. Say—just before you leave. [*He strides upstage nervously, aimlessly.*] But I'd prefer to have her think that you did it in cold blood. Will you all please remember that? [PYLES *comes in.*]

DUKE. O.K., pal. But for the time being, you better sit down. You might get to feeling reckless. [SQUIER *sits down.*]

SQUIER. I want to. Now—I think we'd all better have a drink.

MRS. CHISHOLM. Good!

SQUIER [*To* PYLES]. Would you mind passing glasses to Mr. and Mrs. Chisholm?

PYLES. Sure. [*He goes behind counter for glasses, while* SQUIER *pours himself another.*] Say, boss—let's lam it out of here. I don't like all them big windows. [*He takes glasses down to the* CHISHOLMS.]

DUKE. We got to give them more time.

PYLES. You oughtn't to trust a dame. They probably got lost down there in the Panhandle.

DUKE. They know this country like a book. Doris was the one who picked this place for meeting up.

PYLES. Well—I wish to God she'd show.

DUKE. Where's the cook?

PYLES. She's all right. I locked her up. [PYLES *has been passing glasses around.* GRAMP *has been reading policy carefully. He turns his attention to* PYLES.]

GRAMP. Hey—I'll have a little of that, too.

PYLES [*Pouring a drink*]. Why—certainly.

DUKE. Don't give it to him, Pyles. The girl says he oughtn't to have it.

SQUIER. Better not, Mr. Maple, we'll all need clear heads for what is to come.

GRAMP. *My* head's never been muddled yet.

PYLES [*To* JOSEPH]. Here, brother—you better take it.

JOSEPH. Is it all right, Mr. Chisholm?

PYLES [*Ashamed for his race*]. Listen to him! "Is it all right, Mr. Chisholm?" Ain't you heard about the big liberation? Come on—take your drink, weasel!

CHISHOLM. Go ahead, Joseph.

JOSEPH. Thank you, sir. [PYLES *hands drink to* JOSEPH, *then crosses to right, and sits down on bench by* DUKE. GRAMP *has finished inspection of policy and is putting it in his pocket.*]

SQUIER. Do you think it's legal?

GRAMP. Seems so to me. But I'd like to tell you just one thing, my friend.

SQUIER. And what is that, Mr. Maple?

GRAMP. There ain't a woman alive or ever did live that's *worth* five thousand dollars.

SQUIER. And let me tell *you* one thing —you're a forgetful old fool. Any woman is worth everything that any man has to give—anguish, ecstasy, faith, jealousy, love, hatred, life, or death. Don't you see —that's the excuse for our existence? It's what makes the whole thing possible, and tolerable. When you've reached my age, you'll learn better sense.

MRS. CHISHOLM [*To her husband*]. Did you hear that?

CHISHOLM [*Wearily*]. I heard.

SQUIER [*To* GRAMP]. That lovely girl —that granddaughter of yours—do you know what she is? No—you don't. You haven't the remotest idea.

GRAMP. What is she?

SQUIER. She's the future. She's the renewal of vitality—and courage—and aspiration—all the strength that has gone out of you. Hell—I can't say what she is —but she's essential to me, and the whole damned country, and the whole miserable world. And please, Mrs. Chisholm— please don't look at me quizzically. I know how I sound.

MRS. CHISHOLM [*To* SQUIER]. I'm wondering if you really believe all that— I mean, about women? [*She has already had one stiff drink and is about to have another.*]

SQUIER. Of course I do—and there's a man who agrees with me. [*Indicating* DUKE.] Don't you, Duke?

DUKE. I don't know, pal. I wasn't listening.

SQUIER. Then permit me to speak for you. [*He turns again to* MRS. CHISHOLM.] He could have been over the border long ago, and safe—but he prefers to stay here and risk his life. And do you know why?

MRS. CHISHOLM. Why?

SQUIER. Because he has a rendezvous here with a girl. Isn't that true, Duke?

DUKE. Yes, pal—that's it.

MRS. CHISHOLM [*To* DUKE]. Do you mean to say you never have *time* for romance?

DUKE. Not much, lady.

SQUIER. Certainly he has! Just like the Knights of the Round Table—between dragons.

DUKE. I guess we're *all* a lot of saps. But I wouldn't be surprised if he was the champion. [*He turns to* SQUIER.] Did you think I was kidding when I said I'd be glad to knock you off?

SQUIER. I hope that neither of us was kidding. Did you think *I* was?

DUKE. I just wanted to make sure.

PYLES. Say! What you talking about?

DUKE. Shut up.

SQUIER. You gave me the idea, Duke, when you called me a low-grade son of a bitch. Forgive me, Mrs. Chisholm. I hope you don't object to that phrase.

MRS. CHISHOLM. Not in the least.

DUKE. I take it back. You're all right, pal. You've got good ideas. I'll try to fix it so's it won't hurt.

SQUIER [*Raising his glass*]. You're all right, too, Duke. I'd like to meet you again some day. [*He drinks.*]

DUKE. Maybe it'll be soon.

MRS. CHISHOLM. You know—this frightful place has suddenly become quite cosy. [*She finishes her second drink.*]

SQUIER. That's my doing, Mrs. Chisholm. You ought to thank me for having taken it out of the realms of reality.

MRS. CHISHOLM [*Excitedly*]. I'm going to *see* something at last—and after that dreadful dull day looking at cliff dwellings. [*She turns to her husband.*] Do you realize that we're going to be witnesses at *murder?* He's actually going to shoot him——

SQUIER. Sh—please be careful, Mrs. Chisholm. [GABBY *comes in from left, followed by* JACKIE.] Hello. How's Boze?

GABBY. He'll be all right.

PYLES. Did you tie him up good?

JACKIE. Yeah—in the bathroom. Say, Duke, it's after ten o'clock.

PYLES. Yeah, boss.

DUKE. We'll give 'em a few more minutes.

SQUIER [*Significantly*]. A few minutes.

DUKE [*With a slight grin*]. Not so much more time, pal. [JACKIE *wanders out for a visit with* RUBY.]

GABBY. Listen, Gramp—I've got an idea we ought to sell out right away, tomorrow. It's the best chance we'll ever have, because this place is going to get advertised all over the country and people will be flocking here just to see where Duke Mantee stopped. I'll bet Dana Trimble will boost his offer sure. [*She is standing by table at left.*]

GRAMP [*Significantly*]. You're still aiming to take that trip to France?

GABBY. No—the hell with that! I'm asking you to do it for Dad's sake. Let him get located in Los Angeles—and maybe I'll find that writer with Warner Brothers, and maybe I'll get a job—and then we'll all be rich.

GRAMP. Don't sound likely to me.

GABBY. You can't tell, Gramp. There might be a great future for Dad in the Legion. That's what he wants, and you ought to give him a whack at it.

SQUIER. And would you be content with that?

GABBY [*Savagely*]. I'm not thinking about myself! I don't care what happens to me.

SQUIER. But you *must* think about yourself. You want to be a great painter, don't you? Then you'll have to get used to being a colossal egoist, selfish to the core.

GABBY. Are you going to give me more advice? You and your talk about Nature? I thought you told me never to listen to you.

SQUIER. I did—but——

GABBY. Well, that's all the advice I'm going to take. [*She turns away from him.*]

MRS. CHISHOLM. Do you mind if I speak up, my dear? Perhaps I could tell you some things that——

GABBY. What do *you* know about me?

CHISHOLM. Nothing! If I were you, Edith, I'd keep out of——

MRS. CHISHOLM [*Turning on him*]. You haven't the remotest conception of what's inside me, and you never have had and never will have as long as you live out your stuffy, astigmatic life. [*She turns to* GABBY.] I don't know about you, my dear. But I know what it means to repress yourself and starve yourself through what you conceive to be your duty to others. I've been through that. When I was just about your age, I went to Salzburg—because I'd had a nervous breakdown after I came out and I went to a psychoanalyst there and he told me I had every right to be a great actress. He gave me a letter to Max Reinhardt, and I might have played the Nun in "The Miracle." But my family of course started yapping about my obligation to *them*—who had given me everything, including life. At *least,* they called it "life." They whisked me back to Dayton, to take my place in the Junior League, and the Country Club, and the D.A.R.—and everything else that's foul and obscene. And before I knew it, I was married to *this* pillar of the mortgage loan and trust. And what did *he* do? He took my soul and had it stencilled on a card, and filed. And where have I been ever since? In an art metal cabinet. That's why I think I have a *little* right to advise you.

CHISHOLM [*Closing his tired eyes*]. Dear God!

MRS. CHISHOLM. You needn't look so martyred! You know perfectly well that until this minute I've never complained. I've managed to play the part of a self-effacing——

CHISHOLM [*His eyes are now open*]. Never complained, eh! Forgive me if I indulge in some quiet, mirthless laughter.

MRS. CHISHOLM. What you've wanted is a wife who's an ornamental cipher. And, God knows—I've tried and tried to be just that——

CHISHOLM. When?

MRS. CHISHOLM. I've given you what you wanted—at the cost of my individuality, my self-respect—and—and everything else——

CHISHOLM. At the cost of nothing! I suppose you've never come storming into the office and created a scene just when I was straining every faculty to find ways to pay for——

MRS. CHISHOLM [*To* GABBY]. There—my dear!

CHISHOLM. Your insane extravagance——

MRS. CHISHOLM. Be quiet! [CHISHOLM *abandons the argument, as is his wont.* MRS. CHISHOLM *again to* GABBY.] Perhaps you'll understand now what I mean. Profit by my example and realize that perhaps you have something important to give to the world. Don't let them stifle you with their talk about duty. Go to France—and *find* yourself!

GRAMP. Suppose she learns there's nothing there to find?

MRS. CHISHOLM. Even so—it would be better than endless doubt—which has been my portion. [*She pours herself another drink.* GABBY *sits down at left.*]

SQUIER. You know—it's the damnedest thing about this place. There's something here that stimulates the autobiographical impulse. [*To* DUKE.] What kind of life have *you* had, Duke?

DUKE. A hell of a life.

MRS. CHISHOLM. I don't believe it.

DUKE. Why not, lady? [JACKIE *returns and sits on a stool at counter.*]

MRS. CHISHOLM. Because you've had the one supreme satisfaction of knowing that at least you're a real man.

[CHISHOLM *again shuts his eyes.*]

DUKE. Yeh—that's true. But what has it got me? I've spent most of my time since I grew up in jail, and it looks like I'll spend the rest of my life dead. So what good does it do me to be a real man when you don't get much chance to be crawling into the hay with some dame?

MRS. CHISHOLM [*After a slight, thoughtful pause*]. I wonder if we could find any hay around *here?*

CHISHOLM [*Past vehemence*]. For the love of God, Edith——

JACKIE. *Say!* What's been going on here?

SQUIER. I'm not sure—but I *think* the Duke has had an offer.

MRS. CHISHOLM. He certainly has! And it was made with all sincerity, too.

PYLES. Now, listen, boss—don't you go getting into no hay with her. Because we got to lam it out of here.

DUKE. Thanks very much, lady. When I get settled down in Mexico, maybe I'll send you a postcard, with my address.

SQUIER. Excuse me, Duke—but how's the time getting along?

DUKE. It's just about up, pal.

SQUIER [*Turning to* GABBY]. I must talk to you, Gabrielle.

GABBY. You can wait until after they're gone.

SQUIER. I can't wait. I mean—when they go—I go. I have to tell you now that I love you.

GABBY. Now listen, Alan. I got sort of upset by all that blood, and I don't want to——

SQUIER. I tell you solemnly that I love you, with all the heart that is left in me.

JACKIE. Are we waiting just to listen to this?

MRS. CHISHOLM. He does love you, my dear. He told us so.

SQUIER. Please, Mrs. Chisholm. I'm capable of saying it. [*He turns to* GABBY.] Even if I'm not capable of making you believe that I——

GABBY. Don't make a fool of yourself, Alan. They're all staring at you.

SQUIER. I know they are. But you've got to believe it, and you've got to remember it. Because—you see—it's my only chance of survival. I told you about that major artist, that's been hidden. I'm transferring him to you. You'll find a line in that verse of Villon's that fits that. Something about: "Thus in your field my seed of harvestry will thrive." I've provided barren soil for that seed—but you'll give it fertility and growth and fruition——

PYLES. Listen, boss—I got a wife and four children.

MRS. CHISHOLM. Be quiet—you black gorilla!

PYLES. What you call me? [*He rises, his machine gun at the alert.*]

DUKE. She pegged you, all right, Pyles. Sit down! [*Somewhat reluctantly,* PYLES *obeys.*]

SQUIER. You still think I was being comic?

GABBY. No, Alan. I just think that you—you're kind of crazy. And I guess so am I. And that's why I think we'd be terribly happy together. [SQUIER *looks into her eyes.*]

SQUIER. Don't say that, Gabrielle.

GABBY. Why not—when I believe it, with all my heart?

SQUIER [*After a moment*]. Well—maybe you're right——

GABBY. You're beginning to admit it.

SQUIER. Maybe we will be happy together in a funny kind of way.

GABBY. Alan! [*Impulsively, she goes forward and kneels beside him.*]

JACKIE. Hey!

DUKE. Leave 'em alone!

GABBY. Alan! If you're going away, I'm going with you—wherever it is.

SQUIER [*Taking hold of her hand*]. No, Gabrielle. I'm not going away, anywhere. I don't have to go any farther. Because I think I've found the thing I was looking for. I've found it—here, in the Valley of the Shadow.

GABBY. What, Alan? What have you found?

SQUIER. I can't say what it is, Gabrielle. Because I don't quite know, yet! [*He looks into her eyes for a moment, then turns suddenly to* DUKE.] All right, Duke. We needn't wait any longer.

[*Three sharp toots from the Duesenberg are heard.*]

DUKE. Watch it, boys! [PYLES *and* JACKIE *hastily duck out of range of windows.*]

CHISHOLM. What was that?

JOSEPH. It was our horn, Mr. Chisholm. [JACKIE *is by door,* DUKE *by right window,* PYLES *is crouched, covering those in the room.*]

JASON'S VOICE. Who's that?

RUBY'S VOICE. Stick up your hands! [DUKE *has leveled his machine gun through the slightly open window.*]

DUKE. We got you covered by machine guns. Open that door, Jackie. Come on, boys. Walk in the front door, and *keep 'em up!* Cover the door, Jackie.

JACKIE. I got it.

DUKE. Come on! Keep coming! [JASON *comes in, followed by two fellow legionnaires—one, the* COMMANDER, *a peppery little man, and another who is burly and stupid. All are in the same gaudy uniforms and all look bewildered.*] Get those guns, Jackie. [JACKIE *systematically disarms legionnaires. He tosses guns into ammunition sack.* RUBY *comes to door.*]

RUBY. All clear out here.

DUKE. Is their car in our way?

RUBY. No—it's a good mask.

DUKE. O.K. Get back to the car. [RUBY *disappears into the night.*]

JASON. Is this a stick-up?

JACKIE. What a guesser!

GRAMP. Say—Jason. That there's Duke Mantee. Been here all evening. He and his gang picked this place out of the whole southwest.

DUKE. What's that uniform you're wearing?

JASON. It's the Ralph M. Kesterling Post of the American Legion.

COMMANDER. I'm the commander of this post, buddy, and I want to tell you that all of us men fought in the World War. You wouldn't shoot us down in cold blood?

JACKIE [*Cheerfully*]. Sure we would.

DUKE. Sit down, boys.

ANOTHER LEGIONNAIRE [*Very basso*]. Where?

JACKIE. On your cans, Legion.

DUKE. Down there on the floor—in a bunch—and stay there. [*With some little sacrifice of dignity,* LEGIONNAIRES *sit down on floor in a huddle in center.*] Why did you come here?

JASON. This is where I live.

GABBY. That's my father.

DUKE. Why did you bring the whole regiment with you?

COMMANDER. We were trailing you. And by God we caught up with——

JASON. Shut up, Commander. The less we talk the better for all concerned.

JACKIE. Some legion! Out gunning for the bad men—and look at 'em now!

DUKE. What made you think I'd be around here?

COMMANDER. They caught your pals.

OTHER. Three men and a blonde.

PYLES. Don't you try to go get 'em out now, boss!

DUKE. Where was it? [*There is no reply.* DUKE *continues with unwonted ferocity.*] Come on—tell me—or I'll tear holes a yard wide in them pansy uniforms!

JASON. They caught 'em at Buckhorn.

DUKE. Where's that? [PYLES *pulls map from his pocket.*]

OTHER. It's in New Mexico—'bout ninety—hundred miles southeast of here.

DUKE. When?

JASON. I don't know.

COMMANDER. We heard it half an hour ago. Every man in this state that can bear arms has turned out to——

PYLES. Here it is, boss. Buckhorn—on Route 11.

JACKIE. How'd they get 'em?

COMMANDER. It was the regular army!

OTHER. Your friends run right into a troop of the U.S. Cavalry.

JASON. I warn you, Mantee—you'd better get out of here, for your own good.

DUKE. Is anybody else coming this way?

JASON. I don't know. I swear to God I don't. But there are posses all around here, and I don't want to get this place shot up.

COMMANDER. You got the whole mighty strength of this nation after you now, buddy.

JACKIE. Listen, Legion—when we're got it will be by *real* cops—not by any overgrown Boy Scouts in fancy dress.

JASON. All right—you can talk big, if you want to. But I'll tell you that the woman in that car has been doing some talking.

DUKE [*After a moment*]. What?

JACKIE. It was Doris. She snitched. They always snitch!

DUKE. Shut up! [*To* JASON.] What were you saying?

JASON. I'm telling you for your own good, Mantee—they know where you were heading—they've picked up your trail—and they'll get you——

JACKIE. She *has* snitched! Come on, Duke!

SQUIER. Don't listen to them, Duke' [SQUIER *is leaning forward, watching* DUKE *with great intentness. He sees that* DUKE, *for once, has been propelled into a state of turbulent, agonized indecision.*]

PYLES. Come on, boss—or we're all dead.

COMMANDER. The law's closing in on you!

JACKIE. What's the matter with you, Duke? Why the hell don't you——

DUKE [*With sudden savagery*]. For Christ's sake, shut up! *Shut up!* Give me time to think.

SQUIER [*Urgently*]. No, Duke—don't waste any time thinking. That isn't your game. Don't listen to what they're telling you. You've got to keep going and going and going——

PYLES. Yeah—and go fast.

JACKIE. You've been double-crossed and bitched, and the next thing you'll be laid flat on a marble slab——

DUKE. Where'd they take her?

JASON. I don't know. Maybe to Albuquerque.

JACKIE. If we head for there, they'll take *us!*

SQUIER. You want revenge, don't you! You want to go out of your way again to get that blonde who snitched. Don't do it, Duke. Even if she did betray you, don't you commit a worse crime. Don't betray yourself. Go on, run for the border—and take your illusions with you!

JACKIE. He's right, Duke!

DUKE. I told you to shut up! [*He says that to* JACKIE, *but he is looking hard at* SQUIER, *who is talking with passionate earnestness.*]

SQUIER. You know they're going to get you, anyway. You're obsolete, Duke—like me. You've got to die. Then die for freedom. That's worth it. Don't give up your life for anything so cheap and unsatisfactory as revenge.

PYLES. I hear a car coming, boss. We better lam. [DUKE *looks at* SQUIER *curiously, for a moment.*]

DUKE. All right, pal. I'm going. Now, listen, folks; we've had a pleasant evening here and I'd hate to spoil it with any killing at the finish. So stay where you are until we're out of sight, because we'll be watching. Better cut that phone wire, Jackie. Pack up the ammunition, Pyles. [PYLES *and* JACKIE *are galvanized into action.*]

SQUIER. Wait a minute! You're not forgetting me? [JACKIE *is opening his knife,* PYLES *is picking up ammunition sack, and* DUKE *is covering all, when the Duesenberg horn is heard again.* DUKE, PYLES, *and* JACKIE *duck.*]

DUKE [*Peering out window*]. Car's stopped out in the road. There's a guy with a rifle.

PYLES. Cops?

DUKE. Looks like it.

JACKIE. Hicks or G's?

DUKE. Hicks. Lay low!

COMMANDER. It's the Sheriff! He's got you, Mantee!

JASON. I warned you! You'd better surrender now before they start—— [*A burst of machine-gun fire is heard from left.*]

PYLES. That's Ruby shooting.

DUKE. The God-damn fool. Get out there to that window, Jackie, and tell him to hold his fire. We don't want 'em drilling that car. [JACKIE *starts to go.*] Wait! Tell him to open up if they try to drift around that side.

JACKIE. O.K. [*Stooped over, he goes to door at lower left and out.*]

JASON. You have no right to endanger the lives of innocent people. You'd better surrender.

DUKE. Get behind that counter, Pyles. And keep this mob in here covered.

PYLES. O.K., boss. [*He crouches on left end of counter.* DUKE *is marvelously alert, crouching by window, muzzle of his gun thrust out.*] What they doing now, boss? [DUKE *delivers a short burst of machine-gun fire out the window.*]

DUKE. They're crawling into the sage brush the other side of the road. Where are them pans?

PYLES. The sack's right there beside you. [*A shot from outside shatters one of windowpanes.*] Boy—I knowed this place wasn't safe! [*Wails are heard from* PAULA, *off at left.*]

DUKE. You folks better get down. Lie down, all of you, close together in the middle. Watch 'em, Pyles.

PYLES. I'm watching! [*All hasten to obey, so that they are lying flat on their stomachs, close together.* JACKIE *returns.*]

JACKIE. O.K., Duke.

DUKE. Where's the light switch?

GRAMP. To the right of the door.

DUKE. Turn 'em out, Jackie. [JACKIE *turns out lights.*]

CHISHOLM [*To his wife*]. Do you want any hay now? [*The strip of faces and feet of the prone is illumined by the glow of light from door at right. Through windows and panes of door come bright moonlight and the green neon gleam to illumine, dimly,* DUKE *and* JACKIE.]

DUKE. Get to the kitchen door, Jackie. Hold your fire, unless they try to rush it. They'll try to work around that direction to the shadow of that mesa. It's their only cover. When they get around there, we'll lam.

JACKIE. How many are there?

DUKE. Six or seven. Nothing to worry about. [*Another shot from outside.*] When enough of 'em get across that road, give 'em a couple of bursts to scare 'em and then snap back here. And watch yourself, kid!

JACKIE. O.K., Duke. [*He crosses the line of bodies.*]

COMMANDER. Ouch! [*Still another shot from outside breaks a window.* JACKIE *has gone out at left.* BOZE'S *voice can be heard shouting: "Let me out of here! Let me out of here!"* PAULA *can be heard wailing prayers and imprecations in Spanish.*]

DUKE. Keeping 'em covered, Pyles?

PYLES. I got 'em, boss! I got 'em! [*The subsequent dialogue is punctuated with shots from outside and bursts from* DUKE'S *tommy gun.*]

SQUIER. It's an inspiring moment—isn't it, Gabrielle? The United States of America versus Duke Mantee! [*A volley from* SHERIFF'S *posse and neon light goes out.*]

JASON. They've absolutely wrecked the neon!

GRAMP. It's them deputies shooting. Probably all drunk.

SQUIER. It almost restores in me the will to live—and love—and conquer.

CHISHOLM. Listen, Edith—if I'm killed—

MRS. CHISHOLM. What did you say?

CHISHOLM. I said—if I'm killed—and you're not . . . notify Jack Lavery. He has full instructions.

MRS. CHISHOLM [*Turning away*]. All right.

COMMANDER. Hey—Mantee . . . you're not going to let 'em rush us, are you? [DUKE *replies with another burst.*]

PYLES. Getting any of 'em, boss?

DUKE. Can't get a good angle on 'em. But they're drifting over—and Jackie'll get 'em.

SQUIER. I feel as if I were sitting on top of a mountain . . . in the middle of Penguin Island. Watching . . . watching the odd little creatures. [MRS. CHISHOLM *starts to hum.*] How do you feel about it, darling?

GABBY. I don't know, Alan. And I don't care.

JASON. I wish to God you'd stop that praying.

MRS. CHISHOLM. I'm not praying—I'm singing. [*By now it is apparent that the attackers have been drifting over, the sound of shots comes more from left.*]

PYLES. Why ain't Jackie shooting?

DUKE. The kid knows what he's doing.

COMMANDER. If you let 'em rush us . . . it'll be a massacre.

GABBY. Alan . . . Alan—when you get to France . . . what do you see first?

SQUIER. Customs officers.

GABBY. But what's the first real sight you see?

SQUIER. The fields and forests of Normandy and then——

GABBY. What, Alan?

SQUIER. And then Paris.

PYLES. I better tell Jackie to open up.

DUKE. Stay where you are.

GABBY. Paris! That's the most marvelous place in the world for love—isn't it?

SQUIER. All places are marvelous.

GABBY. Even here.

SQUIER. Especially here, my darling.

JOSEPH [*Swaying and chanting*]. Oh, Lord! Oh, Lord! It is the judgment of thy wrath on these thy poor sinful children. [*More wails from* PAULA *and shouts from* BOZE.]

JASON. The next thing you know those gas pumps will be up in flames.

SQUIER. As long as I live—I'll be grateful to the Duke——

GABBY. Alan . . . Alan . . . will you please kiss me? [*He kisses her.* DUKE *delivers a final prolonged burst, then turns from window.*]

DUKE. O.K., Pyles. We're pulling out. Get Jackie. [PYLES *ducks into kitchen. The shooting from left is now intense.*]

SQUIER. Oh, Lord—Now it's going be all over.

GABBY [*Clinging to him*]. Not for us, Alan—never——

PYLES [*Returning*]. Jackie's got killed.

DUKE. How the hell did he do that?

PYLES. I don't know, boss.

DUKE. Well—we got to leave him. You and you and you and you are coming with us to hang on the running board. We got to have shields. [*He has designated the* CHISHOLMS, JOSEPH, *and the two* LEGIONNAIRES.]

CHISHOLM. Me?

MRS. CHISHOLM. All right! All right! I don't care what happens to me now. I don't care a bit!

COMMANDER. For God's sake, Buddy, don't let us get shot down like——

JOSEPH. Oh, Lord God of Abraham. Oh, Holy Lord——

OTHER LEGIONNAIRE. This is the country I was ready to die for——[*The foregoing is all jumbled together.*]

GRAMP. Me, too?

DUKE. No, not you, Pop. Come on, on your feet. Get moving out through that door. They won't shoot at you! You won't none of you get hurt if you keep your hands up and make plenty of noise. Come on—keep moving!

PYLES. And we're in one hell of a hurry. [*He is herding them out. Their hands are up and they are shouting lustily.*]

ALL. Don't shoot—Don't shoot. For God's sake, buddies, don't shoot!

[DUKE *is in doorway, a crouched silhouette against the moonlit desert. His machine gun is under his left arm, his revolver in his right hand.*]

DUKE [*To those remaining*]. You'd better stay where you are for a while. Good night, folks.

SQUIER [*Springing to his feet*]. Duke!

GABBY. Alan! Keep down!

SQUIER. Duke!

DUKE. Do you still want it?

SQUIER [*Desperately*]. It's no matter whether I want it or not. You've got to——

DUKE. O.K., pal. [*He shoots.* SQUIER *spins against lunch counter.* GABBY *screams.*] I'll be seeing you soon. [*He goes.*]

GRAMP. God Almighty! He meant it. [GABBY *rushes to* SQUIER. *There are more wails from* PAULA *and shouts from* BOZE, *but the shooting has stopped.*]

JASON. Keep *down!* [*The motor of the car is heard starting. Door at left bursts open and* SHERIFF *comes in, holding a rifle. Behind him are* HERB *and two* DEPUTIES, *with rifles, pistols, shotguns.*]

SHERIFF. Where'd they go?

JASON [*Rising*]. Out there.

HERB [*Full of enthusiasm and moon*]. Let's get 'em, Sheriff! Come on, fellers—we'll shoot 'em dead! [SHERIFF *starts for door, and bumps into* JASON.]

GABBY. Gramp! Go get Boze. He knows about first aid. [GRAMP *goes out at left.*]

SHERIFF. Get out of my way, you clumsy——[SHERIFF *goes out front door, followed by* DEPUTIES *and* HERB. *They take cover, and raise their rifles.*]

JASON. Those are innocent people on the running board! [*He switches on lights.*]

HERB. Never mind 'em. Let's shoot the hell out of 'em! [*He shoots.*]

SHERIFF. God damn! Come on. We'll go after 'em. [*He turns out of sight.*]

VOICE OF ANOTHER DEPUTY. Can't drive that car. The tires are all shot.

SHERIFF'S VOICE. Here's a car we can take.

JASON. Wait a minute. That's my car! You've done enough damage to my property.

HERB'S VOICE. Ah—shut up. [SQUIER *lurches toward center table.* GABBY *steadies him and helps him to slump down into a chair.*]

SQUIER. It doesn't hurt—or, at least, it doesn't seem . . . It went into this lung, I think. [*He leans forward on table.*]

GABBY. It's all right, Alan.

SQUIER. It isn't all right, Gabrielle. I'm practically dead.

GABBY. No! Alan! You said you wanted to live.

SQUIER. I know I did——

GABBY. And I'll live with you. I will!

SQUIER [*Looking up at her and smiling, feebly*]. I know I said it. I was blinded, then. But now I can see——

GABBY [*Shouting*]. Boze! Gramp! Somebody! Come here quick!

SQUIER. They were right, Gabrielle . . . I mean the stars. I had to come all this way—to find a reason . . . Oh, —if people only had guts enough, they'd always find . . . [*He covers his eyes with his hand.*] Death is funny-looking when . . . The Duke—understood what it was—I wanted . . . I hope you'll——[*His arms are stretched out on table and his head has been sinking until it rests between them.*]

GABBY. What, Alan? What did you say? [*She takes hold of his shoulder and, frantically, shakes him.*] *Alan* . . . [*He is finally silent. Her lip quivers, but she tightens her face.*] No—don't worry, Alan. I'm not going to be a God-damned cry-baby about it . . . I know you died happy . . . Didn't you, Alan? *Didn't* you? [*After a moment,* BOZE *comes in, followed by* GRAMP. BOZE'S *right hand is in a blood-stained bandage.*]

BOZE. Are you all right, old kid?

GABBY. I guess he's dead.

GRAMP. Sure he is. Mantee couldn't have missed twice.

BOZE. Damned tough. He was a good guy, at that. [*A wail from* PAULA *is again heard.*] What's that?

GABBY. It's Paula. Go in and let her out. [BOZE *goes out at left.* GRAMP *takes insurance policy from his pocket.*]

GRAMP. Listen, Gabby—here's the funny thing. His life insurance for five thousand berries. He made it out to you, and it looks regular. Said he wanted you to spend it on a trip to France to see your mother. Of course, I don't know if it's collectable, but by God, I'm going to get it to Summerfield in the morning. [*He puts policy back in his pocket.*] He was the damnedest feller I ever did see. [*He turns and crosses to left and sits down in his rocking chair.*] Couldn't make him out. [JASON *comes in quickly.*]

JASON. Mantee let 'em off the car 'bout a quarter of a mile up the road. You can see 'em walking back. [*He sees* SQUIER.] Has he——

GRAMP. Yep—he's gone.

JASON [*Removing his cap*]. Poor feller. Well—he died a hero's death. We'll give him an honorable funeral.

GABBY. We'll bury him out there in the petrified forest.

JASON. *What?*

GABBY. That's what he wanted.

GRAMP. Yes—by God—he said so. [JASON *starts up to phone behind counter.*]

JASON. Well, maybe his next of kin will have something to say about that. I've got to 'phone the Sheriff's office. They'll never catch Mantee with my car—unless he wrecks that Duesenberg. . . . Hello——Hello—get me the Sheriff's office in Morenci. . . . Yeh. . . . [GABBY *is still standing close to* SQUIER, *her hands on his shoulder.*]

GABBY [*Almost to herself*]

Thus in your field my seeds of harvestry will
thrive—
For the fruit is like me that I set——

[BOZE *comes in, from kitchen, laughing.*]

BOZE. Boy—it did me good to see that Jackie in a pool of blood——

GABBY [*Louder, almost defiantly*]

God bids me tend it with good husbandry:
This is the end for which we twain are met.

JASON. Hello—who's this? . . . Oh—hello Ernie——

BOZE [*Wildly*]. Don't keep *staring* at him——

JASON. *Jason* Maple. . . . Say—Mantee was here and escaped south in a yellow Duesenberg, Ohio license plate. Sheriff went after him, but you got to watch Route 71 and send out the alarm to watch Route 60. Yes—we had quite some shooting here. . . . [*During this speech the curtain has fallen.*]

Curtain

Thornton Wilder

✻ 1897-

Thornton Wilder was born in Madison, Wisconsin. He spent his childhood in China, returning to the United States to attend Yale University. Upon his graduation in 1920 he went to the Lawrenceville School, where from 1921 to 1928 he was a housemaster and teacher of French. He also took a master's degree from Princeton in 1925.

In that year he made his public appearance as a writer, publishing a novel (THE CABALA) *and furnishing a play to the American Laboratory Theatre* (THE TRUMPET SHALL SOUND). *In 1927 his novel,* THE BRIDGE OF SAN LUIS REY, *brought him a wide audience and a Pulitzer Prize. And thus the pattern of his career was established: teacher-novelist-playwright. From 1930 to 1936 he lectured at the University of Chicago and published his collection of one-act plays from which* THE LONG CHRISTMAS DINNER *is taken. If these plays are conventional in subject matter they are experimental in technique and show his wide acquaintance with the dramatic modes of the eastern as well as the western world and the ancient as well as the modern theatre.*

His world-famous play, OUR TOWN *(1938), shows his ability to combine whatever is useful to him from any dramatic tradition into a unified work which is both unique and universal.* THE SKIN OF OUR TEETH *(1942), which like* OUR TOWN, *was awarded a Pulitzer Prize, shows the influence of the revolutionary techniques of James Joyce's novel,* Finnegan's Wake, *without indulging in its precocious obscurantism. And a nineteenth-century Austrian farce by Johann Nestroy inspired the writing of* THE MERCHANT OF YONKERS, *later revised into the highly successful* THE MATCHMAKER *(1954). One of Wilder's great contributions to modern dramaturgy has been his demonstration of how simple and unsensational truths, forgotten or passed over in the hurry of living, can reassert their importance to a fuller understanding of human experience. In this process the teacher and the artist are happily and everlastingly combined.*

The Long Christmas Dinner

Characters

LUCIA
MOTHER BAYARD
RODERICK
COUSIN BRANDON
CHARLES } *children of Roderick and Lucia*
GENEVIEVE
THE NURSE
LEONORA *wife of Charles*
ERMENGARDE
SAM } *children of Charles and Leonora*
LUCIA II
RODERICK II

NOTES FOR THE PRODUCER

Ninety years are traversed in this play which represents in accelerated motion ninety Christmas dinners in the Bayard household. Although the speech, the manner and business of the actors is colloquial and realistic, the production should stimulate the imagination and be implied and suggestive. Accordingly gray curtains with set pieces are recommended for the walls of the room rather than conventional scenery. In the center of the table is a bowl of Christmas greens and at the left end a wine decanter and glasses. Except for these, all properties in the play are imaginary. Throughout the play the characters continue eating invisible food with imaginary knives and forks. The actors are dressed in inconspicuous clothes and must indicate their gradual increase in years through their acting.

The ladies may have shawls concealed which they gradually draw up about their shoulders as they grow older.

At the rise of the curtain the stage should be dark; gradually a bright light dims on and covers the table. Floods of light also are directed on the stage from the two portals. The flood from stage right should be a "cool" color, and the one from stage left "warm." If possible all lights should be kept off the walls of the room. (It may be possible, when this play is given by itself, to dispense with the curtain, so that the audience arriving will see the stage set and the table laid, though in indistinct darkness.)

Experience has shown that many companies have fallen into the practice of playing this play in a weird, lugubrious manner. Care should be taken that the conversation is normal and that after the "deaths" the play should pick up its tempo at once.

Scene: The dining room of the Bayard home. A long dining table is handsomely spread for Christmas dinner. The carver's place with a great turkey before it is at the right. Down left, by the proscenium arch, is a strange portal trimmed with garlands of fruits and flowers. Directly opposite, down right, is another portal hung with black velvet. The portals denote birth and death, respectively.

Along the rear wall, at the right, is a sideboard, in the center a fireplace with perhaps portrait of a man above it, and on the left a large door into the hall.

At the table there is a chair at each end and three chairs against the walls. The chair at the head of the table right should be high-backed and with arms.

All directions are given from the actor's right and left.

Enter LUCIA *from the hall. She inspects the table, touching here a knife and there a fork. She talks to a servant girl who is invisible to us.*

LUCIA. I reckon we're ready now, Gertrude. We won't ring the chimes today. I'll just call them myself. [*She goes into the hall and calls.*] Roderick. Mother Bayard. We're all ready. Come to dinner.

[*Enter* RODERICK *from the hall, pushing* MOTHER BAYARD *in a wheel chair, which he places at his left at the table.*]

MOTHER BAYARD. . . . and a new horse too, Roderick. I used to think that only the wicked owned two horses. A new horse and a new house and a new wife!

LUCIA. Here, Mother Bayard, you sit between us.

[LUCIA *ties a napkin around* MOTHER BAYARD'S *neck.* RODERICK *sits in chair right,* LUCIA *in chair left of table.*]

RODERICK. Well, Mother, how do you like it? Our first Christmas dinner in the new house, hey?

MOTHER BAYARD. Tz-Tz-Tz! I don't know what your dear father would say! [RODERICK *says a murmured grace and then begins to carve in pantomime the turkey.*] My dear Lucia, I can remember when there were still Indians on this very ground, and I wasn't a young girl either. I can remember when we had to cross the Mississippi on a new-made raft. I can remember when St. Louis and Kansas City were full of Indians.

LUCIA. Imagine that! What a wonderful day for our first Christmas dinner: a beautiful sunny morning, snow, a splendid sermon. Dr. McCarthy preaches a splendid sermon. I cried and cried.

RODERICK [*Extending an imaginary carving fork*]. Come now, what'll you have, Mother? A little sliver of white? [*He serves the turkey during the following speeches with the help of the imaginary servant.*]

LUCIA. Every least twig is wrapped around with ice. You almost never see that. [*Over her shoulder.*] Gertrude, I forgot the jelly. You know—on the top shelf.—Mother Bayard, I found your mother's gravy-boat while we were moving. What was her name, dear? What were all your names? You were . . . a . . . Genevieve Wainright. Now your mother——

MOTHER BAYARD [*As they eat*]. Yes, you must write it down somewhere. I was Genevieve Wainright. My mother was Faith Morrison. She was the daughter of a farmer in New Hampshire who was something of a blacksmith too. And she married young John Wainright——

LUCIA [*Memorizing on her fingers*]. Genevieve Wainright. Faith Morrison.

RODERICK. It's all down in a book somewhere upstairs. We have it all. All that kind of thing is very interesting. Come, Lucia, just a little wine. Mother, a little red wine for Christmas day. Full of iron. "Take a little wine for thy stomach's sake."

LUCIA. Really, I can't get used to wine! What would my father say? But I suppose it's all right.

[*Enter* COUSIN BRANDON *from the hall. He draws up a chair and takes his place by* LUCIA.]

COUSIN BRANDON [*Rubbing his hands*]. Well, well, I smell turkey. My dear cousins, I can't tell you how pleasant it is to be having Christmas dinner with you all. I've lived out there in Alaska so long without relatives. Let me see, how long have you had this new house, Roderick?

RODERICK. Why, it must be——

MOTHER BAYARD. Five years. It's five years, children. You should keep a diary. This is your sixth Christmas dinner here.

LUCIA. Think of that, Roderick. We feel as though we had lived here twenty years.

COUSIN BRANDON. At all events it still looks as good as new.

RODERICK [*Over his carving*]. What'll you have, Brandon, light or dark?—Frieda, fill up Cousin Brandon's glass.

LUCIA. Oh, dear, I can't get used to these wines. I don't know what my father'd say, I'm sure. What'll you have, Mother Bayard?

MOTHER BAYARD. Yes, I can remember when there were Indians on this very land.

LUCIA [*Softly*]. Mother Bayard hasn't been very well lately, Roderick.

[MOTHER BAYARD's *chair, without any visible propulsion, starts to draw away from the table, turns toward the right, and slowly goes toward the dark portal.*]

MOTHER BAYARD. My mother was a Faith Morrison. And in New Hampshire she married a young John Wainright, who was a Congregational minister. He saw her in his congregation one day . . .

LUCIA [*Rising and coming to center stage*]. Mother Bayard, hadn't you better lie down, dear?

MOTHER BAYARD. . . . and right in the middle of his sermon he said to himself: "I'll marry that girl." And he did, and I'm their daughter.

[RODERICK *rises, turns to right with concern.*]

LUCIA [*Looking after her with anxiety*]. Just a little nap, dear?

MOTHER BAYARD. I'm all right. Just go on with your dinner. [*Exit down right.*] I was ten, and I said to my brother——

[*A very slight pause, during which* RODERICK *sits and* LUCIA *returns to her seat. All three resume eating.*]

COUSIN BRANDON [*Genially*]. It's too bad it's such a cold dark day today. We almost need the lamps. I spoke to Major Lewis for a moment after church. His sciatica troubles him, but he does pretty well.

LUCIA [*Dabbing her eyes*]. I know Mother Bayard wouldn't want us to grieve for her on Christmas day, but I can't forget her sitting in her wheel chair right beside us, only a year ago. And she would be so glad to know our good news.

RODERICK. Now, now. It's Christmas. [*Formally.*] Cousin Brandon, a glass of wine with you, sir.

COUSIN BRANDON [*Half rising, lifting his glass gallantly*]. A glass of wine with you, sir.

LUCIA. Does the Major's sciatica cause him much pain?

COUSIN BRANDON. Some, perhaps. But you know his way. He says it'll be all the same in a hundred years.

LUCIA. Yes, he's a great philosopher.

RODERICK. His wife sends you a thousand thanks for her Christmas present.

LUCIA. I forget what I gave her— Oh, yes, the work-basket! [*Slight pause. Characters look toward left portal. Through the entrance of birth comes a* NURSE *holding in her arms an imaginary baby.* LUCIA *rushes toward it, the men following.*] O my darling baby! Who ever saw such a child! Quick, Nurse, a boy or a girl? A boy! Roderick, what shall we call him?

RODERICK. We'll call him Charles after your father and grandfather.

LUCIA. But there are no Charleses in the Bible, Roderick.

RODERICK. Of course, there are. Surely there are.

LUCIA. Roderick!—Very well, but he will always be Samuel to me.

COUSIN BRANDON. Really, Nurse, you've never seen such a child.

[NURSE *starts up stage to center door.*]

LUCIA. What miraculous hands he has! Really, they are the most beautiful hands in the world. All right, Nurse. Have a good nap, my darling child.

[*Exit* NURSE *in the hall.* LUCIA *and* COUSIN BRANDON *to seats.*]

RODERICK [*Calling through center door*]. Don't drop him, Nurse. Brandon and I need him in our firm. [*He returns to his chair and starts to carve.*] Lucia, a little white meat? Some stuffing? Cranberry sauce, anybody?

LUCIA [*Over her shoulder*]. Margaret, the stuffing is very good today.—Just a little, thank you.

RODERICK. Now something to wash it down. [*Half rising.*] Cousin Brandon, a glass of wine with you, sir. To the ladies, God bless them.

LUCIA. Thank you, kind sirs.

COUSIN BRANDON. Pity it's such an overcast day today. And no snow.

LUCIA. But the sermon was lovely. I cried and cried. Dr. Spaulding does preach such a splendid sermon.

RODERICK. I saw Major Lewis for a moment after church. He says his rheumatism comes and goes. His wife says she has something for Charles and will bring it over this afternoon.

[*Again they turn to portal down left. Enter* NURSE *as before.* LUCIA *rushes to her.* RODERICK *comes to center of stage table.* COUSIN BRANDON *does not rise.*]

LUCIA. O my lovely new baby! Really, it never occurred to me that it might be a girl. Why, Nurse, she's perfect.

RODERICK. Now call her what you choose. It's your turn.

LUCIA. Looloolooloo. Aië. Aië. Yes, this time I shall have my way. She shall be called Genevieve after your mother. Have a good nap, my treasure. [*Exit* NURSE *into the hall.*] Imagine! Sometime she'll be grown up and say, "Good morning, Mother. Good morning, Father."— Really, Cousin Brandon, you don't find a baby like that every day.

[*They return to their seats and again begin to eat.* RODERICK *carves as before, standing.*]

COUSIN BRANDON. *And* the new factory.

LUCIA. A new factory? Really? Roderick, I shall be very uncomfortable if we're going to turn out to be rich. I've been afraid of that for years.—However, we mustn't talk about such things on Christmas day. I'll just take a little piece of white meat, thank you. Roderick, Charles is destined for the ministry. I'm sure of it.

RODERICK. Woman, he's only twelve. Let him have a free mind. *We* want him in the firm, I don't mind saying. [*He sits. Definitely shows maturity.*] Anyway, no time passes as slowly as this when you're waiting for your urchins to grow up and settle down to business.

LUCIA. I don't want time to go any faster, thank you. I love the children just as they are.—Really, Roderick, you know what the doctor said: One glass a meal. No, Margaret, that will be all.

RODERICK [*Glass in hand*]. Now I wonder what's the matter with me.

LUCIA. Roderick, do be reasonable.

RODERICK [*Rises, takes a few steps right, with gallant irony*]. But, my dear, statistics show that we steady, moderate drinkers . . .

LUCIA [*Rises, rushes to center below table*]. Roderick! My dear! What . . . ?

RODERICK [*Returns to his seat with a frightened look of relief; now definitely older*]. Well, it's fine to be back at table with you again. [LUCIA *returns to her seat.*] How many good Christmas dinners have I had to miss upstairs? And to be back at a fine bright one, too.

LUCIA. O my dear, you gave us a very alarming time! Here's your glass of milk.—Josephine, bring Mr. Bayard his medicine from the cupboard in the library.

RODERICK. At all events, now that I'm better I'm going to start doing something about the house.

LUCIA. Roderick! You're not going to change the house?

RODERICK. Only touch it up here and there. It looks a hundred years old.

[CHARLES *enters casually from the hall.*]

CHARLES. It's a great blowy morning, Mother. The wind comes over the hill like a lot of cannon. [*He kisses his mother's hair.*]

LUCIA. Charles, you carve the turkey, dear. Your father's not well.

RODERICK. But—but not yet.

CHARLES. You always said you hated carving.

[CHARLES *gets a chair from right wall and puts it right end of table where* MOTHER BAYARD *was.* RODERICK *sits.* CHARLES *takes his father's former place at end of table.* CHARLES, *sitting, begins to carve.*]

LUCIA [*Showing her years*]. And such a good sermon. I cried and cried. Mother Bayard loved a good sermon so. And she used to sing the Christmas hymns all around the year. Oh, dear, oh, dear, I've been thinking of her all morning!

CHARLES. Sh, Mother. It's Christmas day. You mustn't think of such things.—You mustn't be depressed.

LUCIA. But sad things aren't the same as depressing things. I must be getting old: I like them.

CHARLES. Uncle Brandon, you haven't anything to eat. Pass his plate, Hilda . . . and some cranberry sauce . . .

[*Enter* GENEVIEVE *from the hall.*]

GENEVIEVE. It's glorious. [*Kisses father's temple, gets chair and sits center between her father and* COUSIN BRANDON.] Every least twig is wrapped around with ice. You almost never see that.

LUCIA. Did you have time to deliver those presents after church, Genevieve?

GENEVIEVE. Yes, Mama. Old Mrs. Lewis sends you a thousand thanks for hers. It was just what she wanted, she said. Give me lots, Charles, lots.

RODERICK. Statistics, ladies and gentlemen, show that we steady, moderate——

CHARLES. How about a little skating this afternoon, Father?

RODERICK. I'll live till I'm ninety. [*Rising and starting toward right portal.*]

LUCIA. I really don't think he ought to go skating.

RODERICK [*At the very portal, suddenly astonished*]. Yes, but . . . but . . . not yet! [*Exit down right.*]

LUCIA [*Dabbing her eyes*]. He was so young and so clever, Cousin Brandon. [*Raising her voice for* COUSIN BRANDON'S *deafness.*] I say he was so young and so clever.—Never forget your father, children. He was a good man.—Well, he wouldn't want us to grieve for him today.

CHARLES. White or dark, Genevieve? Just another sliver, Mother?

LUCIA [*Drawing on her shawl*]. I can remember our first Christmas dinner in this house, Genevieve. Twenty-five years ago today. Mother Bayard was sitting here in her wheel chair. She could remember when Indians lived on this very spot and when she had to cross the river on a new-made raft.

CHARLES. She couldn't have, Mother.

GENEVIEVE. That can't be true.

LUCIA. It certainly was true—even I can remember when there was only one paved street. We were very happy to walk on boards. [*Louder, to* COUSIN BRANDON.] We can remember when there were no sidewalks, can't we, Cousin Brandon?

COUSIN BRANDON [*Delighted*]. Oh, yes! And those were the days.

CHARLES and GENEVIEVE [*Sotto voce. This is a family refrain*]. Those were the days.

LUCIA. . . . and the ball last night, Genevieve? Did you have a nice time? I hope you didn't *waltz*, dear. I think a girl in our position ought to set an example. Did Charles keep an eye on you?

GENEVIEVE. He had none left. They were all on Leonora Banning. He can't conceal it any longer, Mother. I think he's engaged to marry Leonora Banning.

CHARLES. I'm not engaged to marry anyone.

LUCIA. Well, she's very pretty.

GENEVIEVE. I shall never marry, Mother—I shall sit in this house beside you forever, as though life were one long, happy Christmas dinner.

LUCIA. O my child, you mustn't say such things!

GENEVIEVE [*Playfully*]. You don't want me? You don't want me? [LUCIA *bursts into tears.* GENEVIEVE *rises and goes to her.*] Why, Mother, how silly you are! There's nothing sad about that —what could possibly be sad about that?

LUCIA [*Drying her eyes*]. Forgive me. I'm just unpredictable, that's all.

[CHARLES *goes to the door and leads in* LEONORA BANNING *from the hall.*]

CHARLES. Leonora!

LEONORA. Good morning, Mother Bayard. [LUCIA *rises and greets* LEONORA *near door.* COUSIN BRANDON *also rises.*] Good morning, everybody. Mother Bayard, you sit here by Charles. [*She helps her into chair formerly occupied by* RODERICK. COUSIN BRANDON *sits in center chair.* GENEVIEVE *sits on his left, and* LEONORA *sits at foot of the table.*] It's really a splendid Christmas day today.

CHARLES. Little white meat? Genevieve, Mother, Leonora?

LEONORA. Every least twig is encircled with ice.—You never see that.

CHARLES [*Shouting*]. Uncle Brandon, another?—Rogers, fill my uncle's glass.

LUCIA [*To* CHARLES]. Do what your father used to do. It would please Cousin Brandon so. You know—[*pretending to raise a glass*] "Uncle Brandon, a glass of wine——"

CHARLES [*Rising*]. Uncle Brandon, a glass of wine with you, sir.

COUSIN BRANDON [*Not rising*]. A glass of wine with you, sir. To the ladies, God bless them every one.

THE LADIES. Thank you, kind sirs.

GENEVIEVE. And if I go to Germany for my music I promise to be back for Christmas. I wouldn't miss that.

LUCIA. I hate to think of you over there all alone in those strange pensions.

GENEVIEVE. But, darling, the time will pass so fast that you'll hardly know I'm gone. I'll be back in the twinkling of an eye.

[LEONORA *looks toward left portal, rises, takes several steps.* NURSE *enters, with baby, down left.*]

LEONORA. Oh, what an angel! The darlingest baby in the world. Do let me hold it, Nurse. [*The* NURSE *resolutely has been crossing the stage and now exits at the right portal.* LEONORA *follows.*] Oh, I did love it so.

[CHARLES *rises, puts his arm around his wife, whispering, and slowly leads her back to her chair.*]

GENEVIEVE [*To her mother as the other two cross—softly*]. Isn't there anything I can do?

LUCIA [*Raises her eyebrows, ruefully*]. No, dear. Only time, only the passing of time can help in these things. [CHARLES *returns to his seat. Slight pause.*] Don't you think we could ask Cousin Ermengarde to come and live with us here? There's plenty for everyone and there's no reason why she should go on teaching the First Grade for ever and ever. She wouldn't be in the way, would she, Charles?

CHARLES. No, I think it would be fine.—A little more potato and gravy, anybody? A little more turkey, Mother?

[COUSIN BRANDON *rises and starts slowly toward the dark portal.* LUCIA *rises and stands for a moment with her face in her hands.*]

COUSIN BRANDON [*Muttering*]. It was great to be in Alaska in those days . . .

GENEVIEVE [*Half rising, and gazing at her mother in fear*]. Mother, what is . . . ?

LUCIA [*Hurriedly*]. Hush, my dear. It will pass.—Hold fast to your music, you know. [*As* GENEVIEVE *starts toward her.*] No, no. I want to be alone for a few minutes.

CHARLES. If the Republicans collected all their votes instead of going off into cliques among themselves, they might prevent his getting a second term.

[LUCIA *turns and starts after* COUSIN BRANDON *toward the right.*]

GENEVIEVE. Charles, Mother doesn't tell us, but she hasn't been very well these days.

CHARLES. Come, Mother, we'll go to Florida for a few weeks. [GENEVIEVE *rushes toward her mother.*]

[*Exit* COUSIN BRANDON, *right.*]

LUCIA [*By the portal, smiling at* GENEVIEVE *and waving her hand*]. Don't be foolish. Don't grieve. [*She clasps her hands under her chin; her lips move, whispering; she walks serenely through the portal.*]

GENEVIEVE [*Stares after her*]. But what will I do? What's left for me to do? [*She returns to her seat.*]

[*At the same moment the nurse, with two babies, enters from the left.* LEONORA *rushes to them.*]

LEONORA. O my darlings . . . twins . . . Charles, aren't they glorious! Look at them. Look at them.

[CHARLES *crosses to down left.*]

GENEVIEVE [*Sinks down on the table, her face buried in her arms*]. But what will I do? What's left for me to do?

CHARLES [*Bending over the basket*]. Which is which?

LEONORA. I feel as though I were the first mother who ever had twins.—Look at them now!—But why wasn't Mother Bayard allowed to stay and see them!

GENEVIEVE [*Rising suddenly distraught, loudly*]. I don't want to go on. I can't bear it.

CHARLES [*Goes to her quickly. He whispers to her earnestly taking both her hands*]. But, Genevieve, Genevieve!

How frightfully Mother would feel to think that . . . Genevieve!

GENEVIEVE [*Wildly*]. I never told her how wonderful she was. We all treated her as though she were just a friend in the house. I thought she'd be here forever. [*Sits.*]

LEONORA [*Timidly*]. Genevieve darling, do come one minute and hold my babies' hands. [GENEVIEVE *collects herself and goes over to the* NURSE. *She smiles brokenly into the basket.*] We shall call the girl Lucia after her grandmother—will that please you? Do just see what adorable little hands they have.

GENEVIEVE. They are wonderful, Leonora.

LEONORA. Give him your finger, darling. Just let him hold it.

CHARLES. And we'll call the boy Samuel.—Well, now everybody come and finish your dinners. [*The women take their places.* CHARLES *calls out into the hall.*] Don't drop them, Nurse; at least don't drop the boy. We need him in the firm. [*He returns to his place.*]

LEONORA. Some day they'll be big. Imagine! They'll come in and say, "Hello, Mother!"

CHARLES [*Now forty, dignified*]. Come, a little wine, Leonora, Genevieve? Full of iron. Eduardo, fill the ladies' glasses. It certainly is a keen, cold morning. I used to go skating with Father on mornings like this and Mother would come back from church saying——

GENEVIEVE [*Dreamily*]. I know—saying, "Such a splendid sermon. I cried and cried."

LEONORA. Why did she cry, dear?

GENEVIEVE. That generation all cried at sermons. It was their way.

LEONORA. Really, Genevieve?

GENEVIEVE. They had had to go since they were children and I suppose sermons reminded them of their fathers and mothers, just as Christmas dinners do us. Especially in an old house like this.

LEONORA. It really is pretty old, Charles. And so ugly, with all that iron-work filigree and that dreadful cupola.

GENEVIEVE. Charles! You aren't going to change the house!

CHARLES. No, no. I won't give up the house, but great heavens! it's fifty years old. This spring we'll remove the cupola and build a new wing toward the tennis courts.

[*From now on* GENEVIEVE *is seen to change. She sits up more straightly. The corners of her mouth become fixed. She becomes a forthright and slightly disillusioned spinster.* CHARLES *becomes the plain business man and a little pompous.*]

LEONORA. And then couldn't we ask your dear old Cousin Ermengarde to come and live with us? She's really the self-effacing kind.

CHARLES. Ask her now. Take her out of the First Grade.

GENEVIEVE. We only seem to think of it on Christmas day with her Christmas card staring us in the face.

[*Enter left,* NURSE *and baby.*]

LEONORA [*Rising and crossing down left*]. Another boy! Another boy! Here's a Roderick for you at last.

CHARLES [*Crossing to down left*]. Roderick Brandon Bayard. A regular little fighter.

LEONORA. Good-by, darling. Don't grow up too fast. Yes, yes. Aië, aië, aië—stay just as you are.—Thank you, Nurse.

GENEVIEVE [*Who has not left the table, repeats drily*]. Stay just as you are.

[*Exit* NURSE *into hall.* CHARLES *and* LEONORA *return to their places.*]

LEONORA. Now I have three children. One, two, three. Two boys and a girl. I'm collecting them. It's very exciting. [*Over her shoulder.*] What, Hilda? Oh, Cousin Ermengarde's come! Come in, Cousin.

[*She goes to the hall door and welcomes* COUSIN ERMENGARDE, *already an elderly woman.*]

ERMENGARDE [*Shyly*]. It's such a pleasure to be with you all.

CHARLES [*Pulling out the center chair for her*]. The twins have taken a great fancy to you already, Cousin.

LEONORA. The baby went to her at once.

CHARLES. Exactly how are we related, Cousin Ermengarde?—There, Genevieve, that's your specialty.—First a little more turkey and stuffing, Mother? Cranberry sauce, anybody?

GENEVIEVE. I can work it out: Grandmother Bayard was your . . .

ERMENGARDE. Your Grandmother Bayard was a second cousin of my Grandmother Haskins through the Wainrights.

CHARLES. Well, it's all in a book somewhere upstairs. All that kind of thing is awfully interesting.

GENEVIEVE. Nonsense. There are no such books. I collect my notes off gravestones, and you have to scrape a good deal of moss—let me tell you—to find one great-grandparent.

CHARLES. There's a story that my Grandmother Bayard crossed the Mississippi on a raft before there were any bridges or ferry-boats. She died before Genevieve or I were born. Time certainly goes very fast in a great new country like this. Have some more cranberry sauce, Cousin Ermengarde.

ERMENGARDE [*Timidly*]. Well, time must be passing very slowly in Europe with this dreadful, dreadful war going on.

CHARLES. Perhaps an occasional war isn't so bad after all. It clears up a lot of poisons that collect in nations. It's like a boil.

ERMENGARDE. Oh, dear, oh, dear!

CHARLES [*With relish*]. Yes, it's like a boil.—Ho! ho! Here are your twins.

[*The twins appear at the hall door.* SAM *is wearing the uniform of an ensign or lieutenant.* LUCIA *is fussing over some detail on it.*]

LUCIA. Isn't he wonderful in it, Mother?

CHARLES. Let's get a look at you.

SAM. Mother, don't let Roderick fool with my stamp album while I'm gone. [*Crosses to right.*]

LEONORA. Now, Sam, do write a letter once in a while. Do be a good boy about that, mind.

SAM. You might send some of those cakes of yours once in a while, Cousin Ermengarde.

[LEONORA *rises.*]

ERMENGARDE [*In a flutter*]. I certainly will, my dear boy.

[LEONORA *crosses to center;* SAM *crosses down right.*]

CHARLES [*Rising and facing* SAM]. If you need any money, we have agents in Paris and London, remember.

[LEONORA *crossing down right.*]

LEONORA. Do be a good boy, Sam.

SAM. Well, good-by . . .

[SAM *kisses his mother without sentimentality and goes out briskly through the dark portal. They all return to their seats,* LUCIA *sitting at her father's left.*]

ERMENGARDE [*In a low, constrained voice, making conversation*]. I spoke to Mrs. Fairchild for a moment coming out of church. Her rheumatism's a little better, she says. She sends you her warmest thanks for the Christmas present. The work-basket, wasn't it?—[*Slight pause.*] It was an admirable sermon. And our stained-glass window looked so beautiful, Leonora, so beautiful. Everybody spoke of it and so affectionately of Sammy. [LEONORA's *hand goes to her mouth.*] Forgive me, Leonora, but it's better to speak of him than not to speak of him when we're all thinking of him so hard.

LEONORA [*Rising, in anguish*]. He was a mere boy. He was a mere boy, Charles.

CHARLES. My dear, my dear.

LEONORA. I want to tell him how wonderful he was. We let him go so casually. I want to tell him how we all feel about him.—Forgive me, let me walk about a minute.—Yes, of course, Ermengarde—it's best to speak of him.

LUCIA [*In a low voice to* GENEVIEVE]. Isn't there anything I can do?

GENEVIEVE. No, no. Only time, only the passing of time can help in these things.

[LEONORA, *straying about the room, finds herself near the door to the hall at the moment that her son* RODERICK *enters. He links his arm with hers and leads her back to the table. He looks up and sees the family's dejection.*]

RODERICK. What's the matter, anyway? What are you all so glum about? The skating was fine today.

CHARLES. Roderick, I have something to say to you.

RODERICK [*Standing below his mother's chair*]. Everybody was there. Lucia skated in the corners with Dan Creighton the whole time. When'll it be, Lucia, when'll it be?

LUCIA. I don't know what you mean.

RODERICK. Lucia's leaving us soon, Mother. Dan Creighton, of all people.

CHARLES [*Ominously*]. Young man, I have something to say to you.

RODERICK. Yes, Father.

CHARLES. Is it true, Roderick, that you made yourself conspicuous last night at the Country Club—at a Christmas Eve dance, too?

LEONORA. Not now, Charles, I beg of of you. This is Christmas dinner.

RODERICK [*Loudly*]. No, I didn't.

LUCIA. Really, Father, he didn't. It was that dreadful Johnny Lewis.

CHARLES. I don't want to hear about Johnny Lewis. I want to know whether a son of mine——

LEONORA. Charles, I beg of you——

CHARLES. The first family of this city!

RODERICK [*Crossing below table to left center*]. I hate this town and everything about it. I always did.

CHARLES. You behaved like a spoiled puppy, sir, an ill-bred spoiled puppy.

RODERICK. What did I do? What did I do that was wrong?

CHARLES [*Rising*]. You were drunk and you were rude to the daughters of my best friends.

GENEVIEVE [*Striking the table*]. Nothing in the world deserves an ugly scene like this. Charles, I'm ashamed of you.

RODERICK. Great God, you gotta get drunk in this town to forget how dull it is. Time passes so slowly here that it stands still, that's what's the trouble. [*Turns and walks toward the hall door.*]

CHARLES. Well, young man, we can employ your time. You will leave the university and you will come into the Bayard factory on January second.

RODERICK [*At the door into the hall*]. I have better things to do than to go into your old factory. I'm going somewhere where time passes, my God! [*He goes out into the hall.*]

LEONORA [*Rising and rushing to door*]. Roderick, Roderick, come here just a moment.—Charles, where can he go?

LUCIA [*Rising*]. Sh, Mother. He'll come back. [*She leads her mother back to chair, then starts for the hall door.*] Now I have to go upstairs and pack my trunk.

LEONORA. I won't have any children left! [*Sits.*]

LUCIA [*From the door*]. Sh, Mother. He'll come back. He's only gone to California or somewhere.—Cousin Ermengarde has done most of my packing—thanks a thousand times, Cousin Ermengarde. [*She kisses her mother as an afterthought.*] I won't be long. [*She runs out into the hall.*]

ERMENGARDE [*Cheerfully*]. It's a very beautiful day. On the way home from church I stopped and saw Mrs. Foster a moment. Her arthritis comes and goes.

LEONORA. Is she actually in pain, dear?

ERMENGARDE. Oh, she says it'll all be the same in a hundred years!

LEONORA. Yes, she's a brave little stoic.

CHARLES. Come now, a little white meat, Mother?—Mary, pass my cousin's plate.

LEONORA. What is it, Mary?—Oh, here's a telegram from them in Paris! "Love and Christmas greetings to all." I told them we'd be eating some of their wedding cake and thinking about them today. It seems to be all decided that they will settle down in the East, Ermengarde. I can't even have my daughter for a neighbor. They hope to build before long somewhere on the shore north of New York.

GENEVIEVE. There is no shore north of New York.

LEONORA. Well, east or west or whatever it is.

[*Pause.*]

CHARLES [*Now sixty years old*]. My, what a dark day. [*Pause.*] How slowly time passes without any young people in the house.

LEONORA. I have three children somewhere.

CHARLES [*Blunderingly offering comfort*]. Well, one of them gave his life for his country.

LEONORA [*Sadly*]. And one of them selling aluminum in China.

GENEVIEVE [*Slowly working herself up to a hysterical crisis*]. I can stand everything but this terrible soot everywhere. We should have moved long ago. We're surrounded by factories. We have to change the window curtains every week.

LEONORA. Why, Genevieve!

GENEVIEVE. I can't stand it. [*Rising.*] I can't stand it any more. I'm going abroad. It's not only the soot that comes through the very walls of this house; it's the *thoughts*, it's the thought of what has been and what might have been here. And the feeling about this house of the years *grinding away*. My mother died yesterday—not twenty-five years ago. Oh, I'm going to live and die abroad! [CHARLES *rises.*] Yes, I'm going to be the American old maid living and dying in a pension in Munich or Florence.

ERMENGARDE. Genevieve, you're tired.

CHARLES. Come, Genevieve, take a good drink of cold water. Mary, open the window a minute.

GENEVIEVE. I'm sorry. I'm sorry.

[*She hurries tearfully out into the hall.* CHARLES *sits.*]

ERMENGARDE. Dear Genevieve will come back to us, I think. [*She rises and starts toward the dark portal.*] You should have been out today, Leonora. It was one of those days when everything was encircled with ice. Very pretty, indeed.

CHARLES. Leonora, I used to go skating with Father on mornings like this.—I wish I felt a little better. [CHARLES *rises and starts following* ERMENGARDE *toward the right.*]

LEONORA [*Rising*]. What! Have I got two invalids on my hands at once? Now, Cousin Ermengarde, you must get better and help me nurse Charles.

ERMENGARDE. I'll do my best. [ERMENGARDE *turns at the very portal and comes back to the table.*]

CHARLES. Well, Leonora, I'll do what you ask. I'll write the puppy a letter of forgiveness and apology. It's Christmas day. I'll cable it. That's what I'll do. [*He goes out the portal right. Slight pause.*]

LEONORA [*Drying her eyes*]. Ermengarde, it's such a comfort having you here with me. [*Sits in place at left of* ERMENGARDE, *formerly occupied by* GENEVIEVE.] Mary, I really can't eat anything. Well, perhaps, a sliver of white meat.

ERMENGARDE [*Very old*]. I spoke to Mrs. Keene for a moment coming out of church. She asked after the young people.—At church I felt very proud sitting under our windows, Leonora, and our brass tablets. The Bayard aisle—it's a regular Bayard aisle and I love it.

LEONORA. Ermengarde, would you be very angry with me if I went and stayed with the young people a little this spring?

ERMENGARDE. Why, no. I know how badly they want you and need you. Especially now that they're about to build a new house.

LEONORA. You wouldn't be angry? This house is yours as long as you want it, remember.

ERMENGARDE. I don't see why the rest of you dislike it. I like it more than I can say.

LEONORA. I won't be long. I'll be back in no time and we can have some more of our readings-aloud in the evening. [*She kisses her and goes into the hall.* ERMENGARDE, *left alone, eats slowly and talks to* MARY.]

ERMENGARDE. Really, Mary, I'll change my mind. If you'll ask Bertha to be good enough to make me a little eggnog. A dear little eggnog.—Such a nice letter this morning from Mrs. Bayard, Mary. Such a nice letter. They're having their first Christmas dinner in the new house. They must be very happy. They call her Mother Bayard, she says, as though she were an old lady. And she says she finds it more comfortable to come and go in a wheel chair.—Such a dear letter. . . . And, Mary, I can tell you a secret. It's still a great secret, mind! They're expecting a grandchild. Isn't that good news! Now I'll read a little. [*She props a book up before her, still dipping a spoon into a custard from time to time. She grows from very old to immensely old. She sighs. She finds a cane beside her, and totters out of the right portal, murmuring:*] Dear little Roderick and little Lucia.

[*The audience gazes for a space of time at the table before the lights slowly dim out.*]

Curtain

Tennessee Williams

✻ 1914-

Thomas Lanier Williams was born in Columbus, Mississippi. At the age of 12 he was taken to live in St. Louis, and the shock of the uprooting and the frustrations of adjustment to a new milieu furnished him with the subject matter for THE GLASS MENAGERIE *as well as several of his earlier one-act plays. After a few years he was permitted to return to Mississippi, where he remained until he became an undergraduate at the University of Iowa. After graduation, determined to seek a career as a writer, he changed his name to Tennessee to mark his break with his former life, spent several years at odd jobs, and received a Rockefeller Fellowship during which he wrote his first play to be commercially produced. This was* BATTLE OF ANGELS, *which failed in 1940 in Boston but which brought him to the attention of Metro-Goldwyn-Mayer, by whom he was employed for six months, just long enough to save the money which permitted him to write* THE GLASS MENAGERIE. *When this was produced in New York in 1945, it was received with high acclaim, and critics and audiences realized that an important new talent had entered the American theatre.*

In the fashion typical of all the heirs of Eugene O'Neill, Williams has continued to seek out the most violent and intense conflicts in American life and to write of them in unconventional ways. He uses the stage and its physical properties with imaginative freedom, and makes great demands on actors and directors. These demands have inspired some of the most memorable performances of modern times.

But as a writer he is basically a poet, and he has done much to develop the possibilities for poetic expression in a theatre that was created as a home for relentless realism. His language is often startling and fresh, rich with imagery and literary echoes; yet his poetry is always dramatic, projected into action and character, and made visual in the settings and properties of the production. With Arthur Miller and William Inge he has given new stature to the American drama of the mid-twentieth century, and his influence on other playwrights both in America and abroad has been incalculable.

The Glass Menageric

Characters

THE MOTHER
HER SON
HER DAUGHTER
THE GENTLEMAN CALLER

Scene: An alley in St. Louis.

PART I. Preparation for a Gentleman Caller.

PART II. The Gentleman Calls.

TIME—Now and the Past.

AUTHOR'S PRODUCTION NOTES

Being a "memory play," *The Glass Menagerie* can be presented with unusual freedom of convention. Because of its considerably delicate or tenuous material, atmospheric touches and subtleties of direction play a particularly important part. Expressionism and all other unconventional techniques in drama have only one valid aim, and that is a closer approach to truth. When a play employs unconventional techniques, it is not, or certainly shouldn't be, trying to escape its responsibility of dealing with reality, or interpreting experience, but is actually or should be attempting to find a closer approach, a more penetrating and vivid expression of things as they are. The straight realistic play with its genuine frigidaire and authentic ice-cubes, its characters that speak exactly as its audience speaks, corresponds to the academic landscape and has the same virtue of a photographic likeness. Everyone should know nowadays the unimportance of the photographic in art: that truth, life, or reality is an organic thing which the poetic imagination can represent or suggest, in essence, only through transformation, through changing into other forms than those which were merely present in appearance.

These remarks are not meant as a preface only to this particular play. They have to do with a conception of a new, plastic theatre which must take the place of the exhausted theatre of realistic conventions if the theatre is to resume vitality as a part of our culture.

The Music

Another extra-literary accent in this play is provided by the use of music. A single recurring tune, "The Glass Menagerie," is used to give emotional emphasis to suitable passages. This tune is like circus music, not when you are on the grounds or in the immediate vicinity of the parade, but when you are at some distance and very likely thinking of something else. It seems under those circumstances to continue almost interminably and it weaves in and out of your preoccupied consciousness; then it is the lightest, most delicate music in the world and perhaps the saddest. It expresses the surface vivacity of life with the underlying strain of immutable and inexpressible sorrow. When you look at a piece of delicately spun glass you think of two things: how beautiful it is and how easily it can be broken. Both of those ideas should be woven into the recurring tune, which dips in and out of the play as if it were carried on a wind that changes. It serves as a thread of connection and allusion between the narrator with his separate point in time and space and the subject of his story. Between each episode it returns as reference to the emotion, nostalgia, which is the first condition of the play. It is primarily Laura's music and therefore comes out most clearly when the play focuses upon her and the lovely fragility of glass which is her image.

The Lighting

The lighting in the play is not realistic. In keeping with the atmosphere of memory, the stage is dim. Shafts of light are focused on selected areas of actors, sometimes in contradistinction to what is the apparent center. For instance, in the quarrel scene between Tom and Amanda, in which Laura has no active part, the clearest pool of light is on her figure. This is also true of the supper scene, when her silent figure on the sofa should remain the visual center. The light upon Laura should be distinct from the others, having a peculiar pristine clarity such as light used in early religious portraits of female saints or madonnas. A certain correspondence to light in religious paintings, such as El Greco's, where the figures are radiant in atmosphere that is relatively dusky, could be effectively used throughout the play. (It will also permit a more effective use of the screen.) A free, imaginative use of light can be of enormous value in giving a mobile, plastic quality to plays of a more or less static nature.

Notes on the Characters

AMANDA WINGFIELD (the mother): A little woman of great but confused vitality, clinging frantically to another time and place. Her characterization must be carefully created, not copied from type. She is not paranoiac, but her life is paranoia. There is much to admire in Amanda, and as much to love and pity as there is to laugh at. Certainly she has endurance and a kind of heroism, and though her foolishness makes her unwittingly cruel at times, there is tenderness in her slight person.

LAURA WINGFIELD (her daughter): Amanda, having failed to establish contact with reality, continues to live vitally in her illusions, but Laura's situation is even graver. A childhood illness had left her crippled, one leg slightly shorter than the other, and held in a brace. This defect need not be more than suggested on the stage. Stemming from this, Laura's separation increases till she is like a piece of her own glass collection, too exquisitely fragile to move from the shelf.

TOM WINGFIELD (her son): And the narrator of the play. A poet with a job in a warehouse. His nature is not remorseless, but to escape from a trap he has to act without pity.

JIM O'CONNOR (the gentleman caller): A nice, ordinary, young man.

T. W.

ACT I SCENE 1

The WINGFIELD *apartment is in the rear of the building, one of those vast hive-like conglomerations of cellular living units that flower as warty growths in overcrowded urban centers of lower middle-class population and are symptomatic of the impulse of this largest and fundamentally enslaved section of American society to avoid fluidity and differentiation and to exist and function as one interfused mass of automatism. The apartment faces an alley and is entered by a fire-escape, a structure whose name is a touch of accidental poetic truth, for all of these huge buildings are always burning with the slow and implacable fires of human desperation. The fire-escape is included in the set—that is, the landing of it and steps descending from it. (Note that the stage left alley may be entirely omitted, since it is never used except for* TOM*'s first entrance, which can take place stage right.) The scene is memory and is therefore nonrealistic. Memory takes a lot of poetic license. It omits some details, others are exaggerated, according to the emotional value of the articles it touches, for memory is seated predominantly in the heart. The interior is therefore rather dim and poetic. (As soon as the house lights dim, dance-hall music heard onstage right. Old popular music of, say, 1915–1920 period. This continues until* TOM *is at fire-escape landing, having lighted cigarette, and begins speaking.)*

AT RISE: *At the rise of the house curtain, the audience is faced with the dark, grim rear wall of the* WINGFIELD *tenement. (The stage set proper is screened out by a gauze curtain, which suggests the front part, outside, of the building.) This building, which runs parallel to the footlights, is flanked on both sides by dark, narrow alleys which run into murky canyons of tangled clotheslines, garbage cans and the sinister lattice-work of neighboring fire-escapes. (The alleys are actually in darkness, and the objects just mentioned are not visible.) It is up and down these side alleys that exterior entrances and exits are made, during the play. At the end of* TOM*'s opening commentary, the dark tenement wall slowly reveals (by means of a transparency) the interior of the ground-floor* WINGFIELD *apartment. (Gauze curtain, which* *suggests front part of building, rises on the interior set.) Downstage is the living room, which also serves as a sleeping room for* LAURA, *the day-bed unfolding to make her bed. Just above this is a small stool or table on which is a telephone. Upstage, center, and divided by a wide arch or second proscenium with transparent faded portieres (or second curtain, "second curtain" is actually the inner gauze curtain between the living room and the dining room, which is upstage of it), is the dining room. In an old-fashioned what-not in the living room are seen scores of transparent glass animals. A blown-up photograph of the father hangs on the wall of the living room, facing the audience, to the left of the archway. It is the face of a very handsome young man in a doughboy's First World War cap. He is gallantly smiling, ineluctably smiling, as if to say, "I will be smiling forever." (Note that all that is essential in connection with dance-hall is that the window be shown lighting lower part of alley. It is not necessary to show any considerable part of dance-hall.) The audience hears and sees the opening scene in the dining room through both the transparent fourth wall (this is the gauze curtain which suggests outside of building) of the building and the transparent gauze portieres of the dining-room arch. It is during this revealing scene that the fourth wall slowly ascends, out of sight. This transparent exterior wall is not brought down again until the very end of the play, during* TOM*'s final speech. The narrator is an undisguised convention of the play. He takes whatever license with dramatic convention as is convenient to his purposes.*

TOM *enters dressed as a merchant sailor from alley, stage left (i.e., stage right if left alley is omitted), and strolls across the front of the stage to the fire-escape. (*TOM *may lean against grillwork of this as he lights cigarette.) There he stops and lights a cigarette. He addresses the audience.*

TOM. I have tricks in my pocket—I have things up my sleeve—but I am the opposite of the stage magician. He gives you illusion that has the appearance of truth. I give you truth in the pleasant disguise of illusion. I take you back to an alley in St. Louis. The time that quaint period when the huge middle class of America was matriculating from a school for the blind. Their eyes had failed them, or they had failed their eyes, and so they were having their fingers pressed forcibly down on the fiery Braille alphabet of a dissolving economy.—In Spain there was revolution.—Here there was only shouting and confusion and labor disturbances, sometimes violent, in otherwise peaceful cities such as Cleveland—Chicago—Detroit. . . . That is the social background of this play. . . . The play is memory. [*Music.*] Being a memory play, it is dimly lighted, it is sentimental, it is not realistic.—In memory everything seems to happen to music.—That explains the fiddle in the wings. I am the narrator of the play, and also a character in it. The other characters in the play are my mother, Amanda, my sister, Laura, and a gentleman caller who appears in the final scenes. He is the most realistic character in the play, being an emissary from a world that we were somehow set apart from.—But having a poet's weakness for symbols, I am using this character as a symbol—as the long-delayed but always expected something that we live for.—There is a fifth character who doesn't appear other than in a photograph hanging on the wall. When you see the picture of this grinning gentleman, please remember this is our father who left us a long time ago. He was a telephone man who fell in love with long distance—so he gave up his job with the telephone company and skipped the light fantastic out of town. . . . The last we heard of him was a picture postcard from the Pacific coast of Mexico, containing a message of two words—"Hello—Good-by!" and no address. [*Lights up in dining room.* TOM *exits right. He goes off down-stage, takes off his sailor overcoat and skull-fitting knitted cap and remains off-stage by dining-room right door for his entrance cue.* AMANDA'S *voice becomes audible through the portieres—i.e., gauze curtains separating dining room from living room.* AMANDA *and* LAURA *are seated at a drop-leaf table.* AMANDA *is sitting in center chair and* LAURA *in left chair. Eating is indicated by gestures without food or utensils.* AMANDA *faces the audience. The interior of the dining room has lit up softly and through the scrim—gauze curtains—we see* AMANDA *and* LAURA *seated at the table in the up-stage area.*]

AMANDA. You know, Laura, I had the funniest experience in church last Sunday. The church was crowded except for one pew way down front and in that was just one little woman. I smiled very sweetly at her and said, "Excuse me, would you mind if I shared this pew?" "I certainly would," she said, "this space is rented." Do you know that is the first time that I ever knew that the Lord rented space. [*Dining-room gauze curtains open automatically.*] These Northern Episcopalians! I can understand the Southern Episcopalians, but these Northern ones, no. [TOM *enters dining room right, slips over to table and sits in chair right.*] Honey, don't push your food with your fingers. If you have to push your food with something, the thing to use is a crust of bread. You must chew your food. Animals have secretions in their stomachs which enable them to digest their food without mastication, but human beings must chew their food before they swallow it down, and chew, chew. Oh, eat leisurely. Eat leisurely. A well-cooked meal has many delicate flavors that have to be held in the mouth for appreciation, not just gulped down. Oh, chew, chew—chew! [*At this point the scrim curtain—if the director decides to use it—the one suggesting exterior wall, rises here and does not come down again until just before the end of the play.*] Don't you want to give your salivary glands a chance to function?

TOM. Mother, I haven't enjoyed one bite of my dinner because of your constant directions on how to eat it. It's you that makes me hurry through my meals with your hawk-like attention to every bite I take. It's disgusting—all this discussion of animals' secretion—salivary glands—mastication! [*Comes down to armchair in living room right, lights cigarette.*]

AMANDA. Temperament like a Metropolitan star! You're not excused from this table.

TOM. I'm getting a cigarette.

AMANDA. You smoke too much.

LAURA [*Rising*]. Mother, I'll bring in the coffee.

AMANDA. No, no, no, no. You sit down. I'm going to be the colored boy today and you're going to be the lady.

LAURA. I'm already up.

AMANDA. Resume your seat. Resume your seat. You keep yourself fresh and pretty for the gentlemen callers. [LAURA *sits.*]

LAURA. I'm not expecting any gentlemen callers.

AMANDA [*Who has been gathering dishes from table and loading them on tray*]. Well, the nice thing about them is they come when they're least expected. Why, I remember one Sunday afternoon in Blue Mountain when your mother was a girl . . . [*Goes out for coffee, up right.*]

TOM. I know what's coming now! [LAURA *rises.*]

LAURA. Yes. But let her tell it. [*Crosses to left of day-bed, sits.*]

TOM. Again?

LAURA. She loves to tell it.

AMANDA [*Entering from right in dining room and coming down into living room with tray and coffee*]. I remember one Sunday afternoon in Blue Mountain when your mother was a girl she received —seventeen—gentlemen callers! [AMANDA *crosses to* TOM *at armchair right, gives him coffee, and crosses center.* LAURA *comes to her, takes cup, resumes her place on left of day-bed.* AMANDA *puts tray on small table right of day-bed, sits right on day-bed. Inner curtain closes, light dims out.*] Why, sometimes there weren't chairs enough to accommodate them all and we had to send the colored boy over to the parish house to fetch the folding chairs.

TOM. How did you entertain all those gentlemen callers? [TOM *finally sits in armchair right.*]

AMANDA. I happened to understand the art of conversation!

TOM. I bet you could talk!

AMANDA. Well, I could. All the girls in my day could, I tell you.

TOM. Yes?

AMANDA. They knew how to entertain their gentlemen callers. It wasn't enough for a girl to be possessed of a pretty face and a graceful figure—although I wasn't slighted in either respect. She also needed to have a nimble wit and a tongue to meet all occasions.

TOM. What did you talk about?

AMANDA. Why, we'd talk about things of importance going on in the world! Never anything common or coarse or vulgar. My callers were gentlemen—all! Some of the most prominent men on the Mississippi Delta—planters and sons of planters! There was young Champ Laughlin. [*Music.*] He later became Vice-President of the Delta Planters' Bank. And Hadley Stevenson; he was drowned in Moon Lake.—My goodness, he certainly left his widow well provided for—a hundred and fifty thousand dollars in government bonds. And the Cutrere Brothers—Wesley and Bates. Bates was one of my own bright particular beaus! But he got in a quarrel with that wild Wainwright boy and they shot it out on the floor of Moon Lake Casino. Bates was shot through the stomach. He died in the ambulance on his way to Memphis. He certainly left his widow well provided for, too—eight or ten thousand acres, no less. He never loved that woman; she just caught him on the rebound. My picture was found on him the night he died. Oh and that boy, that boy that every girl in the Delta was setting her cap for! That beautiful [*music fades out*] brilliant young Fitzhugh boy from Greene County!

TOM. What did he leave his widow?

AMANDA. He never married! What's the matter with you—you talk as though all my old admirers had turned up their toes to the daisies!

TOM. Isn't this the first you're mentioned that still survives?

AMANDA. He made an awful lot of money. He went North to Wall Street and made a fortune. He had the Midas touch—everything that boy touched just turned to gold! [*Gets up.*] And I could have been Mrs. J. Duncan Fitzhugh—mind you! [*Crosses left center.*] But—what did I do?—I just went out of my way and picked your father! [*Looks at picture on left wall. Goes to small table right of day-bed for tray.*]

LAURA [*Rises from day-bed*]. Mother, let me clear the table.

AMANDA [*Crossing left for* LAURA's *cup, then crossing right for* TOM's]. No, dear, you go in front and study your typewriter chart. Or practice your shorthand a little. Stay fresh and pretty! It's almost time for our gentlemen callers to start arriving. How many do you suppose we're going to entertain this afternoon? [TOM *opens curtains between dining room and living room for her. These close behind her, and she exits into kitchen right.* TOM *stands up center in living room.*]

LAURA [*To* AMANDA, *offstage*]. I don't

believe we're going to receive any, Mother.

AMANDA [*Offstage*]. Not any? Not one? Why, you must be joking! Not one gentleman caller? What's the matter? Has there been a flood or a tornado?

LAURA [*Crossing to typing table*]. It isn't a flood. It's not a tornado, Mother. I'm just not popular like you were in Blue Mountain. Mother's afraid that I'm going to be an old maid. [*Music.*] [*Lights dim out.* TOM *exits up center in blackout.* LAURA *crosses to menagerie right.*]

ACT I SCENE 2

Scene is the same. Lights dim up on living room.

LAURA *discovered by menagerie, polishing glass. Crosses to phonograph, plays record.*[1] *She times this business so as to put needle on record as music ends. Enter* AMANDA *down alley right. Rattles key in lock.* LAURA *crosses guiltily to typewriter and types.* (*Small typewriter table with typewriter on it is still on stage in living room left.*) AMANDA *comes into room right closing door. Crosses to armchair, putting hat, purse and gloves on it. Something has happened to* AMANDA. *It is written in her face: a look that is grim and hopeless and a little absurd. She has on one of those cheap or imitation velvety-looking cloth coats with imitation fur collar. Her hat is five or six years old, one of those dreadful cloche hats that were worn in the late twenties, and she is clasping an enormous black patent-leather pocketbook with nickel clasps and initials. This is her full-dress outfit, the one she usually wears to the D.A.R. She purses her lips, opens her eyes very wide, rolls them upward and shakes her head. Seeing her mother's expression,* LAURA *touches her lips with a nervous gesture.*

LAURA. Hello, Mother, I was just——

AMANDA. I know. You were just practicing your typing, I suppose. [*Behind chair right.*]

LAURA. Yes.

AMANDA. Deception, deception, deception!

LAURA [*Shakily*]. How was the D.A.R. meeting, Mother?

AMANDA [*Crosses to* LAURA]. D.A.R. meeting!

LAURA. Didn't you go to the D.A.R. meeting, Mother?

AMANDA [*Faintly, almost inaudibly*]. No, I didn't go to any D.A.R. meeting. [*Then more forcibly.*] I didn't have the strength—I didn't have the courage. I just wanted to find a hole in the ground and crawl in it and stay there the rest of my entire life. [*Tears type charts, throws them on floor.*]

LAURA [*Faintly*]. Why did you do that, Mother?

AMANDA [*Sits on right end of daybed*]. Why? Why? How old are you, Laura?

LAURA. Mother, you know my age.

AMANDA. I was under the impression that you were an adult, but evidently I was very much mistaken. [*She stares at* LAURA.]

LAURA. Please don't stare at me, Mother! [AMANDA *closes her eyes and lowers her head. Pause.*]

AMANDA. What are we going to do? What is going to become of us? What is the future? [*Pause.*]

LAURA. Has something happened, Mother? Mother, has something happened?

AMANDA. I'll be all right in a minute. I'm just bewildered—by life——

LAURA. Mother, I wish that you would tell me what's happened!

AMANDA. I went to the D.A.R. this afternoon, as you know; I was to be inducted as an officer. I stopped off at

[1] While "Dardanella" was used in the professional production, any other popular record of the 20's may be substituted. It should be a worn record.

Rubicam's Business College to tell them about your cold and to ask how you were progressing down there.

LAURA. Oh——

AMANDA. Yes, oh—oh—oh. I went straight to your typing instructor and introduced myself as your mother. She didn't even know who you were. Wingfield, she said? We don't have any such scholar enrolled in this school. I assured her she did. I said my daughter Laura's been coming to classes since early January. "Well, I don't know," she said, "unless you mean that terribly shy little girl who dropped out of school after a few days' attendance?" No, I said, I don't mean that one. I mean my daughter, Laura, who's been coming here every single day for the past six weeks! "Excuse me," she said. And she took down the attendance book and there was your name, unmistakable, printed, and all the dates you'd been absent. I still told her she was wrong. I still said, "No, there must have been some mistake! There must have been some mix-up in the records!" "No," she said, "I remember her perfectly now. She was so shy and her hands trembled so that her fingers couldn't touch the right keys! When we gave a speed-test—she just broke down completely—was sick at the stomach and had to be carried to the washroom! After that she never came back. We telephoned the house every single day and never got any answer." [*Rises from day-bed, crosses right center.*] That was while I was working all day long down at that department store, I suppose, demonstrating those—— [*With hands indicates brassiere.*] Oh! I felt so weak I couldn't stand up! [*Sits in armchair.*] I had to sit down while they got me a glass of water! [LAURA *crosses up to phonograph.*] Fifty dollars' tuition. I don't care about the money so much, but all my hopes for any kind of future for you—gone up the spout, just gone up the spout like that. [LAURA *winds phonograph up.*] Oh, don't *do* that, Laura!—Don't play that victrola!

LAURA. Oh! [*Stops phonograph, crosses to typing table, sits.*]

AMANDA. What have you been doing every day when you've gone out of the house pretending that you were going to business college?

LAURA. I've just been going out walking.

AMANDA. That's not true!

LAURA. Yes, it is, Mother, I just went walking.

AMANDA. Walking? Walking? In winter? Deliberately courting pneumonia in that light coat? Where did you walk to, Laura?

LAURA. All sorts of places—mostly in the park.

AMANDA. Even after you'd started catching that cold?

LAURA. It was the lesser of two evils, Mother. I couldn't go back. I threw up on the floor!

AMANDA. From half-past seven till after five every day you mean to tell me you walked around in the park, because you wanted to make me think that you were still going to Rubicam's Business College?

LAURA. Oh, Mother, it wasn't as bad as it sounds. I went inside places to get warmed up.

AMANDA. Inside, where?

LAURA. I went in the art museum and the bird-houses at the Zoo. I visited the penguins every day! Sometimes I did without lunch and went to the movies. Lately I've been spending most of my afternoons in the Jewel-box, that big glass house where they raise the tropical flowers.

AMANDA. You did all that to deceive me, just for deception! Why? Why? Why? Why?

LAURA. Mother, when you're disappointed, you get that awful suffering look on your face, like the picture of Jesus' mother in the Museum! [*Rises.*]

AMANDA. Hush!

LAURA [*Crosses right to menagerie*]. I couldn't face it. I couldn't. [*Music.*]

AMANDA [*Rising from day-bed*]. So what are we going to do now, honey, the rest of our lives? Just sit down in this house and watch the parades go by? Amuse ourselves with the glass menagerie? Eternally play those worn-out records your father left us as a painful reminder of him? [*Slams phonograph lid.*] We can't have a business career. [*End music.*] No, we can't do that—that just gives us indigestion. [*Around right day-bed.*] What is there left for us now but dependency all our lives? I tell you, Laura, I know so well what happens to unmarried women who aren't prepared to occupy a position in life. [*Crosses left, sits on day-bed.*] I've seen such pitiful cases in the South—barely tolerated spinsters living on some brother's wife or a sister's husband—tucked away in some mouse-trap of a room—encouraged by one in-law to go on and visit the next in-law—little bird-like women—without any nest—eating the crust of humility all their lives! Is that the future that we've mapped out for ourselves? I swear I don't see any other alternative. And I don't think that's a very pleasant alternative. Of course—some girls do marry. My goodness, Laura, haven't you ever liked some boy?

LAURA. Yes, Mother, I liked one once.

AMANDA. You did?

LAURA. I came across his picture a while ago.

AMANDA. He gave you his picture, too? [*Rises from day-bed, crosses to chair right.*]

LAURA. No, it's in the yearbook.

AMANDA [*Sits in armchair*]. Oh—a high-school boy.

LAURA. Yes. His name was Jim. [*Kneeling on floor, gets yearbook from under menagerie.*] Here he is in "The Pirates of Penzance."

AMANDA [*Absently*]. The what?

LAURA. The operetta the senior class put on. He had a wonderful voice. We sat across the aisle from each other Mondays, Wednesdays, and Fridays in the auditorium. Here he is with a silver cup for debating! See his grin?

AMANDA. So he had a grin, too! [*Looks at picture of father on wall behind phonograph.*[2] *Hands yearbook back.*]

LAURA. He used to call me—Blue Roses.

AMANDA. Blue Roses? What did he call you a silly name like that for?

LAURA [*Still kneeling*]. When I had that attack of pleurosis—he asked me what was the matter when I came back. I said pleurosis—he thought that I said "Blue Roses." So that's what he always called me after that. Whenever he saw me, he'd holler, "Hello, Blue Roses!" I didn't care for the girl that he went out with. Emily Meisenbach. Oh, Emily was the best-dressed girl at Soldan. But she never struck me as being sincere . . . I read in a newspaper once that they were engaged. [*Puts yearbook back on a shelf of glass menagerie.*] That's a long time ago—they're probably married by now.

AMANDA. That's all right, honey, that's all right. It doesn't matter. Little girls who aren't cut out for business careers sometimes end up married to very nice young men. And I'm just going to see that you do that, too!

LAURA. But, Mother——

AMANDA. What is it now?

LAURA. I'm—crippled!

AMANDA. Don't say that word! [*Rises, crosses to center. Turns to* LAURA.] How many times have I told you never to say that word! You're not crippled, you've just got a slight defect. [LAURA *rises.*]

[2] In the original production this photo was a life-sized head. It lights up from time to time as indicated. The illumination may, if desired, be omitted. If used, it lights here.

If you lived in the days when I was a girl and they had long graceful skirts sweeping the ground, it might have been considered an asset. When you've got a slight disadvantage like that, you've just got to cultivate something else to take its place. You have to cultivate charm—or vivacity—or *charm!* [*Spotlight on photograph.*[3] *Then dim out.*] That's the only thing your father had plenty of—charm! [AMANDA *sits on day-bed.* LAURA *crosses to armchair and sits.*] [*Music.*] [*Blackout.*]

ACT I SCENE 3

Scene: The same. Lights up again but only on right alley and fire-escape landing, rest of the stage dark. (*Typewriter table and typewriter have been taken offstage.*) *Enter* TOM, *again wearing merchant sailor overcoat and knitted cap, in alley right. As music ends,* TOM *begins to speak.*

TOM [*Leans against grill of fire-escape, smoking*]. After the fiasco at Rubicam's Business College, the idea of getting a gentleman caller for my sister Laura began to play a more and more important part in my mother's calculations. It became an obsession. Like some archetype of the universal unconscious, the image of the gentleman caller haunted our small apartment. An evening at home rarely passed without some allusion to this image, this spectre, this hope. . . . And even when he wasn't mentioned, his presence hung in my mother's preoccupied look and in my sister's frightened, apologetic manner. It hung like a sentence passed upon the Wingfields! But my mother was a woman of action as well as words. [*Music.*] She began to take logical steps in the planned direction. Late that winter and in the early spring —realizing that extra money would be needed to properly feather the nest and plume the bird—she began a vigorous campaign on the telephone, roping in subscribers to one of those magazines for matrons called "The Homemaker's Companion," the type of journal that features the serialized sublimations of ladies of letters who think in terms of delicate cup-like breasts, slim, tapering waists, rich creamy thighs, eyes like woodsmoke in autumn, fingers that soothe and caress like soft, soft strains of music. Bodies as powerful as Etruscan sculpture. [*He exits down right into wings. Light in alley right is blacked out, and a headspot falls on* AMANDA, *at phone in living room, music ends as* TOM *stops speaking.*]

AMANDA. Ida Scott? [*During this speech* TOM *enters dining room up right unseen by audience; not wearing overcoat or hat. There is an unlighted reading lamp on table. Sits center of diningroom table with writing materials.*] This is Amanda Wingfield. We missed you at the D.A.R. last Monday. Oh, first I want to know how's your sinus condition? You're just a Christian martyr. That's what you are. You're just a Christian martyr. Well, I was just going through my little red book, and I saw that your subscription to the "Companion" is about to expire just when that wonderful new serial by Bessie Mae Harper is starting. It's the first thing she's written since "Honeymoon for Three." Now, that was unusual, wasn't it? Why, Ida, this one is even lovelier. It's all about the horsey set on Long Island and a debutante is thrown from her horse while taking him over the jumps at the—regatta. Her spine—her spine is injured. That's what the horse did—he stepped on her. Now, there is only one surgeon in the entire world that can keep her from being completely paralyzed, and that's the man she's engaged to be married to and he's tall and he's blond and he's handsome. That's unusual, too, huh? Oh, he's not

[3] See note on page 230.

perfect. Of course he has a weakness. He has the most terrible weakness in the entire world. He just drinks too much. What? Oh, no, Honey, don't let them burn. You go take a look in the oven and I'll hold on . . . Why, that woman! Do you know what she did? She hung up on me. [*Dining-room and living-room lights dim in. Reading lamp lights up at same time.*]

LAURA. Oh, Mother, Mother, Tom's trying to write. [*Rises from armchair where she was left at curtain of previous scene, goes to curtain between dining room and living room, which is already open.*]

AMANDA. Oh! So he is. So he is. [*Crosses from phone, goes to dining room and up to* TOM.]

TOM [*At table*]. Now what are you up to?

AMANDA. I'm trying to save your eyesight. [*Business with lamp.*] You've only got one pair of eyes and you've got to take care of them. Oh, I know that Milton was blind, but that's not what made him a genius.

TOM. Mother, will you please go away and let me finish my writing?

AMANDA [*Squares his shoulders*]. Why can't you sit up straight? So your shoulders don't stick through like sparrows' wings?

TOM. Mother, please go busy yourself with something else. I'm trying to write.

AMANDA [*Business with* TOM]. Now, I've seen a medical chart, and I know what that position does to your internal organs. You sit up and I'll show you. Your stomach presses against your lungs, and your lungs press against your heart, and that poor little heart gets discouraged because it hasn't got any room left to go on beating for you.

TOM. What in hell . . . ! [*Inner curtains between living room and dining room close. Lights dim down in dining room.* LAURA *crosses, stands center of curtains in living room listening to following scene between* TOM *and* AMANDA].

AMANDA.[4] Don't you talk to me like that——

TOM. —am I supposed to do?

AMANDA. What's the matter with you? Have you gone out of your senses?

TOM. Yes, I have. You've driven me out of them.

AMANDA. What is the matter with you lately, you big—big—idiot?

TOM. Look, Mother—I haven't got a thing, not a single thing left in this house that I can call my own.

AMANDA. Lower your voice!

TOM. Yesterday you confiscated my books! You had the nerve to——

AMANDA. I did. I took that horrible novel back to the library—that awful book by that insane Mr. Lawrence. I cannot control the output of a diseased mind or people who cater to them, but I won't allow such filth in my house. No, no, no, no, no!

TOM. House, house! Who pays the rent on the house, who makes a slave of himself to——!

AMANDA. Don't you dare talk to me like that! [LAURA *crosses down left to back of armchair.*]

TOM. No, *I* mustn't say anything! *I've* just got to keep quiet and let you do all the talking.

AMANDA. Let me tell you something!

TOM. I don't want to hear any more.

AMANDA. You will hear more—— [LAURA *crosses to phonograph.*]

TOM [*Crossing through curtains between dining room and living room. Goes upstage of door right where, in a dark spot, there is supposedly a closet.*] Well, I'm not going to listen. I'm going out. [*Gets out coat.*]

AMANDA [*coming through curtains into living room, stands center*]. You are going to listen to me, Tom Wingfield. I'm tired of your impudence.—And another

[4] Tom and Amanda remain in dining room throughout their argument.

thing—I'm right at the end of my patience!

TOM [*Putting overcoat on back of armchair and crossing back to* AMANDA]. What do you think I'm at the end of, Mother? Aren't I supposed to have any patience to reach the end of? I know, I know. It seems unimportant to you, what I'm *doing*—what I'm trying to do —having a difference between them! You don't think that.

AMANDA. I think you're doing things that you're ashamed of, and that's why you act like this. [TOM *crosses to day-bed and sits.*] I don't believe that you go every night to the movies. Nobody goes to the movies night after night. Nobody in their right minds goes to the movies as often as you pretend to. People don't go to the movies at nearly midnight and movies don't let out at two A.M. Come in stumbling, muttering to yourself like a maniac. You get three hours' sleep and then go to work. Oh, I can picture the way you're doing down there. Moping, doping, because you're in no condition.

TOM. That's true—that's very, very true. I'm in no condition!

AMANDA. How dare you jeopardize your job? Jeopardize our security? How do you think we'd manage——? [*Sits armchair right.*]

TOM. Look, Mother, do you think I'm *crazy* about the *warehouse?* You think I'm in love with the Continental Shoemakers? You think I want to spend fifty-five years of my life down there in that—*celotex interior!* with *fluorescent tubes?!* Honest to God, I'd rather somebody picked up a crowbar and battered out my brains—than go back mornings! But I *go!* Sure, every time you come in yelling that bloody *Rise and Shine! Rise and Shine!!* I think how lucky dead people are! But I get up. [*Rises from day-bed.*] I *go!* For sixty-five dollars a month I give up all that I dream of doing and being *ever!* And you say that is all I think of. Oh, God! Why, Mother, if self is all I ever thought of, Mother, *I'd* be where *he* is—GONE! [*Crosses to get overcoat on back of armchair.*] As far as the system of transportation reaches! [AMANDA *rises, crosses to him, and grabs his arm.*] Please don't grab at me, Mother!

AMANDA [*Following him*]. I'm not grabbing at you. I want to know where you're going now.

TOM [*Taking overcoat and starts crossing to door right*]. I'm going to the movies!

AMANDA [*Crosses center*]. I don't believe that lie!

TOM [*Crosses back to* AMANDA]. No? Well, you're right. For once in your life you're right. I'm not going to the movies. I'm going to opium dens! Yes, Mother, opium dens, dens of vice and criminals' hang-outs, Mother. I've joined the Hogan gang. I'm a hired assassin, I carry a tommy-gun in a violin case! I run a string of cathouses in the valley! They call me Killer, Killer Wingfield, I'm really leading a double life. By day I'm a simple, honest warehouse worker, but at night I'm a dynamic czar of the underworld. Why, I go to gambling casinos and spin away a fortune on the roulette table! I wear a patch over one eye and a false moustache, sometimes I wear green whiskers. On those occasions they call me—El Diablo! Oh, I could tell you things to make you sleepless! My enemies plan to dynamite this place some night! Some night they're going to blow us all sky-high. And will I be glad! Will I be happy! And so will you be. You'll go up —up—over Blue Mountain on a broomstick! With seventeen gentlemen callers. You ugly babbling old witch! [*He goes through a series of violent, clumsy movements, seizing his overcoat, lunging to right door, pulling it fiercely open. The women watch him, aghast. His arm catches in the sleeve of the coat as he struggles to pull it on. For a moment he is pinioned by the bulky garment. With an outraged groan he tears the coat off again, splitting the shoulder of it, and hurls it across the room. It strikes against the shelf of* LAURA'S *glass collection, there is a tinkle of shattering glass.* LAURA *cries out as if wounded.*]

LAURA. My glass!—menagerie . . . [*She covers her face and turns away.*]

AMANDA [*In an awful voice*]. I'll never speak to you again as long as you live unless you apologize to me! [AMANDA *exits through living room curtains.* TOM *is left with* LAURA. *He stares at her stupidly for a moment. Then he crosses to shelf holding glass menagerie. Drops awkwardly on his knees to collect fallen glass, glancing at* LAURA *as if he would speak, but couldn't. Blackout.* TOM, AMANDA *and* LAURA *exit in blackout.*]

ACT I SCENE 4

The interior is dark. Faint light in alley right. A deep-voiced bell in a church is tolling the hour of five as the scene commences.

TOM *appears at the top of right alley. After each solemn boom of the bell in the tower he shakes a little toy noisemaker or rattle as if to express the tiny spasm of man in contrast to the sustained power and dignity of the Almighty. This and the unsteadiness of his advance make it evident that he has been drinking. As he climbs the few steps to the fire-escape landing light steals up inside.* LAURA *appears in night-dress, entering living room from left door of dining room, observing* TOM'S *empty bed (day-bed) in the living room.* TOM *fishes in his pockets for doorkey, removing a motley assortment of articles in the search, including a perfect shower of movie-ticket stubs and an empty bottle. At last he finds the key, but just as he is about to insert it, it slips from his fingers. He strikes a match and crouches below the door.*

TOM [*Bitterly*]. One crack—and it falls through! [LAURA *opens door right.*] [5]

LAURA. Tom! Tom, what are you doing?

TOM. Looking for a doorkey.

LAURA. Where have you been all this time?

TOM. I have been to the movies.

LAURA. All this time at the movies?

TOM. There was a very long program. There was a Garbo picture and a Micky Mouse and a travelogue and a newsreel and a preview of coming attractions. And there was an organ solo and a collection for the milk-fund—simultaneously—which ended up in a terrible fight between a fat lady and an usher!

LAURA [*Innocently*]. Did you have to stay through everything?

TOM. Of course! And, oh, I forgot! There was a big stage show! The headliner on this stage show was Malvolio the Magician. He performed wonderful tricks, many of them, such as pouring water back and forth between pitchers. First it turned to wine and then it turned to beer and then it turned to whiskey. I know it was whiskey it finally turned into because he needed somebody to come up out of the audience to help him, and I came up—both shows! It was Kentucky Straight Bourbon. A very generous fellow, he gave souvenirs. [*He pulls from his back pocket a shimmering rainbow-colored scarf.*] He gave me this. This is his magic scarf. You can have it, Laura. You wave it over a canary cage and you get a bowl of goldfish. You wave it over the goldfish bowl and they fly away canaries. . . . But the wonderfullest trick of all was the coffin trick. We nailed him into a coffin and he got out of the coffin without removing one nail. [*They enter.*] There is a trick that would come in handy for me—get me out of this 2 by

[5] Next few speeches are spoken on fire-escape landing.

4 situation! [*Flops onto day-bed and starts removing shoes.*]

LAURA. Tom—shhh!

TOM. What're you shushing me for?

LAURA. You'll wake up Mother.

TOM. Goody goody! Pay 'er back for all those "Rise an' Shines." [*Lies down groaning.*] You know it don't take much intelligence to get yourself into a nailed-up coffin, Laura. But who in hell ever got himself out of one without removing one nail? [*As if in answer, the father's grinning photograph lights up.* LAURA *exits up left. Lights fade except for blue glow in dining room. Pause after lights fade, then clock chimes six times. This is followed by the alarm clock. Dim in forestage.*]

ACT I SCENE 5

Scene is the same. Immediately following. The church bell is heard striking six. At the sixth stroke the alarm clock goes off in AMANDA'S *room off right of dining room and after a few moments we hear her calling, "Rise and shine! Rise and shine! Laura, go tell your brother to rise and shine!"*

TOM [*Sitting up slowly in day-bed*]. I'll rise—but I won't shine. [*The light increases.*]

AMANDA [*Offstage*]. Laura, tell your brother his coffee is ready. [LAURA, *fully dressed, a cape over her shoulders, slips into living room.* TOM *is still in bed, covered with blanket, having taken off only shoes and coat.*]

LAURA. Tom!—It's nearly seven. Don't make Mother nervous. [*He stares at her stupidly. Beseechingly.*] Tom, speak to Mother this morning. Make up with her, apologize, speak to her!

TOM [*Putting on shoes*]. She won't to me. It's her that started not speaking.

LAURA. If you just say you're sorry she'll start speaking.

TOM. Her not speaking—is that such a tragedy?

LAURA. Please—please!

AMANDA [*Calling offstage right from kitchen*]. Laura, are you going to do what I asked you to do, or do I have to get dressed and go out myself?

LAURA. Going, going—soon as I get on my coat! [*She rises and crosses to door right.*] Butter and what else? [*To* AMANDA.]

AMANDA [*Offstage*]. Just butter. Tell them to charge it.

LAURA. Mother, they make such faces when I do that.

AMANDA [*Offstage*]. Sticks and stones can break our bones, but the expression on Mr. Garfinkel's face won't harm us! Tell your brother his coffee is getting cold.

LAURA [*At door right*]. Do what I asked you, will you, will you, Tom? [*He looks sullenly away.*]

AMANDA. Laura, go now or just don't go at all!

LAURA [*Rushing out right*]. Going—going! [*A second later she cries out. Falls on fire-escape landing.* TOM *springs up and crosses to door right.* AMANDA *rushes anxiously in from dining room, puts dishes on dining-room table.* TOM *opens door right.*]

TOM. Laura?

LAURA. I'm all right. I slipped, but I'm all right. [*Goes up right alley, out of sight.*]

AMANDA [*On fire-escape*]. I tell you if anybody falls down and breaks a leg on those fire-escape steps, the landlord ought to be sued for every cent he—— [*Sees* TOM.] Who are you? [*Leaves fire-escape landing, crosses to dining room and returns with bowls, coffee cup, cream, etc. Puts them on small table right of day-bed, crosses to armchair, sits. Counts 3. (Music.) As* TOM *re-enters right, listlessly for his coffee, she turns her back to him, as she sits in armchair. The light on her face with its aged but childish features is cruelly sharp, satirical as a Daumier print.* TOM *glances sheepishly but sullenly at her averted figure and sits on day-bed next to the food. The coffee is scalding hot, he sips it and gasps and spits it back in the cup. At his gasp,* AMANDA *catches her breath and half turns. Then catches herself and turns away.* TOM *blows on his coffee, glancing sidewise at his mother. She clears her throat.* TOM *clears his. He starts to rise. Sinks back down again, scratches his head, clears his throat again.* AMANDA *coughs.* TOM *raises his cup in both hands to blow on it, his eyes staring over the rim of it at his mother for several moments. Then he slowly sets the cup down and awkwardly and hesitantly rises from day-bed.*)

TOM [*Hoarsely*]. I'm sorry, Mother. I'm sorry for all those things I said. I didn't mean it. I apologize.

AMANDA [*Sobbingly*]. My devotion has made me a witch and so I make myself hateful to my children!

TOM. No, you don't.

AMANDA. I worry so much, I don't sleep, it makes me nervous!

TOM [*Gently*]. I understand that.

AMANDA. You know I've had to put up a solitary battle all these years. But you're my right hand bower! Now don't fail me. Don't fall down.

TOM [*Gently*]. I try, Mother.

AMANDA [*With great enthusiasm*]. That's all right! You just keep on trying and you're bound to succeed. Why, you're—you're just full of natural endowments! Both my children are—they're very precious children and I've got an awful lot to be thankful for; you just must promise me one thing. [*Music stops.*]

TOM. What is it, Mother?

AMANDA. Promise me you're never going to become a drunkard!

TOM. I promise, Mother. I won't ever become a drunkard, Mother.

AMANDA. That's what frightened me so, that you'd be drinking! Eat a bowl of Purina.

TOM. Just coffee, Mother.

AMANDA. Shredded Wheat Biscuit?

TOM. No, no, Mother, just coffee.

AMANDA. You can't put in a day's work on an empty stomach. You've got ten minutes—don't gulp! Drinking too-hot liquids makes cancer of the stomach. . . . Put cream in.

TOM. No, thank you.

AMANDA. To cool it.

TOM. No! No, thank you, I want it black.

AMANDA. I know, but it's not good for you. We have to do all that we can to build ourselves up. In these trying times we live in, all that we have to cling to is—each other. . . . That's why it's so important to—— Tom, I—I sent out your sister so I could discuss something with you. If you hadn't spoken I would have spoken to you. [*Sits down.*]

TOM [*Gently*]. What is it, Mother, that you want to discuss?

AMANDA. Laura! [*Tom puts his cup down slowly. Music.*]

TOM. —Oh.—Laura . . .

AMANDA [*Touching his sleeve*]. You know how Laura is. So quiet but—still water runs deep! She notices things and I think she—broods about them. [TOM *looks up.*] A few days ago I came in and she was crying.

TOM. What about?

AMANDA. You.

TOM. Me?

AMANDA. She has an idea that you're not happy here. [*Music stops.*]

TOM. What gave her that idea?

AMANDA. What gives her any idea? However, you do act strangely. [TOM *slaps cup down on small table.*] I—I'm not criticizing, understand that! I know your ambitions do not lie in the warehouse, that like everybody in the whole wide world—you've had to—make sacrifices, but—Tom—Tom—life's not easy, it calls for—Spartan endurance! There's so many things in my heart that I cannot describe to you! I've never told you but I—loved your father . . .

TOM [*Gently*]. I know that, Mother.

AMANDA. And you—when I see you taking after his ways! Staying out late—and—well, you had been drinking the night you were in that—terrifying condition! Laura says that you hate the apartment and that you go out nights to get away from it! Is that true, Tom?

TOM. No. You say there's so much in your heart that you can't describe to me. That's true of me, too. There's so much in my heart that I can't describe to you! So let's respect each other's——

AMANDA. But, why—why, Tom—are you always so restless? Where do you go to, nights?

TOM. I—go to the movies.

AMANDA. Why do you go to the movies so much, Tom?

TOM. I go to the movies because—I like adventure. Adventure is something I don't have much of at work, so I go to the movies.

AMANDA. But, Tom, you go to the movies entirely too much!

TOM. I like a lot of adventure. [AMANDA *looks baffled, then hurt. As the familiar inquisition resumes he becomes hard and impatient again.* AMANDA *slips back into her querulous attitude toward him.*]

AMANDA. Most young men find adventure in their careers.

TOM. Then most young men are not employed in a warehouse.

AMANDA. The world is full of young men employed in warehouses and offices and factories.

TOM. Do all of them find adventure in their careers?

AMANDA. They do or they do without it! Not everybody has a craze for adventure.

TOM. Man is by instinct a lover, a hunter, a fighter, and none of those instincts are given much play at the warehouse!

AMANDA. Man is by instinct! Don't quote instinct to me! Instinct is something that people have got away from! It belongs to animals! Christian adults don't want it!

TOM. What do Christian adults want, then, Mother?

AMANDA. Superior things! Things of the mind and the spirit! Only animals have to satisfy instincts! Surely your aims are somewhat higher than theirs! Than monkeys—pigs——

TOM. I reckon they're not.

AMANDA. You're joking. However, that isn't what I wanted to discuss.

TOM [*Rising*]. I haven't much time.

AMANDA [*Pushing his shoulders*]. Sit down.

TOM. You want me to punch in red at the warehouse, Mother?

AMANDA. You have five minutes. I want to talk about Laura.

TOM. All right! What about Laura?

AMANDA. We have to be making some plans and provisions for her. She's older than you, two years, and nothing has happened. She just drifts along doing nothing. It frightens me terribly how she just drifts along.

TOM. I guess she's the type that people call home girls.

AMANDA. There's no such type, and if there is, it's a pity! That is unless the home is hers, with a husband!

TOM. What?

AMANDA [*Crossing down right to armchair*]. Oh, I can see the handwriting on the wall as plain as I see the nose in front of my face! It's terrifying! More and more you remind me of your father! He was out all [*sits in armchair*] hours without explanation!—Then left! Good-by! And me with the bag to hold. I saw that letter you got from the Merchant Marine. I know what you're dreaming of. I'm not standing here blindfolded. Very well, then. Then do it! But not till there's somebody to take your place.

TOM. What do you mean?

AMANDA. I mean that as soon as Laura has got somebody to take care of her, married, a home of her own, independent—why, then you'll be free to go wherever you please, [*rises, crosses to* TOM] on land, on sea, whichever way the wind blows you! But until that time you've got to look out for your sister. [*Crosses right behind armchair.*] I don't say me because I'm old and don't matter! I say for your sister because she's young and dependent. I put her in business college—a dismal failure! Frightened her so it made her sick at the stomach. I took her over to the Young People's League at the church. Another fiasco. She spoke to nobody, nobody spoke to her. [*Sits armchair.*] Now all she does is fool with those pieces of glass and play those worn-out records. What kind of a life is that for a girl to lead?

TOM. What can I do about it?

AMANDA. Overcome selfishness! Self, self, self is all that you ever think of! [TOM *springs up and crosses right to get his coat and put it on. It is ugly and bulky. He pulls on a cap with earmuffs.*] Where is your muffler? Put your wool muffler on! [*He snatches it angrily from the hook and tosses it around his neck and pulls both ends tight.*] Tom! I haven't said what I had in mind to ask you.

TOM. I'm too late to——

AMANDA [*Catching his arm—very importunately. Then shyly*]. Down at the warehouse, aren't there some—nice young men?

TOM. No!

AMANDA. There must be—some . . .

TOM. Mother—— [*Gesture.*]

AMANDA. Find out one that's clean-living—doesn't drink and—ask him out for sister!

TOM. What?

AMANDA. For sister! To meet! Get acquainted!

TOM [*Stamping to door right*]. Oh, my go-osh!

AMANDA. Will you? [*He opens door. Imploringly.*] Will you? [*He starts out.*] Will you? Will you, dear? [TOM *exits up alley right.* AMANDA *is on fire-escape landing.*]

TOM [*Calling back*]. Yes!

AMANDA [*Re-entering right and crossing to phone. Music*]. Ella Cartwright? Ella, this is Amanda Wingfield. First, first, how's that kidney trouble? Oh, it has? It has come back? Well, you're just a Christian martyr, you're just a Christian martyr. I was noticing in my little red book that your subscription to the "Companion" has run out just when that wonderful new serial by Bessie Mae Harper was starting. It's all about the horsey set on Long Island. Oh, you have? You have read it? Well, how do you think it turns out? Oh, no. Bessie Mae Harper never lets you down. Oh, of course, we have to have complications. You have to have complications—oh, you can't have a story without them—but Bessie Mae Harper always leaves you with such an uplift—— What's the matter, Ella? You sound so mad. Oh, because it's seven o'clock in the morning. Oh, Ella, I forgot that you never got up until nine. I forgot that anybody in the world was allowed to sleep as late as that. I can't say any more than I'm sorry, can I? Oh, you will? You're going to take that subscription from me anyhow? Well, bless you, Ella, bless you, bless you, bless you. [*Music fades into dance music and continues into next scene. Dim out lights. Music.*]

ACT I SCENE 6

Scene: The same.—Only right alley lighted, with dim light.

TOM [*Enters down right and stands as before, leaning against grillwork, with cigarette, wearing merchant sailor coat and cap*]. Across the alley was the Paradise Dance Hall. Evenings in spring they'd open all the doors and windows and the music would come outside.

Sometimes they'd turn out all the lights except for a large glass sphere that hung from the ceiling. It would turn slowly about and filter the dusk with delicate rainbow colors. Then the orchestra would play a waltz or a tango, something that had a slow and sensuous rhythm. The young couples would come outside, to the relative privacy of the alley. You could see them kissing behind ashpits and telephone poles. This was the compensation for lives that passed like mine, without change or adventure. Changes and adventure, however, were imminent this year. They were waiting around the corner for all these dancing kids. Suspended in the mist over Berchtesgaden, caught in the folds of Chamberlain's umbrella—— In Spain there was Guernica! Here there was only hot swing music and liquor, dance halls, bars, and movies, and sex that hung in the gloom like a chandelier and flooded the world with brief, deceptive rainbows. . . . While these unsuspecting kids danced to "Dear One, The World is Waiting for the Sunrise." All the world was really waiting for bombardments. [*Music stops. Dim in dining room: faint glow.* AMANDA *is seen in dining room.*]

AMANDA. Tom, where are you?

TOM [*Standing as before*]. I came out to smoke. [*Exit right into the wings, where he again changes coats and leaves hat.*]

AMANDA [TOM *re-enters and stands on fire-escape landing, smoking. He opens door for* AMANDA, *who sits on hassock on landing*]. Oh, you smoke too much. A pack a day at fifteen cents a pack. How much would that be in a month? Thirty times fifteen? It wouldn't be very much. Well, it would be enough to help toward a night-school course in accounting at the Washington U! Wouldn't that be lovely?

TOM. I'd rather smoke.

AMANDA. I know! That's the tragedy of you. This fire-escape landing is a poor excuse for the porch we used to have. What are you looking at?

TOM. The moon.

AMANDA. Is there a moon this evening?

TOM. It's rising over Garfinkel's Delicatessen.

AMANDA. Oh! So it is! Such a little silver slipper of a moon. Have you made a wish on it?

TOM. Um-mm.

AMANDA. What did you wish?

TOM. That's a secret.

AMANDA. All right, I won't tell you what I wished, either. I can keep a secret, too. I can be just as mysterious as you.

TOM. I bet I can guess what you wished.

AMANDA. Why, is my head transparent?

TOM. You're not a sphinx.

AMANDA. No, I don't have secrets. I'll tell you what I wished for on the moon. Success and happiness for my precious children. I wish for that whenever there's a moon, and when there isn't a moon, I wish for it, too.

TOM. I thought perhaps you wished for a gentleman caller.

AMANDA. Why do you say that?

TOM. Don't you remember asking me to fetch one?

AMANDA. I remember suggesting that it would be nice for your sister if you brought home some nice young man from the warehouse. I think that I've made that suggestion more than once.

TOM. Yes, you have made it repeatedly.

AMANDA. Well?

TOM. We are going to have one.

AMANDA. *What?*

TOM. A gentleman caller!

AMANDA. You mean you have asked some nice young man to come over? [*Rising from stool, facing* TOM.]

TOM. I've asked him to dinner.

AMANDA. You really did?

TOM. I did.

AMANDA. And did he—accept?

TOM. He did!

AMANDA. He did?

TOM. He did.

AMANDA. Well, isn't that lovely!

TOM. I thought that you would be pleased.

AMANDA. It's definite, then?

TOM. Oh, very definite.

AMANDA. How soon?

TOM. Pretty soon.

AMANDA. How soon?

TOM. Quite soon.

AMANDA. How soon?

TOM. Very, very soon.

AMANDA. Every time I want to know anything you start going on like that.

TOM. What do you want to know?

AMANDA. Go ahead and guess. Go ahead and guess.

TOM. All right, I'll guess. You want to know when the gentleman caller's coming—he's coming tomorrow.

AMANDA. Tomorrow? Oh, no, I can't do anything about tomorrow. I can't do anything about tomorrow.

TOM. Why not?

AMANDA. That doesn't give me any time.

TOM. Time for what?

AMANDA. Time for preparations. Oh, you should have phoned me the minute you asked him—the minute he accepted!

TOM. You don't have to make any fuss.

AMANDA. Of course I have to make a fuss! I can't have a man coming into a place that's all sloppy. It's got to be thrown together properly. I certainly have to do some fast thinking by tomorrow night, too.

TOM. I don't see why you have to think at all.

AMANDA. That's because you just don't know. [*Enter living room, crosses to center. Dim in living room.*] You just don't know, that's all. We can't have a gentleman caller coming into a pig-sty! Now, let's see. Oh, I've got those three pieces of wedding silver left. I'll polish that up. I wonder how that old lace tablecloth is holding up all these years? We can't wear anything. We haven't got it. We haven't got anything to wear. We haven't got it. [*Goes back to door right.*]

TOM. Mother! This boy is no one to make a fuss over.

AMANDA [*Crossing to center*]. I don't know how you can say that when this is the first gentleman caller your little sister's ever had! I think it's pathetic that that little girl has never had a single gentleman caller! Come on inside! Come on inside!

TOM. What for?

AMANDA. I want to ask you a few things.

TOM [*From doorway right*]. If you're going to make a fuss, I'll call the whole thing off. I'll call the boy up and tell him not to come.

AMANDA. No! You mustn't ever do that. People hate broken engagements. They have no place to go. Come on inside. Come on inside. Will you come inside when I ask you to come inside? Sit down. [TOM *comes into living room.*]

TOM. Any particular place you want me to sit?

AMANDA. Oh! Sit anywhere. [TOM *sits armchair right.*] Look! What am I going to do about that? [*Looking at day-bed.*] Did you ever see anything look so sad? I know, I'll get a bright piece of cretonne. That won't cost much. And I made payments on a floor lamp. So I'll have that sent out! And I can put a bright cover on the chair. I wish I had time to paper the walls. What's his name?

TOM. His name is O'Connor.

AMANDA. O'Connor—he's Irish and tomorrow's Friday—that means fish. Well, that's all right, I'll make a salmon loaf and some mayonnaise dressing for it. Where did you meet him? [*Crosses to day-bed and sits.*]

TOM. At the warehouse, of course Where else would I meet him?

AMANDA. Well, I don't know. Does he drink?

TOM. What made you ask me that?

AMANDA. Because your father did.

TOM. Now, don't get started on that!

AMANDA. He drinks, then.

TOM. No, not that I know of.

AMANDA. You have to find out. There's nothing I want less for my daughter than a man who drinks.

TOM. Aren't you being a little bit premature? After all, poor Mr. O'Connor hasn't even appeared on the scene yet.

AMANDA. But he will tomorrow. To meet your sister. And what do I know about his character? [*Rises and crosses to* TOM, *who is still in armchair, smooths his hair.*]

TOM [*Submitting grimly*]. Now what are you up to?

AMANDA. I always did hate that cowlick. I never could understand why it won't sit down by itself.

TOM. Mother, I want to tell you something and I mean it sincerely right straight from my heart. There's a lot of boys who meet girls which they don't marry!

AMANDA. You know you always had me worried because you could never stick to a subject. [*Crosses to day-bed.*] What I want to know is what's his position at the warehouse?

TOM. He's a shipping clerk.

AMANDA. Oh! Shipping clerk! Well, that's fairly important. That's where you'd be if you had more get-up. How much does he earn? [*Sits on day-bed.*]

TOM. I have no way of knowing that for sure. I judge his salary to be approximately eighty-five dollars a month.

AMANDA. Eighty-five dollars? Well, that's not princely.

TOM. It's twenty dollars more than I make.

AMANDA. I know that. Oh, how well I know that! How well I know that! Eighty-five dollars a month. No. It can't be done. A family man can never get by on eighty-five dollars a month.

TOM. Mother, Mr. O'Connor is not a family man.

AMANDA. Well, he might be some time in the future, mightn't he?

TOM. Oh, I see. . . . Plans and provisions.

AMANDA. You are the only young man that I know of who ignores the fact that the future becomes the present, the present the past, and the past turns into everlasting regret if you don't plan for it.

TOM. I will think that over and see what I can make of it!

AMANDA. Don't be supercilious with your mother! Tell me some more about this.—What do you call him? Mr. O'Connor, Mr. O'Connor. He must have another name besides Mr.——?

TOM. His full name is James D. O'Connor. The D. is for Delaney.

AMANDA. Delaney? Irish on both sides and he doesn't drink?

TOM [*Rises from armchair*]. Shall I call him up and ask him? [*Starts toward phone.*]

AMANDA [*Crossing to phone*]. No!

TOM. I'll call him up and tell him you want to know if he drinks. [*Picks up phone.*]

AMANDA [*Taking phone away from him*]. No, you can't do that. You have to be discreet about that subject. When I was a girl in Blue Mountain if it was [TOM *sits on right of day-bed.*] suspected that a young man was drinking and any girl was receiving his attentions —if any girl *was* receiving his attentions, she'd go to the minister of his church and ask about his character—or her father, if her father was living, then it was his duty to go to the minister of his church and ask about his character, and that's how young girls in Blue Mountain were kept from making tragic mistakes. [*Picture dims in and out.*] [6]

[6] See note p. 230.

TOM. How come you made such a tragic one?

AMANDA. Oh, I don't know how he did it, but that face fooled everybody. All he had to do was grin and the world was bewitched. [*Behind day-bed, crosses to armchair.*] I don't know of anything more tragic than a young girl just putting herself at the mercy of a handsome appearance, and I hope Mr. O'Connor is *not* too good-looking.

TOM. As a matter of fact he isn't. His face is covered with freckles and he has a very large nose.

AMANDA. He's not right-down homely?

TOM. No. I wouldn't say right-down—homely—medium homely, I'd say.

AMANDA. Well, if a girl had any sense she'd look for character in a man anyhow.

TOM. That's what I've always said, Mother.

AMANDA. You've always said it—you've always said it! How could you've always said it when you never even thought about it?

TOM. Aw, don't be so suspicious of me.

AMANDA. I am. I'm suspicious of every word that comes out of your mouth, when you talk to me, but I want to know about this young man. Is he up and coming?

TOM. Yes. I really do think he goes in for self-improvement.

AMANDA. What makes you think it?

TOM. He goes to night school.

AMANDA. Well, what does he do there at night school?

TOM. He's studying radio engineering and public speaking.

AMANDA. Oh! Public speaking! Oh, that shows, that shows that he intends to be an executive some day—and radio engineering. Well, that's coming . . . huh?

TOM. I think it's here.

AMANDA. Well, those are all very illuminating facts. [*Crosses to back of armchair.*] Facts that every mother should know about any young man calling on her daughter, seriously or not.

TOM. Just one little warning, Mother. I didn't tell him anything about Laura. I didn't let on we had dark ulterior motives. I just said, "How about coming home to dinner some time?" and he said, "Fine," and that was the whole conversation.

AMANDA. I bet it was, too. I tell you, sometimes you can be as eloquent as an oyster. However, when he sees how pretty and sweet that child is, he's going to be, well, he's going to be very glad he was asked over here to have some dinner. [*Sits in armchair.*]

TOM. Mother, just one thing. You won't expect too much of Laura, will you?

AMANDA. I don't know what you mean. [TOM *crosses slowly to* AMANDA. *He stands for a moment, looking at her. Then*——]

TOM. Well, Laura seems all those things to you and me because she's ours and we love her. We don't even notice she's crippled any more.

AMANDA. Don't use that word.

TOM. Mother, you have to face the facts; she is, and that's not all.

AMANDA. What do you mean "that's not all"? [TOM *kneels by her chair.*]

TOM. Mother—you know that Laura is very different from other girls.

AMANDA. Yes, I do know that, and I think that difference is all in her favor, too.

TOM. Not quite all—in the eyes of others—strangers—she's terribly shy. She lives in a world of her own and those things make her seem a little peculiar to people outside the house.

AMANDA. Don't use that word peculiar.

TOM. You have to face the facts.—She is.

AMANDA. I don't know in what way

she's peculiar. [*Music, till curtain.* TOM *pauses a moment for music, then——*]

TOM. Mother, Laura lives in a world of little glass animals. She plays old phonograph records—and—that's about all—— [TOM *rises slowly, goes quietly out the door right, leaving it open, and exits slowly up the alley.* AMANDA *rises, goes on to fire-escape landing right, looks at moon.*]

AMANDA. Laura! Laura! [LAURA *answers from kitchen right.*]

LAURA. Yes, Mother.

AMANDA. Let those dishes go and come in front! [LAURA *appears with dish towel. Gaily.*] Laura, come here and make a wish on the moon!

LAURA [*Entering from kitchen right and comes down to fire-escape landing*]. Moon—moon?

AMANDA. A little silver slipper of a moon. Look over your left shoulder, Laura, and make a wish! [LAURA *looks faintly puzzled as if called out of sleep.* AMANDA *seizes her shoulders and turns her at an angle on the fire-escape landing.*] Now! Now, darling, wish!

LAURA. What shall I wish for, Mother?

AMANDA [*Her voice trembling and her eyes suddenly filling with tears*]. Happiness! And just a little bit of good fortune! [*The stage dims out.*]

Curtain

ACT II SCENE 7

Scene: The same.

Inner curtains closed between dining room and living room. Interiors of both rooms are dark as at beginning of play. (Music.) TOM *has on the same jacket and cap as at first. Same music as at beginning, fading as* TOM *begins.*

TOM [*Discovered leaning against grill on fire-escape landing, as before, and smoking*]. And so the following evening I brought Jim home to dinner. I had known Jim slightly in high school. In high school, Jim was a hero. He had tremendous Irish good nature and vitality with the scrubbed and polished look of white chinaware. He seemed to move in a continual spotlight. He was a star in basketball, captain of the debating club, president of the senior class and the glee club, and he sang the male lead in the annual light opera. He was forever running or bounding, never just walking. He seemed always just at the point of defeating the law of gravity. He was shooting with such velocity through his adolescence that you would just logically expect him to arrive at nothing short of the White House by the time he was thirty. But Jim apparently ran into more interference after his graduation from high school because his speed had definitely slowed. And so, at this particular time in our lives he was holding a job that wasn't much better than mine. He was the only one at the warehouse with whom I was on friendly terms. I was valuable to Jim as someone who could remember his former glory, who had seen him win basketball games and the silver cup in debating. He knew of my secret practice of retiring to a cabinet of the washroom to work on poems whenever business was slack in the warehouse. He called me Shakespeare. And while the other boys in the warehouse regarded me with suspicious hostility, Jim took a humorous attitude toward me. Gradually his attitude began to affect the other boys and their hostility wore off. And so, after a time they began to smile at me too, as people smile at some oddly fashioned dog that trots across their path at some distance. I knew that Jim and Laura had known each other in high school because I had heard my sister Laura speak admiringly of Jim's voice. I didn't know if Jim would remember her or not. Because in high school Laura had been as unobtrusive as Jim had been astonishing. And, if he did remember Laura, it was not as my sister, for when I asked him home to dinner, he smiled and said, "You know, a funny thing, Shakespeare, I never thought of you as having folks!" Well, he was about to discover that I did. . . . [*Music.* TOM *exits right. Interior living-room lights dim in.* AMANDA *is sitting on small table right of day-bed sewing on hem on* LAURA'S *dress.* LAURA *stands facing the door right.* AMANDA *has worked like a Turk in preparation for the gentleman caller. The results are astonishing. The new floor lamp with its rose-silk shade is in place, right of living room next to wall, a colored paper lantern conceals the broken light fixture in the ceiling, chintz covers are on chairs and sofa, a pair of new sofa pillows make their initial appearance.* LAURA *stands in the middle of room with lifted arms while* AMANDA *crouches before her, adjusting the hem of the new dress, devout and ritualistic. The dress is colored and designed by memory. The arrangement of* LAURA'S *hair is changed; it is softer and more becoming. A fragile, unearthly prettiness has come out in* LAURA, *she is like a piece of translucent glass touched by light, given a momentary radiance, not actual, not lasting.* AMANDA, *still seated, is sewing* LAURA'S *dress.* LAURA *is standing right of* AMANDA.]

AMANDA. Why are you trembling so, Laura?

LAURA. Mother, you've made me so nervous!

AMANDA. Why, how have I made you nervous?

LAURA. By all this fuss! You make it seem so important.

AMANDA. I don't understand you at all, honey. Every time I try to do anything for you that's the least bit different you just seem to set yourself against it. Now take a look at yourself. [LAURA *starts for door right.*] No, wait! Wait just a minute—I forgot something. [*Picks two powder puffs from day-bed.*]

LAURA. What is it?

AMANDA. A couple of improvements. [*Business with powder puffs.*] When I was a girl we had round little lacy things like that and we called them "Gay Deceivers."

LAURA. I won't wear them!

AMANDA. Of course you'll wear them.

LAURA. Why should I?

AMANDA. Well, to tell you the truth, honey, you're just a little bit flat-chested.

LAURA. You make it seem like we were setting a trap.

AMANDA. We are. All pretty girls are a trap and men expect them to be traps. Now look at yourself in the glass. [LAURA *crosses right. Looks at mirror, invisible to audience, which is in darkness up right of rear door.*] See? You look just like an angel on a postcard. Isn't that lovely? Now you just wait. I'm going to dress myself up. You're going to be astonished at your mother's appearance. [*End of music.* AMANDA *exits through curtains upstage off left in dining room.* LAURA *looks in mirror for a moment. Removes "Gay Deceivers," hides them under mattress of day-bed. Sits on small table right of day-bed for a moment, goes out to fire-escape landing, listens to dance music, until* AMANDA'S *entrance.* AMANDA, *off.*] I found an old dress in the trunk. But what do you know? I had to do a lot to it but it broke my heart when I had to let it out. Now, Laura, just look at your mother. Oh, no! Laura, come look at me now! [*Enters dining-room left door. Comes down through living-room curtain to living room center. Music.*]

LAURA [*Re-enters from fire-escape landing. Sits on left arm of armchair*]. Oh, Mother, how lovely! [AMANDA *wears a girlish frock. She carries a bunch of jonquils.*]

AMANDA [*Standing center, holding flowers*]. It used to be. It used to be. It had a lot of flowers on it, but they got awful tired so I had to take them all off. I led the cotillion in this dress years ago. I won the cake-walk twice at Sunset Hill, and I wore it to the Governor's ball in

Jackson. You should have seen your mother. You should have seen your mother how she just sashayed around [*crossing around left of day-bed back to center*] the ballroom, just like that. I had it on the day I met your father. I had malaria fever, too. The change of climate from East Tennessee to the Delta —weakened my resistance. Not enough to be dangerous, just enough to make me restless and giddy. Oh, it was lovely. Invitations poured in from all over. My mother said, "You can't go any place because you have a fever. You have to stay in bed." I said I wouldn't and I took quinine and kept on going and going. Dances every evening and long rides in the country in the afternoon and picnics. That country—that country—so lovely—so lovely in May, all lacy with dogwood and simply flooded with jonquils. My mother said, "You can't bring any more jonquils in this house." I said, "I will," and I kept on bringing them in anyhow. Whenever I saw them I said, "Wait a minute, I see jonquils," and I'd make my gentlemen callers get out of the carriage and help me gather some. To tell you the truth, Laura, it got to be a kind of a joke. "Look out," they'd say, "here comes that girl and we'll have to spend the afternoon picking jonquils." My mother said, "You can't bring any more jonquils in the house, there aren't any more vases to hold them." "That's quite all right," I said, "I can hold some myself." Malaria fever, your father and jonquils. [AMANDA *puts jonquils in* LAURA'*s lap and goes out on to fire-escape landing. Music stops. Thunder heard.*] I hope they get here before it starts to rain. I gave your brother a little extra change so he and Mr. O'Connor could take the service car home. [LAURA *puts flowers on armchair right, and crosses to door right.*]

LAURA. Mother!

AMANDA. What's the matter now? [*Re-entering room.*]

LAURA. What did you say his name was?

AMANDA. O'Connor. Why?

LAURA. What is his first name?

AMANDA [*Crosses to armchair right*]. I don't remember——Oh, yes, I do too —it was—Jim! [*Picks up flowers.*]

LAURA. Oh, Mother, not Jim O'Connor!

AMANDA. Yes, that was it, it was Jim! I've never known a Jim that wasn't nice. [*Crosses left, behind day-bed, puts flowers in vase.*]

LAURA. Are you sure his name was Jim O'Connor?

AMANDA. Why, sure I'm sure. Why?

LAURA. Is he the one that Tom used to know in high school?

AMANDA. He didn't say so. I think he just got to know him [*sits on day-bed*] at the warehouse.

LAURA. There was a Jim O'Connor we both knew in high school. If that is the one that Tom is bringing home to dinner——Oh, Mother, you'd have to excuse me, I wouldn't come to the table!

AMANDA. What's this now? What sort of silly talk is this?

LAURA. You asked me once if I'd ever liked a boy. Don't you remember I showed you this boy's picture?

AMANDA. You mean the boy in the yearbook?

LAURA. Yes, that boy.

AMANDA. Laura, Laura, were you in love with that boy?

LAURA [*Crosses to right of armchair*]. I don't know, Mother. All I know is that I couldn't sit at the table if it was him.

AMANDA [*Rises, crosses left and works up left of day-bed*]. It won't be him! It isn't the least bit likely. But whether it is or not, you will come to the table—you will not be excused.

LAURA. I'll have to be, Mother.

AMANDA [*Behind day-bed*]. I don't intend to humor your silliness, Laura. I've had too much from you and your brother, both. So just sit down and compose yourself till they come. Tom has forgotten his key, so you'll *have* to let them in when they arrive.

LAURA. Oh, Mother—*you* answer the door! [*Sits chair right.*]

AMANDA. How can I when I haven't even finished making the mayonnaise dressing for the salmon?

LAURA. Oh, Mother, please answer the door, don't make me do it! [*Thunder heard offstage.*]

AMANDA. Honey, do be reasonable! What's all this fuss about—just one gentleman caller—that's all—just one! [*Exits through living-room curtains. Tom and Jim enter alley right, climb fire-escape steps to landing, and wait outside of closed door. Hearing them approach,* LAURA *rises with a panicky gesture. She retreats to living-room curtains. The doorbell rings.* LAURA *catches her breath and touches her throat. More thunder heard offstage.*]

AMANDA [*Offstage*]. Laura, sweetheart, the door!

LAURA. Mother, please, you go to the door! [*Starts for door right, then back.*]

AMANDA [*Offstage, in a fierce whisper*]. What is the matter with you, you silly thing? [*Enters through living-room curtains, and stands by day-bed.*]

LAURA. Please you answer it, please.

AMANDA. Why have you chosen this moment to lose your mind? You go to that door.

LAURA. I can't.

AMANDA. Why can't you?

LAURA. Because I'm sick. [*Crosses to left end of day-bed and sits.*]

AMANDA. You're sick! Am I sick? You and your brother have me puzzled to death. You can never act like normal children. Will you give me one good reason why you should be afraid to open a door? You go to that door. Laura Wingfield, you march straight to that door!

LAURA [*Crosses to door right*]. Yes, Mother.

AMANDA [*Stopping* LAURA]. I've got to put courage in you, honey, for living. [*Exits through living-room curtains, and exits right into kitchen.* LAURA *opens door.* TOM *and* JIM *enter.* LAURA *remains hidden in hall behind door.*]

TOM. Laura—[*Laura crosses center.*] this is Jim. Jim, this is my sister Laura.

JIM. I didn't know that Shakespeare had a sister! How are you, Laura?

LAURA [*Retreating stiff and trembling. Shakes hands*]. How—how do you do?

JIM. Well, I'm okay! Your hand's *cold,* Laura! [TOM *puts hats on phone table.*]

LAURA. Yes, well—I've been playing the victrola. . . .

JIM. Must have been playing classical music on it. You ought to play a little hot swing music to warm you up. [LAURA *crosses to phonograph.* TOM *crosses up to* LAURA. LAURA *starts phonograph* [7]—looks at JIM. *Exits through living-room curtains and goes off left.*]

JIM. What's the matter?

TOM. Oh—Laura? Laura is—is terribly shy. [*Crosses and sits day-bed.*]

JIM [*Crosses down center*]. Shy, huh? Do you know it's unusual to meet a shy girl nowadays? I don't believe you ever mentioned you had a sister?

TOM. Well, now you know I have one. You want a piece of the paper?

JIM [*Crosses to* TOM]. Uh-huh.

TOM. Comics?

JIM. Comics? Sports! [*Takes paper. Crosses, sits chair right.*] I see that Dizzy Dean is on his bad behavior.

TOM [*Starts to door right. Goes out.*] Really?

JIM. Yeah. Where are *you* going? [*As* TOM *reaches steps right of fire-escape landing*].

TOM [*Calling from fire-escape landing*]. Out on the terrace to smoke.

JIM [*Rises, leaving newspaper in arm-*

[7] A worn record of "Dardanella" or some other popular tune of the 1920's.

chair, goes over to turn off victrola. Crosses right. Exits to fire-escape landing]. You know, Shakespeare—I'm going to sell you a bill of goods!

TOM. What goods?

JIM. A course I'm taking.

TOM. What course?

JIM. A course in public speaking! You know you and me, we're not the warehouse type.

TOM. Thanks—that's good news. What has public speaking got to do with it?

JIM. It fits you for—executive positions!

TOM. Oh.

JIM. I tell you it's done a helluva lot for me.

TOM. In what respect?

JIM. In all respects. Ask yourself: what's the difference between you and me and the guys in the office down front? Brains?—No! Ability?—No! Then what? Primarily, it amounts to just one single thing——

TOM. What is that one thing?

JIM. Social poise! The ability to square up to somebody and hold your own on any social level!

AMANDA [*Offstage*]. Tom?

TOM. Yes, Mother?

AMANDA. Is that you and Mr. O'Connor?

TOM. Yes, Mother.

AMANDA. Make yourselves comfortable.

TOM. We will.

AMANDA. Ask Mr. O'Connor if he would like to wash his hands?

JIM. No, thanks, ma'am—I took care of that down at the warehouse. Tom?

TOM. Huh?

JIM. Mr. Mendoza was speaking to me about you.

TOM. Favorably?

JIM. What do you think?

TOM. Well——

JIM. You're going to be out of a job if you don't wake up.

TOM. I'm waking up——

JIM. Yeah, but you show no signs.

TOM. The signs are interior. I'm just about to make a change. I'm right at the point of committing myself to a future that doesn't include the warehouse or Mr. Mendoza, or even a night school course in public speaking.

JIM. Now what are you gassing about?

TOM. I'm tired of the movies.

JIM. The movies!

TOM. Yes, movies! Look at them. [*He waves his hands.*] All of those glamorous people—having adventures—hogging it all, gobbling the whole thing up! You know what happens? People go to the *movies* instead of *moving*. Hollywood characters are supposed to have all the adventures for everybody in America, while everybody in America sits in a dark room and watches them having it! Yes, until there's a war. That's when adventure becomes available to the masses! Everyone's dish, not only Gable's! Then the people in the dark room come out of the dark room to have some adventures themselves—goody—goody! It's our turn now to go to the South Sea Island—to make a safari—to be exotic, far off . . . ! But I'm not patient. I don't want to wait till then. I'm tired of the movies and I'm about to move!

JIM [*Incredulously*]. Move?

TOM. Yes.

JIM. When?

TOM. Soon!

JIM. Where? Where?

TOM. I'm starting to boil inside. I know I seem dreamy, but inside—well, I'm boiling! Whenever I pick up a shoe I shudder a little, thinking how short life is and what I am doing!—Whatever that means, I know it doesn't mean shoes —except as something to wear on a traveler's feet! [*Gets card from inside coat pocket.*] Look!

JIM. What?

TOM. I'm a member.

JIM [*Reading*]. The Union of Merchant Seamen.

TOM. I paid my dues this month, instead of the electric light bill.

JIM. You'll regret it when they turn off the lights.

TOM. I won't be here.

JIM. Yeah, but how about your mother?

TOM. I'm like my father. The bastard son of a bastard. See how he grins? And he's been absent going on sixteen years.

JIM. You're just talking, you drip. How does your mother feel about it?

TOM. Sh! Here comes Mother! Mother's not acquainted with my plans!

AMANDA [*Offstage*]. Tom!

TOM. Yes, Mother?

AMANDA [*Offstage*]. Where are you all?

TOM. On the terrace, Mother.

AMANDA [*Enters through living-room curtain and stands center*]. Why don't you come in? [*They start inside. She advances to them.* TOM *is distinctly shocked at her appearance. Even* JIM *blinks a little. He is making his first contact with girlish Southern vivacity and in spite of the night-school course in public speaking is somewhat thrown off the beam by the unexpected outlay of social charm. Certain responses are attempted by* JIM *but are swept aside by* AMANDA'*s gay laughter and chatter.* TOM *is embarrassed but after the first shock* JIM *reacts very warmly. Grins and chuckles, is altogether won over.* TOM *and* JIM *come in, leaving door open.*]

TOM. Mother, you look so pretty.

AMANDA. You know, that's the first compliment you ever paid me. I wish you'd look pleasant when you're about to say something pleasant, so I could expect it. Mr. O'Connor? [JIM *crosses to* AMANDA.]

JIM. How do you do?

AMANDA. Well, well, well, so this is Mr. O'Connor? Introduction's entirely unnecessary. I've heard so much about you from my boy. I finally said to him, "Tom, good gracious, why don't you bring this paragon to supper finally? I'd like to meet this nice young man at the warehouse! Instead of just hearing you sing his praises so much?" I don't know why my son is so stand-offish—that's not Southern behavior. Let's sit down. [TOM *closes door, crosses up right, stands.* JIM *and* AMANDA *sit on day-bed,* JIM, *right,* AMANDA *left.*] Let's sit down, and I think we could stand a little more air in here. Tom, leave the door open. I felt a nice fresh breeze a moment ago. Where has it gone to? Mmmm, so warm already! And not quite summer, even. We're going to burn up when summer really gets started. However, we're having—we're having a very light supper. I think light things are better fo'—for this time of year. The same as light clothes are. Light clothes and light food are what warm weather calls fo'. You know our blood gets so thick during th' winter—it takes a while fo' us to adjust ou'selves—when the season changes. . . . It's come so quick this year. I wasn't prepared. All of a sudden—Heavens! Already summer!—I ran to the trunk an'—pulled out this light dress—terribly old! Historical almost! But feels so good—so good and cool, why, y' know——

TOM. Mother, how about our supper?

AMANDA [*Rises, crosses right to* TOM]. Honey, you go ask sister if supper is ready! You know that sister is in full charge of supper. Tell her you hungry boys are waiting for it. [TOM *exits through curtains and off left.* AMANDA *turns to* JIM.] Have you met Laura?

JIM. Well, she came to the door.

AMANDA. She let you in?

JIM. Yes, ma'am.

AMANDA [*Crossing to armchair and sitting*]. She's very pretty.

JIM. Oh, yes, ma'am.

AMANDA. It's rare for a girl as sweet

an' pretty as Laura to be domestic! But Laura is, thank heavens, not only pretty but also very domestic. I'm not at all. I never was a bit. I never could make a thing but angel-food cake. Well, in the South we had so many servants. Gone, gone, gone. All vestige of gracious living! Gone completely! I wasn't prepared for what the future brought me. All of my gentlemen callers were sons of planters and so of course I assumed that I would be married to one and raise my family on a large piece of land with plenty of servants. But man proposes—and woman accepts the proposal!—To vary that old, old saying a little bit—I married no planter! I married a man who worked for the telephone company!—That gallantly smiling gentleman over there! [*Points to picture.*] A telephone man who—fell in love with long-distance!—Now he travels and I don't even know where!—But what am I going on for about my—tribulations? Tell me yours—I hope you don't have any! Tom?

TOM [*Re-enters through living-room curtains from off left*]. Yes, Mother.

AMANDA. What about that supper?

TOM. Why, supper is on the table. [*Inner curtains between living room and dining room open. Lights dim up in dining room, dim out in living room.*]

AMANDA. Oh, so it is. [*Rises, crosses up to table center in dining room and chair center.*] How lovely. Where is Laura?

TOM [*Going to chair left and standing*]. Laura is not feeling too well and thinks maybe she'd better not come to the table.

AMANDA. Laura!

LAURA [*Offstage. Faintly*]. Yes, Mother? [TOM *gestures re:* JIM.]

AMANDA. Mr. O'Connor. [JIM *crosses up left to table and to chair left and stands.*]

JIM. Thank you, ma'am.

AMANDA. Laura, we can't say grace till you come to the table.

LAURA [*Enters up left, obviously quite faint, lips trembling, eyes wide and staring. Moves unsteadily toward dining-room table*]. Oh, Mother, I'm so sorry. [TOM *catches her as she feels faint. He takes her to day-bed in living room.*]

AMANDA [*As* LAURA *lies down*]. Why, Laura, you are sick, darling! Laura—rest on the sofa. Well! [*To* JIM.] Standing over the hot stove made her ill!—I told her that it was just too warm this evening, but—— [*To* TOM.] Is Laura all right now?

TOM. She's better, Mother. [*Sits chair left in dining room. Thunder off-stage.*]

AMANDA [*Returning to dining room and sitting at table, as* JIM *does*]. My goodness, I suppose we're going to have a little rain! Tom, you say grace.

TOM. What?

AMANDA. What do we generally do before we have something to eat? We say grace, don't we?

TOM. For these and all Thy mercies—God's Holy Name be praised. [*Lights dim out. Music.*]

ACT II SCENE 8

Scene: The same. A half hour later. Dinner is coming to an end in dining room.

AMANDA, TOM *and* JIM *sitting at table as at end of last scene. Lights dim up in both rooms, and music ends.*

AMANDA [*Laughing, as* JIM *laughs too*]. You know, Mr. O'Connor, I haven't had such a pleasant evening in a long time.

JIM [*Rises*]. Well, Mrs. Wingfield, let me give you a toast. Here's to the old South.

AMANDA. The old South. [*Blackout in both rooms.*]

JIM. Hey, Mr. Light Bulb!

AMANDA. Where was Moses when the lights went out? Do you know the answer to that one, Mr. O'Connor?

JIM. No, ma'am, what's the answer to that one?

AMANDA. Well, I heard one answer, but it wasn't very nice. I thought you might know another one.

JIM. No, ma'am.

AMANDA. It's lucky I put those candles on the table. I just put them on for ornamentation, but it's nice when they prove useful, too.

JIM. Yes, ma'am.

AMANDA. Now, if one of you gentlemen can provide me with a match we can have some illumination.

JIM [*Lighting candles. Dim-in glow for candles*]. I can, ma'am.

AMANDA. Thank you.

JIM [*Crosses back to right of dining room table*]. Not at all, ma'am.

AMANDA. I guess it must be a burned-out fuse. Mr. O'Connor, do you know anything about a burned-out fuse?

JIM. I know a little about them, ma'am, but where's the fuse box?

AMANDA. Must you know that, too? Well, it's in the kitchen. [JIM *exits right into kitchen.*] Be careful. It's dark. Don't stumble over anything. [*Sound of crash offstage.*] Oh my goodness, wouldn't it be awful if we lost him! Are you all right, Mr. O'Connor?

JIM [*Offstage*]. Yes, ma'am, I'm all right.

AMANDA. You know, electricity is a very mysterious thing. The whole universe is mysterious to me. Wasn't it Benjamin Franklin who tied a key to a kite? I'd like to have seen that—he might have looked mighty silly. Some people say that science clears up all the mysteries for us. In my opinion they just keep on adding more. Haven't you found it yet?

JIM [*Re-enters right*]. Yes, ma'am. I found it all right, but them fuses look okay to me. [*Sits as before.*]

AMANDA. Tom.

TOM. Yes, Mother?

AMANDA. That light bill I gave you several days ago. The one I got the notice about?

TOM. Oh—yeah. You mean last month's bill?

AMANDA. You didn't neglect it by any chance?

TOM. Well, I——

AMANDA. You did! I might have known it!

JIM. Oh, maybe Shakespeare wrote a poem on that light bill, Mrs. Wingfield?

AMANDA. Maybe he did, too. I might have known better than to trust him with it! There's such a high price for negligence in this world today.

JIM. Maybe the poem will win a ten-dollar prize.

AMANDA. We'll just have to spend the rest of the evening in the nineteenth century, before Mr. Edison found that Mazda lamp!

JIM. Candle-light is my favorite kind of light.

AMANDA. That shows you're romantic! But that's no excuse for Tom. However, I think it was very nice of them to let us finish our dinner before they plunged us into everlasting darkness. Tom, as a penalty for your carelessness you can help me with the dishes.

JIM [*Rising.* TOM *rises*]. Can I be of some help, ma'am?

AMANDA [*Rising*]. Oh, no, I couldn't allow that.

JIM. Well, I ought to be good for *something*.

AMANDA. What did I hear?

JIM. I just said, "I ought to be good for something."

AMANDA. That's what I thought you said. Well, Laura's all by her lonesome out front. Maybe you'd like to keep her company. I can give you this lovely old candelabrum for light. [JIM *takes candles.*] It used to be on the altar at the Church of the Heavenly Rest, but it was melted a little out of shape when the church burnt down. The church was struck by lightning one spring, and Gypsy Jones, who was holding a revival meeting in the village, said that the church was struck by lightning because the Episcopalians had started to have card parties right in the church.

JIM. Is that so, ma'am?

AMANDA. I never say anything that isn't so.

JIM. I beg your pardon.

AMANDA [*Pouring wine into glass—hands it to* JIM]. I'd like Laura to have a little dandelion wine. Do you think you can hold them both?

JIM. I can try, ma'am.

AMANDA [*Exits up right into kitchen*]. Now, Tom, you get into your apron.

TOM. Yes, Mother. [*Follows* AMANDA. JIM *looks around, puts wine-glass down, takes swig from wine decanter, replaces it with thud, takes wine-glass—enters living room. Inner curtains close as dining room dims out.* LAURA *sits up nervously as* JIM *enters. Her speech at first is low and breathless from the almost intolerable strain of being alone with a stranger. In her speeches in this scene, before* JIM'*s warmth overcomes her paralyzing shyness,* LAURA'*s voice is thin and breathless as though she has just run up a steep flight of stairs.*]

JIM [*Entering holding candelabra with lighted candles in one hand and glass of wine in other, and stands*]. How are you feeling now? Any better? [JIM'*s attitude is gently humorous. In playing this scene it should be stressed that while the incident is apparently unimportant, it is to* LAURA *the climax of her secret life.*]

LAURA. Yes, thank you.

JIM [*Gives her glass of wine*]. Oh, here, this is for you. It's a little dandelion wine.

LAURA. Thank you.

JIM [*Crosses center*]. Well, drink it —but don't get drunk. [*He laughs heartily.*] Say, where'll I put the candles?

LAURA. Oh, anywhere . . .

JIM. Oh, how about right here on the floor? You got any objections?

LAURA. No.

JIM. I'll just spread a newspaper under it to catch the drippings. [*Gets newspaper from armchair. Puts candelabra down on floor center.*] I like to sit on the floor. [*Sits on floor.*] Mind if I do?

LAURA. Oh, no.

JIM. Would you give me a pillow?

LAURA. What?

JIM. A pillow!

LAURA. Oh . . . [*Puts wine-glass on telephone table, hands him pillow, sits left on day-bed.*]

JIM. How about you? Don't you like to sit on the floor?

LAURA. Oh, yes.

JIM. Well, why don't you?

LAURA. I—will.

JIM. Take a pillow! [*Throws pillow as she sits on floor.*] I can't see you sitting way over there. [*Sits on floor again.*]

LAURA. I can—see you.

JIM. Yeah, but that's not fair. I'm right here in the limelight. [LAURA *moves a little closer to him.*] Good! Now I can see you! Are you comfortable?

LAURA. Yes. Thank you.

JIM. So am I. I'm comfortable as a cow! Say, would you care for a piece of chewing gum? [*Offers gum.*]

LAURA. No, thank you.

JIM. I think that I will indulge. [*Musingly unwraps it and holds it up.*] Gee, think of the fortune made by the guy that invented the first piece of chewing gum. It's amazing, huh? Do you know that the Wrigley Building is one of the sights of Chicago?—I saw it summer before last at the Century of Progress.—Did you take in the Century of Progress?

LAURA. No, I didn't.

JIM. Well, it was a wonderful exposition, believe me. You know what impressed me most? The Hall of Science. Gives you an idea of what the future will be like in America. Oh, it's more wonderful than the present time is! Say, your brother tells me you're shy. Is that right, Laura?

LAURA. I—don't know.

JIM. I judge you to be an old-fashioned type of girl. Oh, I think that's a wonderful type to be. I hope you don't think I'm being too personal—do you?

LAURA. Mr. O'Connor?

JIM. Huh?

LAURA. I believe I *will* take a piece of gum, if you don't mind. [JIM *peels gum—gets on knees, hands it to* LAURA. *She breaks off a tiny piece.* JIM *looks at what remains, puts it in his mouth, and sits again.*] Mr. O'Connor, have you—kept up with your singing?

JIM. Singing? Me?

LAURA. Yes. I remember what a beautiful voice you had.

JIM. You heard me sing?

LAURA. Oh, yes! Very often. . . . I —don't suppose—you remember me—at all?

JIM [*Smiling doubtfully*]. You know, as a matter of fact I did have an idea I'd seen you before. Do you know it seemed almost like I was about to remember your name. But the name I was about to remember—wasn't a name! So I stopped myself before I said it.

LAURA. Wasn't it—Blue Roses?

JIM [*Grinning*]. Blue Roses! Oh, my gosh, yes—Blue Roses! You know, I didn't connect you with high school somehow or other. But that's where it was, it was high school. Gosh, I didn't even know you were Shakespeare's sister! Gee, I'm sorry.

LAURA. I didn't expect you to.—You —barely knew me!

JIM. But, we did have a speaking acquaintance.

LAURA. Yes, we—spoke to each other.

JIM. Say, didn't we have a class in something together?

LAURA. Yes, we did.

JIM. What class was that?

LAURA. It was—singing—chorus!

JIM. Aw!

LAURA. I sat across the aisle from you in the auditorium. Mondays, Wednesdays, and Fridays.

JIM. Oh, yeah! I remember now—you're the one who always came in late.

LAURA. Yes, it was so hard for me, getting upstairs. I had that brace on my leg then—it clumped so loud!

JIM. I never heard any clumping.

LAURA [*Wincing at recollection*]. To me it sounded like—thunder!

JIM. I never even noticed.

LAURA. Everybody was seated before I came in. I had to walk in front of all those people. My seat was in the back row. I had to go clumping up the aisle with everyone watching!

JIM. Oh, gee, you shouldn't have been self-conscious.

LAURA. I know, but I was. It was always such a relief when the singing started.

JIM. I remember now. And I used to call you Blue Roses. How did I ever get started calling you a name like that?

LAURA. I was out of school a little while with pleurosis. When I came back you asked me what was the matter. I said I had pleurosis and you thought I said Blue Roses. So that's what you always called me after that!

JIM. I hope you didn't mind?

LAURA. Oh, no—I liked it. You see, I wasn't acquainted with many—people . . .

JIM. Yeah. I remember you sort of stuck by yourself.

LAURA. I never did have much luck at making friends.

JIM. Well, I don't see why you wouldn't.

LAURA. Well, I started out badly.

JIM. You mean being——?

LAURA. Well, yes, it—sort of—stood between me . . .

JIM. You shouldn't have let it!

LAURA. I know, but it did, and I——

JIM. You mean you were shy with people!

LAURA. I tried not to be but never could——

JIM. Overcome it?

LAURA. No, I—never could!

JIM. Yeah. I guess being shy is something you have to work out of kind of gradually.

LAURA. Yes—I guess it——

JIM. Takes time!

LAURA. Yes . . .

JIM. Say, you know something, Laura? [*Rises to sit on day-bed right.*] People are not so dreadful when you know them. That's what you have to remember! And everybody has problems, not just you but practically everybody has problems. You think of yourself as being the only one who is disappointed. But just look around you and what do you see—a lot of people just as disappointed as you are. You take me, for instance. Boy, when I left high school I thought I'd be a lot further along at this time than I am now. Say, you remember that wonderful write-up I had in "The Torch"?

LAURA. Yes, I do! [*She gets yearbook from under pillow left of day-bed.*]

JIM. Said I was bound to succeed in anything I went into! Holy Jeez! "The Torch"! [*She opens book, shows it to him and sits next to him on day-bed.*]

LAURA. Here you are in "The Pirates of Penzance"!

JIM. "The Pirates"! "Oh, better far to live and die under the brave black flag I fly!" I sang the lead in that operetta.

LAURA. So beautifully!

JIM. Aw . . .

LAURA. Yes, yes—beautifully—beautifully!

JIM. You heard me then, huh?

LAURA. I heard you all three times!

JIM. No!

LAURA. Yes.

JIM. You mean all three performances?

LAURA. Yes!

JIM. What for?

LAURA. I—wanted to ask you to—autograph my program. [*Takes program from book.*]

JIM. Why didn't you ask me?

LAURA. You were always surrounded by your own friends so much that I never had a chance.

JIM. Aw, you should have just come right up and said, Here is my——

LAURA. Well, I—thought you might think I was——

JIM. Thought I might think you was —what?

LAURA. Oh——

JIM [*With reflective relish*]. Oh! Yeah, I was beleaguered by females in those days.

LAURA. You were terribly popular!

JIM. Yeah . . .

LAURA. You had such a—friendly way——

JIM. Oh, I was spoiled in high school.

LAURA. Everybody liked you!

JIM. Including you?

LAURA. I—why, yes, I—I did, too. . . .

JIM. Give me that program, Laura. [*She does so, and he signs it.*] There you are—better late than never!

LAURA. My—what a—surprise!

JIM. My signature's not worth very much right now. But maybe some day —it will increase in value! You know, being disappointed in one thing and being discouraged is something else. Well, I may be disappointed but I am not discouraged. Say, you finished high school?

LAURA. I made bad grades in my final examinations.

JIM. You mean you dropped out?

LAURA [*Rises*]. I didn't go back. [*Crosses right to menagerie.* JIM *lights cigarette still sitting on day-bed.* LAURA *puts yearbook under menagerie. Rises, picks up unicorn—small glass object—her back to* JIM. *When she touches unicorn, music.*] How is—Emily Meisenbach getting along?

JIM. That kraut-head!

LAURA. Why do you call her that?

JIM. Because that's what she was.

LAURA. You're not still—going with her?

JIM. Oh, I never even see her.

LAURA. It said in the Personal section that you were—engaged!

JIM. Uh-huh. I know, but I wasn't impressed by that—propaganda!

LAURA. It wasn't—the truth?

JIM. It was only true in Emily's optimistic opinion!

LAURA. Oh . . . [*Turns right of* JIM. JIM *lights a cigarette and leans indolently back on his elbows smiling at* LAURA *with a warmth and charm which lights her inwardly with altar candles. She remains by the glass menagerie table and turns in her hands a piece of glass to cover her tumult. Cut music.*]

JIM. What have you done since high school? Huh?

LAURA. What?

JIM. I said what have you done since high school?

LAURA. Nothing much.

JIM. You must have been doing something all this time.

LAURA. Yes.

JIM. Well, then, such as what?

LAURA. I took a business course at business college . . .

JIM. You did? How did that work out?

LAURA [*Turns back to* JIM]. Well, not very—well. . . . I had to drop out, it gave me—indigestion. . . .

JIM [*Laughs gently*]. What are you doing now?

LAURA. I don't do anything—much. . . . Oh, please don't think I sit around doing nothing! My glass collection takes a good deal of time. Glass is something you have to take good care of.

JIM. What did you say—about glass?

LAURA [*She clears her throat and turns away again, acutely shy*]. Collection, I said—I have one.

JIM [*Puts out cigarette. Abruptly*]. Say! You know what I judge to be the trouble with you? [*Rises from day-bed and crosses right.*] Inferiority complex! You know what that is? That's what they call it when a fellow low-rates himself! Oh, I understand it because I had it, too. Uh-huh! Only my case was not as aggravated as yours seems to be. I had it until I took up public speaking and developed my voice, and learned that I had an aptitude for science. Do you know that until that time I never thought of myself as being outstanding in any way whatsoever!

LAURA. Oh, my!

JIM. Now I've never made a regular study of it [*sits armchair right*] mind you, but I have a friend who says I can analyze people better than doctors that make a profession of it. I don't claim that's necessarily true, but I can sure guess a person's psychology. Excuse me, Laura. [*Takes out gum.*] I always take it out when the flavor is gone. I'll just wrap it in a piece of paper. [*Tears a piece of paper off the newspaper under candelabrum, wraps gum in it, crosses to day-bed, looks to see if* LAURA *is watching. She isn't. Crosses around day-bed.*] I know how it is when you get it stuck on a shoe. [*Throws gum under day-bed, crosses around left of day-bed. Crosses right to* LAURA.] Yep—that's what I judge to be your principal trouble. A lack of confidence in yourself as a person. Now I'm basing that fact on a number of your remarks and on certain observations I've made. For instance, that clumping you thought was so awful in high school. You say that you dreaded to go upstairs?

You see what you did? You dropped out of school, you gave up an education all because of a little clump, which as far as I can see is practically non-existent! Oh, a little physical defect is all you have. It's hardly noticeable even! Magnified a thousand times by your imagination! You know what my strong advice to you is? You've got to think of yourself as *superior* in some way! [*Crosses left to small table right of day-bed. Sits.* LAURA *sits in armchair.*]

LAURA. In what way would I think?

JIM. Why, man alive, Laura! Look around you a little and what do you see? A world full of common people! All of 'em born and all of 'em going to die! Now, which of them has one-tenth of your strong points! Or mine! Or anybody else's for that matter? You see, everybody excels in some one thing. Well—some in many! You take me, for instance. My interest happens to lie in electrodynamics. I'm taking a course in radio engineering at night school, on top of a fairly responsible job at the warehouse. I'm taking that course *and* studying public speaking.

LAURA. Ohhhh. My!

JIM. Because I believe in the future of television! I want to be ready to go right up along with it. [*Rises, crosses right.*] I'm planning to get in on the ground floor. Oh, I've already made the right connections. All that remains now is for the industry itself to get under way—full steam! You know, *knowledge*—zszzppp! *Money*—Zzzzzzpp! POWER! Wham! That's the cycle democracy is built on! [*Pause.*] I guess you think I think a lot of myself!

LAURA. No—o-o-o, I don't.

JIM [*Kneels at armchair right*]. Well, now how about you? Isn't there some one thing that you take more interest in than anything else?

LAURA. Oh—yes . . .

JIM. Well, then, such as what?

LAURA. Well, I do—as I said—have my—glass collection . . . [*Music.*]

JIM. Oh, you do. What kind of glass is it?

LAURA [*Takes glass ornament off shelf*]. Little articles of it, ornaments mostly. Most of them are little animals made out of glass, the tiniest little animals in the world. Mother calls them the glass menagerie! Here's an example of one, if you'd like to see it! This is one of the oldest, it's nearly thirteen. [*Hands it to* JIM.] Oh, be careful—if you breathe, it breaks! [*The* BELL SOLO *should begin here.*]

JIM. I'd better not take it. I'm pretty clumsy with things.

LAURA. Go on, I trust you with him! [JIM *takes horse.*] There—you're holding him gently! Hold him over the light, he loves the light! [JIM *holds horse up to light.*] See how the light shines through him?

JIM. It sure does shine!

LAURA. I shouldn't be partial, but he is my favorite one.

JIM. Say, what kind of a thing is this one supposed to be?

LAURA. Haven't you noticed the single horn on his forehead?

JIM. Oh, a unicorn, huh?

LAURA. Mmmm-hmmmmm!

JIM. Unicorns, aren't they extinct in the modern world?

LAURA. I know!

JIM. Poor little fellow must feel kind of lonesome.

LAURA. Well, if he does he doesn't complain about it. He stays on a shelf with some horses that don't have horns and they all seem to get along nicely together.

JIM. They do. Say, where will I put him?

LAURA. Put him on the table. [JIM *crosses to small table right of day-bed, puts unicorn on it.*] They all like a change of scenery once in a while!

JIM [*Center, facing upstage, stretching arms*]. They do. [*Dance music.*] Hey! Look how big my shadow is when I stretch.

LAURA [*Crossing to left of day-bed*]. Oh, oh, yes—it stretched across the ceiling!

JIM [*Crosses to door right, exits, leaving door open, and stands on fire-escape landing. Sings to music.* (*Popular record of day for dance hall.*) *When* JIM *opens door, music swells*]. It's stopped raining. Where does the music come from?

LAURA. From the Paradise Dance Hall across the alley.

JIM [*Re-entering room, closing door right, crosses to* LAURA]. How about cutting the rug a little, Miss Wingfield? Or is your program filled up? Let me take a look at it. [*Crosses back center. Music, in dance hall, goes into a waltz. Business here with imaginary dance program card.*] Oh, say! Every dance is taken! I'll just scratch some of them out. Ahhhh, a waltz! [*Crosses to* LAURA.]

LAURA. I—can't dance!

JIM. There you go with that inferiority stuff!

LAURA. I've never danced in my life!

JIM. Come on, try!

LAURA. Oh, but I'd step on you!

JIM. Well, I'm not made out of glass.

LAURA. How—how do we start?

JIM. You hold your arms out a little.

LAURA. Like this?

JIM. A little bit higher. [*Takes* LAURA *in arms.*] That's right. Now don't tighten up, that's the principal thing about it—just relax.

LAURA. It's hard not to.

JIM. Okay.

LAURA. I'm afraid you can't budge me.

JIM [*Dances around left of day-bed slowly*]. What do you bet I can't.

LAURA. Goodness, yes, you can!

JIM. Let yourself go, now, Laura, just let yourself go.

LAURA. I'm——

JIM. Come on!

LAURA. Trying!

JIM. Not so stiff now—easy does it!

LAURA. I know, but I'm——!

JIM. Come on! Loosen your backbone a little! [*When they get to upstage corner of day-bed—so that the audience will not see him lift her—*JIM'*s arm tightens around her waist and he swings her around center with her feet off floor about 3 complete turns before they hit the small table right of day-bed. Music swells as* JIM *lifts her.*] There we go! [JIM *knocks glass horse off table. Music fades.*]

LAURA. Oh, it doesn't matter——

JIM [*Picks horse up*]. We knocked the little glass horse over.

LAURA. Yes.

JIM [*Hands unicorn to* LAURA]. Is he broken?

LAURA. Now he's just like all the other horses.

JIM. You mean he lost his——?

LAURA. He's lost his horn. It doesn't matter. Maybe it's a blessing in disguise.

JIM. Gee, I bet you'll never forgive me. I bet that was your favorite piece of glass.

LAURA. Oh, I don't have favorites—[*Pause.*] much. It's no tragedy. Glass breaks so easily. No matter how careful you are. The traffic jars the shelves and things fall off them.

JIM. Still I'm awfully sorry that I was the cause of it.

LAURA. I'll just imagine he had an operation. The horn was removed to make him feel less—freakish! [*Crosses left, sits on small table.*] Now he will feel more at home with the other horses, the ones who don't have horns. . . .

JIM [*Sits on arm of armchair right, faces* LAURA]. I'm glad to see that you have a sense of humor. You know—you're—different than anybody else I know? [*Music.*] Do you mind me telling you that? I mean it. You make me feel sort of—I don't know how to say it! I'm usually pretty good at expressing things, but—this is something I don't know how to say! Did anybody ever tell you that you were pretty? [*Rises, crosses to* LAURA.] Well, you are! And in a different way from anyone else. And all the nicer because of the difference. Oh, boy, I wish that you were my sister. I'd teach you to have confidence in yourself. Being different is nothing to be ashamed of. Because other people aren't such wonderful people. They're a hundred times one thousand. You're one times one! They walk all over the earth. You just stay here. They're as common as—weeds, but —you, well you're—*Blue Roses!*

LAURA. But blue is—wrong for—roses . . .

JIM. It's right for you!—You're pretty!

LAURA. In what respect am I pretty?

JIM. In all respects—your eyes—your hair. Your hands are pretty! You think I'm saying this because I'm invited to dinner and have to be nice. Oh, I could do that! I could say lots of things without being sincere. But I'm talking to you sincerely. I happened to notice you had this inferiority complex that keeps you from feeling comfortable with people. Somebody ought to build your confidence up—way up! and make you proud instead of shy and turning away and—blushing—— [JIM *lifts* LAURA *up on small table on "way up."*] Somebody —ought to—[*Lifts her down.*] somebody ought to—kiss you, Laura! [*They kiss.* JIM *releases her and turns slowly away, crossing a little down right. Then, quietly, to himself: As* JIM *turns away, music ends.*] Gee, I shouldn't have done that—that was way off the beam. [*Gives way down right. Turns to* LAURA. LAURA *sits on small table.*] Would you care for a cigarette? You don't smoke, do you? How about a mint? Peppermint—Life-Saver? My pocket's a regular drugstore. . . . Laura, you know, if I had a sister like you, I'd do the same thing as Tom. I'd bring fellows home to meet you. Maybe I shouldn't be saying this. That may not have been the idea in having me over. But what if it was? There's nothing wrong with that.—The only trouble is that in my case—I'm not in a position to—— I can't ask for your number and say I'll phone. I can't call up next week end—ask for a date. I thought I had better explain the situation in case you—misunderstood and I hurt your feelings . . .

LAURA [*Faintly*]. You—won't—call again?

JIM [*Crossing to right of day-bed, and sitting*]. No, I can't. You see, I've—got strings on me. Laura, I've—been going steady! I go out all the time with a girl named Betty. Oh, she's a nice quiet home girl like you, and Catholic and Irish, and in a great many ways we—get along fine. I met her last summer on a moonlight boat trip up the river to Alton, on the *Majestic.* Well—right away from the start it was—love! Oh, boy, being in love has made a new man of me! The power of love is pretty tremendous! Love is something that—changes the whole world. It happened that Betty's aunt took sick and she got a wire and had to go to Centralia. So naturally when Tom asked me to dinner—naturally I accepted the invitation, not knowing—I mean—not knowing. I wish that you would—say something. [LAURA *gives* JIM *unicorn.*] What are you doing that for? You mean you want me to have him? What for?

LAURA. A—souvenir. [*She crosses right to menagerie.* JIM *rises.*]

AMANDA [*Offstage*]. I'm coming, children. [*She enters into dining room from kitchen right.*] I thought you'd like some liquid refreshment. [*Puts tray on small table. Lifts a glass.*] Mr. O'Connor, have you heard that song about lemonade? It's

Lemonade, lemonade,
Made in the shade and stirred with a spade—
And then it's good enough for any old maid!

JIM. No, ma'am, I never heard it.

AMANDA. Why are you so serious, honey? [*To* LAURA.]

JIM. Well, we were having a serious conversation.

AMANDA. I don't understand modern young people. When I was a girl I was gay about everything.

JIM. You haven't changed a bit, Mrs. Wingfield.

AMANDA. I suppose it's the gaiety of the occasion that has rejuvenated me. Well, here's to the gaiety of the occasion! [*Spills lemonade on dress.*] Oooo! I baptized myself. [*Puts glass on small table right of day-bed.*] I found some cherries in the kitchen, and I put one in each glass.

JIM. You shouldn't have gone to all that trouble, ma'am.

AMANDA. It was no trouble at all. Didn't you hear us cutting up in the kitchen? I was so outdone with Tom for not bringing you over sooner, but now you've found your way I want you to come all the time—not just once in a while—but all the time. Oh, I think I'll go back in that kitchen. [*Starts to exit up center.*]

JIM. Oh, no, ma'am, please don't go, ma'am. As a matter of fact, I've got to be going.

AMANDA. Oh, Mr. O'Connor, it's only the shank of the evening! [JIM *and* AMANDA *stand upper center.*]

JIM. Well, you know how it is.

AMANDA. You mean you're a young working man and have to keep workingmen's hours?

JIM. Yes, ma'am.

AMANDA. Well, we'll let you off early this time, but only on the condition that you stay later next time, much later—— What's the best night for you? Saturday?

JIM. Well, as a matter of fact, I have a couple of time-clocks to punch, Mrs. Wingfield, one in the morning and another one at night!

AMANDA. Oh, isn't that nice, you're so ambitious! You work at night, too?

JIM. No, ma'am, not work but—Betty!

AMANDA [*Crosses left below day-bed*]. Betty? Who's Betty?

JIM. Oh, just a girl. The girl I go steady with!

AMANDA. You mean it's serious? [*Crosses down left.*]

JIM. Oh, yes, ma'am. We're going to be married the second Sunday in June.

AMANDA [*Sits on day-bed*]. Tom didn't say anything at all about your going to be married?

JIM. Well, the cat's not out of the bag at the warehouse yet. [*Picks up hat from telephone table.*] You know how they are. They call you Romeo and stuff like that.—It's been a wonderful evening, Mrs. Wingfield. I guess this is what they mean by Southern hospitality.

AMANDA. It was nothing. Nothing at all.

JIM. I hope it don't seem like I'm rushing off. But I promised Betty I'd pick her up at the Wabash depot an' by the time I get my jalopy down there her train'll be in. Some women are pretty upset if you keep them waiting.

AMANDA. Yes, I know all about the tyranny of women! Well, good-by, Mr. O'Connor. [AMANDA *puts out hand.* JIM *takes it.*] I wish you happiness—and good fortune. You wish him that, too, don't you, Laura?

LAURA. Yes, I do, Mother.

JIM [*Crosses left to* LAURA]. Good-by, Laura. I'll always treasure that souvenir. And don't you forget the good advice I gave you. So long, Shakespeare! [*Up center.*] Thanks, again, ladies.—Good night! [*He grins and ducks jauntily out right.*]

AMANDA [*Faintly*]. Well, well, well. Things have a way of turning out so badly—— [LAURA *crosses to phonograph, puts on record.*] I don't believe that I would play the victrola. Well, well—well, our gentleman caller was engaged to be married! Tom!

TOM [*Off*]. Yes, Mother?

AMANDA. Come out here. I want to tell you something very funny.

TOM [*Entering through right kitchen door to dining room and into living room, through curtains, down center*]. Has the gentleman caller gotten away already?

AMANDA. The gentleman caller made a very early departure. That was a nice joke you played on us, too!

TOM. How do you mean?

AMANDA. You didn't mention that he was engaged to be married.

TOM. Jim? Engaged?

AMANDA. That's what he just informed us.

TOM. I'll be jiggered! I didn't know.

AMANDA. That seems very peculiar.

TOM. What's peculiar about it?

AMANDA. Didn't you tell me he was your best friend down at the warehouse?

TOM. He is, but how did I know?

AMANDA. It seems very peculiar you didn't know your best friend was engaged to be married!

TOM. The warehouse is the place where I work, not where I know things about people!

AMANDA. You don't know things anywhere! You live in a dream; you manufacture illusions! [TOM *starts for rear door.*] Where are you going? Where are you going? Where are you going?

TOM. I'm going to the movies.

AMANDA [*Rises, crosses up to* TOM]. That's right, now that you've had us make such fools of ourselves. The effort, the preparations, all the expense! The new floor lamp, the rug, the clothes for Laura! All for what? To entertain some other girl's fiancé! Go to the movies, go! Don't think about us, a mother deserted, an unmarried sister who's crippled and has no job! Don't let anything interfere with your selfish pleasure! Just go, go, go—to the movies!

TOM. All right, I will, and the more you shout at me about my selfish pleasures, the quicker I'll go, and I won't go to the movies either. [*Gets hat from phone table, slams door right, and exits up alley right.*]

AMANDA [*Crosses up to fire-escape landing, yelling*]. Go, then! Then go to the moon—you selfish dreamer! [*Music. Interior light dims out. Re-enters living room, slamming right door.* TOM'*s closing speech is timed with the interior pantomime. The interior scene is played as though viewed through soundproof glass, behind outer scrim curtain.* AMANDA, *standing, appears to be making a comforting speech to* LAURA, *who is huddled on right side of day-bed. Now that we cannot hear the mother's speech, her silliness is gone and she has dignity and tragic beauty.* LAURA'*s hair hides her face until at the end of the speech she lifts it to smile at her mother.* AMANDA'*s gestures are slow and graceful, almost dance-like, as she comforts her daughter.* TOM, *who has meantime put on, as before, the jacket and cap, enters down right from offstage, and again comes to fire-escape landing, stands as he speaks. Meantime lights are upon* AMANDA *and* LAURA, *but are dim.*]

TOM. I didn't go to the moon. I went much farther. For time is the longest distance between two places. . . . I left Saint Louis. I descended these steps of this fire-escape for the last time and followed, from then on, in my father's footsteps, attempting to find in motion what was lost in space. . . . I traveled around a great deal. The cities swept about me like dead leaves, leaves that were brightly colored but torn away from the branches. I would have stopped, but I was pursued by something. It always came upon me unawares, taking me altogether by surprise. Perhaps it was a familiar bit of music. Perhaps it was only a piece of transparent glass. . . . Perhaps I am walking along a street at night, in some strange city, before I have found companions, and I pass the lighted window of a shop where perfume is sold. The window is filled with pieces of colored glass, tiny transparent bottles in delicate colors, like bits of a shattered rainbow. Then all at once my sister touches my shoulder. I turn around and look into her eyes. . . . Oh, Laura, Laura, I tried to leave you behind me, but I am more faithful than I intended to be! I reach for a cigarette, I cross the street, I run into a movie or a bar. I buy a drink, I speak to the nearest stranger—anything that can blow your candles out!—for nowadays the world is lit by lightning! Blow out your candles, Laura . . . [LAURA *blows out candles still burning in candelabrum and the whole interior is blacked out.*] And so—good-by! [*Exits up alley right. Music continues to the end.*]

Curtain